Nursing Management in the New Paradigm

Catherine E. Loveridge, PhD, RN

Associate Professor
School of Nursing
San Diego State University
San Diego, California

and

Susan H. Cummings, MN, RN

President
Cummings Associates
Adjunct Faculty
School of Nursing
San Diego State University
San Diego, California

AN ASPEN PUBLICATION®
Aspen Publishers, Inc.
Gaithersburg, Maryland
1996

Library of Congress Cataloging-in-Publication Data

Nursing management in the new paradigm / [edited by] Catherine E.
Loveridge and Susan H. Cummings.
p.   cm.
Includes bibliographical references and index.
ISBN 0-8342-0620-X
1. Nursing services—United States—Administration. 2. Nursing—
United States—Forecasting. 3. Medical care—United States—Cost
control. 4. Medical care—United States—quality control.
I. Loveridge, Catherine E. II. Cummings, Susan H.
[DNLM: 1. Nursing, Supervisory. 2. Nursing Care—organization &
administration. 3. Nurse Administrators. WY 105 N97479 1996]
RT89.N798   1996
362.1′73′0973—dc20
DNLM/DLC
for Library of Congress
95-38551
CIP

Aspen Publishers, Inc., grants permission for photocopying for limited personal
or internal use. This consent does not extend to other kinds of copying, such as
copying for general distribution, for advertising or promotional purposes, for
creating new collective works, or for resale. For information, address Aspen
Publishers, Inc., Permissions Department, 200 Orchard Ridge Drive, Suite 200,
Gaithersburg, Maryland 20878.

Editorial Resources: David A. Uffelman
Library of Congress Catalog Card Number: 95-38551
ISBN: 0-8342-0620-X

Printed in the United States of America

2   3   4   5

Table of Contents

Contributors

Jennifer M. Biggs, MS, RNC, CPHQ
Patient Care Manager
Adult Health Services
University Medical Center
Tucson, Arizona

Maryann Cone, RN, MS
Director
Ambulatory Services
Sharp HealthCare
San Diego, California

Susan H. Cummings, MN, RN
President
Cummings Associates
Adjunct Faculty
School of Nursing
San Diego State University
San Diego, California

Becky DeVillier, MSN, DSN
Assistant Administrator
USA Children's and Women's Hospital
Mobile, Alabama

Judith G. Eckhart, DNSc, RN
Instructor
Nursing Education Department
Palomar College
San Marcos, California

Donna Fosbinder, DNSc, RN
Associate Professor
Coordinator
Graduate Program in Nursing
    Administration
Brigham Young University College of
    Nursing
Provo, Utah

Aloma R. Gender, RN, MSN, CRRN
Assistant Administrator
Director of Nursing
San Diego Rehabilitation Institute
San Diego, California

Alice A. Kayuha, RN, MSN
Coordination of Care Service Line
    Director
North Bay Customer Service Area
Kaiser Permanente
San Rafael, California

Catherine E. Loveridge, PhD, RN
Associate Professor
School of Nursing
San Diego State University
San Diego, California

Jim O'Malley, MSN, RN
Senior Vice President
Nursing Services
Allegheney General Hospital
Associate Dean for Clinical Studies
School of Nursing
Duquesne University
Pittsburgh, Pennsylvania

Cynthia A. Parkman, BSN, MSN
Clinical Nurse
Acute Care Services
Sharp Memorial Hospital
San Diego, California

Tim Porter-O'Grady, EdD, PhD, FAAN
Senior Partner
Tim Porter-O'Grady Associates, Inc.
Senior Consultant
Affiliated Dynamics, Inc.
Assistant Professor
Emory University
Atlanta, Georgia

Robert L. Seidman, PhD
Associate Professor
Graduate School of Public Health
San Diego State University
San Diego, California

Myrna L. Warnick, MSN, RN
Associate Professor
Brigham Young University College of Nursing
Provo, Utah

Preface

Health care in the United States is being transformed by social and economic forces. The traditional physician–patient and nurse–patient relationships of earlier generations have been reformed by changes in financing illness care, a transition to building healthier communities, advanced technology, and consumer expectations. These changes have affected nursing by altering the delivery systems through which nursing care is provided. Redesigned health care systems project an array of settings and organizational relationships in which nursing and health services will be offered. Quality, cost-efficient programs emphasizing access and continuity of care will be successful in the future. Traditional patient care delivery systems and organizational management methods will be ineffective in this environment. Redesigned systems require imagination in translating manager and leader functions. Every professional nurse will need to be prepared for leadership and management responsibilities.

Entry-level professional nurses will be assuming management and leadership roles in redesigned health care delivery systems. *Nursing Management in the New Paradigm* is a textbook for undergraduate professional nursing students and will also be of value to nurses whose role expectations include entry-level management and leadership responsibilities. Kuhn (1970) defines paradigm as the common elements held by the practitioners of a scientific community, which include the shared beliefs, common education and apprenticeship, shared values, and shared exemplars (examples of outstanding performance. Successful nurses in the future, in addition to developing clinical skills, will develop skills for self-management, managing others, and integrating multiple roles in an organizational system.

We believe that the best way to present this information is within a framework that supports systems thinking. Achoff (1991) describes systems thinking as a new way to organize and understand multiple factors. Systems thinking places emphasis upon the interaction among elements in performance of a task rather than the individual performance of task elements. The systems age demands a new way of thinking: synthesis rather than analysis, meaning that one can understand systems better by examining how they function in the larger operations of which they are a part.

In previous texts on nursing management, skills such as communication are presented as isolated processes to be understood and applied. In this text, communication is woven throughout the book within the context of management and leadership roles and activities appropriate for the beginning professional nurse. Skill sets are described in the context in which they are practiced. These include coordination, consultation, coaching, empowerment, professional accountability, role development, teamwork, flexibility, problem solving, and decision making.

This book is organized in three sections: "Organization for Health Care," "The Business of Health Care," and "The Future of Health Care." Each chapter includes theoretical principles, practical implementation strategies, research findings to support practice, summaries of key concepts to reinforce learning, and idea-generating questions and situations to stimulate individual and group learning.

Part I, "Organization for Health Care," provides the foundation for understanding the structures that are evolving to support health care delivery in an era of great change. The chapter on organizational design discusses the elements of organizational design and their integration as a basis for understanding how organizations operate. The chapter on organizational systems focuses on how systems support the achievement of an organization's goals and mission and introduces key organization and nursing systems. Irrespective of the setting where client care is provided, structures exist that identify how nursing care will be delivered within a defined health care delivery model. The chapter on patient care delivery systems describes, compares, and contrasts methodologies to provide nursing care services within hospitals, schools, and communities. Staffing determinations that reflect patient requirements for nursing care, identification of nursing care costs, and how various methodologies for delivering patient care can be monitored for quality add to the discussion of the organized delivery of patient care services. The chapter on leadership roles of the professional nurse focuses on leadership theory and its application in the new paradigm of health care. Power and decision-making concepts critical to a leader's success are examined as they affect individual and organizational outcomes. Patient care manager roles, key patient care management skills, and group dynamics are explored in the chapter on the role of the professional nurse in patient care management. This chapter builds on the nurse's foundation of information and skills necessary to meet the challenges of patient care management in the future. The new paradigm of communication, consultation, coordination, and coaching is explored as it relates to patient care management. Facilitating individual and organizational outcomes through others is the focus of the chapter on the role of the professional nurse in organizational management. Similarities and differences between patient and organizational management provide the basis for exploration and development of self-management and organizational management skills.

Key to the success of health care organizations in the future will be their ability to manage their resources effectively and efficiently. Professional nurses must be cognizant of economic and financial issues as they affect patient care delivery and individual and organizational outcomes. Part II, "The Business of Health Care," explores issues related to the professional accountability of resource management. The chapter on health care economics provides a basis for understanding the economic challenges and opportunities within the health care marketplace in the 1990s. Resource allocation is explored in the chapter on budgeting and management of health care finances. Knowledge of financial terminology, the budget process, and monitoring of financial reports will be key to the success of nurses in the future as societal mandates focus on quality, cost-efficient care. The chapter on quality improvement focuses on one of the most frequently discussed topics in health care today. Quality assurance, utilization management, peer review, program evaluation, utilization of research, and quality improvement are explored as elements of a comprehensive quality program and as keys to organizational survival in an ever-changing, highly competitive health care environment. The chapter on human resource management focuses on effective deployment of human resources as a critical element in creating organizations that are competitive from both a cost and a quality perspective. Functions of the human resources department and nursing department functions in human resource management are discussed within the context of a framework for human resource management.

Change is the only constant in health care as we move into the 21st century. Nurses have the opportunity to create and influence the future. Part III, "The Future of Health Care," explores the phenomenon of change and changes that are affecting nurses as well as client care delivery. The chapter on planned change explores the process of change and planned change theory. Initiation and implementation of change as well as successful coping with change and resistance to change will be imperative to nursing success with clients and organizations. The chapter on building shared visions challenges our thinking about the visioning process, the articulation of visions, planning strategies, and the impact of shared visions on individual and organizational success. Technological innovations related to therapeutic interventions, diagnostics and evaluation, and information systems are the subject of the chapter on the changing role of technology. Technological advances markedly affect every aspect of care delivery, raise legal and ethical questions, and challenge nurses to balance technology and caring. The chapter on advanced practice nursing explores the multiple challenges to nursing, especially for those in advanced practice roles, as interdependent, team-based practice becomes a reality.

The professional nurse of today and tomorrow will be expected to use clinical, management, and personal leadership skills in ensuring the delivery of high-quality, cost-effective client care in divergent health care delivery systems. This book is dedicated to those professionals.

Catherine E. Loveridge   *Susan H. Cummings*
San Diego, CA   *San Diego, CA*

REFERENCE

Achoff, R. (1991). *Achoff's fables.* New York: Wiley.

Kuhn, T. (1970). *The structure of scientific revolutions* (2nd ed.). Chicago: University of Chicago Press.

PART I

Organization for Health Care

CHAPTER 1

Organizational Design

Catherine E. Loveridge

CHAPTER OBJECTIVES

At the completion of this chapter, the beginning professional nurse will be able to:
1. understand the elements of organizational design
2. define organizational culture
3. recognize several models of organizational structure
4. identify elements of organizational structure
5. understand the integration of services through organizational integrity

CRITICAL THINKING CHALLENGE

Many changes have occurred in health care since you began studying for the nursing profession. Think about the first unit to which you were assigned for clinical practice in your first year of nursing school. Compare that unit with the unit to which you are now assigned in terms of organizational design, organizational culture, and organizational structure.

We often think of the concept of design as a "look" one might find, as in fashion design or a logo that represents the trademark of a certain company. In organizational design, one refers to the "look" of the elements of the organization, which include the mission of the organization, the environment, the organizational structure, and human resources, all of which operate in an environment of social and political change.

This chapter discusses the elements of organizational design and will help the reader identify the ways in which these elements are integrated to indicate how the organization operates. The structure is, in many cases, the visible reflection of the total organizational design. Many organizational designs that are present today will be obsolete by the beginning of the next century. Nevertheless, whatever name is given to organizational designs, the elements presented here will be present and identifiable to the astute observer.

BACKGROUND

To understand organizational design, it is necessary to examine relevant history. The Industrial Revolution brought with it not only new machinery, new products, and expanded capacity for production but also a new approach to studying work. Before this time, work was performed by individual laborers or skilled craftspeople, who were employed by wealthy individuals. Another source of labor was prisoners of war and slaves, who were engaged in public works projects under the authority of the government of the time. Little attention was paid to the organization of workers or to the functions necessary to produce the final product. Mechanization, however, changed all that.

First, the nature of work was changed with the introduction of machines, which were capable of removing some of the drudgery of labor while increasing output substantially. Second, a huge market for goods was created, which stimulated the growth of providers of goods and services as well as the consumers of these products. Providers were now interested in increasing their profit margins and began to turn their attention toward methods to improve their efficiency of operation. Adam Smith (1937) stated the rationale for the **division of labor.** By analyzing the trade of the pin maker, he found that 10 men employed in a factory could produce about 12 pounds of pins a day. This equaled about 48,000 pins. Each of the 10 men might be considered to make ¹⁄₁₀th this amount, or 4,800 pins a day. If the men worked independently, however, they probably could not make 20 pins. In this way, dividing the work among many workers improved the overall efficiency of the operation.

Just as changes in the industrial society of the past forced a reconfiguration of the workforce and the emergence of a middle class composed of workers, so too are the changes in today's society forcing reorganization of health care services.

LEVELS OF ORGANIZATIONAL DESIGN

In examining how organizations are designed, it is important to focus on the visible elements of that design to understand how the system maintains its integrity.

The first level of organizational design is the individual position. In the position description, information regarding the purpose of the work and the environment in which it is performed is described. Personal, professional, and technical skills and attributes of the worker are included. In this way, the individual begins to understand the expectations, priorities, and goals of the organization.

The next level of organizational design is the group or unit. In the group design, the skills of individual members are coordinated to improve the effectiveness of the entire group. Examples of this level of design include multidisciplinary patient care teams, intravenous therapy teams, and trauma teams (see Chapter 3 for greater detail about nursing care delivery systems).

In the next level, several groups are clustered to improve expertise and flexibility in response to changing conditions. An example of this is an obstetrics suite, which includes labor and delivery, nursery, and postpartum services. Each individual is prepared to respond to demands from any unit.

The division level organizes several clusters to expand services without duplicating effort. An example of this is a service line organization that provides oncology services to recently diagnosed and acutely ill clients in ambulatory as well as hospitalized settings.

The system level design identifies an entity organized under one ownership. Examples of this level include a hospital or a long-term care facility.

The network level of design is emerging in many regions of the country. This design recognizes affiliated systems that work together following agreed-to procedures but maintain their individual ownership. Examples of this include visiting nurse associations and some hospitals, physician practice groups and hospitals, and acute care hospitals and extended care facilities (Shortell & Kaluzny, 1994).

KEY CONCEPT Levels of organizational design include:
- individual
- group
- cluster of groups
- division
- system
- network

ELEMENTS OF ORGANIZATIONAL DESIGN

Although the levels of organizational design include increasingly complex perspectives, the elements of the design that distinguish one organization from another can be found at each level.

The elements of organizational design include the mission of the organization, the environment in which the organization operates, the structure of the organization, the human resources available to the organization, and the social and political forces affecting the operation of the organization.

The **mission** of the organization is defined as a statement that identifies the business in which the organization is engaged. It often includes the values and ideology of the organization in terms of client care and personnel. The mission statement of the Veterans Administration (VA) Nursing Service shown below provides an example. This mission statement, derived from the mission of the organization, was developed with input from the entire nursing division. Once such a mission statement has been adopted, it is reviewed periodically by the organization to ensure its continued relevancy to the care that is currently being provided.

Mission Statement from San Diego VA Medical Center

The VA Nursing Service provides care that will assist veterans to maintain or regain health, to learn to live with disabilities, or to die with dignity and comfort. Nursing Service establishes humanistic, outcome-oriented nursing programs and participates on the health care team to promote effective patient care. Fostering the development of nursing personnel is essential to this mission.

Courtesy of Department of Veterans Affairs, Department of Nursing Service, San Diego, California.

Evidence of the mission of the organization is seen at the individual level in the position description's focus on quality patient care by well-educated professionals. The group level implements the mission through development of multidisciplinary teams that provide a wide range of services to veterans. A cluster of groups coordinates expert services to ensure integrated care to veterans through the ambulatory and hospitalized phases of their illness. A division may be developed to deliver care to paralyzed veterans that promotes their abilities and skills and supports their reentry into the workforce. Such coordinated efforts reflect the mission of the organization.

The **environment** of the organization describes the conditions in society that permit or inhibit an organization's development. Internal environmental factors such as employee commitment, conflict resolution, and the degree of complexity of the work create a need for training, coordination, and communication at all levels. In the external environment, the extent of stable and predictable demand for services affects the growth and development of the organization. In today's competitive, cost-containment environment, organizations must transform themselves to meet changing needs.

The internal environment shapes the design of the organization by directing communication and coordination processes. For example, in a health care facility in which a collective bargaining agreement is in place, communication patterns between the staff nurse and the unit manager may also include the union representative in resolving work-related conflicts.

The external environment shapes the organizational design by creating new demands. For example, the shift to prospective payment for services caused many hospitals to decrease lengths of stay for patients and to expand ambulatory service centers. This required a change in the communication and coordination processes between the acute care hospital and the ambulatory centers.

The **structure** of the organization refers to the way in which the component units of the organization are related to one another to accomplish the goals of the organization. These components include standardization, centralization of authority, specialization, coordination, communication, and innovation.

Human resources affect organizational design by requiring the arrangement of skills and expertise in accordance with the demand for that expertise at the bedside and throughout the organization. To provide 24-hour, 7-day-a-week service to clients, processes for communication and coordination are necessary to ensure accountability. Various designs for nursing care delivery systems to accomplish this are described in detail in Chapter 3.

The **social and political forces** affecting organizational design are numerous. Everyone who works in health care recognizes the rapid changes that are affecting health care. For example, demographics of the patient population indicate a demand for services for the elderly in alternative settings to traditional hospital care. Many physician practices have changed from private practice arrangements to large, multispecialty group practices. Financing of health care services has evolved from fee-for-service payments to contracted arrangements through group insurance purchases of covered services. Nursing care has changed from a focus on acute, episodic care to information-based managed care throughout a lifetime. Nurses themselves have responded by developing innovative services within organizations and beyond. Educational preparation for the new demands includes technical, professional, and advanced practice programs (O'Malley, Loveridge, & Cummings, 1989).

ORGANIZATIONAL CULTURE

Organizational culture, like ethnic or national culture, is based on shared values and beliefs. What distinguishes organizational culture is its focus on work life (del Bueno, 1986). Symbols, assumptions, and behaviors all assume a shared meaning in the context of the organization's culture. Some of these culture characteristics are visible, and some are deeply imbedded assumptions about the relationships between the organization and the larger community. Regardless of the depth of cultural influence, activities and decisions made by the organization are influenced by, and understood fully only within the context of, the organizational culture.

An example of a visible culture characteristic is the logo, the symbol that a hospital uses on its communication materials. In Figure 1–1, the kite, a child's toy, is central to the logo. The use of the term *health center* rather than *hospital* alone, communicates an attitude of wellness rather than illness. These reflect the values held by the organization.

The next level of culture includes the shared values of what ought to be done. This is reflected in policies regarding uniform dress and social interaction. For example, in some facilities first names are used routinely, whereas in other facilities a more formal use of title and last name is the norm.

The third level of culture is described as the basic assumptions that cannot be challenged but guide behavior. These may include beliefs about the relationship of the organization to its employees and the community. For example, if an organization includes scientific research as part of its mission, then expectations of research-based practice for all disciplines will be rewarded more than tradition-based practice.

KEY CONCEPT   Characteristics of the organizational culture include:
- first level—symbols and logos
- second level—shared values
- third level—basic assumptions

Organizations in transition often experience difficulties in making changes in long-held basic assumptions, values, and their image in the community.

Figure 1–1 Logo from Children's Hospital and Health Center. Courtesy of Children's Hospital and Health Center, San Diego, California.

For example, public hospitals, which operated to serve the indigent and needy with subsidies provided from tax revenues, are experiencing the need to change their patient mix to attract funded patients so that they can secure needed revenue to maintain services to paying and nonpaying clients. Practices associated with marketing health care to the public assume an important role that did not exist in the past.

LEARNING   Describe the organizational culture of the facility in which you are having
CHALLENGE   clinical experience. Identify symbols, assumptions, values, and practices, and give examples of each. Compare organizational culture assessments with those of a peer who is describing a different facility.

ELEMENTS OF ORGANIZATIONAL STRUCTURE

Organizational structure is defined as the formal pattern of relationships among positions, directing the processes and functions of the organization. The components of the structure include standardization, centralization of authority, specialization, coordination, communication, and innovation.

Standardization is defined as a dimension of structure indicating the degree to which the organization relies on rules and procedures to guide the behavior of employees (Dienemann, 1990). An example of standardization is a department policy that explains the procedure for an employee to request vacation time.

Centralization of authority is defined as a dimension of structure indicating the degree to which the locus of authority is contained in one or a limited number of positions (Loveridge, 1988). An example of centralization of authority is the chain of accountability displayed in the organizational chart.

Specialization is defined as a dimension of structure specifying the extent to which the duties of each role are clearly specified. This may be narrowly defined to specific tasks within an organization (e.g., phlebotomist) or more broadly defined as a specific function (e.g., financial duties) (Aldrich, 1979). An example of specialization is the detailed description of work found in position descriptions of employees.

Coordination is defined as a dimension of structure that identifies the process of combining the efforts of subsystems to achieve the goals of the organization (Lawrence & Lorsch, 1967). An example of coordination is the clinical pathway developed for an oncology client.

Communication is defined as a dimension of structure in which information is transmitted throughout the organization to provide data for decision making, to motivate employees, to exercise control, and to express satisfaction or dissatisfaction with operations (Rakish, Longest, & Darr, 1993). An example of communication is the activities of a quality improvement committee focused on the development of a protocol for orthopedic care.

Innovation is defined as a dimension of structure that describes the extent to which the organization supports and encourages the development of unexpected and creative solutions (Adams, 1994). An example of innovation is an organization's commitment to the implementation of nursing research findings in clinical practice.

These elements of organizational structure assume different degrees of prominence in different organizational models. The most common of these models include the functional model, the bureaucratic model, the matrix model, and the shared governance model.

MODELS OF ORGANIZATIONAL STRUCTURE

The **functional model of organizational structure** relies on dividing up activities to maximize standardization and routinization of repetitive tasks. An example of this type of organization is found at the nursing unit level by assignment of a medication or treatment nurse who is responsible for administering medication to all clients on the unit (Figure 1–2). The intent of this type of organization is to improve efficiency by streamlining processes (e.g., medication administration).

In this model, **line and staff activities** are also evident. Line activities are those activities directly involved in the principal work of the organization. In the example shown in Figure 1–2, the unit manager, charge nurse, and direct care providers are involved in line activities. Staff activities are those activities provided to support the work of the line. For example, in nursing, the

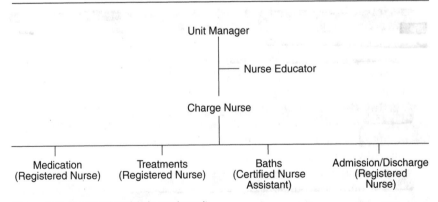

Figure 1–2 Functional model of a nursing unit.

nurse educator who is responsible for the orientation of new nurses would be considered in a staff position. Usually, no subordinates report directly to those in staff positions.

Two additional components of the functional model are **chain of command** and **unity of command**. The scalar chain of command describes the flow of authority in an unbroken line from the highest level, usually the executive, to the lowest. The second principle, unity of command, specifies that no subordinate should be responsible to more than one superior. In organizations in which professional nurses are employed, these components of a functional organization are of limited usefulness because professionals are responsible not only to the organization as employees hired to provide specific services but also to society in fulfilling a commitment that is the basis of the bond established between society and the profession.

KEY CONCEPTS

Advantages of the functional model include:
- clear assignment of roles and responsibilities
- mutual support among people doing similar work
- minimized duplication of tasks
- maximized use of specialized equipment and techniques

Disadvantages of the functional model include:
- limited point of view (focused on a specific task)
- difficult coordination of tasks because of isolation
- resistance to change, requiring coordinated action
- difficulty in adapting this mechanical model to human services

Another approach to efficiency was proposed by Weber (1978). He designed a model of organization called a **bureaucracy**. His early writings described this ideal type of organization as one that assumes a closed system existence as well as a high degree of rationality in the enterprise. He believed that rules, procedures, and regulations should be derived from the goals of the organization. Tasks should be subdivided among members of the group so that the sphere of activity matches the members' competence. Positions should be arranged in a pyramid, with each position having more authority than the one below it in the hierarchy. Decision making should be based on rules and criteria attached to each position. Members of the organization should participate on the basis of contractual agreements and be remunerated in the form of salaries for their contribution. Although criticized by many for its limitations, the bureaucratic model of organization has prevailed throughout most of the 20th century.

In the bureaucracy, coordination requires that people responsible for subdivisions of work be placed in authority positions where work is coordinated by orders from superiors to subordinates, reaching from the top to the bottom of the enterprise. The scalar chain of command in a bureaucracy is represented by the principles of office hierarchy. This principle states, "...levels of graded authority mean a firmly ordered system of super- and subordination in which there is a supervision of lower offices by the higher ones" (Weber, 1978, p. 38).

A problem with bureaucracies and health care is the conflict inherent in organizations that employ professional workers. It has been noted that, when professionals are members of an organization, the question arises as to whether their expertise and position in the hierarchy derive from their knowledge of organizational operations or from their professional discipline (Perrow, 1979). If their expertise derives from their discipline, then their allegiance is to society, not to the organization. If their expertise is related to organizational operations, then to what extent should their authority extend to discipline-related decision making?

The bureaucratic model of organization includes many features of the functional model, but it is more complex. The term *bureaucracy* has often been used to indicate difficulties in getting things done. In reality, many features of a bureaucracy are desirable, but the ways in which these elements have been put into practice often cause the problems associated with the term. Figure 1–3 shows a diagram of a bureaucracy.

Other characteristics include the principle of fixed and official jurisdictional areas, generally ordered by rules or administrative regulations; man-

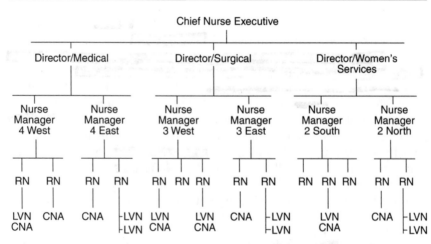

Figure 1–3 Bureaucratic model of a nursing department. RN, registered nurse; LVN, licensed vocational nurse; CNA, certified nurse assistant.

agement of the office based upon written documents or files, which are preserved in their original form; the fact that management is a primary duty of the office holder and as such requires specific management expertise and full-time commitment; and the fact that management of the office follows general rules that can be learned and are applied equitably, so that no favoritism or special privilege is permitted (Weber, 1978).

Although this organizational model has contributed a great deal to the improvement of industrial production, it presents significant challenges to human service organizations. The philosophy of a bureaucracy is based on the belief that the dominance of an idea will produce such single-mindedness of purpose that each individual will fit his or her work into the master plan with skill and enthusiasm. The process of developing such single-minded commitment was not addressed when the bureaucratic model was defined.

A limited view of the role of the professional nurse employee has resulted in centralized decision making, in which authority is vested in the department rather than shared with the individual clinician, standardized policies and procedures replace individualized care, management replaces leadership, and quality equates to adequate rather than excellent. Reliance on rules that assist in confronting complex rather than simple problems results in confusion when rapid change is required to meet uncertain conditions.

The **matrix organizational design** was developed to improve the responsiveness and focus of organizations. Characteristics of this design include the distribution of authority and resources to the operational level of the organization, dual reporting and accountability channels, and multidisciplinary membership. An example of a matrix organization is displayed in Figure 1–4.

The matrix model of organization provides the expertise needed to provide quality care through the functional leadership dimension. At the same time, cost and efficiency are controlled through the service or product dimension. Although this model is being used more frequently in complex organizations, it still presents challenges for the professional employee. The unity of command that is characteristic of organizations is violated by this model. Dual channels of authority can be confusing to both managers and employees and can lead to interpersonal and role conflict (Decker & Sullivan, 1992). For this model to be successful, it is imperative for people assuming these roles to negotiate role responsibilities with the persons to whom they report. See Chapter 6 for further discussion of role negotiation.

Newer organizational structure models have evolved in hospitals where industrial designs have proved inadequate to address professional employee issues. These models include shared governance at the department level of the organization and self-directed work teams at the unit level of operation.

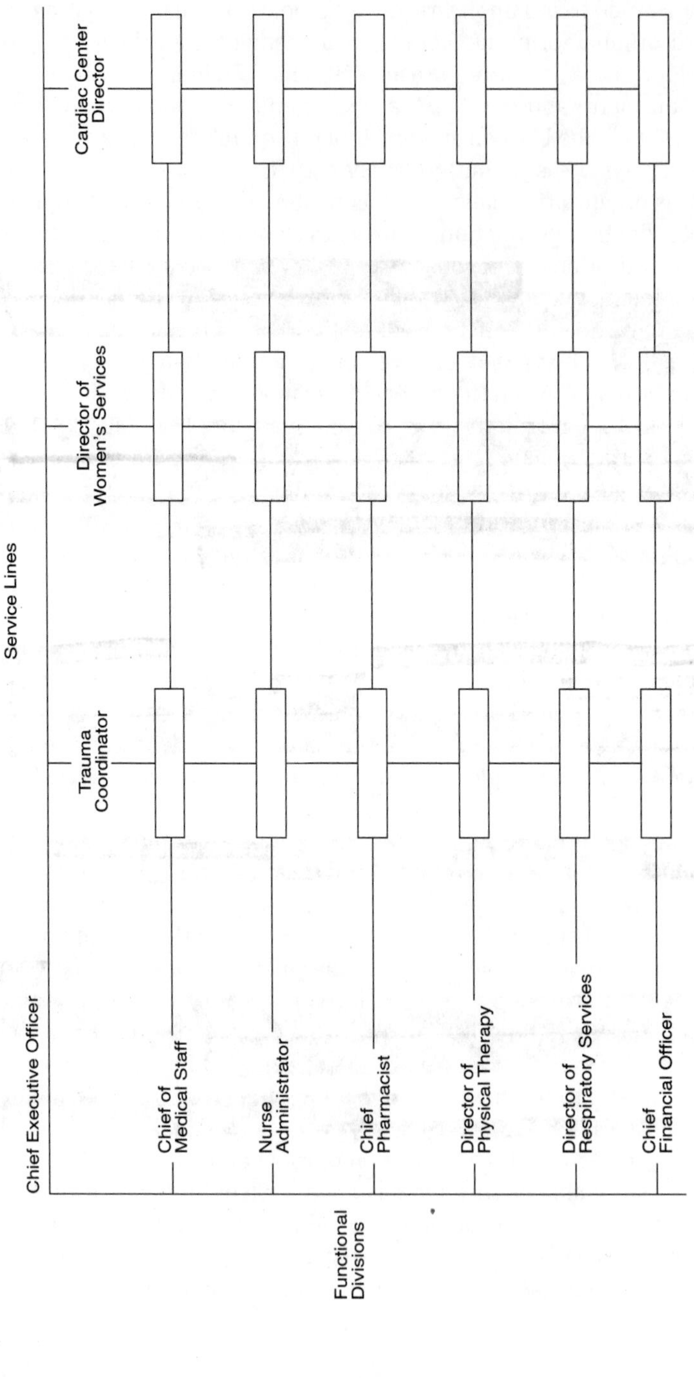

Figure 1–4 Matrix model of a health care organization.

Shared governance is the term used to describe an organizational structure in which accountability directs the relationships of communication, coordination, coaching, and counseling. The professional is accountable in the following ways (Porter-O'Grady, 1990):

- The professional has a social mandate to use expert judgment in caring for the client.
- The professional is accountable to society to monitor those who are practicing nursing and to assure the public that practitioners are properly educated to assume the responsibilities of the role.
- The professional is accountable for exercising authority regarding decisions affecting nursing practice and for working collaboratively with members of other disciplines in providing client care.

To achieve these accountabilities, the organizational structure must empower staff to take responsibility in making decisions that will affect the nursing care of clients. The organization formalizes its commitment to shared governance through a vote of the staff and the development of bylaws designed to direct the way in which authority, responsibility, coordination, and communication will be allocated throughout the new structure.

Porter-O'Grady (1984) suggests a councilor structure as a model to achieve these goals. **Councils** differ from committees in that committees advise and recommend specific actions to managers but do not have the authority to implement their decisions. Councils, however, are invested with the authority to make decisions and are responsible for the impact of the decisions made. When shared governance is initiated, the coordinating council discusses with the nurse executive each council's responsibilities, accountabilities, and domain of activities. Inherent in this process is clarification and delineation of:

- council decision-making responsibilities
- shared decision-making responsibilities with managers and administration
- decisions that will be the primary responsibility of administration

The councilor model is developed through representative groups at the unit level, which then coordinate activities through the department level. Staff members are elected to each council and serve a term of membership as specified in the bylaws. During their term, they solicit input from the unit staff regarding the areas of council responsibility and communicate results of deliberation about issues and decisions. The unit-based councils accomplish the work of shared governance at the patient care level. The unit councils elect a representative from each council to represent the unit at the department level. Department level councils reflect the same alignment as the unit structure. Councils include the following types:

- **Nursing practice council**—This council is responsible for the development and implementation of standards of nursing practice in the institution. It determines roles and responsibilities of all levels of nursing care providers; reviews and approves all issues related to policy development regarding the clinical practice of nursing; represents clinical nurses at all forums in which decisions affecting clinical nursing practice are made; participates in resolution of interdisciplinary problems affecting clinical practice (Porter-O'Grady, 1992); and represents clinical nursing practice perspectives at the decision-making nursing department administrative forums.

- **Quality improvement council**—This council is responsible for monitoring compliance with the standards for nursing practice in the institution as developed and implemented by the nursing practice council. In addition, the council is responsible for selecting appropriate assessment and evaluation strategies for monitoring nursing activities and developing corrective actions when standards have not been met or when standards are changed to improve nursing practice. This council also has responsibility for establishing performance expectations or standards and for determining the credentialing and privileging process (Porter-O'Grady, 1992). The quality improvement council is also involved in interdisciplinary and institutional quality assurance activities.

- **Nursing education council**—This council is responsible for ensuring high levels of competency among the nursing staff. Responsibilities are met through the development and delivery of educational programs directed toward meeting the standards of clinical practice and through incorporating new skills and clinical research findings into clinical practice (Porter-O'Grady, 1992). This council also assumes responsibility for effective, efficient communication within the nursing organization.

- **Nursing management council**—This council is responsible for ensuring appropriate administrative, financial, material, system, and human resources to support the clinical practice of nursing. This obligation is met through implementing the decisions of the councils, developing interunit communication mechanisms, allocating sufficient resources to support the clinical mission of the unit, and identifying organizational obstacles to clinical practice and methods to overcome those obstacles (Porter-O'Grady, 1992).

- **Research council**—A research council may be established to address the professional accountability of research. This council has responsibility for research activities in the nursing department related to the conduct of research, utilization of research in clinical practice, and communication of research findings throughout the organization (Porter-O'Grady, 1992). Often, a representative of this council is invited to participate on the institutional committee for the protection of human subjects.

- **Coordinating council or executive council**—This council is responsible for coordinating the developmental and decision-making activities of each individual council, establishing mechanisms for decision-making communication, and resolving conflicts. It is composed of the chairpersons of each individual council and the nursing executive (Porter-O'Grady, 1992).

See Figure 1–5 for an example of a shared governance model of organization.

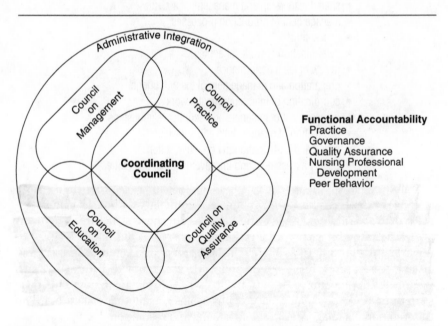

Functional Accountability
Practice
Governance
Quality Assurance
Nursing Professional
   Development
Peer Behavior

Figure 1–5 Nursing operational framework organizational structure. *Source:* Reprinted from *Shared Governance for Nursing: A Creative Approach to Professional Accountability* by T. Porter-O'Grady & S. Finnigan, p. 105, Aspen Publishers, Inc., © 1984.

Self-directed work teams offer a unit-level approach to improving accountability by the staff in clinical practice. In this organizational model, staff are represented on committees and councils (e.g., research, education, quality improvement, and clinical practice) that are responsible for developing policies and making decisions regarding their areas of responsibility. These teams may be multidisciplinary in membership. In addition, these self-directed work teams often assume responsibility for aspects of operational management.

Self-directed work teams on patient care units are often implemented simultaneously with patient-focused care redesign. In traditional health care organizations, specialization and bureaucratic hierarchies have not supported organizational realignment with self-directed work teams. Patient-focused redesigns, however, have caused health care organizations to look at organizational structures that facilitate empowerment within the unit-based multidisciplinary group providing the most patient services.

KEY CONCEPT
Characteristics of self-directed work teams include the following (Wellins, Byham, & Wilson, 1991):

- shared leadership and management activities
- management of production processes
- goal setting
- determination of work schedules
- review of team performance
- preparation and management of the unit budget
- coordination of interdepartmental work
- management of materials and supplier relationships
- acquisition of needed skills and knowledge
- hiring and participation in corrective actions
- quality assessment and improvement responsibilities

Self-directed work teams that include multiskilled caregivers and support staff on patient care units often assume accountability for first-level management activities independent of the manager. In these structures, the manager, who often has responsibility for several units, consults with the staff regarding patient information, acts as a coach and facilitator for staff, and often learns of problem resolution and work group activities after strategies have been implemented. Relationships with physicians change in these structures as well. As teams mature, physicians consult the team rather than the traditional manager for problem solving and resolution.

Challenges for staff are inherent in self-directed work teams. In addition, managers who are responsible for patient care units with self-directed work teams also face many challenges:

- managing multiskilled workers
- facilitating interdepartmental communication, problem solving, and organizational integration
- managing in old and new paradigms simultaneously
- transitioning their own role to a coach and facilitator
- orchestrating the 3- to 5-year transition to mature self-directed work teams
- providing team members with education and coaching related to organizational management functions and processes
- ensuring that individual and organizational outcomes are attained

A comparison of the major organizational models along with the components of organizational structure is presented in Table 1–1.

HEALTH CARE DELIVERY SYSTEM REDESIGN

These organizational models can also be identified in health care systems that focus on a broader continuum of care beyond the traditional hospital setting. As health care in the United States moves from an illness focus to a preventive and health focus, services such as screening and wellness education, diagnostic procedures, and home health care are being offered to a growing population through health delivery systems and networks that require new organizational structures.

Individuals and groups in these diverse settings are integrated through case management, information systems, and finance systems. Through **case management**, integration occurs at the point at which service is provided. Physicians, nurses, and other members of the health team provide their expertise to patients and families in a cooperative effort to promote health and prevent illness in the individual and the population. Case management further coordinates resources from the organization to facilitate cost containment and quality outcomes for those same individuals and populations. **Information systems** serve to integrate services by providing a timely resource about the individual as well as trended data about populations' health and illness characteristics to provide the most appropriate interventions. **Financial systems** serve to integrate services by monitoring resource utilization critical to the provision of quality care.

Redesigned health care delivery models can be organized either as systems or as networks. The **systems** own facilities and may directly employ physicians and other caregivers, competing with other systems for client membership. **Networks,** on the other hand, develop contracts that provide

Table 1-1 Key Concepts of Organizational Structure and Their Place in Organizational Models

Concept	Standardization	Centralization	Specialization	Coordination	Communication	Innovation
Functional	Maximized for uniformity	Authority flows from highest to lowest positions	Development of specialists for repetitive work	Departments report to an administrator who integrates activities	Upward communication from departments and downward directives from administration	Limited to leadership group
Bureaucracy	Written procedures guide practice	Authority flows from highest to lowest positions	Staff positions serve line positions	Span of control in positions arranged in a hierarchy to permit direction from superiors	Formal channels through chain of command	Limited to span of operation
Matrix	Integration of procedures for effective results	Dual authority from functional and service lines	Multidisciplinary use of special expertise	Maximized due to integration of several disciplines	Maximized across organization	Maximized due to synergism
Shared Governance	Policies and procedures developed by those governed by them	Accountability for practice placed with practitioners, organizational responsibilities shared with administration	Roles for expert clinicians designed by staff group	Councils include representatives from all groups	Coordinating council disseminates all decisions to members	Encouraged through council support

partnerships among physician groups, institutions, and payers, which cooperate in the provision of services for client groups and populations, thereby sharing financial risks. An example of a system is an acute care hospital corporation that owns a home care department, a long-term skilled nursing facility, an ambulatory care center, a 1-day surgery center, and a health promotion program. In some cases, physician groups are employees of the corporation or a group practice contracted for service. An example of a network is an acute care hospital that contracts with a visiting nurse service for home health care, a long-term skilled nursing facility, a hospice center, physicians, and health plans and health maintenance organizations to achieve health care outcomes (Coile, 1994).

CONCLUSION

The organization is designed to integrate the efforts of individuals and groups to accomplish the work to be done. Each organization has its own culture, which provides meaning to the decisions made and the directions taken in accomplishing the mission. Several of the organizational structures presented emphasize command and control perspectives, or empowerment perspectives, which reflect beliefs about how systems operate and how people work together. Further discussion of systems operation is found in Chapter 2. The chapters that follow elaborate further on the methods used and the skills needed to practice professional nursing successfully in the emerging systems of today and tomorrow.

RESEARCH FOUNDATION   Loveridge, C.E., Weiss, M., & Webb, L. (1995). *A contingency theory test of nursing administration. Communicating Nursing Research: Innovation and Collaboration: Responses to Health Care Needs. 28* (3), Boulder, CO: Western Institute of Nursing.

Information on which to base organizational redesign decisions is scarce. Nevertheless, redesign, restructuring, and reengineering efforts have proceeded. In an effort to improve the quality of redesign decisions and to evaluate those restructures that had already taken place, the San Diego State University (SDSU) Institute for Nursing Research, a consortium of eight area hospitals with the SDSU School of Nursing, developed a project. The institute was initiated in 1988 to promote collaboration in the conduct, dissemination, and utilization of nursing research that would contribute to the quality of patient care and services. The research reported here is from a pilot study conducted to examine organizational effectiveness of nursing units.

Study problems:

1. Determine which variables of nursing technology and organizational structure correlate most strongly with outcome measures of organizational effectiveness.

2. Determine whether there is a nonmonotonic (curvilinear) relationship between organizational structure and effectiveness over a range of nursing technology.

Data were collected from 261 nurses from 37 nursing units in two member hospitals of the institute. Multiple regression analysis was performed on data aggregated to the unit level. Results of the reduced regression analysis of nurse job satisfaction indicated that 60% of the variance in job satisfaction and 39% of the variance in job enjoyment were explained by the main effects and interaction effects of structure and technology.

Because these results were significant ($p = .01$), a partial derivative of the regression coefficient was examined for curvilinearity. Two curvilinear relationships were found. Such findings mean that the relationship between structure and effectiveness is not constant over the range of technology. This means that costs associated with improving the structural variables of standardization and decentralization are a worthwhile investment on nursing units where more than 50% of the patients have uncertain, variable problems. On units with less than 50% of these complex patients, such investments would be unwise.

These findings have several implications. First, collaborative research can be conducted successfully in competitive hospital environments. Second, there is no one best structure for nursing care delivery systems. The nursing care delivery system must be designed at the unit level. The structure should be based on the patient care needs of each unit. Although other studies show that decentralized structures produce greater job satisfaction and enjoyment among staff, it must be remembered that these studies are based on a linear relationship. These data demonstrate that the interaction of structure and technology sometimes has an impact on effectiveness in a curvilinear manner. Therefore, investments made in organizational restructuring may not produce expected savings if the technology is not fitted to the structure. Additional data are needed to determine whether these findings are consistent with clinical, quality, utilization, and financial outcomes.

REFERENCES

Adams, C.E. (1994). Innovative behavior in nurse executives. *Nursing Management, 25*(5), 44–47.

Aldrich, H. (1979). *Organizations and environments.* Englewood Cliffs, NJ: Prentice-Hall.

Coile, R., Jr. (1994). Guiding the integrated delivery network: Seven models for cooperation. *Health Care Forum, 37* (6), 16–23.

Decker, P., & Sullivan, E. (1992). *Nursing administration: A micro/macro approach for effective nurse executives.* Norwalk, CT: Appleton & Lang.

del Bueno, D. (1986). Organizational culture: How important is it? *Journal of Nursing Administration, 16* (10), 15–20.

Dienemann, J. (1990). *Nursing administration: Strategic perspectives and application.* Norwalk, CT: Appleton & Lang.

Lawrence, P., & Lorsch, J. (1967). Differentiation and integration in complex organizations. *Administrative Science Quarterly, 11* (3), 1–47.

Loveridge, C. (1988). Contingency theory: Explaining staff nurse retention. *Journal of Nursing Administration, 18* (6), 22–25.

Loveridge, C., Weiss, M., & Webb, L. (1995). A contingency theory test of nursing administration. *Communicating nursing research: Innovation and collaboration: Responses to health care needs. 28* (3), Boulder, CO: Western Institute of Nursing.

O'Malley, J., Loveridge, C., & Cummings, S. (1989). The new nursing organization. *Nursing Management, 20* (2), 29–32.

Perrow, C. (1979). *Complex organizations: A critical essay.* Glenview, IL: Scott, Forsman.

Porter-O'Grady, T. (1984). *Shared governance for nursing: A creative approach to professional accountability.* Gaithersburg, MD: Aspen.

Porter-O'Grady, T. (1990). Nursing governance in a transitional era. In N. Chaska (Ed.), *The nursing profession: Turning points* (pp. 432–439). St. Louis: Mosby.

Porter-O'Grady, T. (1992). *Shared governance implementation manual.* St. Louis: Mosby–Year Book.

Rakish, J.S., Longest, B., & Darr, K. (1993). *Managing health service organizations* (3rd ed.). Baltimore: Health Professions.

Shortell, S., & Kaluzny, A. (1994). *Health care management: Organization design and behavior* (3rd ed.). Albany, NY: Delmar.

Smith, A. (1937). *An inquiry into the nature and causes of the wealth of nations, 1776.* New York: Modern Library.

Taylor, F.W. (1978). The principles of scientific management. In J.M. Shafritz & P.H. Whitbeck (Eds.), *Classics in organizational theory* (pp. 9–22). Oak Park, IL: Moore.

Weber, M. (1978). Bureaucracy. In J.M. Shafritz & P.H. Whitbeck (Eds.), *Classics of organizational theory* (pp. 37–43). Oak Park, IL: Moore.

Wellins, R., Byham, W., & Wilson, J. (1991). *Empowered teams.* San Francisco: Jossey-Bass.

CHAPTER 2

Organizational Systems

Alice A. Kayuha

CHAPTER OBJECTIVES

At the completion of this chapter, the beginning professional nurse will be able to:
1. discuss how systems support the achievement of an organization's mission and goals
2. identify the elements of a system and discuss how each is separate yet related to all other elements
3. describe the ways in which a change to any component can affect all other points in the system as well as other systems within the organization
4. identify and discuss key organization and nursing systems found in the hospital

CRITICAL THINKING CHALLENGE

Organizational systems and biological systems have often been compared. Identify ways in which an organizational system is like a biological system. Think about the structure, function, and purpose of the systems you are comparing.

Systems are a familiar concept to nurses. As a part of their clinical instruction, nurses are introduced to thinking of the physiology of the body as the result of a number of interrelated systems. Understanding the body's complexities begins with learning how each of its anatomical pieces—the structure—fits with the others to create a process. The outcome of each system is based on the function of each of its units.

There are three elements that make up a system: structure, function, and purpose. Thinking of how these are identified in the cardiovascular system will help elucidate how they form a system. First, the **structure** equates to the anatomical components of the heart, such as the chambers, valves and muscle, and the vascular attachments (e.g., arteries and veins). These are connected together to form the cardiovascular system. The **function** of these structural elements is to pump blood throughout the body. Their fundamental **purpose** is to transport nutrients to the cells that make up the body. The process they create is designed to eject blood into the vessels for delivery to the cells to deposit oxygen and pick up carbon dioxide for transport to the lungs. Once there, the red blood cells are reoxygenated, and the cycle begins again. Recognizing how body systems operate can assist the nurse to understand how systems in an organization affect its operations.

APPLICATION OF BIOLOGICAL SYSTEMS TO ORGANIZATIONAL SYSTEMS

In the same way that the elements of structure, function, and purpose lead to a specific outcome in the body systems, departments or employees in an organization come together to achieve a specific goal. This comparison of biological systems to organizational systems was developed as **general systems theory** by Ludwig Von Bertalanfly (1968). He identified that organizations, whether living or societal, have characteristics such as wholeness, growth, differentiation, hierarchical order, dominance, control, and competition. Three components come together to achieve the goal of the system: input, throughput, and output. **Input** is the stimulus that enters the system at its first step and activates it. **Throughput** is the portion of the system that processes the input to create a product or service. **Output** is the last step in the system and produces the product or service. In some instances, the output step may be the input step in another system. Because of this, all systems in the organization become subject to the influence of changes in other systems in the organization.

General systems theory lends itself to an understanding of the complexity of today's organizations in a way that cannot be addressed by the conventional one-way, cause-and-effect scientific approach. This theory identifies the need to think in terms of the mutual interactions of the elements of an organization (Von Bertalanfly, 1968). Applying the concept of looking at the components and the order in which they occur creates an organized way of examining a process. By breaking the whole down to see the parts, one can sense patterns, identify the relationships among the components, and simplify complex interactions so that they can be better understood. As a result, the building blocks of the system can be analyzed and adjusted to improve effectiveness without changing the outcome or interfering with other systems.

In the cardiovascular system, valves within the heart are one component of the system that influence the overall effectiveness of the system. In fact, the first symptom of a breakdown in this component of the system may well not appear to be a failure in the cardiovascular system. It may be that the first presenting symptom the patient notices is shortness of breath. Without taking systems analysis into consideration, this complaint seems more likely to be related to the pulmonary system than the cardiac system. To diagnose this problem, however, the practitioner begins by looking at all the potential causes. This includes examining all the surrounding and connecting structures to ascertain whether they are functioning properly. It also means looking at those events that occur before and after the incident. In this case, the examiner finds that the problem is occurring as a result of a back-up in a related system and not in the pulmonary system, as it appeared at first glance.

This example demonstrates the interrelatedness of systems. For a presenting problem to be investigated adequately, the adjoining systems need to be scrutinized as intently as the system in question. In this instance, analysis uncovers that the element to be corrected is a component of the cardiovascular system, not the pulmonary system, as might be supposed on first inspection. A structural component of the heart pump—a valve—is failing to open completely and carry out its function to eject blood, which results in a throughput problem. The decreased output that occurs causes a back-up in the system, which affects the pulmonary system. Surgery to correct the valve deficit improves output, which enhances throughput and prevents back-up. Consequently, adjoining systems such as the pulmonary system also benefit. If the practitioner were to focus on treating the shortness of breath without going through an analysis of the system, the wrong solution would be devised, and the problem would become worse. Figure 2–1 displays examples of normal and defective systems.

This same thinking process is applicable to organizational systems. It helps identify elements of an organizational system and provides a mechanism for organizations to solve problems and correct deficits so that departments (an element of structure) can carry out their functions (the throughput) in order for the purpose (the output) of the organization to be achieved. By looking at problems as symptoms of system deficits, managers can begin to address

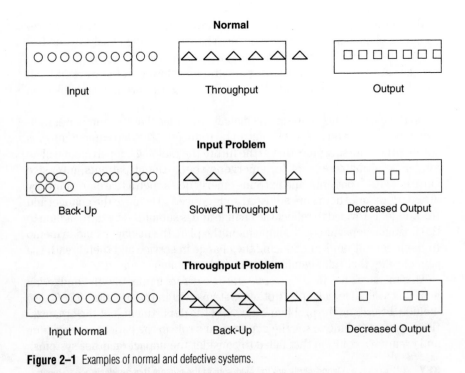

Figure 2–1 Examples of normal and defective systems.

problems as issues with organizational systems rather than issues with the performance of the people who carry out the organization's functions.

Without this orderly approach to problem solving, there is a risk that the solution to one problem will only create another, larger problem or that the perceived resolution to one situation will cause the development of an even bigger hornet's nest in a connecting system. For example, the chief financial officer, head of the financial system, decides that all departments must make a 5% reduction in the cost of doing business during the upcoming fiscal year. In response to this directive, the radiology department manager looks over the options that are available for achieving this requirement. This manager proceeds by defining the instruction in its simplest terms: How can a 5% reduction be made in the radiology department. This poses a predicament because the operating budget of a department contains two areas from which to make this reduction: personnel and supplies. Because the number of radiology procedures is not expected to change, the manager decides that the needed reduction cannot come from the supplies associated with performing procedures. With this option eliminated, that leaves only the staffpower side of the budget. If staffpower is reduced, however, that means that a corresponding change in service must occur. The manager then analyzes the frequency with which certain functions of the department occur and determines that the need for inpatient radiography is lower on the weekend and surmises that this is related to the fact that surgeries are not scheduled on weekends.

On the basis of this analysis, the manager decides that the number of radiology technicians on the weekend can be reduced if the department informs the inpatient nursing units that in the future the radiology department will no longer be available except for emergency department patients, intensive care unit (ICU) patients, and extreme emergencies such as cardiorespiratory arrest. Personnel hours are adjusted and reduced to achieve the change, and the budget is revised to reflect the change and is submitted by the deadline to the financial department. To implement the plan, the manager sends a memo to the inpatient units announcing the change in service and then breathes a sigh of relief that this seemingly impossible problem is solved.

This manager has made several strategic errors in meeting the budgeting goal that will adversely affect other systems within the organization. These include describing the problem in terms of the department, not the organizational system; failing to see the department's role in the patient care system; and creating a solution that failed to consider the impact on other systems.

KEY CONCEPTS
- Departments are the elements of the system that are designed to meet the goals of an organization.
- Because one department may serve as the throughput for the output of another departmental system, there is a strong likelihood that a change in one department will affect the system in another department.
- Any department changes that affect service or output are likely to affect related systems.

LEARNING CHALLENGE
What did the radiology department manager overlook in developing the budget? What departments are likely to be affected by changes in the nursing department? Identify the nursing units that would be affected by a change in the admitting practices of the emergency department.

In the foregoing example, the manager considered only the systems of the radiology department when developing a solution. The role and function of the department and its contribution to the structure of the organization were overlooked. In addition, the function of the department was defined without consideration of the department's contribution to the achievement of the goals of the organization. By limiting the definition of the problem to "reduce the department budget by 5%," the manager overlooked the fact that performing radiological examinations so that patients can receive appropriate medical intervention and be restored to health is the function of the department. By rationing this service to achieve the budget reduction, attaining that end becomes more difficult.

In a short time, the consequences of this solution begin to have a ripple effect on the other departments in the hospital. It can result in longer hospital stays because patients have to wait until Monday to access the radiology tests that may determine appropriate treatment. As a consequence, this affects the nursing department budget because staff must be maintained to care for the patient. In addition, the budgets of other ancillary departments are influenced because they must continue to provide services such as meals, housecleaning, and linen for the patient. Furthermore, an increase in tests to be performed on Monday may occur. Overtime in the radiology department may be required to respond to this workload change. This, too, can adversely affect the budget and could nullify the expected savings. In this instance, what looked like a plan to economize could lead to unexpected costs. The adjustment of workload without consideration of the impact on other departments in the organization shifted costs and failed to achieve the cost savings the financial officer was seeking.

Although this example may seem extreme, it is frequently the practice of the inexperienced manager. A manager who considers systems would take into consideration the impact and implications of a change from the perspective of organizational structure. If the issue is thought over from a systems point of view, the implications of one department's solutions for another system within the organization are more apparent because the interrelatedness of department activities can be seen. System analysis helps the manager focus on the contribution of a department to the achievement of the organization's specific goal and points out actions that might interfere with that intent. Recognizing the link of departments to achieve positive outcomes for the organization promotes collaboration in problem solving and improved communication among managers. Surprises and rework are reduced.

The complexity of today's health care environment demands creative solutions that will maintain the health of the system as well as the patients whom it serves. Systems thinking and the improved collaboration and communication that it fosters in the organization can only increase the likelihood of that happening.

ORGANIZATIONAL STRUCTURE AS A SYSTEM

Most organizations are arranged according to functions, traditionally by departments, divisions, or units. Organizational charts are graphic representations of how organizational systems are arranged. On the surface they appear to be defining primarily structure by illustrating the titles of departments and the titles of the people in charge. They also depict systems of communication, authority, and decision making, however. In fact, they are the formal representation of how the organization, the largest system, has chosen to arrange those functions and subsystems that must come together for the organization to act as a system to realize its goals.

In daily use, organizational charts are looked at most often to determine lines of authority and reporting relationships. They usually take a pyramid shape, with one person at the top and several expanding layers of management between the top and the front line, where the service is provided or the product manufactured. Hammer and Champy (1994) suggest that this shape is best suited for organizations that are experiencing high growth and have an interest in control and planning; they also suggest that it may no longer be pertinent in today's organizations.

Organizational charts can also serve a useful purpose for the working nurse manager. They can be a valuable resource in determining the systems that the nursing department affects and in deciding who needs to be included in planning changes because of the possible impact on their system. Furthermore, it will clarify who needs to approve decisions or participate in making them. Alternative organizational structures are discussed in greater detail in Chapter 1.

The structure of the organization is designed to arrange the subsystems within the organization as divisions, departments, and units. Most typically, they are based on function. For example, the hospital system meant to deliver babies becomes the labor and delivery unit. Even its title defines its function. In another example, the operating room is defined as a department because that is where surgery is performed. Hammer and Champy (1994) suggest, however, that these organizational arrangements are artifacts of another age that was founded on the industrial concept of organizing work based on tasks. They propose that today's organizations should be built around processes that are based on customers' needs rather than on the tasks to be performed. If this concept were applied in health care, labor and delivery would no longer be a department but a step in the system for maternal care. Maternal care would become the place where a woman comes for her prenatal care, delivery, and postpartum recovery and would flow into well-baby care and transition to the pediatric services system. The new system would now be based on the process of having a baby and meeting the customer's needs, not on the function of the birth. By serving the customer, the system is more likely to achieve the organization's goal of satisfying customers. This type of structure is designed to meet the customer's needs, achieve the goals of the organization, and perform the functions related to patient care.

PREVENTING SYSTEM BREAKDOWN

In general systems theory, as discussed earlier, systems are made up of three elements: input, throughput, and output. In addition, there is a **feedback** loop so that adjustment can be made to prevent system breakdown. Failure in throughput will either cause back-up for entry into the system or a delay in output from the system. A common biological example familiar to all nurses is cardiac failure. Failure in the cardiac pump, the agent of throughput, results in congestive heart failure. Depending on which part of the pump is damaged, the failure can manifest itself as pulmonary congestion, a back-up of the entry to the system, or reduced cardiac output, a deficit in the output portion of the system. If either goes uncorrected, there is soon widespread failure of the entire system, and right-sided or left-sided failure becomes cardiac failure. Ultimately, other systems are affected.

Another cardiac example demonstrates how a reduction of input can result in system failure. Hemorrhage reduces input into the system. To compensate the throughput portion, the heart pump increases to maintain output at an optimum level. If the input deficit goes uncorrected, the system begins to fail. In this case, the function of the system—transport of nutrients to the cells—is unachievable because the transport mechanism—blood—is not being input adequately. If uncorrected, the system collapses.

LEARNING CHALLENGE In health care, managers witness minor system breakdowns that can lead to major organizational complications on a daily basis. A domino effect occurs when prescriptions for a patient scheduled for discharge are delayed in the pharmacy, just as it does when the output from the ventricle is decreased and a back-up occurs in the atrium and lungs. The decreased output from the pharmacy affects the throughput of the nursing unit. This delay in turn causes a delayed discharge that creates a back-up in the recovery room because a bed is not available for a patient transfer. This event then affects the input to the patient care system on the inpatient nursing unit. Identify other events in hospital departments that might lead to similar back-ups.

The above example also demonstrates the interrelatedness of systems in the hospital. In a short time, any system failure begins adversely to affect those systems with which it communicates. Once again, the cardiac system serves as a good biological example. When the cardiac pump fails, the cardiac output is reduced. This output acts as the input for the renal system, and failure of renal throughput begins to occur. Soon the renal system problem begins to affect the input to the fluid and electrolyte balance of the chemical system, which in turn affects cellular function and the metabolic system. Eventually, these sequences lead to full system failure, and the organism dies.

In an organization, the path to collapse is similar. A breakdown in the scheduling system leads to a reduction of available staff. The responsibility to meet patients' needs remains, however. As a result, the organization must resort to the use of overtime to maintain the patient care system. This increases the costs but not the output. The impact of increased cost in turn begins to make itself felt in the financial system, which can affect the overall function of all elements of the organizational system, including departments other than nursing.

KEY CONCEPTS
- These biological and organizational examples point out how any change in a system will affect all its components as well as the components of all systems that communicate with the changing system.
- If systems are to remain sound, managers must consider the effect on parallel and communicating systems when planning for change.

METHODS TO ANALYZE A SYSTEM

Most managers are faced with changing a system more frequently than developing one. The best way to change a system, however, is to treat it as though a new one was being developed. For example, how might maternity services be changed from the traditional method of dividing services between inpatient and outpatient, prenatal and postnatal care, and the labor and delivery event? In addition, some settings still set up care of the newborn as a separate, not integrated, system. The first step in making this change is to decide the scope of services to be covered. The traditional industrial approach, which is based on function, would analyze the system as it exists for prenatal care, delivery services, and postpartum care and would continue to separate systems based on the tasks to be performed. Hammer and Champy (1994), on the other hand, define the system based on the customer's needs or, in other words, the **process** of pregnancy. This redefining of services requires reengineering that breaks down the unit barriers that now exist, that is to say a change in the skill of the nursing personnel in order to deinstitutionalize the birthing process so that the patients' needs are better met. This is an example of a system that is based on customer needs more than organizational needs, but still supports organizational goals.

When examined closely, most current hospital systems are more provider focused than patient focused. Historically, hospitals have marketed their services primarily to physicians because it was the physicians who determined which hospital a patient would use and therefore brought in the revenue. As a result, many internal systems were designed to meet the convenience of the provider more than the patient. Recently, however, a few hospitals have begun to manipulate systems to create what is being called **patient-focused care**. Townsend (1993) describes this as a new paradigm of care that links components of system redesign work through a common, defining purpose. In other words, meeting the patient's needs becomes the center of system planning. Services begin to be decentralized to the patient care areas rather than remaining centralized into hospital departments. Hospital services begin to come to the patient rather than the patient moving throughout the building to access services.

For example, in the functional model patients are transported to the radiology department for all procedures. In the new model, the radiology technician is stationed on the patient care unit and participates in other patient care activities when not performing radiological procedures. The patient no longer experiences the discomfort of moving from one department to another through long corridors to receive specialized care from strangers. Proponents of these new patient care models believe that the majority of patients with similar reasons for hospital admission require comparable laboratory and radiology services. By moving these services to the patient care units, the productivity of these technicians can be improved as well.

These changes to models of care are too recent to determine their success. Even so, this change to basing systems on the patient care process is being received favorably by many administrators. Staff who are being asked to cross-train and step outside their existing job descriptions are less certain that the change is positive, but no change ever occurs without things having to be done differently. Evaluating the effectiveness of these system changes will take time. It is hoped that the effectiveness of the system will come from the feedback from the patients who receive the services so that their input will guide the adjustments to perfect the systems.

General system theory also makes possible the design of models. Therefore, principles can be transferred from one field to another without necessitating duplication of the discovery of the same principle in different fields that are isolated from each other (Von Bertalanfly, 1968). The application of critical paths to the clinical setting is an example of taking a technique from one industry and using it in another.

Critical path methodologies originated in the construction and engineering fields and have been used there for many years (Coffey, Richards, Remmert,

LeRoy, Schoville, & Baldwin, 1992). They provide a way to organize the sequence of events of large, complex projects so that they are efficiently managed and delays limited while quality is maximized. When used in the health care setting, they become a mechanism for graphically depicting the interrelatedness of services that are required for a patient to move through the labyrinth that health care has become. The use of critical paths for patients, however, requires a fundamental change in the way in which health care providers identify patients' needs. During the past several years, there has been an increased focus on individualizing the patient's care. As a result, practitioners have been more focused on the differences among patients. In contrast, **critical paths** focus on the similarities of patient needs. The planning of critical paths is based on predicting standardized needs and a common progression in recovery for a patient group. As a result, for some practitioners it is difficult not to see critical paths as "cookbook medicine." Human nature also interferes with accepting that there is more that is common to patients with the same diagnosis than is different. Because the focus is the individual patient's need, the clinician focuses on the differences and overlooks the patterns and trends that exist within that patient group. In addition, we are all more likely to remember the patient who did not follow the expected course and challenged our abilities better than the patient whose care was uneventful. In many instances, being confronted with the unexpected creates discomfort. To counteract this troublesome situation, procedures are incorporated into practice to make sure that this emergency does not recur. These soon become patterns and rituals of everyday care and emphasize the differences among patients. As a result, it seems that the similarities among patients are few and far between.

KEY
CONCEPT

To develop clinical paths:
- identify patient groups with like diagnoses and outcomes
- identify the disciplines involved in providing care for these patients
- identify the standards that influence the care of these patients
- identify all the information that is known about the patient group
- review the current practices for these patients, and separate ritual from need
- bring the various disciplines together to discuss the care of the patient group
- focus on what is similar about the patients, not what is different

When one begins to look at patient groups for their similarities, it becomes apparent that there are more common issues than expected. It must be kept in mind that critical paths are a method for tracking the interrelatedness of systems and that developing any system begins with identifying how routine steps will occur. The standard must be known in order to identify the deviation.

The labor and delivery unit can be used as an example of the application of this concept. Traditionally this has been considered one of the least predictable areas in the hospital. If the paradigm is shifted to focus on what is common and known about the patients who use the labor and delivery service, however, the picture changes. Consider what is common to the patients in labor and delivery. First, all the patients are female and have the same diagnosis: pregnancy. That defines them as a patient group, which means that certain elements of their care should be similar. The predicted time frame within which the delivery should occur is also known. Although the exact time at which it will occur cannot be predicted, the end point of the time frame is well defined. If labor does not start naturally by week 42 of the pregnancy, labor will be induced. Furthermore, the stages of labor and the patient's needs during each stage are well known. Finally, the delivery will occur either vaginally or by cesarean section. Other sources are available to identify patient similarities. Because of the need to register births and report birth statistics to government agencies, most labor and delivery units collect extensive statistics. They include, minimally, the date and the number and method of delivery. Often, these statistics also contain information about average laboring time and patterns of activity for the day, shift, month, and season. Data that profile the maternity patient can be retrieved from other sources, such as the medical record, as well. Demographics such as age, number of pregnancies, preterm labor patients, and so forth are available. The one thing that cannot be predicted, however, is who will come through the door in the next 5 minutes. Ironically, it is this one piece of missing information that convinces us that this area is highly unpredictable. For this patient group, and for many others, examining the data provides direction and helps build the systems for improving patient care.

In this instance, reviewing the data points out some emerging patterns. Analysis of deliveries by the day of the week may indicate a change in the rate on the weekends. The most common time for admissions may point out that most patients come into the hospital in the morning. A review of the census on each shift can help determine which shift has the most patients in labor and guide decisions about staffing patterns. Consideration of the cesarean section rate and separation of the scheduled cases from the urgent cases will indicate the need for contingency planning to handle emergencies. As a result, the budget management should be improved, which will benefit the financial system. As in earlier examples, a change in one system ripples throughout the organization and affects many systems.

LEARNING   Other units in the hospital are also considered unpredictable and too diverse
CHALLENGE   to permit any preplanning. How would you go about analyzing the patient
groups in an ICU? What are the similarities of patients in the ICU? What are
the routines that occur in an ICU? Can you identify any routines in the ICU
that could be characterized as rituals? What other systems would be affected
by a change in routines in the ICU?

Critical paths have several characteristics that distinguish them from algorithms and practice parameters. They are comprehensive, demonstrate the interaction of services, and do not reflect the decision making of just one group of providers. Also, they identify timelines during which events should occur. Furthermore, critical paths are developed in collaboration with other health care providers. In many cases, someone (most of the time a nurse) acts as a manager of the case (Coffey et al., 1992).

Critical paths vary from institution to institution in their format. Although there is no generic format, most critical paths include some form of timeline on a horizontal axis (which may be described in minutes, hours, days, or zones) complemented by a list of services or interventions that the patient will need on the vertical axis. Table 2–1 depicts an example of a critical path for a cesarean section patient.

Another method for developing critical paths, as in other systems, begins with examining the data. A review of the charts of patient groups identifies common milestones in recovery and similarities in the use of hospital services. This will also help determine factors that influence the length of stay. Although reducing length of stay is not the primary purpose of writing critical paths, times have changed, and no one wants a patient to be in the hospital longer than is necessary.

Another source for these data is the hospital utilization department. A breakdown of the charts of patients who fall on either side of this expected length of stay can help identify the exceptions as well as possibilities for improvement. For example, examining the records of patients who have short stays may point out some methods in their care that could lead to a shortened stay when incorporated into the care of all patients in that group. On the other hand, looking at the situations that lead to an extended stay can identify organizational system problems that influence the stay. These become opportunities for improvement. From all this information, the time standard around which the critical path is developed is based on the expected outcome for the noncomplicated patient.

Table 2-1 Sample Critical Path for the Diagnosis of Cesarean Section

	Time Postpartum					
	8 Hours	8–12 Hours	12–24 Hours	24–48 Hours	48–72 Hours	Expected Outcome
Labs	UA & H/H results on chart		Draw H/H results on chart			H&H within normal limits
Renal	Foley placed in L&D	Remove Foley	Check for 3 voids (>150 mL), straight cath prn for retention	Voiding independently	Voiding independently	Voiding independently
Diet/GI	Clear liquids if no N&V	Clear liquids	Clear liquids	Advance diet as tolerated	Regular diet	Regular diet
Activity/musculoskeletal	Bedrest, TC&DB q2h moving all extremities	Dangle or up in chair	Ambulate with assistance q shift	Ambulate independently	Ambulate independently, shower	Care of self and infant
Medication	IV medication to control nausea	IV medication to control nausea	IV medication to control nausea	Stool softeners, laxatives prn	RhoGAM and/or MMR if indicated, DC prescription to pharmacy	Able to verbalize understanding of DC medications (name, reason, dosage, schedule)
Pain management	PCA	PCA	PCA	Pain controlled by oral meds	Pain controlled by oral meds	Able to verbalize pain management, including medication
IV therapy	IV with Pitocin	DC Pitocin, IV infusing	IV infusing	Heparin Lock IV if taking fluids	DC Heparin Lock	No IV

continues

Table 2–1 Continued

	Time Postpartum					
	8 Hours	8–12 Hours	12–24 Hours	24–48 Hours	48–72 Hours	Expected Outcome
Treatment/intervention	Tri-flow q hour while awake, fundus, dressing and lochia check on admission and q2h	Tri-flow q hour while awake, fundus, dressing and lochia check q2h, pericare	Tri-flow q hour while awake, fundus, dressing and lochia check q2h, pericare	Remove dressing, assess incision q shift, self-pericare, fundus and lochia checks q shift, observe bonding	Observe bonding, assess incision, remove staples, place Steri-Strips, fundus and lochia check q shift	Incision clean and dry, no signs of infection, Steri-Strips intact, fundus firm, lochia small to moderate
Teaching	Signs of increased bleeding, infant security, tri-flow, infant identification	Infant safety, bulb suctioning, feeding, bonding, tri-flow, lactation referral if breastfeeding	Self-pericare, breast care, cord care, circumcision care, infant complications, temperature taking; reinforce previous teaching; assess understanding	Reinforce previous teaching, assess learning, attend discharge teaching class, provide mother/baby books	Identification of complications, incision care; demonstrates learning of previous teaching; assess learning; follow-up care for infant and mother; car safety	Verbalizes signs and symptoms of complications of mother or infant and appropriate follow-up, able to demonstrate knowledge of cord care and circumcision care
Discharge planning	Assess discharge needs, social service referral if indicated			Discuss discharge transportation, home needs	Dietary or home health referral if indicated, lactation consult if appropriate	Referrals completed before discharge

KEY
CONCEPT Critical path development includes the following:

  • Analyze patient charts to identify milestones in recovery.
  • Use organizational data systems to provide historical information.
  • Look closely at the charts of patients whose length of stay was shorter or longer than expected. They could indicate where changes in the system are needed.

Critical paths, when used for patient care, include a method to identify **variances** from the path. These detours are identified because they occur outside the predicted time period. They may have occurred either earlier or later than expected. In all instances, once the variance is identified, the reason for it can be pinpointed in one of three categories. One area is related to the patient. Obviously, there are times when the patient's course does not follow the predicted path. In other instances, the variance is the result of a breakdown in one of the systems of the organization. The last category is when the variance occurs because of a provider's decision to manage the patient differently than the critical path suggests. Over time, analysis of these variances will identify areas for improvement. Patient variances may indicate that the time frames that are established were either too ambitious or too conservative. These new data can indicate patterns and trends that will point out how to adjust the care for future patients. By pinpointing system variances, the process of deciding where system changes need to be made is simplified. Finally, this method will make data available to measure outcomes for various providers that will lend support to the development of practice guidelines. It is hard to ignore data that identify the need for change.

FLOWCHARTS

Another technique that lends itself to the development of a system and is also useful in developing a critical path is the **flowchart**. Flowcharts are a method for system analysis that uses standardized symbols that graphically depict a process. Figure 2–2 displays the standard symbols. The symbols are connected by arrows that indicate the sequence of steps and the direction in which the activity will flow. Flowcharts also have start and end points. These define the boundaries of the process to be diagrammed; these may really be where one system connects with another. For critical paths, they help determine the systems with which the critical path will join or intersect.

Flowcharts are useful tools for several reasons. A high-level flowchart is one with fewer details and helps identify the sequencing of steps that must occur within a system for a process to take place. Activities are entered in a rectangular symbol, and the direction of activity is indicated by direction ar-

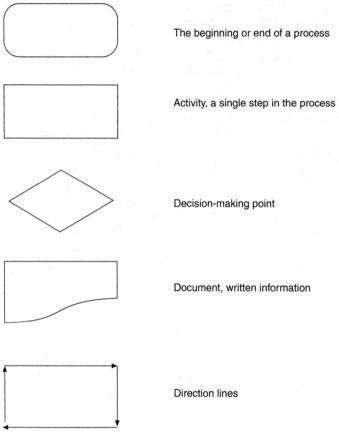

Figure 2–2 Flowchart symbols.

rows between the boxes. Decision points are also identified in the chart and are indicated in a diamond. High-level flowcharts begin by charting key steps in a process. These steps are then analyzed and charted for final details. This exercise helps clarify points in the process where needless, circuitous, time-wasting loops occur. Figure 2–3 is a high-level flowchart of the steps to set up the operating room in preparation for a cesarean section.

Flowcharts must be drawn and reviewed by those who are familiar with the system, and they develop best when accompanied by dialogue. Questions such as "What do you do next?" or "How do you do that?" help refine the process to tease out the detail needed. This exercise also benefits the outcome

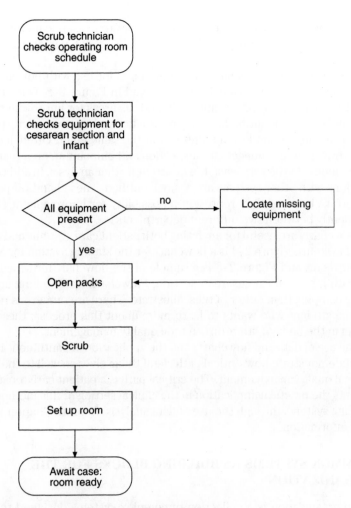

Figure 2–3 High-level flowchart, cesarean section room ready.

because it forces all the participants to think about the steps that must occur and the sequence of each; many times it serendipitously identifies misconceptions of how things happen. There is a saying in management: If you want to know how a system works, try to change it. Another benefit of this critical thinking process is that it helps identify those steps that are dependent upon a certain person rather than on an ongoing process. In many cases, this is not discovered until the person leaves the organization. Something that everyone thought was a part of a more formalized system disappears with the person, and the system collapses. In this example it is the person's system, not the organization's.

Standardized symbols have been developed for use with flowcharts. The most commonly used symbols are displayed in Figure 2–2. Once the flowchart is finalized, **loops** are apparent, and the areas for improvement in the system are easily identified. Loops are situations where the activity branches out of the process and then reenters it at the same point. Often, loops indicate rework or an unnecessary inspection and pinpoint an area that may be superfluous. At the very least, they warrant further analysis. In addition, connections with other systems are easily identified. These hand-off points are important because they represent a possibility for improvement (they are frequently between two different departments).

Flowcharts are useful for analyzing both patient care systems and management systems. Figure 2–4 is a flowchart for the staffing system for a nursing department, and Figure 2–5 is a sample of the flowchart for scheduling an operating room for a cesarean section. Flowcharts can be long and much more complex than either of these illustrate. There are numerous resources for the student who wants to learn more about this process; these can be found in the body of literature on total quality management.

The use of data and flowcharts and the application of continuous improvement demonstrate how critical paths lend themselves so well to the concept of total quality management. The critical path is a patient care tool that represents the practical application in the clinical setting of this method for improving systems through the use of data analysis. Refer to Chapter 9 for further information.

COMMON SYSTEMS AS BUILDING BLOCKS FOR THE ORGANIZATION

An organization is a collection of complex systems designed to reach a goal. It can be as small as two people or as large as thousands. Regardless of size, the goal must be clear to everyone involved if it is going to be achieved. Organizations also represent collective leadership. This means that the message of organizational directives comes from many different people, often at different times and in different locations. Size, time, locations, and different leaders all contribute to the risk that the goal of the organization may be unclear to employees or first-line managers, who are making vital decisions on a daily basis that can determine the success or failure of the company. Success is dependent on every manager using the same criteria for decision making, whether it is the chief executive officer of the hospital or the night nursing

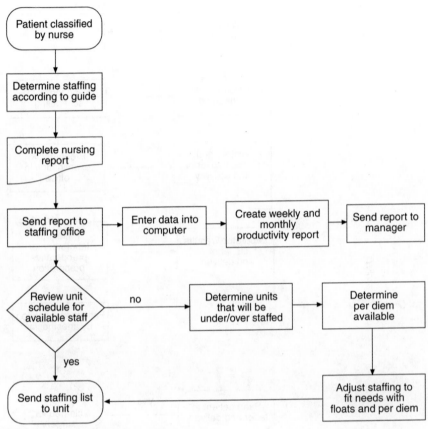

Figure 2–4 Nursing department staffing system.

supervisor, who is determining staffing ratios for the next shift. In addition, large organizations are less likely to reflect the image of any one person, although this does not eliminate the potential for influence of a strong leader, as was demonstrated by Lee Iacocca at Chrysler Corporation.

Most commonly, though, large organizations become a collection of people who come together to achieve a purpose, and as a result the organization seems to develop a collective personality all its own that is separate and apart from the people who work there. This does not occur unintentionally. To accomplish this, organizations put in writing statements that are meant to create a social order that will clarify the goals of the organization and influence the way the leadership conducts business with its customers and employees. These written documents are its mission, philosophy, and vision statements.

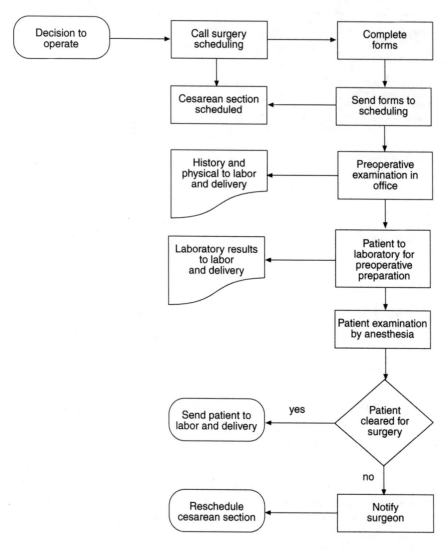

Figure 2–5 Scheduling a cesarean section.

These will propagate the culture that the organization wants to embrace. Like all social orders, organizations develop the basic elements of a culture, such as values, mores, taboos, legends, myths, symbols, status, and so forth. These statements of vision, mission, and philosophy, when developed collectively by the leaders in the organization, come together to define what the organization stands for. They become the social system of the organization.

Mission

The **mission statement** defines the general goals of the organization in broad terms. Most mission statements are one sentence but contain a lot of substance. The following example shows how a mission statement might be worded:

> The mission of the nursing department of this hospital is to provide quality care that is based on scientific knowledge, fosters patient comfort in an individualized and personalized manner, and is designed to support the organizational goals and vision.

Mission statements should be reviewed periodically to determine whether they are current, have been accomplished, or need modification. They are not static statements. Consider a military mission; it defines an objective and a method for measuring when the objective has been achieved: "Send 22 planes to bomb and destroy an enemy encampment." This makes it evident that the mission will change when the objective is achieved or changes. In one instance, the planes may achieve their objective. In another, there may be representatives at a peace conference who will sign a treaty before the military objective is achieved, in which case the mission will need to change.

In health care, payment formats, patient groups, and locations for care delivery are being changed by legislators, consumers, and directors in the board rooms every day. The need to update a mission statement may be as vital to a health care organization as it is to a military general. Because the mission in health care is based on meeting the needs of customers, it must reflect the changing climate outside the organization. The organization that defines its mission based on its internal environment may find itself without customers because the customers' needs have changed and the organization is not changing to meet them. Refer to Chapter 1 for a more detailed discussion of mission.

Vision

The concept of vision draws a picture for the members of an organization of what the organization wants to be that it believes it is not now. Kouzes and Posner (1988) define a **vision statement** as an ideal and unique image of the future. They believe that inspiring a vision is one of the critical traits of successful leaders. Senge (1990) believes that the vision transforms work into the pursuit of a larger purpose and embodies the style, climate, and spirit of the organization. He describes it as being exhilarating and as creating a spark of excitement that lifts the organization out of the mundane and changes the relationship of its people from "us and them" to just "us." It creates a common identity for the people working in the organization and promotes people working together.

Visions for corporations may be drafted by a committee or the leadership of the organization, so that it represents the collective image of the future. Whether a vision is developed by a committee or a single person, the more it is able to paint a picture of what the future will look like for those who share the vision, the more likely it is that it will be embraced and, better yet, achieved. People are less likely to be able to relate to visions that are stated in lofty terms. They will seem vague and unattainable and will not unite people to achieve a common goal. At the very least, they will not ignite that spark of excitement that makes ordinary people accomplish extraordinary things (Senge, 1990). Visions are useful to the organizational leadership because they serve as a benchmark against which to test decisions. Hammer and Champy (1994) cite the vision of Federal Express during its infancy as expertly expressed: "We will deliver the package by 10:30 the next morning." They believe this is an excellent example because it is about operations, has measurable objectives, and changed the basis for competition in the industry. The vision for Southern California Kaiser Permanente appears in Exhibit 2–1.

A vision addresses more than one element of the business. If a management decision looks too far removed from what is stated in the vision, staff will lose their enthusiasm for what the vision is trying to create. Reality and the image will be too disparate. For example, a vision statement that describes a company that provides secure jobs for employees will be faced with conflict should layoffs have to occur. This comes about even when the layoffs are necessary to ensure that jobs are secure for employees in the future. Even though there may be no other choice, the leadership should be sensitive to how this conflict between action and vision will be perceived by staff. A spark of excitement can be doused quickly in these circumstances, and it will require extraordinary leadership to rekindle the flame. Refer to Chapter 12 for a more detailed description.

Philosophy

The **philosophy statement** is a statement of beliefs. The values of the organization are embodied in this document. The philosophy of the nursing department, for example, provides a description of how the patient will be

Exhibit 2–1 Organization Vision Statement

Our Vision

Preamble: This vision of our future reflects the goals and aspirations of all the people who share in a common desire to make Kaiser Permanente the first choice among employees, physicians, and members.

We serve as a health care team and value the contributions of each member.

We are compassionate and caring, devoted to the health and well-being of our members.

We provide superior value in health care.

We are a unique partnership of medicine and business, which is the key to our success.

We are the first choice for a career in the health care field.

We foster innovation by valuing ideas.

We provide leadership to the health care industry and serve as a model for the efficient delivery of quality health care.

We are committed to the success of our communities as well as the success of our organizations.

Courtesy of Kaiser Permanente, Southern California Region.

treated. Many times it will be based on a theory for nursing and will describe how care will be delivered within the tenets of that theory. It should be in concert with and reflect the department's role in achieving the organization's vision. Like the mission and vision statements, it should be reviewed periodically to ensure that it still reflects the beliefs of the organization. Conversely, the implementation of new programs should be measured against it to ensure that the new programs are in keeping with the beliefs of the organization. A sample of a nursing department philosophy is displayed in Exhibit 2–2.

All these components come together to form the social system of the organization. To some they may seem like exercises and only flowery words, but the process and activity necessary to create them elicit discussions among the leadership that breed consensus for goals and confirm the direction that the organization wants to take. These exchanges of views are valuable because the documents they produce will be instrumental in charting the course for the organization. This outcome is another reason why it is important for these reviews to take place regularly or when changes in leadership occur.

Vision, mission, and philosophy become benchmarks against which to test organizational decisions and programs. For example, goals should be set to

Exhibit 2–2 Nursing Department Integrated Vision Road Map

Vulnerabilities

Becoming the Employer of Choice	Demonstrating Value	Decision Making/ Organization Design

Vision

We serve as a health care team and value the contributions of each team member.

We are compassionate and caring, devoted to the health and well-being of members.

We provide superior value in health care.

We are a unique partnership of medicine and business, which is a key to our success. We are the first choice for a career in the health care field.

We provide leadership to the health care industry and serve as a model for the efficient delivery of quality health care.

We foster innovation by valuing new ideas.

We are committed to the success of our communities as well as the success of our organization.

Medical Service Area Strategic Goals

- Member satisfaction with access to minor illness/same-day service
- Member satisfaction with personalized care
- Hospital utilization
- Improved member health
- Access to care
- Cost
- Employee/physician satisfaction

Nursing Services Mission

The nursing service provides patients with nursing care, builds and supports relationships with providers and departments in the organization, achieves patient-focused outcomes, and is reflective of the high standard of performance of the nursing staff.

Nursing Services Core Values

Patient Centered

We value care delivery systems and processes that meet patient and family needs and goals. These outcomes include: service quality, clinical quality,

continues

Exhibit 2–2 Continued

patient-centered decision making, safe environment, interdisciplinary coordination, interdepartmental communication, continuity of care.

Results Orientation

We value the achievement of specific targeted outcomes. These outcomes are: cost effective, efficient, defined, innovative.

Performance

We value our individual and team activities. These behavioral outcomes include: initiative, competence, continuous improvement, creativity, accountability, high quality, commitment to change.

Relationship

We value the connection between processes that depend on, involve, or follow each other. These behavioral outcomes are: acceptance of thought diversity, integrity, teamwork, collaboration, positive image, service philosophy, integrated resources.

Nursing Services Strategic Focus

Member satisfaction with personalized care
- Personalized care

Hospital utilization
- Care delivery
- Kare Paths
- Documentation

Improved member health
- Existing quality improvement plan

Access to care
- Operating room access

Cost
- Payroll
- Nonpayroll

Employee/physician satisfaction
- Employee satisfaction task force
- Collaborative practice teams

Unit-Specific Strategic Focus

Member satisfaction with personalized care
- Personalized care

Improved member health/patient-centered care
- Unit determined

Cost
- Payroll
- Nonpayroll

Employee/physician satisfaction
- Unit climate survey results
- Unit-based collaborative practice teams

Courtesy of Kaiser Permanente, San Diego Medical Center Nursing Department.

achieve the vision. When developing organizational goals, the leadership should ask questions such as "Is this goal in keeping with the vision, philosophy, and mission of the organization?" and "Does it treat customers as we say we believe they should be treated?" Formally going through this process begins to anchor the tenets of the social system to the operating systems of the organization. Refer to Chapter 1 for a more detailed discussion of philosophy.

Policymaking

Policies equate to rules and regulations that govern society at large and should be in writing. They are the application of the vision, mission, and philosophy to the operational systems of the organization. In a practical sense, they communicate the vision, mission, and philosophy by implanting them into practice. They also describe how situations and issues will be handled by the organization and are based on these belief systems. They act as a reference for decision makers, managers, and employees for the purpose of ensuring that rules are invoked consistently. In addition, a policy statement acts as a method for enacting the philosophy of the organization. For example, an organization that states that it believes that all patients are a member of a family and that families will be included in the care of patients should have a liberal visiting policy. A restrictive policy with stringent time limits and rigid visitor categories would not be in concert with this belief statement. Another example of an inconsistency would be a nursing department policy that requires approval by the nursing supervisor of all calls to physicians in a department with a philosophy that states its belief in self-governance and the empowering of employees.

Many policies are mandated by regulatory and credentialing agencies and must be evidenced in writing. The absence of such a policy can lead to a loss of approval by the agency. Examples of some agencies that influence policies are Medicare, the Joint Commission on Accreditation of Healthcare Organizations, the state Department of Health, and others. Of a less formal nature, community standards will also influence the creation of policies. Practices that are introduced in one institution as an innovation may be embraced by the consumer with such enthusiasm that other organizations soon receive the message that their policies need to be adjusted so that they are in line with the community and meet customer expectations.

Procedures

Procedures operationalize the policies of the organization. They are the detailed instructions for the methods to be used in carrying out specific tasks. Procedures include policy statements that define the conditions under which the procedure can be applied. They are always in writing. In addition, they reflect the application of the mission, vision, and philosophy at the operational level. In other words, they translate mission, vision, and philosophy into actions. Procedures ensure that practice occurs within regulatory guidelines and that practice is consistent throughout the organization. Like all other documents that influence the care of patients, they must be reviewed on a regular basis to ensure that they mirror current practice and policy.

SYSTEMS TO MANAGE PERSONNEL

The **organizational chart** is a graphic display of the management of the organization and how it is organized. It demonstrates the lines of authority, decision-making, and communication patterns that make up the systems that manage personnel. Like all other systems in the organization, the management system is designed to support achieving the goals of the organization. The organizational chart, like all other documents, should reflect the values, beliefs, and goals that are embodied in the mission, vision, and philosophy statements. For example, an organization that says its vision is to achieve shared governance with its employees should not have an organizational chart that depicts many layers of management and supervision between the direct caregivers and the top position in the organization. Chapters 1 and 10 review this topic in more detail.

INFORMATION SYSTEMS

Documentation is probably the most familiar information system for nurses. Nurses make entries into the **medical record** at regular intervals. This in turn contributes to the system for retrieving information about individual patients and groups of patients. Charting this information takes a considerable amount of the nurse's time.

Although the medical chart was once a method for communicating the ongoing condition of the patient to other caregivers, it has now become the information resource for many other disciplines. Because the **nursing record** chronicles the patient's care in great detail and in a time-focused fashion, it has become, in addition to a communication tool, a legal document, a resource for accounting and billing purposes, and a method to demonstrate regulatory compliance. Because of these added uses, the amount of information that is documented is voluminous, and numerous chart forms have been developed to meet these specific needs.

In addition, despite the fact that most hospitals treat similar patient groups in a similar fashion, nurses create new chart forms to make them more specific to their institution and unit of practice. For example, a nursing assessment is required in many settings at least once during a 24-hour period. Yet what makes up a nursing assessment and how it is configured vary widely and are dependent upon the opinions and beliefs of the nurses who developed and designed the form. In fact, most revisions take place with minimal research into the need to document all the details that appear on a nursing flowsheet. In addition, many medical records are separated into sections for the various disciplines to document care. In essence, each discipline creates its own subsystem for charting patient care. As a result, few documentation "systems" can be found. At best, they are a collection of loosely connected chart forms that describe a patient's health care experience.

Electronic Medical Record

Many practitioners are hoping that the **electronic medical record** will resolve this issue. Computers demand a systematic approach for data entry. Because of this, information must be entered in a specific sequence that demands the completion of required fields before the computer will permit the user to move to the next screen. Proponents of the electronic medical record see this form of charting as the resolution to a lot of documentation compliance problems.

There are electronic issues that may create other problems, however. For example, computer displays are limited by the size of the screen. As a result, information entered into the chart by other disciplines may not be reviewed as frequently because of the mechanical steps required. Chances are that documentation by other disciplines will be found on another screen. This could interfere with the communication between disciplines unless the electronic system eliminates charting by category of discipline and moves toward integrated charting or incorporates a system to alert other providers to review an entry. Davenport (1994) believes that effective information management must begin by thinking about how people use information, not how people use machines.

Computer Systems

The clinical application of computers is in its infancy, but the possibilities are limitless. Currently, the most effective systems are linked to routine practices such as laboratory test results, management of medication orders through the pharmacy, order entry for nutrition or radiology, and bed management activities. In many instances, these systems may be mainframed but not necessarily linked to each other. For example, when a patient is put on a medication that has food interactions associated with it, the pharmacy system will not automatically notify the nutrition department to restrict serving this food to the patient. Notifying the nutrition department remains dependent on existing manual systems. As the systems become more sophisticated and integrated, these are examples of automatic patient care improvements that will become routine.

Decision Support Systems

Decision support systems are defined as those that make data available by computer in areas such as finance, staffing and productivity, material resource utilization, patient mix, quality indicators, and length of stay. Such information can be used by the beginning professional nurse to identify trends in client outcomes and care processes and to discover opportunities for improvement. Transforming data into information means asking the right questions and requesting information that will support problem solving and decision making. Such questions might include the following:

- What is the outcome that you want?
- What is the information that is needed to make the decision?
- What is the time frame for data collection?
- How are the data collected?
- How are the data sorted and analyzed?
- How are the data formatted to support the decision-making process?
- How can the effectiveness of the decision be measured?

Effective use of information systems to support clinical and management decisions is predicated on obtaining quality information, having input into the types of data being entered into the system, and using ongoing education to maintain sound operation practices.

FINANCIAL SYSTEMS

Nursing managers are central to the management of budgets in hospitals. The cost center is the smallest unit of budget and often represents a patient care unit. There are three components of the financial system that they deal with most frequently: the operational, capital equipment, and capital improvement budgets.

Operational Budget

There are a variety of methods for developing an **operational budget**. In many instances, despite the fact that the budget is to manage care in the future, history is used to forecast future activity. In the nursing department, where a significant portion of the costs are for labor, the staffing system and budget system are intertwined. Managing and monitoring the budget are a constant frustration for nursing managers because they require setting the cross hairs of dollar usage on the moving targets of staff and patient census. Daily and unrelenting vigilance is required to make all the pieces fit together throughout the fiscal year. Achieving this requires sophisticated monitoring systems that will provide accurate data as close to the event as possible so that early intervention to correct budget variances can be activated. The cost of care cannot be ignored in this climate of health care reform and given the outcry from the public to control costs.

Capital Equipment

The second category of budget that nursing managers handle is the **capital equipment budget**. By definition, this is usually any single piece of medical equipment that costs in excess of $500. This budget usually includes an annual request cycle joined to an approval process. With the increase in technologically based care, the competition for these funds has become fierce.

Capital Improvement

Each institution defines the dollar amount that is allocated to the **capital improvement budget** for remodeling and upgrading the facility. Like the equipment budget, the remodeling budget usually includes an annual request cycle joined to an approval process. Also in this category, the competition for funding is feverish.

Summary

All areas of budget management require good planning and ongoing monitoring. Budget management presents one of the greatest challenges to the new nurse manager because it seems so removed from patient care. Nevertheless, the successful manager will not lose sight of the commitment to provide patient care. Refer to Chapter 8 for greater detail.

PATIENT CARE DELIVERY SYSTEMS

Patient care delivery systems are closely related to staffing systems that must be supported by the budget systems. In addition, the care delivery system that is used must be consistent with the mission, vision, and philosophy of the organization. The care delivery system creates order in how patients will receive their nursing care. Throughout its past, nursing has periodically changed the model that it uses to deliver care. New hybrid models are emerging from a history that has stretched from case assignment to primary nursing. Organizations are experimenting with new models that focus more on patient outcomes and less on who provides the care.

CONCLUSION

Clinically driven critical paths are an example of another process change that is helping nurses see the patient in a continuum of health care. The method to develop them emphasizes the need for efficiently run systems to effect optimal outcomes for the patient. The collaboration required, coupled with the increased awareness of the interaction of well-run systems, calls for a fundamentally different way of looking at patient care needs. The caregiver is refocused to identify where the patient is on the path to recovery rather than on what the caregiver needs to do for a particular shift. The implementation of critical paths and the teamwork required to put them together provide a system for nursing to dismantle the current nursing practice, so that it can focus on patterns that lead to reengineering systems for care rather than designing systems to address the exceptions. Refer to Chapter 3 for greater detail.

Systems thinking is becoming increasingly important in the management of organizations. Every nurse needs to ask these questions: "If I change this, how will it affect the system it is a part of? What occurs at the step before the change I am considering, and what follows it? What communicating systems will be affected by this change? Who needs to know about this change?" If these practices are adopted consistently, the outcome will be improved systems that support quality patient care and provide a healthy working environment for employees.

RESEARCH FOUNDATION   Guild, S., Ledwin, R., Sanford, D., & Winter, T. (1994). Development of an innovative nursing care delivery system. *Journal of Nursing Administration, 24*, 23–29.

Guild, Ledwin, Sanford, and Winter (1994) describe a study that was used to evaluate a current system of nursing care delivery to develop recommendations for a new system for an expansion of obstetrical beds. They describe the process used by a project team to form the new system, which incorporated the components of an organization. To create the fabric of the system, the task force began defining a patient- and family-centered philosophy of care that would serve as the guiding principle of the care system to be developed. In addition, the task force identified the essential components of an effective system that were needed to support these values.

Information from a review of the literature and external hospital surveys was gathered. In addition, internal interviews of key services were carried out. This represented the step of analyzing the impact on connecting systems. Key individuals were asked what they liked about the current system, what they would like to see changed, and what suggestions for innovative ideas for improvement they might have. The information was analyzed by using a database computer system. The recommendations for the care delivery system that resulted blended known nursing care models to meet the specific needs of each care site and patient population. The result of this study was a new system that represented a service line based on the customer's needs rather than on organizational barriers such as units or departments. This study is an example of making the process, not the organization, the object of reengineering (Hammer and Champy, 1994).

REFERENCES

Coffey, R., Richards, J., Remmert, C., LeRoy, S., Schoville, R., & Baldwin, P. (1992). An introduction to critical paths. *Quality Management and Health Care, 1* (1), 45–54.

Davenport, T. (1994). Saving ITs soul: Human-centered information management. *Harvard Business Review, 72* (2), 119–131.

Hammer, M., & Champy, J. (1994). *Reengineering the corporation.* New York: Harper Business.

Kouzes, J.M., & Posner, B.Z. (1988). *The leadership challenge: How to get extraordinary things done in organizations.* San Francisco: Jossey-Bass.

Senge, P.M. (1990). *The fifth discipline: The art and practice of the learning organization.* New York: Doubleday Currency.

Townsend, M. (1993). Patient-focused care: Is it for your hospital? *Nursing Management, 24* (9), 74–80.

Von Bertalanfly, L. (1968). *General systems theory: Foundation, development, applications.* New York: Braziller.

SUGGESTED READING

Hall, G., Rosenthal, J., & Wade, J. (1993). How to make reengineering really work. *Harvard Business Review, 71* (6), 119–131.

Kim, D. (1993, July/August). The leader with the "beginner's mind." *Healthcare Forum Journal,* pp. 32–37.

Klir, G. (1969). *An approach to general systems theory.* Cincinnati, OH: Van Nostrand Reinhold.

Klir, G. (1985). *Architecture of system problem solving.* New York: Plenum.

Kovner, C., Hendrickson, G., Knickman, J., & Finkler, S. (1993). Changing the delivery of nursing care: Implementation issues and qualitative findings. *Journal of Nursing Administration, 23* (11), 24–34.

Tonges, M., & Madden, M. (1993). "Running the vicious cycle backward" and other systems solutions to nursing problems. *Journal of Nursing Administration, 23* (1), 39–44.

Woodyard, L., & Sheetz, J. (1993). Critical pathway patient outcomes: The missing standard. *Journal of Nursing Care Quality, 8* (1), 51–57.

CHAPTER 3

Delivering Client Care

Judith Eckhart

CHAPTER OBJECTIVES

At the completion of this chapter, the beginning professional nurse will be able to:

1. compare and contrast several common types of nursing care delivery systems found in hospitals, schools, and community settings
2. explain how diagnostic-related groupings created an expanded focus on the costs associated with delivering client care
3. analyze the differences between prototype evaluation and factor evaluation patient classification systems
4. explain how acuity systems are used to identify the amount of nursing care clients need and to determine the appropriate number of nursing staff to meet these needs
5. define methods utilized to monitor nursing care delivery systems for quality

CRITICAL
THINKING
CHALLENGE

You are a staff nurse on a 35-bed medical-surgical unit. Your unit is responsible for developing its annual budget. In the past, you have not been able to use the current patient classification system to determine the cost of the nursing care services. The hospital is in the process of installing an extensive computer system that has the capacity to include a computerized acuity system or patient classification system. As your unit's representative on the nursing department's ad hoc committee, what information do you need to include in the acuity system so that your unit can readily identify the costs associated with providing nursing care services?

BACKGROUND

Wherever client care is provided, in a hospital, a school, or a community clinic, some structure exists to identify the means for delivering nursing care. This structure can be defined as the facility's **nursing care delivery system** (NCDS). The NCDS explains and defines the type of nursing care utilized at the specific institution. Large institutions, such as hospitals, consist of multiple departments and require careful coordination of client care. In smaller facilities, such as home health services, nurses function independently and have a great deal of flexibility in the format used to deliver client care. Nevertheless, each system utilizes some type of NCDS to organize and deliver nursing care.

The cost of delivering nursing care is one of the health care costs that has been increasing over the years. The Social Security Amendment Act of 1983 (P.L. 98-21) included the establishment of a prospective payment program known as **diagnostic-related groupings** (DRGs) (Shaffer, 1983). DRGs were targeted toward hospitals being reimbursed through Medicare funding (refer to Chapter 8). For an institution to remain cost effective and stay in business within the DRG format, facilities have found that they must carefully monitor the cost of providing client care.

Since the implementation of DRGs, many insurance companies have also adopted some form of prospective payment plan. As of 1989, 70% of hospitalized patients were covered by some form of DRG payment plan (Munoz, Josephson, Tenenbaum, Goldstein, Shears, & Wise, 1989). The limitations DRGs place on an institution's financial reimbursement have forced hospitals to limit the amount of money spent by all departments. This has resulted in NCDSs developing more cost-effective models for providing client care.

Nursing represents a substantial portion of a hospital's budget. Stanley and Luciano (1984) noted that nursing can amount to between 35% and 50% of a hospital's operating expenses. Even though the proportion of nursing care costs to the hospital's budget varies among institutions, it is a large enough portion of the budget that it cannot be ignored when the facility's expenses are being identified. How the nursing care is organized (i.e., how the patient care is delivered) is a component that must be understood when one is attempting to provide cost-effective health care services.

In this chapter, a few common NCDSs are examined. Some methodologies utilized to provide nursing care services within hospitals, schools, and community-based programs are discussed. In addition, an explanation is given about how nursing care systems can classify patients, determine staffing, and identify direct nursing care costs. Information is also provided on how various methodologies for delivering client care can be monitored for quality.

THE DEVELOPMENT OF NURSING CARE DELIVERY SYSTEMS

Within any nursing organization, care is delivered to the clients according to some structured methodology. The NCDS identifies the way in which patient care is provided. Hospitals have been a major setting for the delivery of client care. Some common formats of NCDSs have been defined and utilized in hospital institutions. Schools and community settings also organize the delivery of patient care, but their methods have required some techniques not found in hospital environments.

The first modern-day NCDS utilized in hospitals was known as **functional nursing**. Functional nursing identifies a specific role for each caregiver. The staffing is fairly consistent and includes the following individuals for an entire small unit of about 20 to 24 clients:

- one charge nurse, a registered nurse (RN)
- one medication nurse, an RN
- one treatment nurse, a licensed vocational nurse (LVN) or licensed practical nurse (LPN)
- nursing assistants (NAs) or others to provide bedside care

The number of NAs needed depends upon the number of clients on the unit, but it is not uncommon for an NA to assist with providing bedside care to 9 or 10 clients. Figure 3–1 is a graphic illustration of the organizational structure seen within the functional nursing format.

Within the functional nursing model, the charge nurse helps monitor changes in the client's condition and supervises the employees. The medication RN not only provides medications but also charts on the client's record. An advantage of this method is the low cost of implementation. It utilizes staff, such as LVNs and NAs, whose salaries are not as high as RNs' salaries. The patient care, however, is fragmented because each client has a variety of

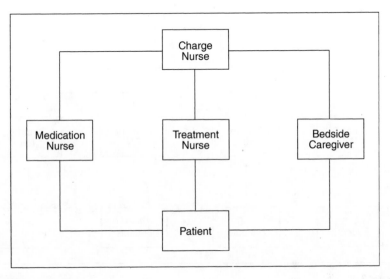

Figure 3–1 Functional nursing.

caregivers. In addition, the format, based on task orientation, is monotonous for the employees and leads to rapid employee turnover.

During the 1950s, an NCDS known as **team nursing** became popular. With team nursing a specific group of patients, generally about 8 to 10, are cared for by a team of nurses. Figure 3–2 illustrates how a team consists of an RN with an LVN or NA.

The head nurse supervises the unit, coordinates the client care with other hospital departments, and determines the staffing needs for the unit. The staff RN is in charge of the team and responsible for delegating tasks to the other team members (LVNs and NAs). Some advantages of team nursing over functional nursing are as follows:

- the client care is less fragmented
- the RN has fewer clients to monitor
- care plans are written with input from the various team members
- the RN has more time to assess and plan each client's care

One of the major problems with this system is the lack of client contact on the part of the RN. In addition, this methodology requires a larger number of RNs. This increases the cost of providing the nursing care, making this NCDS more expensive than functional nursing.

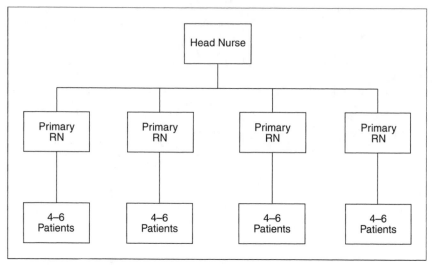

Figure 3–2 Team nursing.

During the 1970s, a concept known as **primary nursing** emerged. With this NCDS methodology, each RN is responsible for all the nursing care provided to a specific number of clients. With increased autonomy, the RN can plan and implement each client's nursing care. The RN is now able to provide direct patient care. An example of the organizational structure used for primary nursing is presented in Figure 3–3.

Primary nursing has been one of the most popular forms of NCDS. The head nurse with this system supervises the unit and provides for adequate staffing ratios. The primary RN is allowed to provide individualized, personal care to the clients. Some advantages of primary nursing include:

- increased satisfaction from clients and RNs
- quicker recognition and prevention of complications because the RN is directly supervising client care
- more opportunity for client teaching while care is being provided
- better preparation of the clients and their families so that care can be provided at home and clients can be discharged sooner

The primary RN develops the care plan that is then followed by the associate nurse, or the relief RN, when the primary RN is not on duty. The major disadvantage of this methodology is that there are tasks performed by RNs that do not require RN expertise. Therefore, the cost of delivering the care is

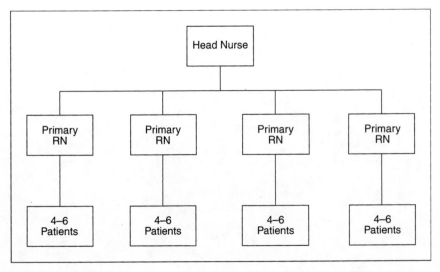

Figure 3–3 Primary nursing.

more expensive than for functional or team nursing since the RN is paid a higher salary than an LVN or NA.

During the 1980s, the DRG reimbursement system was implemented nationally. The increased emphasis on the cost of delivering client care became a major consideration for health care institutions. The traditional NCDSs were examined, and efforts were made to identify how more cost-effective, quality client care could be provided. In an attempt to maximize the value of various health care resources, it was found that additional coordination between the client and the health care system would be useful. The latest NCDS format, **case management**, was developed with this increased coordination in mind. Case management concepts have been utilized previously in small institutions, such as community-based or home health nursing. Their introduction into large organizations, such as hospitals, however, did not occur until between the late 1980s and the early 1990s.

The case manager is an RN who monitors a client's health status both within the hospital and at home. Case management revolves around the idea that the case manager can coordinate appropriate health care services and therefore provide more cost-effective client care. This allows for increased continuity and better selection of appropriate health care services, resulting in lower health care costs with no adverse effects on quality patient outcomes. Figure 3–4 portrays an example of how a case manager utilizes various agencies to provide appropriate patient care services.

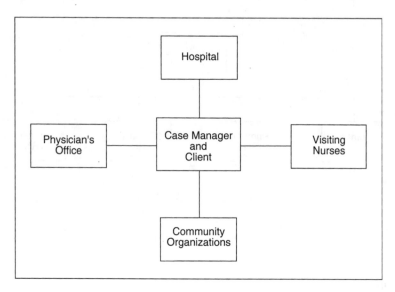

Figure 3–4 Case management.

Within the case management NCDS, there are three major concepts that need to be understood:

1. Case management functions can be superimposed on other NCDSs, such as primary or team nursing.
2. Various people can be trained to be case managers, such as staff RNs, clinical nurse specialists, discharge planners, or utilization review nurses.
3. Individual case managers may operate within specific settings, such as critical care or home health areas. As the client moves through the health care system, the case manager may transfer the client to another case manager in the new setting, or he or she can maintain responsibility to the client indefinitely.

The types of NCDSs seen in the hospital setting continue to evolve as the needs of the system change. Some facilities have found it more useful to use a combination or an integration of several NCDSs. There are advantages and disadvantages to every NCDS because no one method can meet nursing care needs in every situation. What is important, however, is to use a system, either a basic type of NCDS or an integrated methodology, that has been carefully reviewed and can best meet the needs of the clients within the specific environment.

Currently, hospitals are focusing on delivering cost-effective care, maintaining quality, and utilizing the professional skills of the RN in the most productive manner possible. To provide appropriate nursing care services, hospitals have been tasked to develop flexibility in the implementation of nursing care while attempting to offer the most cost-effective NCDS possible. In the constantly changing health care environment, the delivery of cost-effective, quality client care is a challenge. A properly developed NCDS that is appropriate for the setting is one of the necessary components for meeting the challenge. A specific NCDS is not going to guarantee, however, that the appropriate nursing care is being provided and that it is cost effective. Organizations also need to know how to classify their patients, how to provide cost-effective staffing, how to identify the cost of providing their nursing services, and how to verify that the NCDS is a quality system.

KEY
CONCEPTS

- The development of the DRG system for funding in large health care institutions has resulted in a cost-conscious health care environment.
- In any health care setting, client care is organized in some form of NCDS. The most common types of NCDSs are functional nursing, team nursing, primary nursing, and case management.

ACUITY SYSTEMS IN HOSPITALS

To assure the public that a health care facility has met acceptable, quality medical and nursing care standards, there are organizations that provide regulatory review services to an institution. Some agencies are state bodies, such as the state Board of Health; others are national organizations, such as the **Joint Commission on Accreditation of Healthcare Organizations** (Joint Commission). After monitoring numerous hospitals and health care facilities throughout the state or the country, these regulatory agencies have established minimal standards that must be met if the institution wishes to receive the regulatory agency's stamp of approval.

Most hospitals strive to be accredited by the Joint Commission, which is a nongovernmental group (refer to Chapter 9). Although accreditation is a voluntary process, receiving Joint Commission accreditation informs the public that the hospital has been found to provide quality client care. Accreditation is one of the criteria that is utilized when a hospital is evaluated for financial reimbursement by third party payers, for state licensure, or for authorization of various educational programs (Gillies, 1989).

To receive Joint Commission accreditation, an institution must meet a number of standards. When dealing with the delivery of client care, some of the Joint Commission standards state that the patient-specific plan of care must be implemented in accordance with the organization's policies and procedures and within the staff's scope of practice, and the care provided must be appropriate to the client's specific needs and the severity level of the client's condition (Joint Commission, 1994).

To comply with these Joint Commission standards, hospitals have taken several actions. First, they monitor staffing to ensure that there are a sufficient number of RNs on duty at all times to provide adequate client care. In addition, the hospitals have developed tools to reflect the severity of the client's condition known as **patient classification systems** (PCSs) or **acuity systems**.

An acuity system can be used with any NCDS. The way the nursing care is delivered is not directly related to how sick the clients are or their acuity rating. The PCS identifies the amount of nursing care required for each patient and how many nurses are needed on each shift to provide adequate nursing care. It has been determined that acuity systems can also be used to identify the cost of the nursing care services being provided.

Because each hospital provides health care services to a local population, an acuity system needs to be site specific. There is no single format for a PCS that can be applied to all organizations. Therefore, each facility must develop or adapt a PCS that appropriately suits the needs of its institution.

There are numerous acuity systems that have been developed commercially and adopted by hospital facilities. These systems may be loosely grouped into two basic formats, first identified by Abdellah and Levine (1965), as prototype evaluation and factor evaluation rating methods. Both types of PCSs are developed from critical indicators or descriptors reflecting common types of nursing care provided to clients (Giovannetti, 1979).

A **critical indicator** is a specific task that is commonly needed for the clients on that unit. Indicators vary, some depending upon the type of unit and some on the type of patient being treated. For example, on an obstetrics unit a critical indicator could include changing a sanitary napkin or checking a client's fundus. In an intensive care unit, however, few patients would require those services, so that a more appropriate critical indicator might be monitoring a Swan-Ganz catheter or an arterial line.

Prototype evaluation systems rate a client simultaneously on the specific critical indicators listed on the PCS. The critical indicators are used to separate clients into categories requiring more or less nursing care. Each category is designed to be broad but mutually exclusive. Table 3–1 shows an example of a prototype evaluation PCS (this is a generic example and is not intended to be comprehensive enough to apply to all hospital units).

The nurse using the prototype evaluation PCS rates the client simultaneously on a variety of patient care needs. The category that best describes

Table 3–1 Generic Prototype Evaluation Acuity System

Category	Class I	Class II	Class III	Class IV
Assessments	VS q shift, self-care	VS qid, daily standing wt., no tubes	VS q4h, bed scale wt., neuro checks q2–4h, 1–2 tubes	VS q2h, neuro checks q1h, 3 or more tubes
Mobility	Up ad lib	Ambulates or chair with one-person assistance	Ambulates or chair with two-person assistance	Ambulates or chair with three-person assistance, two- to three-person assist on and off gurney
Hygiene and elimination	Self-care	BSC or bedpan with one-person assist, partial bath, Foley care, Fleets enema	BSC or bedpan with two-person assist, complete bath, SSE, complete linen change with two people	Incontinent care, complete bed bath, enemas til clear, several linen changes per shift
Diet	Feeds self, NPO	Positioning by one person for meal, set up tray	Positioning by two persons for meals, assist with feeding	Feeder, tube feeding, high risk of aspiration
Medications and tubes	Meds 1–2 trips/shift	Meds 3–5 trips/shift, IV or HL with 1 IVPB/shift	Meds 6–7 trips/shift, IV or HL with 2 IVPB/shift, hang 1 U of blood	Meds 8 or more trips/shift, IV Hyperal or heparin, 3 or more IVPB/shift, hang 2 U of blood or more
Treatments	Simple dsg change qd	Simple dsg change q8h, assist with simple procedure	Complex dsg change q4h, empty colostomy bag, assist with 2 procedures	Colostomy irrigation, assist with complex procedure, more than 1 complex dsg change q4h, suction q1–4h
Teaching and emotional	A&O × 3, simple teaching	Anxious, reinforced teaching, Posey vest or wrist restraints, some family interaction	Disoriented or hostile, some language barrier, Posey and wrist restraints, frequent interaction with family, teaching new material or discharge instruction	Needs constant monitoring, major language barrier, teaching complex procedures, extensive family interaction
Other	None	Telemetry monitoring	Blood and body fluid precautions	Code, postmortem care

Total score

the amount of nursing care needed by the client at the time of the rating determines the patient's classification. If a client can fit into two categories at the same time, the nurse makes a subjective decision and assigns the level that he or she believes is the most appropriate. Table 3–1 can be used with the following two examples to understand how to apply a prototype PCS. The first client is Mrs. A, a 45-year-old white woman with low acuity. The second is Mr. B, a 75-year-old African American man with a high acuity rating.

Mrs. A is 3 days post-cholecystectomy. She is able to be up with minimal assistance and is tolerating a full liquid diet. Her intravenous (IV) line has been converted to a heparin lock (HL), and she is not receiving any IV medications. She is stable, but because of the surgery her vital signs (VS) are to be taken four times a day. She needs some assistance with her bath and takes pain pills about every 6 hours. She is passing flatus and voiding without difficulty. Her incision is clean and intact with minimal drainage from a Penrose drain, which is expected to be removed tomorrow before discharge. Her family visits once a day. She has been told that when she returns home she should not need any specific dietary restrictions or any special dressing changes.

Mrs. A falls into several categories using the prototype PCS. Her assessment rating is class III because she needs VS every 4 hours and has one tube, the HL. For mobility, she is class II as she can be up with minimal assistance. In terms of hygiene and elimination, Mrs. A is class II based upon the fact that she needs some assistance with her bath and with getting out of bed to go to the bathroom. She should be able to feed herself, but because of the recent surgery she probably needs some assistance getting positioned for meals. Therefore, she is class II for diet. For medications, she is class I. Although Mrs. A has an HL, it is not used for medications, and she only needs pain pills once or twice a shift. With minimal drainage from the Penrose, she should only need a simple dressing change each day. Therefore, in terms of treatments, she is rated as class I. Her teaching and emotional needs are also class I since she has a few family interactions and does not appear to be anxious or to have any specific emotional concerns. She does not qualify for any of the categories under the heading "Other."

The total summary for Mrs. A includes three class I ratings, three class II ratings, and one class III rating. For the acuity rating, she is considered class II because the one class III rating balances out the three class I ratings.

Mr. B has a history of hypertension. He was admitted 24 hours earlier for severe rectal bleeding and is receiving multiple blood transfusions. With a history of hypertension, his VS must be closely monitored and taken at least every 4 hours. Because of extensive blood loss, he is weak and needs two people to help him get into a chair. He is continent but needs extensive help up to the commode. Because of the rectal bleeding, the physician has ordered that he not eat or drink. He is to receive 2 units of blood over the next 6 hours and is on IV fluids for hydration. He is anxious about the bleeding and has numerous questions about the safety of the blood. His family has been sitting with him most of the day, and they are also concerned about the blood transfusions. Because of the rectal bleeding, he has been placed on blood and body fluid precautions.

When Table 3–1 is used to determine Mr. B's rating, it is seen that he falls into several categories. His assessment rating is class IV because he needs frequent VS during the administration of the blood products. Since he is weak and needs two people for assistance into a chair, his mobility rating is class III. For hygiene and elimination he is also class III because he needs two people to help him to the commode and, due to his weakness, also requires a complete bath. He is class I for diet since he is not eating or drinking. For medications he falls into class IV because of the 2 units of blood he is to receive during the shift. He has no treatments at this time. For the teaching and emotional category, Mr. B is class II as he is anxious and there are several family interactions occurring. Under the category of "Other," he classifies as class III because he is on blood and body fluid precautions.

The completed rating for Mr. B involves two class IV, three class III, one class II, and one class I. When these are analyzed along with a complete assessment, Mr. B is rated as class III for the acuity system.

From these examples, one can see how different clients require different amounts of nursing care and how they can be classified in terms of their acuity, or their nursing care needs. A prototype evaluation PCS is a way to rate clients simultaneously in several related aspects of their nursing care. These rating systems are usually easy to implement and do not require extensive training to be understood. They can be subjective, however, and it may be difficult for two independent raters to consistently produce the same rating on the same patient. Once the clients on a unit are rated and classified, the information can be used to determine the number of nurses needed to care for the group of clients. This is explained in detail later in this chapter.

The second format that can be utilized in an acuity or PCS system is known as the **factor evaluation** method. This methodology rates the client separately on various critical indicators instead of simultaneously, as seen with the prototype evaluation method. Each category of client needs (i.e., assessment, mobility, hygiene, etc.) is given a separate score. A total overall rating or score is then computed. Although this method is more time consuming to complete, it is less ambiguous and more objective than the prototype evaluation method. Figure 3–5 is an example of a generic factor evaluation PCS and, like Table 3–1, is not intended to be comprehensive.

D	E	N	Client Care Categories
			Assessments
			1 VS q shift
			2 VS QID
			2 VS q4h
			3 VS q2h
			1 neuro check q8h
			2 neuro check q2–4h
			3 neuro check q1h
			1 daily standing wt
			2 daily bed scale wt
			1 1–2 tubes
			2 3 or more tubes
			Mobility
			1 up ad lib
			2 up only BID or TID with 1 person assist
			3 up QID with 1 person assist
			3 up only BID with 2–3 person assist
			4 up TID or QID with 2–3 person assist
			2 assist pt. on & off the gurney
			Hygiene & Elimination
			1 self care
			2 partial bath
			3 complete bath
			5 multiple baths per shift—incontinent
			2 BSC or bedpan with 1 person assist
			3 BSC or bedpan with 2 person assist
			1 Foley cath care
			1 Fleets enema
			2 SSE enema
			3 enemas til clear
			Diet
			1 NPO
			1 feeds self, able to position self
			2 feeds self, 1 person assist for positioning
			3 assist feed, 2 person assist for position
			4 feeder or tube feeding, aspiration risk
			Medications & Tubes
			1 1–2 med trips/shift
			2 3–5 med trips/shift

Figure 3–5 Generic factor evaluation acuity system.

D	E	N	Client Care Categories
			3 6–7 med trips/shift
			4 8 or more med trips/shift
			2 IV or HL with 1 IVPB/shift
			3 IV or HL with 2 IVPB/shift
			4 IV of Hyperal or Heparin
			4 3 or more IVPB/shift
			3 hang 1 unit of blood/shift
			4 hang 2 or more units of blood/shift
			Treatments
			1 simple dsg change qd
			2 simple dsg change q8h
			3 complex dsg change q4h
			3 more than 1 complex dsg change q4h
			2 assist with simple procedure
			3 assist with 2 simple procedures
			4 assist with complex procedure
			3 empty colostomy bag
			4 colostomy irrigation
			4 suction q1–4h
			Teaching & Emotional
			1 simple teaching (5 min)
			2 continual reinforced teaching (10 min)
			3 teaching new material or discharge instruction
			4 complex teaching, multiple parts (20 min)
			3 some language barrier
			4 major language barrier
			1 alert & oriented x 3
			2 very anxious and agitated
			3 disoriented or hostile
			4 needs constant monitoring
			2 some general family interaction
			3 frequent family interaction
			4 extensive family interaction
			2 Posey vest or wrist restraints
			3 Posey vest and wrist restraints
			Other
			2 telemetry monitoring
			3 blood & bodily fluids precautions
			4 code or postmortem care
			Total Score

Figure 3–5 Continued

For Figure 3–5, the items that pertain to the patient are identified, and the point value for each item is recorded under the appropriate shift. The numerical values assigned to each section of the acuity tool can then be summed and utilized in one of two methodologies: in a checklist format or as **relative value units** (RVUs) (Lewis & Carini, 1984).

When the factor evaluation acuity tool is used as a checklist, the items relevant to the client are checked off, and the total points assigned to each item are added. This method requires prior analysis of the unit to determine the range of points applicable to each acuity classification. For example, assume that Mrs. A and Mr. B are patients on the 2 North unit. Studies on 2 North have determined that clients can be categorized into classes based upon the following point system:

- class I, 0–10 total points
- class II, 11–25 total points
- class III, 26–40 total points
- class IV, 41 total points or more

To review, Mrs. A, 3 days post-cholecystectomy, is up with minimal assistance, on full liquids, needs VS every 4 hours, and takes pain medications about every 6 hours. She is voiding without difficulty, is passing flatus, and has a Penrose drain. She is expecting to return home soon. Mr. B, with a history of hypertension, is being treated for severe rectal bleeding. He is weak and needs two people for assistance getting out of bed. He is not eating or drinking and is to receive 2 units of blood during the next 6 hours. He and his family are anxious about the transfusions, and he has been placed on blood and body fluid precautions.

When the PCS in Figure 3–5 is used as a checklist, the total point value for Mrs. A is 12 points (VS every 4 hours, up ad lib, partial bath, feeds self with one-person assist for positioning, 1–2 med trips/shift, simple dressing change daily, simple teaching, alert and oriented, and some general family interaction). Based upon the rating scale for 2 North, this makes Mrs. A a class II patient. That is the same rating that was obtained from Table 3–1, the prototype evaluation method.

Mr. B requires more extensive nursing care. When his points are added together, he has 27 points (VS every 2 hours, 1–2 tubes, up 3–4 times a day with two- to three-person assist, complete bath, no oral intake, 2 units of blood per shift, teaching new material, anxious, frequent family interaction, and blood and body fluid precautions). This places him into class III, which is also the same rating received with the prototype evaluation form in Table 3–1. As with the prototype evaluation PCS, these classification ratings can then be used to determine the number of staff needed for the shift.

In addition to using the factor evaluation PCS as a checklist, the numerical values can also be treated as RVUs. With an RVU system, the numbers assigned to each item or each critical indicator are equated to the amount of time required to do the various tasks. The time allotments are identified from time and motion studies done on the unit. During time and motion studies, an independent observer carefully times and records the time spent by each caregiver in performing various nursing care services. The amount of time required to chart each task is included in the time calculation for the study. Once the average amount of time required to do each task on that specific unit is determined, the corresponding numbers are then assigned to the PCS.

For example, if it is determined that each RVU reflects 3 minutes of care, all the values are calculated using a 3:1 ratio (i.e., 1 = 3 minutes, 2 = 6 minutes, as so on). If the time and motion study shows that a partial bed bath takes an average of 5 to 6 minutes, it receives 2 RVUs. Tasks done repeatedly during the shift must reflect the additional time required to complete the care for a client.

The RVU methodology with the factor evaluation PCS can be explained using Figure 3–5. When the RVU system is utilized for Mrs. A, the same 12 points are found as were noted with the checklist format. The points are then multiplied by 3 minutes per point to reflect that Mrs. A requires 36 minutes of nursing care for the shift. For Mr. B, his 27 points reflect 81 minutes of nursing care per shift. This reveals a quantitative difference in the patient care needs between the two clients. Once the number of minutes required for each client on the unit is known, the number of staff needed to meet the clients' needs can be determined.

As the examples show, clients can be categorized in terms of their acuity rating, or the amount of nursing care they require, by using either a prototype evaluation or a factor evaluation PCS. The ratings received with the prototype evaluation format and the checklist method of the factor evaluation system should be the same. The RVU format of the factor evaluation PCS provides a direct comparison of the amount of time required to provide nursing care for different clients.

The advantage of the prototype evaluation method is that it is quick to complete, but it allows for a more subjective rating. The factor evaluation acuity system requires more time to complete and more extensive training for the staff. The major advantage of the factor evaluation PCS is that it is more objective in determining the amount of time or assistance required by the patient.

Both types of PCS meet the Joint Commission's requirement that patients be classified according to the severity of their condition or the amount of nursing care required. As mentioned earlier, either method can be employed regardless of the type of NCDS used. Whether the delivery of patient care is being done with case management, primary nursing, team nursing, or some variation of these, the classification system still reflects the amount of nursing care required.

An appropriate PCS must be able to do more than simply classify the patients. For an acuity system to supply only one function is not cost effective. The Joint Commission requires that, in addition to determining the amount of nursing care each patient needs, the facility must also provide adequate staff so the nursing care can be implemented within the staff's scope of practice. This means that the hospital must supply a sufficient number of RNs on each unit, although a specific RN-to-patient ratio is not identified for all types of units. It also means that the hospital needs to have some way to determine the appropriate number of staff required to supply the patient care. Based upon information collected through the PCS, either the prototype evaluation or the factor evaluation format, staffing ratios as well as direct nursing care costs can be delineated.

KEY CONCEPT   • The basic formats used in acuity systems are prototype evaluation and factor evaluation rating methods.

LEARNING CHALLENGE   Utilizing two clients you have cared for in the past week, identify their acuity level using the prototype evaluation and the factor evaluation classification tools in Table 3–1 and Figure 3–5. Are the ratings similar? Describe the differences.

USING AN ACUITY SYSTEM TO DETERMINE STAFFING

In the current health care environment, in attempts to minimize expensive hospitalization costs, clients are not admitted promptly to a hospital once they become ill. They are often treated at home and seen at their physician's office. Therefore, once it has been identified that the individual needs to be hospitalized, he or she often has a higher acuity rating than was traditionally seen. Another way to keep hospital costs low is to discharge clients early and not allow them to recuperate fully in the hospital. Once stable, clients are discharged and a home health nurse association provides additional nursing care outside the institution.

Because clients have higher acuity ratings while they are hospitalized, the hours of nursing care necessary to meet the clients' needs have also increased. As more complex nursing care is required, nursing contact hours must also increase. This results in more money being spent to deliver the client care. Since the DRG system has limited financial reimbursement to hospitals, it becomes increasingly important for hospitals to be certain that the client care being provided is cost effective with acceptable levels of quality.

To ensure quality nursing care, the Joint Commission requires that a hospital provide a sufficient number of nurses on each shift to meet the clients' needs. Generally, facilities within a local area tend to maintain similar **nurse-to-patient ratios**, so that community standards are fairly uniform. The ratios, however, must be based upon the nursing care needs of the clients, and a PCS can be used to determine how much staff is necessary to meet the clients' nursing care needs.

To identify the necessary number of staff for a 24-hour period, staffing ratios for nursing care have traditionally been determined by the following formula:

HPPD × Number of patients = Hours of staff assigned/24 hours

where HPPD is the hours per patient day, or the average amount of time spent providing nursing care to each patient per day; the number of patients is the number on the unit at a given point in time (usually at midnight); and the hours of staff is the hours available for the 24-hour day. The number of staff is calculated by dividing the hours of staff assigned in 24 hours by the length of the shift (e.g., 90 hours of staff/8-hour shift = 11.25 number of staff over the 24-hour period of time).

Once the number of staff needed for 24 hours is identified, the nursing department or the nursing unit must then determine how many staff are needed for each shift. If the number of staff required during 24 hours was divided by 3 for three 8-hour shifts, the same amount of staff would be needed on all three shifts. Usually day and evening shifts are found to need more staff than the night shift, so that a percentage of the 24-hour total is calculated for each shift. For example, the nursing department may decide to use 35% of the total for days, 35% for evenings, and 30% for nights.

Once it is known how many employees are needed for each shift, the problem becomes one of determining what type of employees are required. Historically, the mix of employees has been subjectively determined based upon the type of staff available, the budget restraints for the unit, and the client's acuity. Current acuity systems do not have any techniques to identify exactly what type of staff is required for a given class of patient. They can, however, provide a more objective method for identifying how many hours of care need to be provided.

Because patient acuity can change quickly and the number of patients on the unit varies during a 24-hour day, an acuity rating should be done every shift on each patient. When the amount of time needed to provide the nursing care per shift is known, the required staffing can be determined by shift instead of for the 24-hour period.

When the prototype evaluation or a checklist factor evaluation PCS is utilized, the clients are categorized by classes, as discussed previously. Additional studies are then required to identify the average amount of time spent providing nursing care to patients of the different classes. As mentioned, time and motion studies can be conducted to obtain this information. For in-house time and motion studies, the specific amount of time spent providing nursing care is carefully recorded by an independent observer. Over time, the average amount of time spent by nurses for each class of patients can be computed.

Once it is known how much time is spent, on the average, for each class of patients, the number of clients per class can be multiplied by the average number of hours needed for that specific classification rating. This reflects the amount of time needed to provide services to the patients in that category. This is then repeated for each class on the unit. When the numbers of hours for all the classes have been computed, they can be summed to identify the total hours needed to provide nursing care to that group of clients.

To show how staffing can be done with the PCS, Exhibit 3–1 displays classifications for the day shift for all the clients on 2 North using a prototype evaluation or a checklist factor evaluation PCS. The PCS shows that there are currently 3 class II, 14 class III, and 3 class IV patients. It should be noted that there are no class I clients listed using the PCS. Class I clients are considered to be stable since they need only a minimal amount of nursing care within a 24-hour period. Therefore, to contain costs these clients are discharged as soon as possible. Based upon a hypothetical time and motion study conducted for 1 year on the unit, it has been determined that the following average times per class are reasonable:

Exhibit 3–1 Classification Ratings per Bed on 2 North for Day Shift

Room 201, Bed A—empty	Room 207, Bed A—class III
Bed B—class III	Bed B—class IV
Room 202, Bed A—class III	Room 208, Bed A—class III
Bed B—class II	Bed B—empty
Room 203, Bed A—class IV	Room 209, Bed A—class III
Bed B—class IV	Bed B—class III
Room 204, Bed A—class III	Room 210, Bed A—class II
Bed B—class III	Bed B—class III
Room 205, Bed A—class II	Room 211, Bed A—empty
Bed B—class III	Bed B—class III
Room 206, Bed A—class III	Room 212, Bed A—empty
Bed B—class III	Bed B—class III

- class I = 2 hours of nursing care/24-hour shift
- class II = 3 hours of nursing care/24-hour shift
- class III = 4.5 hours of nursing care/24-hour shift
- class IV = 6 hours of nursing care/24-hour shift

To identify the staff needed for a 24-hour period, it is necessary to assume that the client will basically maintain the same classification during that time period. Because the clients are rated every shift, staffing can be recalculated as their condition changes. The next step in determining the number of staff needed is to multiply the number of hours per class by the number of patients currently in each class. For Exhibit 3–1, the day shift on 2 North, the hours of care required are as follows:

- class II = 3 hours × 3 patients = 9 hours of care
- class III = 4.5 hours × 14 patients = 63 hours of care
- class IV = 6 hours × 3 patients = 18 hours of care
- Total hours of care needed for the 24-hour period = 90 hours

Once the hours of care for the day are known, that value must be multiplied by the percentage of the staff allocated to each shift. For example, 35% of the staff are allotted to days and to evenings:

$$90 \text{ hours of care} \times 0.35 = 31.5 \text{ hours of care}$$

In addition, 30% of the staff are allocated to nights:

$$90 \text{ hours of care} \times 0.3 = 27 \text{ hours of care}$$

Now the hours of care for the shift are divided by the number of hours in the shift to identify the number of employees needed to staff the unit. With 8 hours per shift, the following calculation applies:

$$\frac{31.5 \text{ hours of care}}{8 \text{ hours of time/shift}} = 3.94, \text{ or 4 employees}$$

$$\frac{27 \text{ hours of care}}{8 \text{ hours of time/shift}} = 3.37, \text{ or 3 employees}$$

Therefore, based upon the prototype evaluation or a checklist factor evaluation PCS for 2 North with 3 class II, 14 class III, and 3 class IV patients, four employees are needed to provide the current nursing care needs for day and evening shifts. For the night shift, three employees are needed. As the levels of the patients change, the amount of staff required may also vary. That is one of the reasons why the PCS must be updated each shift.

When staffing is determined using an RVU method of the factor evaluation PCS, the calculations vary to some extent. Since each task reflects a predetermined time allotment, the staffing is only calculated on a per-shift basis, not for a 24-hour period. Time and motion studies are conducted before the RVU methodology is utilized to verify the average amount of time spent for each RVU. In the example of 2 North, the amount of time was determined to be 3 minutes per RVU. Exhibit 3–2 reveals the number of RVUs assigned to each client for the day shift based upon the PCS.

On the day shift, 2 North currently has 645 RVUs of care to provide. The number of RVUs can be multiplied by the minutes per RVU to obtain the number of minutes of care required for the shift. The minutes of care per shift, 1,935 minutes, can then be converted to the hours of care required for the shift, or 32.25 hours. That value is then divided by the hours per shift to identify the number of employees. For example:

$$645 \text{ RVU} \times 3 \text{ minutes/RVU} = 1,935 \text{ minutes of care}$$

$$\frac{1,935 \text{ minutes of care}}{60 \text{ minutes/hour}} = 32.25 \text{ hours of care}$$

$$\frac{32.25 \text{ hours of care}}{8 \text{ hours/employee}} = 4.03 \text{ employees}$$

Exhibit 3–2 RVU Assignments per Bed on 2 North for Day Shift

RVU (Class)	RVU (Class)
Room 201, Bed A—empty	Room 207, Bed A—26 (III)
Bed B—35 (III)	Bed B—43 (IV)
Room 202, Bed A—27 (III)	Room 208, Bed A—28 (III)
Bed B—12 (II)	Bed B—empty
Room 203, Bed A—45 (IV)	Room 209, Bed A—31 (III)
Bed B—47 (IV)	Bed B—29 (III)
Room 204, Bed A—26 (III)	Room 210, Bed A—20 (II)
Bed B—35 (III)	Bed B—38 (III)
Room 205, Bed A—18 (II)	Room 211, Bed A—empty
Bed B—34 (III)	Bed B—36 (III)
Room 206, Bed A—38 (III)	Room 212, Bed A—empty
Bed B—40 (III)	Bed B—37 (III)

Total RVU for this specific shift = 645 RVUs

The value of 4.03 employees per shift is slightly higher than the 3.94 employees identified by the PCS methods using class ratings. With the RVU system, the numerical values assigned to each patient are more exact than the class ratings, and that can alter the number of staff. If more class III patients are at the high end of the rating scale, the RVU system will reflect more points. This will generally result in the RVU system showing a larger number of staff. The same is true when the patients are at the low end of the class rating scale; the RVU method will then give them fewer points, and usually the staffing values will be smaller.

Maintaining accurate, up-to-date information about the acuity levels on each unit allows for appropriate but not excessive staffing patterns to meet the clients' needs. This minimal staffing pattern helps keep the cost of delivering nursing care at the most cost-effective level possible. The Joint Commission stipulates that clients must have adequate staff to provide the care and that the care must be implemented in accordance with the qualifications of the nursing staff (i.e., within their scope of practice). An objective and reliable PCS is one methodology that can be used to allocate patient assignments. Once the number of staff needed for the shift has been determined, the acuity system can also be used to assign the staff in an equitable manner.

USING AN ACUITY SYSTEM TO ASSIGN PATIENTS

Within the hospital environment, the nursing budget is a large portion of the total budget. With the continual focus on delivering cost-effective nursing care services, assignments for the staff must also be made in a cost-effective manner. This task can be facilitated by an accurate and reliable acuity system.

When making cost-effective assignments, the RN must consider several factors. Some of the major considerations are the acuity level of each client, the physical location of the clients, the qualifications of the staff members coming on duty, and the clients' diagnoses. The easiest way to determine the acuity level of each client is by using an appropriate PCS. This is a faster method than trying to make rounds and assess each patient individually. After each client has been assigned a classification rating, either with the prototype evaluation or with the checklist method of the factor evaluation PCS, the clients can be assigned to a nurse based upon their class.

In addition to balancing the class ratings, the RN must consider the patients' physical location. It is not easy for a staff nurse to organize an assignment when the patients are physically scattered around the unit. To optimize the staff's time and provide for better patient monitoring, the nurse's assignment should include patients located in the same general area.

In addition, assignments must take into consideration the qualifications of the oncoming staff. The Joint Commission has stipulated that client care must be provided in accordance with the staff member's scope of practice. This means that appropriate levels of staff must be available to provide adequate client care.

The final point that must be addressed is knowledge about the clients' diagnoses. Unnecessary exposure, either direct or indirect, of high-risk clients to some medical conditions can be life threatening. For example, a client with an antibiotic-resistant infection should not be assigned to the same nurse who is caring for an immunosuppressed client.

Exhibit 3–1 can be used to demonstrate how assignments can be made. On 2 North there are currently 20 patients: 3 class II, 14 class III, and 3 class IV. The floor's capacity is 24 patients. Exhibit 3–1 also identifies where the patients are located. In this example, the diagnoses of the specific clients will not be a factor because there are no immunocompromised clients currently on the unit. The staff coming on duty consists of four RNs. A fairly equitable assignment could be done in the following fashion:

- one RN = rooms 201B, 202A and B, 203A, and 204A (1 class II, 3 class III, 1 class IV, and 1 empty bed)
- one RN = rooms 203B, 204B, 205A and B, and 206A (1 class II, 3 class III, and 1 class IV)
- one RN = rooms 206B, 207A and B, 208A, and 209A (4 class III, 1 class IV, and 1 empty bed)
- one RN = rooms 209B, 210A and B, 211B, and 212B (1 class II, 4 class III, and 2 empty beds)

The types of patients are fairly well distributed based upon the rating system assigned through the PCS. The empty beds are also fairly well divided. The fourth RN has two empty beds and no class IV patients, so that RN should expect the first admission.

When an acuity system uses the RVU method of the factor evaluation format, the assignments are based upon the number of RVUs assigned to each patient. Again, consideration must be given to the clients' acuity levels, the clients' locations, the staff's qualifications, and the clients' diagnoses. With the RVU method, however, unlike the situation with the class ratings, each nurse may not have the same number of patients, but all nurses should be assigned similar numbers of RVUs.

The information in Exhibit 3–2 applies when one is making assignments based upon the RVU ratings. First, the total number of RVUs for the shift is calculated. This number is then divided by the number of staff. On 2 North for this shift, there are 645 RVUs and four RNs coming on duty. This computes to

161.25 RVUs, or about 161 RVUs per person for the shift. Again for this example, the clients' diagnoses will not be an issue.

After the points per employee are known, the patients' RVUs are summed until the rating is moderately close to the expected average. Here an assignment would look as follows:

- one RN = rooms 201B, 202A and B, 203B, and 204B (156 RVUs)
- one RN = rooms 203A, 204A, 205A and B, and 206A (161 RVUs)
- one RN = rooms 206B, 207A and B, 208A, and 209A (168 RVUs)
- one RN = rooms 209B, 210A and B, 211B, and 212B (160 RVUs) ˙

The assignments made utilizing the RVUs are quite similar to the ones made using classes, but there are some changes. The first admit now would be expected by the first RN since that assignment has fewer RVUs than the others. The empty beds are not as much of a consideration with this format because the number of RVUs reflects the expected amount of work. When patients are to be admitted, consideration is given to which RN has the fewest RVUs and which RN has discharged a client.

When utilizing an RVU methodology, one must identify the maximum number of RVUs an employee can accomplish during an 8-hour shift. When working an 8-hour shift, an employee is at work for 8.5 hours with 0.5 hour allowed for a meal. The resulting 8 hours is what the employee is paid for and reflects the amount of time considered when the maximum number of RVUs is established. To make the calculation, the number of hours in the shift is multiplied by the number of minutes in an hour. That value is then multiplied by the number of minutes per RVU:

$$8 \text{ hours/shift} \times 60 \text{ minutes/hour} = 480 \text{ minutes/shift}$$

$$480 \text{ minutes/shift} \times 1 \text{ RVU/3 minutes} = 160 \text{ RVUs/shift}$$

In the example from 2 North, the RNs are working between 156 and 168 RVUs. This reflects 468 to 504 minutes, or 7.8 to 8.4 hours, per employee. Based upon these calculations, the employees should be able to complete their patient care within the allotted time frame. When the number of assigned RVUs markedly exceeds the 160 that can be done in an 8-hour shift, the supervisor can expect that the employee may need some overtime to accomplish the assignment, or the unit may need additional staff.

When one is utilizing the PCS to make assignments, it is necessary that the acuity information be accurate. If the data are not accurate, the assignments will not reflect the expectations for the oncoming shift. On any unit the status of patients can change rapidly, but to start the shift staff nurses like reasonable equity in the assignments.

KEY CONCEPT
- Acuity systems can be utilized to determine appropriate staffing levels and to develop realistic staff assignments.

LEARNING CHALLENGE
You are working in an acute care, hospital setting where a prototype evaluation PCS is utilized. The unit has 45 beds, 39 of which are currently occupied. What factors need to be considered to determine the assignments for the shift?

USING AN ACUITY SYSTEM TO DETERMINE DIRECT NURSING COSTS

Once the number of staff required for the unit is confirmed, the cost of providing direct nursing care services can be identified. Nursing care costs can be recognized as direct costs and indirect costs. Direct costs are the variable expenses associated with providing actual patient care. The **direct nursing care costs** vary depending on the client and any changes in the client's nursing care needs. Direct costs are defined differently depending upon the institution. For consistency, however, they should include costs for all caregivers on the unit (e.g., the charge nurse, all staff nurses, and any bedside caregivers), the ward secretary, and the benefit package for all these individuals.

Indirect nursing care costs are fixed costs related to nondirect nursing care services or nursing support services. These costs also vary in their definition but, for consistency, should include all nursing overhead items, such as nursing administration and nursing education. When one is identifying the total nursing care costs for each patient, the direct and the indirect nursing costs must be included.

An acuity system can identify the cost of providing direct nursing care services to a client. To utilize a PCS in identifying nursing care costs, a facility must first ascertain the price of providing 1 hour of direct nursing care on a specific unit. This is calculated in several steps. First, the average hourly salary of each group of employees (RNs, LVNs, and NAs) must be identified. Then the average mix of employees used to staff the specific unit must be determined. Subsequently, the average composite hourly salary based upon the specific employee mix for the unit can be calculated. At this point there will be a unit-specific, hourly value for the cost of delivering nursing care on the unit.

In the previous scenario dealing with 2 North, it was noted that four RNs were required to provide care for the day shift. The use of an all-RN staff has been defined as a form of primary nursing. Recall, for this example, that Figure 3–3 depicts primary nursing as having one head nurse and four primary RNs. To calculate the cost of providing direct nursing care to the entire unit for one shift, the average salary for a primary RN will be set at $21 and for the head nurse at $23. This unit, for simplicity, will not be staffed with a ward secretary. The benefit package for these employees will be computed at 30% of their hourly rate. The cost of 1 hour of direct nursing care services on the unit, including direct, hands-on care and benefits for the employees, is calculated as follows:

- four primary nurses   = $21.00/hour × 4   = $84.00/hour
- one head nurse   = $23.00/hour × 1   = $23.00/hour
- salary costs for the unit   = $107.00/hour
- benefits   = $107.00 × 0.30   = $32.10/hour
- total direct nursing costs
  for the unit   = $107.00 + $32.10 = $139.10/hour

Once the hourly rate for direct care is known, the next phase is to identify the amount of nursing care required by each client. This is accomplished using a PCS. To determine how much care is provided, the average amount of nursing time spent caring for patients within each class rating must be calculated. Once an organization knows the average number of nursing hours per class, the cost per class rating can be identified. As with the time and motion studies, the average costs must be calculated over time.

Continuing with the example from 2 North, the 20 clients were previously identified by class (refer to Exhibit 3–1). There are 3 class II, 14 class III, and 3 class IV clients. For simplicity, it will be assumed that the 20 clients remain at the same classification for a 24-hour period. Earlier in this chapter it was noted that the average times per class are as follows:

- class II = 3 hours of direct nursing care/24 hours
- class III = 4.5 hours of direct nursing care/24 hours
- class IV = 6 hours of direct nursing care/24 hours

Once the average number of hours of care per class is known and the average cost per hour of providing direct nursing care is determined, the final step can be taken. The two values can then be multiplied to identify the cost of providing direct nursing care services to a specific class of patients on a specific unit. For example, 1 day of direct nursing care costs for each class is calculated as follows:

- class II, 3 hours of care × $139.10/hour = $417.30/day
- class III, 4.5 hours of care × $139.10/hour = $625.95/day
- class IV, 6 hours of care × $139.10/hour = $834.60/day

The cost for a client at any given class level is then calculated. The cost per hospitalization can be identified once it is known how many days the client spent in each class. By adding each day's costs, the cost for the direct nursing care services over the entire hospital stay can be computed.

The technique is similar when the PCS uses the RVU methodology. The composite salary for providing direct nursing care on a specific unit must first be determined. Then, instead of identifying the direct nursing care costs per class, the organization must calculate the average cost per RVU. Because direct nursing care services vary depending on the type of client being served, the average cost for 1 RVU must be unit specific. The monetary figure will reflect the cost of providing direct nursing care for 1 RVU on a specific unit.

Next, the acuity system is used to identify the respective number of RVUs assigned to each client. The number of RVUs needed during a 24-hour period for each client are then totaled. Finally, the number of RVUs for that 24-hour period is multiplied by the unit-specific composite salary for 1 RVU of direct nursing care. This shows the cost per day for direct nursing care services for a specific client.

It is then possible to identify the cost of providing direct nursing care services to a client throughout the hospital stay. The overall cost of nursing care services per hospitalization is needed when one is developing a budget for the facility. To determine the cost of providing nursing care during the entire hospital stay, the daily numbers of RVUs are added and then multiplied by the cost per RVU.

Within the current health care environment, providing cost-effective nursing care is vital. Once an organization knows the cost of providing direct nursing care services to each class of clients or for each RVU of care, it is possible to predict direct nursing care expenses for a unit. For example, if long-term analysis shows that clients have higher acuity ratings during the winter months, the organization can expect expenses to rise accordingly. This information is useful when one is working on budgets. To understand more about how nursing costs affect a hospital budget, refer to Chapter 8.

NURSING CARE DELIVERY SYSTEMS IN SCHOOLS

The delivery of nursing care services within the school system has recently undergone extensive changes. Historically, school nurses provided general health services and basic health education (Yates, 1994). This involved health screenings, educational classes, basic first aid, and referral services for students within the school district. Although general screenings were performed routinely, students often had to arrange to meet with the nurse for additional counseling, first aid, or any referrals. When the nurse was responsible for more than one facility, it could be difficult for the students to make contact with the nurse. The budget for school nurses and the health care services they provide has usually been determined by the local school board and the local school tax base. Therefore, funds are most often limited, and expansion of services is often not possible.

Recent changes have been made in the delivery of health care services to school-age children. Some major changes resulted from the enactment of two public laws, the Education for All Handicapped Children Act of 1975 (P.L. 94-142) and the Individuals with Disabilities Education Act (P.L. 101-476). These laws altered and expanded the scope of health care services that are to be provided within the school system. School systems are now required to provide education and specific health care for children with disabilities (Yates, 1994).

Children with chronic health problems, such as spina bifida or severe asthma, are now allowed to attend public schools (Passarelli, 1994). School nurses must provide necessary services, such as administering medications or emptying a catheter bag, or they must train school personnel to perform these tasks. The nurse must also be available for consultation if any child's medical condition deteriorates.

There are some environmental factors that have affected the school system. In America today, increasing numbers of families have little or no medical insurance. This results in large numbers of school-age children who have no basic, routine medical services. Typical services not received are immunizations, routine health screenings, and treatment for minor illnesses. The school nurse is often the only source of medical service for these children. In response to the growing problems seen within the school-age population, two similar NCDSs have been started within the schools. One is known as the school-based clinic, and the other is the school-linked clinic (Passarelli, 1994).

Types of School Delivery Systems

The trend toward delivering more broad-based health care services to school-age children has required increasing flexibility and creativity within the health care community. The two new types of clinics, school-based and school-linked, are designed to address more comprehensive health care concerns for students.

The **school-based clinic** provides a way to deliver basic medical and nursing care to individuals who are not able to pursue independent health care services. The basic premise is to bring a variety of health care services to the school environment. This makes it easier and possible for the student to utilize the services. Often, the health care team is multidisciplinary and will include a physician, an RN or a nurse practitioner (NP), and a social worker (Passarelli, 1994). Other services, when they are available, may also be provided, such as nutrition counseling or psychological support. Even though many of the employees providing services may work only part time, they can still provide a wide range of services to which students might not have routine access.

Within the school-based system, the students must approach the clinic for assistance. The team is not able to tell students they must report for treatment unless a condition exists that is highly contagious and places other students at risk for infection. Unless it is an emergency, parental permission is also required before the student can be seen and treated.

The types of cases seen within school-based clinics vary depending upon the age and composition of the student population. Most school-based clinics are being established in low-income school districts. These are the people who do not have ready access to health care. Students most often seek services for teenage pregnancy, bulimia, anorexia, drug reactions, various educational programs, assessment for child abuse, and counseling (Council of Scientific Affairs, 1990; Passarelli, 1994).

With the influx into educational settings of students requiring increased medical technology, the complexity of the school nurse's job is increasing. Some students may need health care services that represent more involved nursing procedures, such as giving medications, suctioning, or catheterizing the student. The school nurse is generally responsible for coordinating and providing these health care services.

One of the major benefits of the school-based clinics is the availability of different members of the multidisciplinary team. This provides more continuity of care for the student within the clinic. It also makes it easier for many students to obtain a variety of health care services that they would not usually be able to access.

Another method for delivering health care services in the school system is known as the **school-linked clinic**. Here the nurse at the school is linked to local services, such as physicians, social workers, or nutritionists. The other services are not established on the school grounds but can be accessed quickly as needed. The school nurse makes referrals and provides follow-up care for the students by accessing the various linked services on their behalf.

There are several advantages to the use of school-linked clinics. They are less expensive for the school system than school-based programs. With a school-linked clinic, the nurse is the only member of the health care team consistently on the school payroll. The other health care team members are not on site and are paid only as needed. In addition, the linked network provides a means by which students can be referred and seen for medical problems. A commitment to the school-linked system by all members of the health care team ensures that the students will be seen when they are referred by the nurse. In this setting, students without financial means are not denied care or referred elsewhere.

The school-based and school-linked clinics can directly assist in health promotion and prevention. Dealing with students of all ages and being able to meet the needs of all medically challenged individuals allow for the delivery of more comprehensive health care services. Part of providing appropriate health care services means the school clinic must have appropriate numbers of employees and medically trained staff.

Determining Staffing in School Systems

Staffing in the school environment is not determined in the same manner as for hospitals. The educational system is not accredited through the Joint Commission, but instead must abide by government and local laws generated for the schools. These laws and regulations may vary widely from one school system to another.

Generally, the number of staff employed for school health services is determined by the average number of students the system expects to treat. Depending upon the size of the school system, most school budgets have traditionally been too small to provide for a full-time RN on site. Many facilities utilize an NA or medical assistant to do routine monitoring of students seeking health care services. The NA or medical assistant can take vital signs and gather some basic information about the problem. The RN, who may oversee several schools, can then be consulted as needed.

With the trend toward school-based or school-linked clinics, and with the increasing number of medically dependent students, it is preferred to have an RN or NP on site. Because the RN or NP is qualified to perform a larger variety of medical procedures, he or she can provide more comprehensive medical care and make more appropriate, rapid interventions for various health care problems. If the school is quite large and has a school-linked system, an additional staff assistant such as an NA or medical assistant may be appropriate. This would depend upon the average number of students routinely seen for medical treatment. On the other hand, with a school-based clinic several additional staff members would be present, so that the immediate medical attention would not necessarily be given by the RN.

To determine the level and number of staff needed for a school-based or school-linked clinic, the type of patient being seen must be examined carefully. Records must be maintained to reflect the general category of service required by each student. For example, how many students receive immunizations, vision screening, nutritional counseling for pregnancy, catheterization, or educational classes for prevention of drug use? Over time, if the types of patients being seen can be shown to require more extensive services, justification can be developed for the addition of another RN or LVN.

Often, staffing is greatly affected by the health care portion of the school's budget. Because additional staff cannot be hired without appropriate funding, which is difficult to obtain, the financial impact of delivering health care services in the school system must be examined closely.

Determining Funding in School Systems

Traditionally, school health services have been funded from the general education budget, which is generated and regulated by local property taxes. Therefore, areas in low socioeconomic neighborhoods have less money for health care services within the educational system. With the new trend toward school-based and school-linked clinics, several additional sources of funding are being accessed (Passarelli, 1994; Yates, 1994). Requests for federal grants can be written to obtain financial support to start, maintain, or expand a school-based or school-linked system. In addition, some supplemental funding can be sought by asking health care workers to volunteer time on a regular basis to the clinic. If the increasing need for additional services and the continual use of specific services can be documented, this documentation can be used as justification for additional funding.

Within the school environment, additional health care services are also being provided to students with disabilities. The school can pursue Medicaid funding to cover some of these expenses, such as physical therapy, nursing, and speech services ("Medicaid Reimbursement," 1993). Creativity is required to discover as many funding sources as possible.

Determining the Cost of Nursing Care Services

Within the school system, the cost of providing nursing care services has primarily represented the salary of the health care provider. This has been determined by the hourly rate of the RN or NA providing services to the students. The cost of providing individual services to students has not been examined extensively because the health care services were only provided by the one individual on site.

With the onset of the multidisciplinary team stationed at the school in the school-based clinics, the costs of the nursing care services could be differentiated and computed. The RN would have to track the time spent with each student. Multiplying the total number of hours spent each month seeing patients by the worker's hourly wage will identify the cost per hour of delivering nursing care. Because students are not billed for health care services provided through the school, there is no motivation to specifically identify the cost of nursing care services at this time.

Within the school system, the development of school-based and school-linked clinics will improve medical access for numerous students. When the students' health care needs can be dealt with more rapidly, the chances for complications will decrease. To expand the various school programs, creativity is required to find more funding sources. In addition, as the services expand and more complex nursing care is needed, more justification for RN staffing needs to be generated. Changes are going to continue within the school programs, and it is necessary for nursing to be involved in the development of the nursing care delivery process. This will ensure that the nursing needs of the students can be met with the maximum efficiency and the minimum cost.

LEARNING CHALLENGE   You are working in a large school-based clinic. As the RN in charge, you are not able to see every student who comes in, but you have two NAs who do initial screening and some basic care. One NA has been with the clinic for 2 years, the other has been with the clinic for 3 years. You have instructed the two NAs to refer any student to you who needs additional testing, counseling, or more than basic health care. One of the NAs, the one who has worked with you for 2 years, continues to refer every student she sees. What action could you take to assist the NA in classifying the students who need your attention?

NURSING CARE DELIVERY SYSTEMS IN THE COMMUNITY

Within the community, there are numerous types of health care services that involve nurses delivering patient care. **Public health nurses** have always taken an active role in overseeing the health care needs of clients within their local communities. In addition, home health care organizations provide **visiting nurse services** for clients needing care in their own homes. Some areas have free clinics or government-supported **health care clinics**. These organizations supply basic health care services with minimal or no fees for those needing care. **NP clinics** are also being established as another way to provide more cost-effective health care services. They provide service in areas where physicians are not located or where the population cannot afford expensive medical attention.

The way in which patient care is organized and delivered in the community setting varies depending upon the specific system and the type of population being served. Some services focus on health promotion and prevention (Tripp & Stachowiak, 1992); others deal with providing care to clients on ventilators and other high-technology equipment in the home setting (Parette, 1993). Some agencies use a primary nurse for the delivery of patient care services; others have found a case management format to be more effective.

All the community services have to operate within a budget to stay in business. To provide appropriate, cost-effective health care services, the issues of staffing, funding, and the cost of providing nursing care services must be addressed. The way in which this is accomplished depends to a great extent on the type of funding. In this regard, the community health setting has great diversity, much like the school-based delivery environment.

Determining Staffing in the Community Setting

Within the community, many patient care services are offered through some form of clinic setting. Public health nurses often are associated with a free clinic or government clinic. NP clinics may also be available. Staffing within a clinic setting is similar to that in a school system. A specific number of NPs, RNs, LVNs, and NAs are hired to staff the facility based upon the average number of patients expected.

If the clinic is large, some flexible staffing patterns may occur that will allow employees to work 2- to 4-hour shifts as needed. Clients often do not make appointments in a clinic setting, however, so the volume is difficult to predict. Therefore, a set number of staff is generally kept on duty at all times.

In home health agencies or visiting nurse services, the staffing is determined by the number of patients who are to be seen on any given day. Based on experience, the standard amount of time generally allotted for a visit by the visiting nurse is 45 minutes (Churness, Kleffel, Onodera, & Jacobson, 1988). The patient caseload for the day is often four to six patients, depending upon the amount of driving that must be done to visit the patients.

Under the new DRG reimbursement process, hospitals tend to discharge patients more quickly. As a result, the acuity of clients treated at home has been markedly increasing. With increasing acuity, a caseload of four to six clients per day may be too high. A PCS or acuity tool in home health settings can be useful for making assignments based upon acuity ratings. The PCS can also identify the cost of providing these nursing care services (Churness, Kleffel, Jacobson, & Onodera, 1986; Pavasaris, 1989).

An acuity system may be used in a similar fashion to that found in the hospital setting. An acuity system (refer to Table 3–1 and Figure 3–5) can easily identify the amount of nursing care needed by each patient. Because the client is in the home setting, the critical indicators will need to be modified to reflect specific tasks and care that would appropriately be provided at home. These indicators could include the amount of assistance needed with items such as activities of daily living, use of oxygen equipment, wound care, dressing changes, and range of motion.

To determine staffing, the PCS can rate clients in classes or use an RVU methodology. As previously discussed for hospital settings, the home care agency must also determine the average amount of time spent providing nursing care services within each class rating or per RVU. Once the amount of time needed to provide nursing care services to the client can be identified, a more cost-effective and appropriate staff assignment can be made. For example, when the acuity tool shows that a client requires 2 hours of nursing care, the staffing assignment can be modified to allow the staff member the necessary time to provide the care.

The rating for the PCS needs to be conducted every visit to keep the rating as current and relevant as possible. When the patient acuity shows the need for additional patient care, the agency would then have the data necessary to justify billing for additional nursing care services.

Determining Funding in the Community Setting

Funding for nursing services in community settings is as varied as the services provided. One type of funding is done through free clinics or government-supported clinics. Here no fee or a minimal fee is collected from the person seeking medical care. The care is funded or supplemented by government agencies, so individuals with inadequate insurance or without health insurance can be treated. Many of the patient care services provided in this setting are billed to Medicare or Medicaid. Supplementing the cost of medical and nursing care provided at the clinic is more cost effective than having the client use hospital emergency departments for routine services.

Another way in which community-based groups are funded is through private insurance companies. Home health agencies and visiting nurse groups often join together with local hospitals and physicians. The hospitals or physicians refer clients to the home health groups or the visiting nurse agencies. If the client has insurance, the community groups can bill the insurance company for reimbursement.

Home health agencies or visiting nurse associations can provide a more cost-effective option than hospitalizing each client. A home visit also allows for a thorough assessment of the home environment, so that possible problems can be found before they cause complications. Home visits also provide time for interaction with and teaching of the family members. Often, family members or significant others can be taught how to provide basic health care services. Then the client can be cared for at home with minimal or no expense to either the insurance company or a government-funded program.

Independent clinics run by NPs are another option for community health care services. Their funding comes from a combination of insurance companies, government-supported programs, and cash paid by the clients for services. To obtain any funding other than cash, however, the NP must be closely aligned with some physician. Currently, insurance companies do not allow NP clinics to bill directly under their own identification code. All billing forms must include the identification number of the physician who is involved with the clinic.

Another method of funding occurs when patients pay cash for necessary health care services. This method can usually only be done when the expenses are fairly small. In many community settings, clients are seen and treated even though they cannot pay for the services (Josten, Strohschein, & Smoot, 1993). These patients are known as bad debts because the care is provided without any reimbursement. If an organization provides service to large numbers of bad debt cases, its financial stability can be jeopardized (refer to Chapter 8 for information about budget management). To stay in practice, all facilities must make enough money to pay the debts they incur while providing health care services.

Within the community setting, some clinics or special programs can apply for grants and other special funding. As with all health care services, creativity is required to utilize as many different funding options as possible so the appropriate patient care services can be provided. Each organization must carefully monitor its funding sources so that it can continue to operate. If the agency does not break even financially, it cannot remain in business.

Determining the Cost of Nursing Care Services

The cost of nursing care within the community setting depends upon the organization providing the service. For community-based clinics, determining the cost of nursing care is similar to the methods discussed for the school system. The exact number of minutes spent seeing clients and providing nursing care services must be recorded. Then the nurses' salaries can be divided by the time spent to determine the cost per minute or per hour of care.

In the home health agencies, when an acuity methodology is used the technique for calculating the cost of the nursing care is similar to that used in the hospital setting. If the average amount of time spent for each classification of patient is known and the average salary of the health care worker is given, the cost of providing the nursing care services can be identified. If the agency uses an RVU system, the cost for each RVU can be calculated. Either way, the care for each visit or the overall care for each client can be determined.

Within the various community-based organizations, there is no uniform method for providing nursing care services. Client care is delivered based upon the type of agency and the population being served. It is important, however, for each group to monitor its cost effectiveness carefully so that it can continue to provide the broad base of services currently available.

KEY CONCEPT	• Creativity is required to identify funding sources for patient care services in school or community agencies.
LEARNING CHALLENGE	You are an RN working in a home health organization. The agency also utilizes LVNs for maintenance visits and to provide basic nursing care needs. As the RN, you have responsibility for making all assignments. One LVN has just refused a patient in the assignment you have given her because the patient has acquired immunodeficiency syndrome. What action would you take with the LVN? What additional action would you take within the organization?

MONITORING ACUITY SYSTEMS

To obtain a license to provide health care and to utilize outside funding, health care institutions must meet various regulatory standards. These standards are usually referred to as **quality standards**. The programs created by institutions to ensure that they meet quality standards are generally known as quality assurance or quality control programs (refer to Chapter 9). The types of **quality monitoring** done depend upon the type of organization providing the care. In the hospital setting, the Joint Commission requires that quality be monitored continually and corrective changes be made to the services as necessary. In school and community settings, where programs are not accredited, quality standards will be established by the government agency providing the funding.

Standards have been developed by various national nursing organizations that can be used to determine whether the care being delivered is quality care. The standards are often broad statements that reflect codes for nursing conduct or patients' rights. These broad, general statements serve as guidelines that can be adapted to meet the specific scenario for any nursing or health care institution. The **American Nurses Association** and the **International Council of Nurses** have both established standards that reflect several aspects of delivering care to clients (Wright, 1987). Each organization that is supplying patient care must then specifically define how the standards are reflected in the services it provides.

Within any organization that is delivering patient care, **audits** must be conducted on a regular basis. An audit consists of independently examining the documented client care. Patient charts are examined for specific factors that can be used to determine whether the care provided was quality care. The specific items that are being monitored vary depending upon the focus of the audit. Audits can be conducted to monitor trends or potential problems in the delivery of patient services. The focus of an audit can be the structure used to deliver nursing care services, the process by which the care is provided, or the outcome experienced by the patient. Chapter 9 includes more specific information about the various types of audits that can be performed.

One common practice used to monitor patient care for quality is to analyze the comments made by the patients and their families. Patient satisfaction surveys, letters, or phone calls can be examined. For sources of concern identified in an interview, appropriate actions are taken. Perhaps the issue is that not enough time is allotted for a home visit or that the assignment on a hospital unit is so large proper care cannot be provided. In such cases, perhaps the staffing patterns should be reevaluated and attention given to reorganizing the workload.

Another technique used to monitor quality is the identification of the length of time a patient remains outside the health care system. If a client returns to the hospital within 1 to 2 weeks of being discharged, the previously provided care may need to be reexamined. Quality concerns that should be investigated include the adequacy of discharge planning, appropriate use of community resources, and client contact by referral services. If clients are not able to receive the needed services at home, they will require more follow-up visits to the hospital or clinic, and during these visits they may be more acutely ill than when they were discharged.

When a PCS is used to identify the type of nursing service to provide, the acuity tool should also be monitored for quality. For quality within an acuity system, it is necessary that the critical indicators be appropriate and that the patients be classified with consistency. **Interrater reliability**, or equivalence (Polit & Hungler, 1993), is a common assessment used to monitor the quality of a PCS. To determine interrater reliability, a patient's nursing needs and care are rated simultaneously by two independent observers. If both reviewers obtain the same or similar rating, the acuity instrument can be shown to consistently reflect and measure the client's nursing care needs. If the instrument does not provide similar results, the PCS should be examined and revised.

Within the current health care environment, cost saving measures are continually being implemented. While providing cost-effective client care, it is necessary for nursing to be sure the quality of that care is not degraded. Cost-effective methods of delivering client care should not sacrifice quality. Auditing various aspects of the health care delivery system for quality will provide protection for the clients against poor-quality services. Monitoring nursing services can also assist the nurses by making them aware of items that need to be revised or improved to ensure the quality of the nursing care being provided.

KEY CONCEPT
- Patient care services in all health care settings need to be monitored for quality. This is done to protect the client and to maintain the integrity of the quality care being provided.

CONCLUSION

When planning a budget or deciding what cost-effective strategies to implement, a manager must be aware of what costs are being accrued by the department. Since nurses are not required to have a strong educational background in finance, it is often necessary for nursing managers to receive additional training in budgets and finances. Nurses are well trained in client care, so when financial information can be related to client care it may be easier for nurse managers to understand. The major benefit that nursing derives from costing out services is the increased ability to justify, monitor, and control costs within the current cost-conscious health care environment. The costs that nursing cannot justify or control, it stands to lose.

RESEARCH FOUNDATION   Eckhart, J. (1992). Meta-analysis on costing out nursing services. *Dissertation Abstracts International*, 53/04-B, 1783, AAD 92-23366.

With the increased focus on the cost of nursing services, various studies have been done on the subject. One such study was performed by Eckhart in 1992. Eckhart looked at the methods of costing nursing services in acute care hospital settings. Using a mathematical technique known as meta-analysis, Eckhart studied the cost of nursing care services documented in 73 primary studies. Total and direct nursing care costs were correlated with four variables:

1. direct nursing care hours required
2. total hospital costs accumulated
3. patient length of stay in the hospital
4. DRG reimbursements received by the institution

The meta-analysis utilized Pearson's r coefficient, or product-moment correlation coefficient, to compute the correlations among all the above listed variables. The purpose of Pearson's r is to identify the intensity of the relationship between two variables. The range for Pearson's r coefficient is from -1.00 to $+1.00$. The closer the calculated coefficient is to the absolute value of 1.00, the stronger the relationship is between the two variables. Positive values represent strong direct relationships, and negative values represent inverse relationships. For the study, correlations of absolute value greater than 0.80 between two variables were considered strong correlations.

The meta-analytic study found that total nursing care costs correlated with the variables as follows:

- 0.85 to direct nursing care hours
- 0.99 to hospital costs
- 0.65 to length of stay

Direct nursing care costs were found to correlate in a similar fashion:

- 0.94 to direct hours
- 0.95 to hospital costs
- 0.83 to length of stay

No significance was found in correlations between nursing costs and DRG reimbursements.

The percentage of the total hospital costs represented by the total and direct nursing costs was also calculated. Within the 73 primary studies, total nursing costs were found to be 22.15% of hospital costs, and direct nursing costs were 15.68%. These percentages show nursing costs to be a large portion of a hospital budget. This implies that control of nursing costs is a major part of controlling the overall hospital budget.

The major inconsistency found within the 73 studies examined dealt with the definitions of direct and total nursing costs. Some studies did not identify what services were included in direct or total nursing care costs. The studies that carefully identified which services were included in the costs were not consistent in their definitions. Although strong correlations were found for several of the items listed above, it should be remembered that the quality of the study was directly dependent on the consistency of the definitions used in each of the 73 studies.

REFERENCES

Abdellah, F., & Levine, L. (1965). *Better patient care through nursing research.* New York: Macmillan.

Churness, V., Kleffel, D., Jacobson, J., & Onodera, M. (1986). Development of a patient classification system for home health nursing. In F. Shaffer (Ed.), *Patient and purse strings: Patient classification and cost management* (pp. 319–330). New York: National League for Nursing.

Churness, V., Kleffel, D., Onodera, M., & Jacobson, J. (1988). Reliability and validity testing of a home health patient classification system. *Public Health Nursing, 5* (3), 135–139.

Council of Scientific Affairs. (1990). Providing medical services through school-based health programs. *Journal of School Health, 60* (3), 87–91.

Gillies, D. (1989). *Nursing management: A systems approach* (2nd ed.). Philadelphia: Saunders.

Giovannetti, P. (1979). Understanding patient classification systems. *Journal of Nursing Administration, 9* (2), 4–9.

Joint Commission on Accreditation of Healthcare Organizations. (1994). *Accreditation manual for hospitals.* Chicago: Author.

Josten, L., Strohschein, S., & Smoot, C. (1993). Managing uncompensated home care. *Journal of Community Health Nursing, 10* (3), 149–160.

Lewis, E., & Carini, P. (1984). *Nurse staffing and patient classification: Strategies for success.* Gaithersburg, MD: Aspen.

Medicaid reimbursement for school nursing services. (1993). *Journal of School Nursing, 9* (3), 37–39.

Munoz, E., Josephson, J., Tenenbaum, N., Goldstein, J., Shears, A., & Wise, L. (1989). Diagnosis-related groups, costs, and outcome for patients in the intensive care unit. *Heart & Lung, 18* (6), 627–633.

Parette, H. (1993). High risk infant case management and assistive technology: Funding and family enabling perspectives. *Maternal–Child Nursing Journal, 21* (2), 53–64.

Passarelli, C. (1994). School nursing: Trends for the future. *Journal of School Nursing, 10* (2), 10–21.

Pavasaris, B. (1989). Patient classification tool in home health care. *Home Healthcare Nurse, 7* (1), 28–33.

Polit, D., & Hungler, B. (1993). *Essentials of nursing research: Methods, appraisal, and utilization* (3rd ed.). Philadelphia: Lippincott.

Shaffer, F. (1983). DRGs: History and overview. *Nursing & Health Care, 4* (7), 388–396.

Stanley, M., & Luciano, K. (1984). Eight steps to costing nursing services. *Nursing Management, 15* (10), 35–38.

Tripp, S., & Stachowiak, B. (1992). Health maintenance, health promotion: Is there a difference? *Public Health Nursing, 9* (3), 155–161.

Wright, R. (1987). *Human values in health care: The practice of ethics.* New York: McGraw-Hill.

Yates, S. (1994). The practice of school nursing: Integration with new models of health service delivery. *Journal of School Nursing, 10* (1), 10–19.

CHAPTER 4

Leadership in Nursing

Catherine E. Loveridge

CHAPTER OBJECTIVES

At the completion of this chapter, the beginning professional nurse will:

1. understand the importance of leadership in health care today
2. understand the relationship between leadership and management
3. be able to compare and contrast selected leadership theories
4. be able to compare and contrast selected management theories
5. understand the nurse's leadership role in client care, professional issues, and political systems
6. understand the use of power as a leadership skill

CRITICAL THINKING CHALLENGE

Your organization has made a commitment to redesign the patient care delivery system as a patient-focused model of care. You have been asked to participate in the unit planning committee. How will you display your leadership abilities in addressing the changes to take place in the redesigned delivery system?

Leadership is an essential topic for the beginning nurse to understand in preparing for the professional role. Leadership is more than a position in an organization; it is an approach to life, an attitude that says "I know where I'm going." This attitude is required in the changing health care system of today.

At one time, health care systems were stable and required the nurse to develop and follow the nursing care plan while resources were provided to complete needed activities. This is no longer the case. As increasing technological advancements compete for limited human and material resources, organizations struggle with their bureaucratic structures to chart a path toward the future. Often, the plans for the future are compromised by the exigencies of the present. Crisis management replaces long-term planning in the struggle for survival. From these forces, a need for visionaries, communicators, and implementors arises. Professional nurses are uniquely prepared to respond to this requirement.

The exercise of leadership skills is not limited to those people at the top of organizations. Leadership pervades the activities of all professionals by challenging them to develop a vision of the desired future, first with the client, then with the organizational changes necessary to accommodate needed collaboration, and finally with the health care system and the larger society through political activity. Leadership begins with understanding the many facets of the concept and learning to apply the principles to everyday personal and clinical experience. In applying leadership principles to the mutual interaction model of nurse–client relations, one finds the nurse uniquely positioned to understand the client's needs, values, and goals.

The nurse exercises leadership skills by using professional knowledge to create a vision of what client outcomes are likely if particular health behaviors are chosen by the client. Through respect for the client's integrity and desires, a collaborative plan is developed. This plan is then communicated to colleagues. As an instrumental member of the health care team, the nurse exercises leadership skills through communication and collaboration with other health care professionals. Client outcomes become the focus of action to aid the client in achieving the desired health status. In addition, collaborative efforts are more effective than individual or single department action in creating change in a complex organizational system.

As a citizen and health care professional, the nurse exercises leadership through community service and political activity. Finding a way to use one's particular talents to serve the organization, the nursing profession, and the community demonstrates one's leadership ability. This service might include stimulating discussion about health care needs of citizens, exercising the right to vote to elect candidates supporting a desired vision of health care, serving on civic boards, and running for public office.

MANAGEMENT AND LEADERSHIP

Management authority evolves from the manager's position in the organization. Leadership authority evolves from the individual's ability to influence the behavior of others, regardless of the position held in the organization. Although it is often suggested as ideal to have the two abilities located in the same individual, a closer examination of the differences in the perspectives of these individuals is warranted.

The manager's responsibility is to assess situations in a rational manner; identify goals and strategies to achieve objectives; assemble resources; design and implement a plan of action; organize, direct, and control activities aimed toward goal attainment; and maintain acceptable productivity and employee satisfaction levels. These activities require skills in problem analysis, collaboration, coordination, compromise, conflict resolution, negotiation, and perseverance. By its very nature, the effect of good management is to maintain momentum and balance within the organization.

The leader's role is different. Often the leader is the risk taker, upsetting the status quo with extraordinary ideas guaranteed to disrupt organizational routine. By sparking imaginations and changing expectations, the leader changes the way people think about what is possible, desirable, and necessary.

These activities can only thrive in an environment that is open to new ideas and tolerant of eccentricities. In complex organizations, tension exists between the manager's efforts to maintain a balance and the leader's efforts to change direction. The need for both is evident if growth and progress are to occur.

LEARNING CHALLENGE   Think about a manager and a leader with whom you have worked. Do you think that managers and leaders need different skills? What skills do managers need? What skills do leaders need? Discuss the behaviors associated with each of these roles and how they are similar or different.

DEFINITION OF LEADERSHIP

Leadership is defined as the ability to influence others in the determination and achievement of goals. Although this is simply stated, the meaning implies the exercise of creative thinking, excellent communication skills, and the will to act.

Creative thinking requires letting go of the structured, rational approach to viewing the world and allowing the intuitive, futuristic vision of how things might be to take over. Often called "blue sky" thinking, it frees the individual to explore mentally what kind of outcome would be the most desirable, regardless of limitations that may exist in the environment. It follows from the belief that one is more likely to achieve a goal if that goal is visualized.

The second critical component in defining leadership is communication. Skill is needed to inform all parties involved in the action of the vision and to gain their commitment to it. Clients come to the nurse with varying degrees of knowledge about their health and the interventions available to them. The nurse needs to convey sufficient information for the client to make informed choices. Colleagues need opportunities to contribute their expertise to the client's outcomes. Through collaboration, each profession brings its own perspective to the plan of care, enriching the results. The nurse exercises leadership by contributing to the discussions, clarifying ideas, valuing the insights offered by other participants, and creating consensus about what is to be done.

The most visible part of leadership is action. Once commitment has been made to the plan, the leader carries out the necessary action. This may involve direct nurse-client intervention, organizational activity, or public service. Evaluation of the action, readjustment of the plan, and continued communication among all participants complete the exercise of leadership.

KEY CONCEPTS
- Leadership is the ability to influence others in the determination and achievement of goals.
- Leadership requires creative thinking, excellent communication skills, and the will to act.

EVOLUTION OF LEADERSHIP THOUGHT

Two basic approaches laid the foundation for thinking about leadership in early research on the topic. One approach was to examine the person who was identified as a leader. The second approach was to examine the organization in which leadership was exercised.

In historical times, the prevailing culture valued a personal relationship between the leader and those who were led. Outward signs, such as an imposing physical appearance and greater education, were identified as characteristics of leaders. Because members of the ruling classes were often taller, stronger, and healthier than those of the lower classes who worked in the fields, it is not surprising that these characteristics were identified as evidence of leadership destiny. In addition, education was available only to the wealthiest families, thus further identifying the ruling classes as smarter than others (Fiedler & Garcia, 1987).

In contrast to this personal view of leadership, Weber (1946) defined leadership in the context of the organization. He named this organizational structure a **bureaucracy** because each department or "bureau" was limited to specific activities. In this perspective, the role of the leader is clearly defined through the duties and responsibilities inherent in the leadership position. Loyalty is given to the organization and its goals, not to the individual leader. Both these perspectives have their merits and bear closer examination because of their influence on the development of leadership in nursing.

Trait Theory

The earliest conception of the personal theories of leadership focused on the traits identified as being associated with leaders in government, the military, and industry. According to the **trait theory**, individuals are born with specific traits, such as aggressiveness, intelligence, initiative, drive, and ambition. These traits were proposed as correlates of successful leadership. It is interesting to note that these characteristics are also associated with masculine behavior as described in early times as well as today.

Another example of the trait approach to the study of leadership was the **Great Man theory**. It was believed that, if one studied the lives of great men, a pattern of characteristics and behaviors correlated with successful leadership would emerge. A significant point to examine is the cultural bias associated with the term *Great Man* as opposed to the gender-neutral term *Great People*. Those examined for these characteristics were leaders in government, the military, and industry, areas in which women were not significantly represented. It is clear that women were not considered appropriate subjects for the study of leadership.

Although much of this perspective has been replaced with more comprehensive theories, there is a lingering impact of this approach on current thinking about leadership. Captains of industry, military commanders, government officials, and hospital administrators are predominantly male. Their judgments affect nursing and health care through the policies developed throughout society.

These findings have significance for nursing because nursing is a predominantly female profession. Leadership exercised in the context of one's gender and relationships becomes undervalued or unrecognized in comparison with the traits that have been promoted as indicators of leadership. Nevertheless, nursing has prevailed against this bias by recognizing charismatic leaders such as Nightingale and Rogers (Chaska, 1990), organizational leaders such as Clifford and Kerfoot, and political leaders such as Gebbie and Hinshaw. At the local level, leaders include the many women who advocate for quality patient care, such as advanced practice nurses and nursing case managers.

LEARNING   What factors in your personal life have influenced your leadership ability?
CHALLENGE   Consider your position in your family, your class, your school, and your
community. What experiences have shaped the way you think about
leadership?

Management Theory

At the opposite end of the spectrum of leadership thought are the studies
that focus on organizational systems. In this perspective, the key to completing successfully the work of groups of people was the way in which people
were organized, their scope of responsibility, and their training for the job to
be done. In his development of **scientific management theory**, Taylor
(1916) described the benefits that could derive from focusing on the efficient
completion of a task by the best-prepared worker in the shortest amount of
time to increase productivity and general effectiveness of the organization.

Weber (Gerth & Mills, 1946) designed an organization providing levels of
graded authority in which each level was responsible for supervision of the
level below it. This bureaucracy has been the dominant organizational structure of the 20th century. In this system, the leader is defined by his or her
position in the hierarchy. Personal attributes are subordinate to strict adherence to official duties and responsibilities.

Before World War II, hospitals adopted a scientific management approach
to maximize the skills of a short supply of nurses. The result was the development of functional nursing, a method of assigning a large group of patients to
a staff of registered nurses (RNs), licensed vocational nurses (LVNs), and
nurse assistants. All staff would report to a head nurse for assignment and
supervision (see Chapter 1 for a broader discussion of functional nursing).

In following Taylor's objectives of efficiency, nurse assistants provided
care for the least ill clients assigned to the unit and performed tasks such as
making beds and bathing clients. LVNs could contribute technical assistance,
such as dressing changes and other selected procedures. The RNs on the
staff were responsible for the care they provided to the sickest clients on the
unit and for professional skills required by clients cared for by LVNs and
aides. In this small unit of the larger hospital bureaucracy, the head nurse
was responsible for the quality of care received by all clients, for supervising
the work of all staff, and for providing direct nursing care when necessary.

Several aspects of this management strategy affected the development of
nursing leadership. First, professional values of individual client care were
subordinated to the efficiency of several workers providing parts of care to
any one client. This resulted in a distancing of the client from the nurse, a
blurring of accountability, and a missed opportunity for collegial practice to

flourish. Second, the route to recognition of leadership ability was seen as leading away from direct nursing care of clients to supervision of others, management of larger units, and administration. Third, nurses were viewed as interchangeable workers, able to fill slots in staffing schedules without regard to specialty, preference, and expertise.

Nursing leaders recognized these forces and responded with the development of primary nursing, a philosophy of care that places the nurse and client in a partnership for recovery and advancement of health. Collaborative practices have also developed throughout the nation, providing job satisfaction and professional recognition for clinical nurses choosing to provide direct care to clients.

As hospitals reorganize patient care units to reflect a commitment to patient-focused care, the nurse has become a key coordinator of services and an essential member of patient care teams. Not only are excellent communication skills required to collaborate with multidisciplinary workers on the team, but leadership skills that require flexibility in sharing leader responsibilities are also essential. These skills are discussed in greater detail in Chapters 5 and 6.

Summary

Although both trait theory and the scientific management approach to the study of leadership attempted to provide criteria for identifying leadership performance, they neglected to account for the individual personal differences that exist among people. They also neglected to address the best method to lead professional employees who are directed by a code of professional standards developed outside the walls of the organization.

LEARNING CHALLENGE   Select five well-known leaders in the community and have small groups independently identify the leadership characteristics of each individual. Reassemble the groups and compare characteristics of all the leaders. Students can identify patterns of leadership behavior among people in different walks of life.

CONTEMPORARY THEORIES OF LEADERSHIP

Human Relations

The perspective that is gaining more relevance in today's workplace focuses on both the leader and the people being led. It extends the focus of the personal leadership theorists to the people with whom the leader interacts. It was originally developed by human relations theorists, who felt that a major fault of the bureaucratic system was its failure to recognize the human element in its focus on task completion.

In a landmark study conducted near Chicago at the Hawthorne Works of the Western Electric Company, it was discovered that, when employees received special attention from managers, productivity increased (Marquis & Huston, 1994). The original purpose of the study was to determine the relationship of the amount of illumination in the factory to productivity. The findings showed that, in cases of both increased illumination and near darkness, productivity increased during the study. This Hawthorne effect demonstrated that people will increase positive behavior when they believe that their behavior is being studied.

Team nursing was a response to the human relations approach to leadership. In team nursing, a team leader (an RN) was responsible for the care delivered by a team composed of RNs, LVNs, and nursing assistants. The team would consistently be assigned to the same patients, provide input to the team leader regarding modifications to the plan of care, and record and report pertinent observations and changes in client condition. This recognition of staff contributions improved morale and the continuity of client care (Giovannetti, 1978), yet larger problems of professional accountability remained.

Human resources theory evolved from the attention to the worker and used the insights gained from psychologists to contribute to the study of people in the workplace. Understanding the motives and aspirations of working people would enable leaders to become more effective. Argyris (1964) described a range of behaviors called the **immaturity–maturity continuum**. Immature behavior includes dependency, passivity, short-range perspectives, and a lack of self-awareness. At the other end of the continuum, mature behavior includes independence, the capacity for multiple interests, a developed ability to view the long-term implications of actions, and self-control. To encourage mature behavior, organizations need to restructure.

Theory X and Theory Y

These ideas were reinforced by McGregor (1960) in his study of managerial attitudes toward employees. He found that the way managers thought about their employees directed the way in which they treated them. He labeled this perspective **Theory X and Theory Y**. Theory X managers considered their employees basically lazy and unwilling to complete their work unless they were continually supervised and directed. On the other hand,

Theory Y managers believed that their employees were self-motivated, enthusiastic, and eager to work to meet personal and organizational objectives.

These ideas are important in the study of nursing leadership because they provide the foundation for understanding the past and planning the future. As nursing faces the challenges of a changing health care system, it is important to be ready with workable options for the future that will reflect knowledge gained through education and experience.

Leadership is needed to expand the opportunity to contribute to the advancement of health. The health care consumer is changing, as is the health care organization provider. Leadership exercised in this new dynamic will reflect the greater role of the client in his or her own health care. Mutual goal setting will replace the client's passive role, and collaboration will replace bureaucracy as organizations respond to these changes.

An example of this kind of organizational restructuring is **shared governance**. In this type of structure, workers are empowered to make critical decisions regarding the operation of the organization. Leadership is shared by clinicians and managers, so that the unique talents of each are developed to their fullest extent. Success requires the development of leadership skills in all participants. In some cases, this may require the reeducation of managers to reflect the new philosophy of sharing power. Such a philosophy requires understanding the relationship between the two approaches to leadership that have been described, the personal approach and the organizational approach. See Chapter 1 for more discussion of shared governance as an organizational structure.

LEADERSHIP MEASUREMENT

Because leadership is often experienced more than visualized, measurement of the concept has been difficult. To understand the dynamics involved, does one examine the person, the situation, or the organization? The following examples demonstrate the development of ideas reflecting different aspects of measuring leadership.

Ohio State Leadership Scales

Among the early research in the field, the Ohio State Leadership studies published in the 1950s provided information regarding the behavior of leaders in satisfying common group needs. The survey of leaders in business, the military, and education discovered that initiating structure and consideration were the two important dimensions of leadership. **Initiating structure** included the leader's behavior in establishing patterns of organization, channels of communication, and methods of procedure. The category of **con-**

sideration included behavior reflecting respect, friendship, and warmth between the leader and the persons led.

Figure 4–1 indicates the placement of leaders according to their responses on the Leader Behavior Description Questionnaire. The four types of leaders identified were as follows:

- quadrant 1: high initiating structure, high consideration
- quadrant 2: high initiating structure, low consideration
- quadrant 3: low initiating structure, low consideration
- quadrant 4: low initiating structure, high consideration

In this analysis, the quadrant 1 leader is considered the most effective leader because both organizational processes and human resources are equally important. The quadrant 2 leader emphasizes organizational values over those of the employees, and the quadrant 4 leader reverses those emphases. The quadrant 3 leader fails to meet expected behavior in either domain.

Michigan Leadership Studies

Similar findings emerged from studies conducted at about the same time at the University of Michigan (Katz et al., 1950). Surveys indicated that leaders could be classified as either employee centered or job centered. In system 1, the exploitative autocracy, the leader emphasized task completion at the expense of employees' personal needs. System 2, the benevolent autocracy,

---

Initiating Structure

		Low	High
Consideration	High	Low structure High consideration <div align=right>4</div>	High structure High consideration <div align=left>1</div>
	Low	3 Low structure Low consideration	2 High structure Low consideration

Figure 4–1 Ohio State Leadership Scale. *Source:* Reprinted from *Management: Concepts and Applications* by L.C. Megginson, D.C. Mosley, & P.H. Pietri, Jr., p. 410, with permission of Harper Collins, © 1986.

emphasized leader decision-making authority with some attention to the personal needs of employees. The system 3 leader, the consultative leader, demonstrated consideration of the input of employees in decisions affecting their work. The system 4 leader, the participative leader, shared authority for decision making with employees. Lewin (1947) determined that supervisors with the best performance were those who emphasized creating a work environment in which mutual respect, trust, and a commitment to high performance goals were maintained.

Leadership Grid

Blake and McCanse (1991), formerly Blake and Mouton, further developed the interaction of task orientation and people orientation in leader behavior. They developed the Leadership Grid shown in Figure 4–2. This grid has a horizontal axis, representing concern for results, and a vertical axis, representing concern for people. The leader evaluates his or her leadership concerns on a scale of 1 and 9 on both dimensions. This rating positions the leadership style on the grid. In each of these measures, leaders evaluate levels of concern from low to high regarding organizational production as it interacts with human resources. For example, managers displaying a 9,1 Authority–Compliance management behavior see people as tools for production with low concern for others. They demand tight, unilateral control to complete tasks and consider creativity and human relations a low priority. On the other hand, people displaying 1,9 Country Club management behaviors have great concern for people and low concern for results. They try to avoid conflict and keep people happy even at the expense of achieving results.

Nurses and Leadership Measurement

In the more traditional hospital environment, nurses might be perceived as good leaders if they maintain the organizational status quo without regard to morale or concerns of the staff employees. Such an individual would be in quadrant 2 of the Ohio State Leadership Scales, an autocrat according to the Michigan Leadership Studies, and a 9,1 manager on the Leadership Grid.

However accurate these tools might be in measuring individual behaviors, they neglect to provide useful insights about the circumstances that might require a leader to emphasize one domain over another. For example, newly formed organizations require the establishment of organizational rules to structure internal and external relationships. In developing shared governance models of organizational structure, staff nurses and nurse managers decide how to change communication and decision-making channels to support the objective of sharing power. The design of policies and procedures for operation takes initial priority. Those policies and procedures affect people,

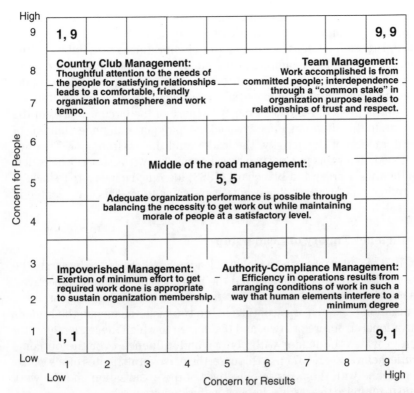

Figure 4–2 Leadership grid. *Source:* The Leadership Grid figure from *Leadership Dilemmas: Grid Solutions* by Robert R. Blake and Anne Adams McCanse (formerly the Managerial Grid figure by Robert R. Blake and Jane S. Mouton), Houston: Gulf Publishing Company, p. 29. © 1991 by Scientific Methods, Inc. Reproduced by permission of the owners.

however, and therefore require attention to the human element. All participants need to consider the effects of their actions on their clients, their profession, their colleagues, and the organization. In this example, each employee has the opportunity to be a leader. Successful leaders blend their knowledge of organizational demands and human resources to produce the best outcome.

SITUATIONAL LEADERSHIP

An additional perspective can be gained through the measurement of leadership behaviors. The dominant elements are people-oriented or task-oriented behaviors. In studies examining how to combine the best of these behaviors effectively, it was found that the situation in which leadership behavior emerges plays an important part.

Each situation presents its own set of circumstances that influence the results obtained. For example, in the emergency department, an unconscious client requires immediate attention, implementation of life-support procedures, and the well-practiced skills of a team of professionals. Attention to technical procedures takes priority because of the circumstances of the moment. In this situation, effective leadership requires an understanding of the interaction of the activity, the leader, and the environment. Theories developed under this perspective have become known as situational leadership theories. Hersey and Blanchard (1988) identified a measure to include determination of several dimensions at the same time. This is presented in Figure 4–3.

Contingency Theory of Leadership

In 1976, Fiedler proposed a model of leadership that tried to integrate the personal leader, the employee, and the bureaucratic system perspectives. The **contingency model** states that the effectiveness of a leader or of the organization depends, or is contingent, on two major elements: the leader's motivational structure or style, and the degree to which the leadership situation provides the leader with control and influence over the outcome (Schriesheim & Kerr, 1977). In this case, the personal attributes of the leader are matched with the tasks or objectives of the organization and the work group to optimize the results. Implicit in this definition is knowledge of motivation, group dynamics, and the exercise of power. The leader must understand his or her own motivation and style to exercise leadership effectively. In addition, the work group dynamics require understanding so that communication succeeds. Finally, the organization must commit sufficient resources for completion of the activity. For example, a Theory Y leader believes in the commitment and industry of workers. This leader would most likely be motivated to accomplish a goal by bringing out the best in the individual workers. The work group would need to be technically competent and skilled in communication so that efforts could be coordinated. The leader would need the organizational authority or position to command the necessary resources to accomplish the task.

Path–Goal Theory of Leadership

House (1971) developed an integrating theory that identified motivational aspects of the leader's role. He proposed that the leader is effective insofar as he or she provides subordinates with coaching, guidance, and incentives that

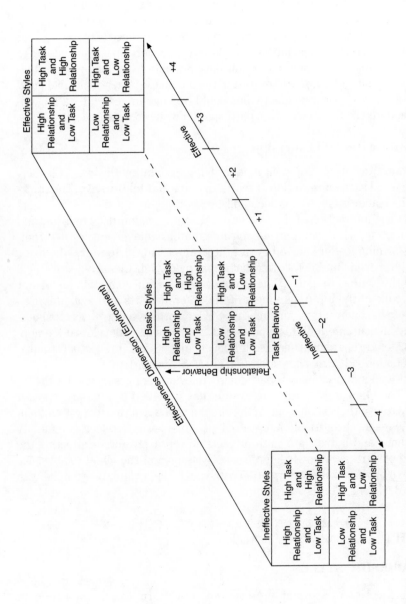

Figure 4-3 Tridimensional leader effectiveness model. Reprinted with permission of Prentice Hall, Englewood Cliffs, New Jersey. *Source:* From Paul Hersey and Kenneth Blanchard, *Management of Organizational Behavior: Utilizing Human Resources*, 6th ed., p. 131, © 1993.

are not readily available in the work environment. When goals are identified for the employee, the leader's role is to make a path toward the goal that is easier to travel by reducing obstacles and increasing opportunities for employee satisfaction en route. For example, a staff nurse interested in quality assurance would benefit from increased exposure to those activities. A unit leader exercising House's **path–goal theory** of leadership would encourage the staff nurse's participation in unit-based quality assurance responsibilities. By enabling this nurse to represent the unit in the larger department and division, quality assurance activities could be encouraged and staffing accommodated so that the nurse's participation would be ensured.

Transformational Leadership

A more recent development in identifying integrating theories of leadership has led to the description of **transformational leadership**. The transforming leader is one who is accomplished at bringing out the best in others so that the interaction of the leader and the group is mutually uplifting and encouraging, with each party inspiring greater achievement in the other. Transforming leaders move beyond the **transactional leader**, who leads through convincing the follower that attaining organizational objectives will fulfill the follower's goals. The transforming leader combines his or her knowledge of the interrelatedness of the different parts of the organization with a focus on intuitive thinking that will lead others to the envisioned outcomes. Measurement of this type of leadership has been developed. Components include charisma, idealized influence, inspiration, intellectual stimulation, and individualized consideration (Bass & Avolio, 1990).

This leadership strategy is particularly relevant for nursing and for the future. The changing health care system has provided the opportunity for nurses to use their knowledge of the client and the health care system to integrate resource information for the client. Ambulatory services, community programs, and industrial health projects all represent forces affecting the health of citizens. Knowledge of these systems and the client enables the nurse to provide sound information with which clients and their families can make decisions. This is leadership.

KEY CONCEPT   • Integrated theories of leadership consider the goal, the leader, the followers, and the situation.

LEADERSHIP STYLES

The theories of leadership presented above form the basis of thought about how work is accomplished through other people. The manner in which these activities are carried out, or the behavior of the leader, is called leadership style. The most common definitions of leadership style were developed by Lewin (1947) at the Group Dynamics Center of the Massachusetts Institute of Technology in the 1940s. Lewin identified three major styles of leadership: autocratic, democratic, and laissez faire.

In the **autocratic style**, the leader assumes the role of commander and issues directives that are expected to be accomplished without hesitation. Power is based on the authority of the position, and the leader exercises this power through the granting of rewards or punishment. The autocratic leader is unable to accept suggestions that differ from his or her own views. Eventually, the lack of freedom and appreciation experienced by workers in this type of environment leads to dissatisfaction, loss of motivation and productivity, and system breakdown. Among the few situations in which this behavior is appropriate are emergencies and active combat.

In the **democratic style** of leadership, the group reserves for itself the final authority to make decisions. The success of this style depends upon the group's knowledge of group dynamics and the work to be accomplished so that realistic standards and priorities can be set. In addition, the leader must be patient in allowing the group to work at its own pace while guiding and encouraging cohesion and mutual trust among all members. This style is most favored by professionals who derive great satisfaction from the work itself and are less motivated to rely on a leader for positive feedback.

In the **laissez faire style** of leadership, the group functions independent of the leader. The leader provides information when asked, but performance is not evaluated or influenced either positively or negatively. This style often creates tension and dissatisfaction among the group members because insufficient feedback regarding their work is provided.

The leadership style receiving current attention is the collaborative or participative style of leadership. Collaboration implies that all parties have talents and contributions to make regarding goal setting and the plans and strategies used to achieve those goals. It is the leader's responsibility to encourage these contributions so that a high-quality decision can be achieved.

LEADERSHIP IN PROFESSIONAL ISSUES

Leadership in nursing requires extending one's influence beyond the local issues of a particular hospital or community to the larger realm of the profession. In a study conducted by Kinsey (1986), characteristics of a group of nurse leaders were compared with those of a group studied 10 years previously. In both groups, communication skills were considered the characteristic most needed for leadership, with creativity, risk taking, and interpersonal skills following in importance. This communication effort took the form of presiding at meetings, publishing in professional journals and books, taking part in political activities, and conducting research. Of note in this study was the large percentage of participants who cited a mentor in their professional development. Mentoring is a relationship between two people, a mentor and a protege. The mentor serves as teacher and coach, positive role model, and sponsor within an organization or a profession. This activity defines a contribution of leadership that is presently receiving much attention (Marquis & Huston, 1994). Its success is continuing to be realized.

The overarching responsibility of nursing leaders today is to capture the imagination of professional nurses and to encourage them to develop their potential fully as clinicians and collaborators in health care. The nursing values of caring and advocating the rights of clients are needed more than ever today.

LEADERSHIP IN CLIENT CARE

Nurses are providing leadership in client care through the development of alternative delivery models, such as case management. Through this system, the advanced clinician or manager is placed at the center of coordination of resources and collaboration of professionals. Achievement of specified outcomes within the length of stay is the goal for which collaborative leadership is required.

Leadership in self-directed work teams challenges the professional nurse to be both a leader and a follower. Leadership skills involve participation in group problem solving, goal setting, and conflict resolution and in recommending changes in practice that will improve the patient's quality of care or the operation of the unit. This type of leadership requires excellent communication skills, a sound clinical knowledge base, and sufficient assertiveness to secure needed information and resources. The followership component includes listening to and valuing the ideas of other people, who may have different perspectives and roles from those of nurses, and learning together how to create an effective work team. Such developmental activity takes material resources, time, and commitment to the objective.

The philosopher Hegel (1979) pointed out long ago that the school of leadership is followership. To be a good leader, the leader must have the experience of following others. In fact, followers give leaders their authority to lead by the very fact of accepting their direction. In today's health care system, complex relationships develop through the collective efforts of professionals, clients, and system experts. The nurse learns the professional role through active participation in this ongoing collaboration for client care.

Leadership in client care is also being provided through the growth of nursing clinical research. More hospitals are developing research programs within their own organizations as well as in collaboration with schools of nursing individually or in consortium arrangements.

LEADERSHIP IN ETHICAL PRACTICE

To meet the obligation of leadership in health care today, one should understand the issues of ethical practice. According to Davis and Aroskar (1991), health care ethics:

> [raises] the question of what is right or what ought to be done in a health science situation when a moral decision is called for. Such situations range from moral decisions in the clinical setting focused on one patient and his family to those concerned with policy decisions as to distribution of resources. Specifically, health care ethics addresses four interrelated areas: 1) clinical, 2) allocation of scarce resources, 3) human experimentation, and 4) health policy. (p. 4)

DECISION MAKING

Deciding how to make a decision and who should be involved in making that decision is as important as choosing the appropriate steps to take to reach a conclusion. **Decision making** is defined as "a deliberative, cognitive process consisting of sequential steps that can be refined and analyzed" (Gillies, 1994, p. 418). The decision itself is the last step in the process of analysis of possible choices that will lead to differing outcomes.

KEY CONCEPT

Steps in the decision-making process include the following (Gillies, 1994):
- Identify organizational goals and priorities.
- Define the problem or challenge that requires a decision.
- Define the criteria to be used to judge whether an acceptable decision is achieved.
- Generate alternative solutions.
- Compare alternative choices against each other to determine fit with selection criteria.
- Select one alternative.
- Weigh the pros and cons of committing to this alternative.
- Take action.
- Evaluate the results of the action taken.

Determining who participates in the decision-making process refocuses attention on the leader's style and the needs of the situation. Vroom and Yetton (1973) developed a model that examines characteristics of the leader, the followers, and the situation to choose the best method for decision making:

- *Autocratic I*—The manager makes the decision with the information available.
- *Autocratic II*—The manager seeks information from subordinates to make the decision.
- *Consultative I*—The manager tells subordinates about the problem and seeks information from them to solve the problem.
- *Consultative II*—The manager tells the group about the problem and seeks information to solve the problem. The information provided by the group may or may not be used by the manager in making the decision.
- *Group II*—The manager presents the problem to the group and explores with the group what action should be taken. The group makes the final choice, and the manager supports the decision.

It is evident from earlier discussions about empowered organizations that the group II approach is more appropriate for newer organizations than the autocratic and consultative methods of the past. Organizational bylaws, however, may guide the professional nurse in determining how best to proceed in making decisions. Additional decision-making strategies are discussed in Chapter 9.

POWER

Effective leadership assumes that one understands the nature of power in relationships and the larger organization. Traditionally, **power** is the capacity one has to influence others to accomplish something they would not normally accomplish (Kotter, 1979). Commonly accepted bases for power (French & Raven, 1959) include legitimate power, expert power, referent power, coercive power, and reward power.

Legitimate power is linked to an officially titled position within an organization. The degree of legitimate power associated with a particular position is somewhat influenced by followership. **Expert power** is derived through one's knowledge, expertise, and experience. Clinical specialists and others in staff roles within an organization function from an expert power base. **Referent power** is derived from association with powerful individuals and from others' perceptions that an individual is powerful. Individuals who associate themselves with powerful people proceed from this perspective by assuming that they are powerful because their friends are powerful. **Reward** and **coercive power** are derived from opposite bases. Reward power is related to the perception that one will receive a benefit from performing as desired. Coercive power is based on the fear that if one does not meet another's expectations punishment will follow.

It is important to recognize the changes in the understanding of power that have been suggested by futurists such as Toffler (1990), who suggests that a power shift is occurring globally that can be identified by political instability, fierce organizational competition, and a move to information-based systems that will determine future success. Power will belong to those who have restructured to enhance the contributions of a diverse workforce in a new relationship with owners and the public.

Power and Gender

As we move toward a new definition of power, it is necessary to understand the impact of gender in defining and changing power relationships. Gender differences related to power are evident in health care organizations. Women are socialized in family and societal roles to believe that their responsibility is to facilitate others' successes. Men, on the other hand, have been socialized to relate to others in terms of rank and status (Cummings,1995). Therefore, in female-dominated professions such as nursing, power may be perceived within the profession in different terms than it is outside the profession in the larger organizational leadership ranks.

Common stereotypes of women include "mother," "Iron Maiden," and "Superwoman." In the mother role, the woman is perceived as being sacrificing, fostering dependence, being passive, and being the peacemaker. The Iron Maiden role describes a competitive, controlling, distant, and critical individual who sabotages collaboration. The Superwoman role demands perfection; is overcommitted, isolated, and unappreciated; and refuses to delegate. Each of these roles can be assumed by a woman over a period of time. Although they may be recognizable within the department, they are perceived as dysfunctional in the male-dominated larger organization.

Power Strategies

Using power requires a recognition of the importance of perceptions and competence. Power strategies are those activities that can effectively enhance the individual's ability to influence the organization. Some of these strategies include the following:

- *Look powerful.* Role-appropriate symbols, such as dress, influence others' perceptions of an individual's power. In the old paradigm of bureaucratic organization, head nurses and nursing directors wore white uniforms as symbols of their power. In the new paradigm of empowered organizations, nurse leaders wear business attire as symbols of power equal to that of others in health care administrative and leadership roles. An additional facet of looking powerful is conveying self-confidence in verbal and nonverbal behavior.

- *Enhance your skill and knowledge.* Continual learning increases one's power and value within an organization as well as enhances one's employability. Knowledge of the internal organization's power operations will make one more effective within that organization but will not necessarily transfer to another organization. Continued expansion of one's perspective about health care forces and issues will increase one's value beyond the initial organization as well.

- *Increase your visibility as a leader.* Information is power. In organizations, much information is communicated through committee activity. Membership on key committees enhances one's status within the organization as well as one's ability to know what is important to the organization. This knowledge can be used to communicate organizational values to followers, which demonstrates more effective leadership.

- *Use networking and consultation.* Networking is an informal communication channel among individuals with similar professional goals who may or may not work in the same organization. Consultation is more formalized communication between an expert (consultant) and a consultee who is seeking assistance with a work-related issue within the competence of the expert. Both sources permit the expert to broker information to individuals and groups. Sharing information is a power-building strategy, especially in information-based organizations. Once computerized information systems are in place, power-building strategies will focus on using the available information to assist others in solving problems.

- *Empower others.* Encouraging, coaching, and mentoring not only develop leadership skills in those being coached but also energize the relationship and the entire organization.

POLITICAL LEADERSHIP

Political behaviors are evident in every organization. As Tichy (1993) writes, "Organizations' political systems are reflected in who gets ahead, how they get rewards, and who has the power to make decisions" (p. 45). Politics and political behavior often carry with them negative connotations; nevertheless, effective use of political behaviors can enhance power and facilitate individual and organizational outcome attainment. Power and politics are intimately linked: Political blunders often result in a loss of power, whereas effective political behaviors can enhance a power base. Political behaviors really focus on acquisition of power and resources and can result in a desired outcome being attained in a situation where there is little consensus about options.

KEY CONCEPT   Political behavior has multiple dimensions, which include both positive and negative activity. It is important to recognize when power is being used in a negative manner.

Positive:
- the individual's or group's desire for power
- developing coalitions to support an issue
- building support through alignment with powerful people
- exchanging favors or creating obligations
- bargaining and negotiating related to organizational issues
- developing knowledge of who has power and who has access to power

Negative:
- neutralizing stakeholders through activities such as verbal attacks, blaming, and scapegoating
- using information to overwhelm others, withholding information, or selective disclosure of information (telling lies is a detrimental political behavior and usually results in decreased trust and lost power)
- amassing resources when they are highly valued or scarce
- keeping information from competitors through outside political activity

Effective political strategies for acquiring and maintaining power include interpersonal skills. The ability to acquire, analyze, and disseminate information can markedly enhance one's success and effectiveness as a leader. Developing a reputation as an ethical and reliable source of information is essential for success.

del Bueno and Freund (1986) also cite coalitions, bargaining and trade-offs, posturing, and bluffing as effective political strategies. A **coalition**, a group of individuals with a common purpose or goal, exerts greater influence through the group's collective power compared with individual power. Coalitions and networking are valuable not only to gather information but, from the perspective of group power, to support positive issues as well as to receive individual or group support in adverse situations. **Bargaining** and trade-offs usually focus on tangible resources, such as space and equipment, as well as intangibles, such as ideas and strategies. Bargaining and trade-offs may result in win–win situations or with one party obligated to another. **Posturing** and **bluffing** (e.g., asking for more than is required) are effective in keeping others off balance by making them guess about the real issue or desired outcome.

Effective use of political strategies is also predicated on understanding the issues and their associated benefits and losses for key stakeholders. One caveat about political behavior is that power can be as easily lost as gained.

CONCLUSION

Leadership is a complex topic that has been studied for some time. Early researchers attempted to find one set of traits that were common to leaders under all conditions. This focus lacked consideration of other forces affecting leadership and was abandoned. Organizational theory approaches such as scientific management and bureaucratic structures emphasized the role of the organization in shaping leadership. These, too, lacked attention to the human element of the enterprise. Human resource theorists focused attention on the relationship of the leader to those being led. These studies of interactive relationships formed the basis for later research in collaboration and transformational leadership. The Ohio State University and University of Michigan studies were concerned with leader behavior and identified the basic orientations as people-focused or task-focused behaviors. Fiedler (1964) expanded on these studies by including the situational factors in the context of which leadership is exercised. This was augmented by the path–goal theory of leadership, in which the effective leader acts as a coach and encourager of those being led.

Transformational leadership extracts the most effective elements of earlier research. Creating a vision of the outcomes to be achieved and collaborating with others to attain those outcomes identify the leadership behavior that is needed for the next century. As nursing responds to the challenges of the new century, strong professional leadership is required. Collaborative practice in hospitals and community agencies as well as political activities call for the development of transformational leadership skills. Understanding the foundation of leadership will position the nurse to continue to develop those skills that provide the greatest benefit to clients and society. Understanding power is a requirement of effective leaders.

RESEARCH   Risner, P.B., & Anderson, M.L. (1994). Project nurse manager: An intrapre-
FOUNDATION   neurial role. *Nursing Economics, 12* (5), 261–265.

Nurse intrapreneurs are the key to innovations and cost-effective health care in the 1990s. A project in one midwestern teaching hospital identified the development, interaction, structure, and function of the role. Project examples and benefits were also presented. Projects such as product evaluation, unit renovation, and the development of a new facility validated the need for a project manager who would be a liaison between service departments. This role required vision and insight to involve the appropriate people in effecting change. The role needed to establish a trusting relationship among multiple disciplines and to support the sharing of information and expertise.

Nurses who are interested in shifting from leader to team leader to worker may find that, rather than seeking opportunities outside the facility, they may wish to look for innovative ways to use their talents within the organization.

REFERENCES

Argyris, C. (1964). *Integrating the individual and the organization.* New York: Wiley.

Bass, B.M., & Avolio, B.J. (1990). *Transformational leadership development: Manual for the Multifactor Leadership Questionnaire.* Palo Alto, CA: Consulting Psychologists Press.

Blake, R.R., & McCanse, A.E. (1991). *Leadership dilemmas—grid solutions.* Houston, TX: Gulf Publishing.

Chaska, N.L. (1990). *The nursing profession: Turning points.* St. Louis: Mosby.

Cummings, S. (1995). Atilla the Hun versus Atilla the Hen: Gender socialization of the American nurse. *Nursing Administration Quarterly, 19* (2), 19–29.

Davis, A.J., & Aroskar, M.A. (1991). *Ethical dilemmas and nursing practice* (3rd ed.). Norwalk, CT: Appleton & Lang.

del Bueno, D., & Freund, C. (1986). *Power and politics in nursing administration: A case book.* Owings Mills, MD: Rynd Communications.

Fiedler, F.E. (1976). *Improving leadership effectiveness: The leader match concept.* New York: Wiley.

Fiedler, F.E., & Garcia, J. (1987). *New approaches to effective leadership: Cognitive resources and organizational performance.* New York: Wiley.

French, J., & Raven, B. (1959). The bases of social power. In D. Cartwright (Ed.), *Studies in social power* (pp. 150–167). Ann Arbor, MI: University of Michigan Press.

Gerth, H., & Mills, C.W. (1946). *Max Weber: Essays in sociology.* Oxford, England: Oxford University Press.

Gillies, D. (1994). *Nursing management: A systems approach* (3rd ed.). Philadelphia: Saunders.

Giovannetti, P. (1978). *Patient classification systems in nursing: A description and analysis* (DHEW Publication No. 78-22). Washington, DC: Department of Health, Education and Welfare.

Hegel, J. (1979). *Aesthetik. English selections. Hegel's introduction to aesthetics.* Translated by T.M. Knox. Oxford, England: Clarendon Press.

Hersey, P., & Blanchard, K. (1988). *Management of organizational behavior: Utilizing human resources* (5th ed.). Englewood Cliffs, NJ: Prentice-Hall.

House, R.J. (1971). A path–goal theory of leader effectiveness. *American Science Quarterly, 3*, 321–329.

Katz, D., Maccoby, N., & Morse, C. 1950. *Productivity, supervision, and morale in an office situation.* Ann Arbor, MI: University of Michigan.

Kinsey, D.C. (1986). The new nurse influentials. *Nursing Outlook, 23* (8), 34–38.

Kotter, J. (1979). *Power in management.* New York: AMACOM.

Lewin, K. (1947). Frontiers in group dynamics: Concept, method, and reality in social science, social equilibria, and social change. *Human Relations, 1* (1), 1–23.

Marquis, B.L., & Huston, C.J. (1994). *Management decision making for nurses* (2nd ed.). Philadelphia: Lippincott.

McGregor, D. (1960). *The human side of enterprise.* New York: McGraw-Hill.

Schriesheim, C., & Kerr, S. (1977). Theories and measures of leadership: A critical appraisal of current and future directions. In J.G. Hunt & L.L. Larson (Eds.), *Leadership: The cutting edge* (pp. 9–56). London: Feffer.

Taylor, F. (1916). *Principles of scientific management.* Cleveland, OH: Bulletin of the Taylor Society.

Tichy, N. (1993). Managing organizational transformations. *Human Resources Management, 22*, 45–60.

Toffler, A. (1990). *Powershift.* New York: Bantam.

Vroom, V.H., & Yetton, P.W. (1973). *Leadership and decision-making.* Pittsburgh, PA: University of Pittsburgh Press.

Weber, M. (1978). Bureaucracy. In J.M. Shafrity & P.H. Whelbeck (Eds.), *Classes of organizational theory* (pp. 37–43). Oak Park, IL: Moore.

CHAPTER 5

Role of the Professional Nurse: Patient Care Manager

Cynthia A. Parkman

CHAPTER OBJECTIVES

At the completion of this chapter, the beginning professional nurse will be able to:

1. describe changes in health care organizations that affect and define the role of the professional nurse in patient care management
2. describe role expectations for the professional nurse
3. describe the use of nursing process and related skills in patient care management
4. define the management process as it relates to patient care management
5. define management skills that are essential to staff nurses
6. compare and contrast roles of the staff nurse, shift manager, and unit manager in patient care management

7. describe the key patient care management skills of communication, coordination, consultation, coaching, and delegation
8. identify key terms in group dynamics, including group, team, teamwork, and group dynamics
9. describe group developmental concepts
10. describe characteristic problems of groups and teams
11. differentiate between functional and dysfunctional communication patterns in groups
12. describe group stressors and how groups adapt and change

CRITICAL THINKING CHALLENGE

In a moderate-size acute care facility, the number of basic nursing assistants (NAs) made available on the nursing units has increased in the past 2 years from one NA to 32 patients to a current standard of one NA to 10 to 12 patients on the day shift. In addition, expanded assistant roles of patient technicians (PATs) have been instituted on the unit in the past 2 months. These individuals took a 4-week training session to become technical assistants to the registered nurses (RNs). The number of RN staff has decreased slightly in proportion to the increase in NA and PAT usage. The number of RNs remains greater than the number of NAs.

As the RN/assistant ratio has changed, the roles of the basic NA and the PAT have taken on broader patient care significance than before. The manager feels that the changes have been on the whole positive for the unit, and the staff report that the support roles have enabled the RN to have time for professional, noncustodial patient care responsibilities.

In spite of the positive role changes perceived by the staff, communication on the unit has also changed, and not for the better. Staff nurses find it difficult to control the work of the NAs or to direct their tasks for their own caseloads. The PATs consult with their respective RNs throughout the shift. The NAs have developed a close-knit rapport with each other and exhibit an "us against them" attitude in completion of supportive tasks. The RNs frequently complain to peers about the attitudes of the NAs, yet they approach them with a soft touch. When a nurse asks an NA to do specific items, the NA says "I'll get to it when I can" and sets off on his or her own plan. The PATs (two on the day shift) find it difficult to get the NAs, some of whom used to be their peers, to listen to them.

The staff nurse group perceives the NA group to be quite cohesive and feels that they should role model cooperation for the NAs. From a nursing management skills standpoint, the RNs hesitate to take action on any NA failure to act, and the NAs know this. One principle of group dynamics is that a group may learn to control its leader(s) (Hayes, 1992), as the NA group may be doing here.

Clearly, the RNs lack some essential management skills in their work with the NA staff and in helping the PATs work effectively with the NA group. Your challenge is to:

1. identify the stage of group development this staff appears to be in, and give examples to support your response
2. identify the necessary patient care management skills in working with this group, and discuss their importance in this vignette
3. approach the problem using a consultation process; specify what type of consultation is appropriate and the steps to utilize to approach the unit problem discussed
4. devise an approach to educate and prepare the RN staff for management skills, clarify roles and responsibilities on the unit and build positive group dynamics among the groups of caregivers
5. discuss your answers with others in your group or class, and compare responses

ROLE OF THE BEGINNING PROFESSIONAL NURSE TODAY

Nursing roles have changed considerably within the past 10 to 15 years. Today the nurse must be able to adapt personal resources to the job situation as quickly and effectively as possible. Shortened patient lengths of stay, higher patient acuities, and limitations on reimbursement to organizations providing medical care are a few of the major social changes affecting a nurse's role in any setting. The new graduate nurse who is beginning a professional role today has options for a variety of practice settings. Acute care hospitals, intermediate care, ambulatory care, long-term care, and home health care and community health care (with necessary certification) are common practice areas for nurses.

The definition of the nurse's role is, in general, "an organized set of expected behaviors of a nurse in any given position" (Douglass, 1992, p. 61). Douglass asserts that the expected role behaviors of a nurse arise from various sources. For example, the nurse:

- meets institutional requirements (rules, regulations, and job descriptions)
- meets patient/client needs (patients' rights)
- maintains professional values and attitudes
- works within group norms
- establishes effective communication strategies in social interactions

Role theory is an excellent tool for understanding nursing (and management) positions (Stevens, 1983).

In addition to role expectations, a nurse's role is shaped by the multiple facets of performance in the management of patient care. In a typical day, there are multiple role facets for a nurse to perform, such as managing, coordinating, collaborating, planning, and communicating with patients, families, and others who affect patient care (Douglass, 1992). Although Douglass asserts that in a healthy organization everyone knows his or her role, Chaska (1992) contends "the staff nurse role—what it is and what it is not—is a continuing problem plaguing the delivery of care" (p. 185). There has been a considerable expansion of functions and tasks for nurses in the staff nurse role. The nurse is charged with more decision-making authority in patient care than previously, and there are efforts to maximize professional autonomy in the organizations in which staff nurses practice (Chaska, 1992). Chaska further asserts, "as the staff nurse role becomes defined clearly within the overall system of care, the most important consideration will be the relationship aspects of the role, that is, how the staff nurse interacts with other health care personnel such as head nurses, clinical specialists, and physicians" (p. 186). The staff nurse and other health care professionals are interacting roles that exist as part of the patient care management environment.

This chapter explores the professional nurse role in patient care management. The primary sections of this chapter look at the various patient care manager roles, key patient care management skills, and the complex topic of group dynamics in health care settings. Emphasis is placed upon the level of understanding that a new professional nurse or a returning nurse needs to meet the challenges of patient care management in the 1990s and beyond. The concepts discussed are intended to build upon current knowledge and to stretch the learner's concept of the professional nurse role in patient care management today.

KEY DEFINITIONS

The new professional nurse is defined in this chapter as a registered nurse (RN) who has successfully completed baccalaureate education and whose role conception is associated with principles and standards of the profession (Chaska, 1992) combined with strong patient care values. In addition, the professional nurse applies the process of "critical thinking—a process of defining and analyzing problems—with the emphasis on questioning information rather than merely accepting it" (Pinkerton & Schroeder, 1988, p. 51). These three attributes—professional standards, strong patient care values, and critical thinking—are the underlying role aspects necessary to forge an understanding of the professional nurse role in patient care management.

The term *patient care management* also needs defining to elucidate this topic. One way to simplify the phrase is to cut it in half, into *patient care* and *management*. **Patient care** is the sum total of the clinical activities and events that are performed by nurses, support personnel, and others on behalf of the patient to promote optimal health and outcomes. Attention is given not only to physiological and emotional needs but also to psychological, sociological, and spiritual needs, which may be significant priorities for individual patients (Douglass, 1992). **Management**, when used in relation to patient care, is more a process than a simple thing one does. Although no one definition of management has been universally accepted in nursing, the term has generally referred to achieving organizational objectives through a process of working with and through others (Stevens, 1983) or, in other words, getting things done through other people. A broader definition of the term *management* is more appropriate in the management of patient care. Words borrowed from nursing case management principles fit nicely with a clinical definition of management: coordination, integration, and monitoring of patient care (Cohen & Cesta, 1993). In addition, patient care management is a process of planning (using the nursing process), organizing, and directing human and physical resources and technology (Douglass, 1992).

NURSING PRACTICE ENVIRONMENT

Before proceeding further, it is important to consider the nursing practice environment (i.e., the hospital setting and its structure and philosophy) and how this has evolved in recent years. The changes in nursing practice environments are important to the new nurse, who must be ready to practice in settings that may range from traditional/hierarchical structures to staff empowerment/decentralized structures. Nursing practice environments have changed in concert with changes in overall organizational structure.

Organizational Structure

In the past, most hospitals functioned in a highly organized, bureaucratic structure in which control was from the top down and lines of authority were spelled out. The pyramid (Figure 5–1) has been the classic shape typical of bureaucratic organizations. The people are classified in a hierarchy according to rank, capacity, or authority, with authority being assigned to vertical levels and ranks. Those with the greatest decision-making authority and control are at the top, and those with the least authority are at the bottom.

*Most Authority

Pyramid

Least Authority

Figure 5–1 Bureaucratic hierarchy model.

In bureaucratic organizations, centralized control is practiced. Centralized control used to be the most common model in hospitals, but decentralized organizations are now popular. "It is only in the past few years that structures have begun to emerge that will carry nursing from the direct supervision mechanisms . . . to more progressive mechanisms to organize and deliver services" (Campbell, 1992, p. 56).

The organization structure and system for any hospital need to match the philosophy, goals, and objectives of the organization and be compatible with the needs of those charged with fulfilling those goals and objectives (Douglass, 1992). When the major forms of organizational structures are compared and contrasted (Table 5–1), important differences are evident. The characteristics listed in Table 5–1 are extreme examples of each type of structure. Modern health care settings are dynamic and must reevaluate structures and systems periodically to remain viable. Thus, it may be possible to see parts of the bureaucratic, participatory, or collaborative structure in a single organization at a given time.

Over time, many organizations change and develop as new views on structures and management beliefs are created in response to the health care environment, internal goals and needs, and professionalism of the staff. For example, over a 10-year period an acute care nursing department in a large metropolitan hospital evolved from a traditional hierarchical structure to a professional practice/staff empowerment model of management and governance in response to continued changes in nursing and health care (Parkman & Loveridge, 1994). Over time, management of nursing changed from a nursing bureaucracy to a professional governance model in which staff became empowered to make decisions about nursing practice, from staff education and practice issues to clinical research and evaluation (Parkman & Loveridge, 1994).

Table 5–1 Comparison of Characteristics of Three Major Nursing Organization Structures

Collaborative Management	Participatory Management	Bureaucratic Management
Balance of power, defined roles and responsibilities	Manager is facilitator	Manager is controller
Professional practice	Staff members relate to one another and then to the organization	Staff relate to organization individually
Communication is horizontal rather than vertical	Communication system is open	Communication is one-way; obedience is demanded
Interdependence of groups to accomplish mission and goals of organization and how these relate to subgroups	Social forces and quality of service are more important than economic factors	Economic factors are the primary motivation
Decision making is delegated to areas of interest	Work groups define objectives	Management defines objectives
Cooperative/reciprocal nature, negotiation	Conflict is accepted and managed; problem resolution	Conflict is discouraged or avoided
Teams/councils create outcomes		
Shared governance is common		
(Stichler, 1992)		

Professional Governance

Professional (or **shared**) **governance** may be seen by some as a fresh expression of the participatory organization structure. "Shared governance is not a new brand of participative management" (Porter-O'Grady, 1992, p. 36). It is much more than participative management; it is an example of a collaborative management structure that focuses upon balancing of power, reciprocating, and interpersonal valuing (Stichler, 1992).

During the past 10 to 15 years, many hospitals in this country have embraced the shared governance philosophy and as a result have redefined the very nature of management and the nurse's role in the organization. "Shared governance reduces the emphasis on hierarchical relationships and highlights the professional's right to be involved in governance of the profession" (Stichler, 1992, p. 17). Refer to Chapter 1 for further information about organizational change and shared governance.

As the varied elements of professional governance have been adopted and practiced in multiple nursing organizations, and as *staff empowerment* has become a buzzword, the traditional hierarchical model has slowly become outdated. What does this mean for the new professional nurse? Inherent in staff empowerment models is the expression of necessary skills of leadership and decision making in all areas affecting nursing practice. The shared governance approach in nursing makes a great deal of sense when one considers that the nurse requires leadership and management skills from the first day of employment. In business settings, employees are expected to learn to be a successful subordinate; in health care settings, nurses are expected to make decisions that help patients reach their optimal level of functioning (Douglass, 1992).

Accomplishing nursing and patient goals is a demanding task in every setting. In staff empowerment models, the professional nurse is capable of expressing and adhering to professional standards and values related to nursing. There is therefore a more professional fit between the goals and objectives of the organization and the goals and values/beliefs of the professional nurse.

NURSING PROCESS AND SKILLS IN PATIENT CARE MANAGEMENT

Decision-Making Process

Nurses accomplish the work of nursing (e.g., nursing care goals, priority setting, and patient care) most successfully when a decision-making process is utilized. Critical thinking and strong patient care values may be seen as interdependent attributes of the professional nurse. The very process of decision making ensures the nurse develops a commitment to a course of action in sequential steps. In this course of action, the nurse places the patient's need at the center of the decision-making process. The scientific or pragmatic approach entails four steps (Douglass, 1992):

1. Identify the problem.
2. Generate alternative solutions.
3. Select a solution.
4. Evaluate the results of the solution.

The decision-making format familiar to the professional nurse is the nursing process and is a format similar to that of the pragmatic approach. The nursing process has five components that nurses use systematically to problem solve for a particular patient. The nursing process sets the practice of nursing in motion (Carpenito, 1992). The steps of the nursing process are:

1. assessing
2. selecting of nursing diagnoses

3. planning care
4. implementing the plan of care
5. evaluating the outcome of care

The steps are listed individually but are related to one another and occur in a cyclic process. Each step relies upon the accuracy of the preceding one. Figure 5–2 is an example of this continuous relationship.

The new professional nurse can increase his or her process skills through practice and an associated increase in knowledge and experience. This review of the nursing process is not meant to be an in-depth review but rather to refer the nurse to further skills that build upon the critical problem-solving process. It is assumed that the new nurse will understand the nursing process as the minimum basis for approaching the management of patients in his or her care. The nursing process provides a framework in which to observe and assess patients systematically to derive valid diagnoses and effective interventions (Carpenito, 1992).

Managerial Skills

In addition to utilizing the nursing process, there are other management skills needed by all nurses that have an impact on their nursing performance. Douglass (1992) lists four specific managerial skills that enable the nurse to lead and manage most effectively: **technical**, **human**, **conceptual**, and **diagnostic**. Table 5–2 displays the key aspects of these four skills.

Technical skill has to do with what is done, things, and the ability to use technology. Nurses are expected to have or acquire proficiency in a wide range of skills that relate to every part of the human being (Douglass, 1992). Human skill is about working with people, how things are done, and the abil-

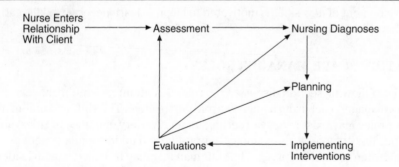

Figure 5–2 Steps of the nursing process cyclical relationship.

Table 5–2 Leadership and Management Skills Necessary for Nursing Practice at Any Level

Technical Expertise	Human Skills	Conceptual Skills	Diagnostic Skills	Coach and Mentor Skills
Tools	Select	See total picture	Plan	Hands-on process
Techniques	Motivate self and	Link own work	Organize	Plan mutually
Procedures	others	with that of	Direct	acceptable action
	Lead	others	Evaluate	Create supportive
			Control	and helpful
				climate
What . . . things	How . . . people	Why . . . whole picture	Why . . . whole picture	How . . . people

Source: Reprinted from *The Effective Nurse: Leader and Manager,* 4th ed., by L.M. Douglass, p. 212, with permission of Mosby-Year Book, © 1992.

ity to work with others in goal achievement. Conceptual skill pertains to why things are done and viewing the organization as a whole picture. It is linking the work of nursing with the work of other departments or personnel in patient goal achievement. Diagnostic skill refers to the ability to specify why something occurred and to get to the heart of the issue at hand. It includes analysis and examination of particular circumstances or conditions.

The very nature of both conceptual and diagnostic skills makes them mature skills that one learns through experience, time, and intellectual ability. The development of technical and human skills comes first and serves as a basis for developing more mature skills (Douglass, 1992).

The fifth managerial skill listed in Table 5–2 that the more experienced nurse may acquire is the coach and mentor skill. The staff nurse who has a leader who coaches in a day-by-day manner and serves as a mentor in the development of new skills is motivated to begin to learn necessary skills early in his or her career.

PATIENT CARE MANAGER ROLES

The following section discusses the roles of staff nurse, shift manager, and unit manager, each from a manager role perspective. The shift and unit manager roles may exist in a given setting under a variety of names or titles, and in this text they serve as examples of first-line and middle management positions often seen in hospitals. The shift manager may be called a team leader, charge nurse, supervisor, resource nurse, or manager in different settings.

As organization structures have changed and evolved toward more professional/collaborative structures, so have attitudes toward just whose role fits in the managerial domain. Stevens (1983) saw a clear distinction between staff and management positions in terms of who has employee responsibilities: "While all nurses *manage*, in that they organize care delivery for their patients, a management position is differentiated from a staff position in that it entails major responsibility for other employees" (p. 5). More recently, Douglass (1992) asserted "whatever the role, *all* nurses lead and manage to some degree" (p. 1). Through a decision-making process, the goals for patient care are accomplished by nurses through delegation and direction of others. All nurses are leaders when they influence others to achieve specific goals in the provision of nursing care for one or more patients (Douglass, 1992).

Staff Nurse as Manager

The new graduate nurse holds an individual perception of the staff nurse role as schooling is completed and professional employment begins. This perception may in part be based on past experiences and on anticipation of what lies ahead. Buckenham (1988) found in research on the student, staff, and manager view of the nurse role that the role of the nurse is a developing role perception for students and often is not well understood until the senior year of schooling. Taunton and Otteman (1986), in studying the multiple dimensions of the staff nurse role, found that the staff nurse role conception is complex. Part of this complexity may arise from bureaucratic and professional role conflicts, which are a source of stress for today's staff nurses (Taunton & Otteman, 1986). The staff nurse is both a position specific to hospitals and a nursing role in that setting. Chaska (1992) defines the staff nurse as a "generalist, clinical nursing role held by a registered nurse in a first-level clinical nursing position in a hospital setting" (p. 187). This definition clearly articulates who is considered in the staff nurse role and that it is generally seen as an entry-level position. Douglass (1992) refers to staff nurses as RNs who "provide the bulk of primary nursing practice in a variety of settings . . . with graduates licensed to function as beginning practitioners" (p. 67). Stevens (1983) viewed the entry-level role as staff hired primarily to meet the needs of the organization in caring for patients.

One can agree that, in general, the **staff nurse role** is a position-related role. A position-related role has three basic elements: the job description (the job one is hired to do), the social expectations, and personal enactment (Stevens, 1983). The new nurse will find that the staff nurse role entails more than the job description and is shaped by both the norms (expectations) of the work group and the personal attributes and values one brings to the role (work groups are discussed later in this chapter).

Accountability

In general, the staff nurse is accountable to the organization for meeting its needs in relation to quality patient care and to the patient for the care provided during the assigned shift. A key responsibility in meeting patient goals is applying the nursing process—putting it into action with each patient. Typically, the staff nurse job description incorporates each step of the nursing process into its format. Table 5–3 is an example of the nursing process used in an entry-level nursing position description. For example, the staff nurse utilizes the assessment step of the nursing process through the admission patient history and assessment, initial shift assessments, and so forth in the course of care. Each step of the nursing process helps define key elements of the staff nurse role in managing patient care.

Managing Self

The staff nurse manages himself or herself in providing patient care. Two challenges in self-management are time management and managing the caseload. A patient caseload is assigned to the nurse, and the nurse has to determine the most efficient and effective ways to accomplish tasks and care for the assigned patients. A caseload's complexity may be characterized by the acuity level of each patient, treatments anticipated per the plan of care, patient teaching needs, and documentation. A caseload of five semiambulatory patients with moderate, predictable care needs is not the same as a caseload of five bedridden patients with varying care needs.

Time refers to both the hours of the given shift and the allotment of minutes or hours to particular patient care activities. Each patient has any num-

Table 5–3 Nursing Process Reflected in Staff Nurse Position Description

Assessing	Selecting Diagnoses	Planning	Implementing	Evaluating
Admission patient history and assessment, includes physical and psychosocial data	Using assessment database, select primary nursing diagnoses and problems for patient, initiate patient care plan and related nursing diagnoses	Demonstrate knowledge of principles underlying nursing interventions through planning care	Implement patient care according to written plan of care	Evaluate and document physical and emotional responses to care; revise plan of care as appropriate

ber of nursing therapies, medications, patient teaching needs, and other expected care needs throughout the shift. It is important to consider the ideal time and the actual time in caring for patients. The routine aspects of patient care may fit into the ideal time plan that the nurse expects for the shift. Unexpected events alter the ideal plan and may decrease the actual time a nurse has for getting all the work done. Problems with time management are common on units that have a high level of unpredictability, and self-management is a significant issue.

In the recent past, new graduate nurses were often hired onto units that typically cared for a more predictable patient population, such as a general medical unit, and were only hired onto specialty units, such as oncology or neurology, after a year or so of basic medical-surgical experience. Changes in health care have increased the overall acuity and unpredictability of patients in virtually every area of specialty, and there are no longer generic units in which to groom the new graduate. Most nursing units care for patients with complex conditions or associated illnesses. For example, it is not uncommon for the orthopedic nurse to care for a patient who has had surgery and also happens to have a preexisting serious illness, such as cancer or chronic obstructive pulmonary disease. Care needs to be given in a compressed time period as a result of broad changes in insurance plans and reimbursement for care. Time limitations are a factor in care, requiring priorities to be set among competing tasks, and patient outcomes should be the primary concern in staff nurse role delineation (Chaska, 1992).

Fortunately, the more complex patients seen in hospitals today afford the new nurse a broad range of opportunities for technical and human skill attainment. In addition, systems and methods of care delivery have evolved as patient characteristics have changed. Nurses now have standardized, preprinted assessment tools, care plans, and discharge teaching forms to streamline assessment, planning, and documentation of care and patient education.

Managing Others

The past primary nursing models meant that professional nurses had to do everything themselves, which Cohen and Cesta (1993) call the parallel play syndrome. When primary nurses deliver all the care to patients themselves, they are not managers, but independent professionals (Stevens, 1983). Most nurses learn pieces of the management process by managing individual workloads and providing nursing care for patients (Douglass, 1992). Independence used to be expected, but with increased complexity and technology a multidisciplinary approach to patient care is becoming the norm (Cohen & Cesta, 1993). A social worker, a psychiatric nurse specialist, a clinical pharmacist, and others may be directly involved in the patient's care.

In addition, assistant and technician roles are used in organizations to help get patient care accomplished in an equitable fashion. The staff nurse can expect to work with various assistive nursing personnel in hospital settings, commonly referred to as unlicensed assistive personnel. The nurse is expected to manage the nursing assistants and other technicians who care for patients on the unit in his or her module or caseload. The management skills of direction and delegation are essential and are discussed with other key skills in this chapter.

The staff nurse collaborates with peers on the shift in various patient care tasks and may use management skills in negotiating for help or seeking advice on particular patients. The effective group is able to negotiate roles and tasks, as is discussed later in this chapter.

A large part of patient care is managing patient and family needs in the caseload. Patient goals are the staff nurse's primary focus, and the goals are often accomplished through active involvement of the patient's family members. Family members provide important assessment and nursing history details that the patient may not be able to provide, and they are key players in discharge plans and patient education. Involvement of the family is not a luxury but a necessity for two reasons. First, the shortened length of stay means that the patient often returns home with significant care or self-management needs that family members often help tend to or oversee. Second, each patient is unique and is part of some type of family support system and needs to be approached from that perspective to individualize the teaching and discharge plans.

Summary

The staff nurse is accountable to the organization and the patient, and manages himself or herself and others through the use of management skills at the beginning technical and human skill levels. Clinical nursing education stresses relations with patients. Senior-level baccalaureate programs introduce strategies for working with nursing staff and the assistant roles that the staff nurse is expected to manage.

Shift Manager

The **shift manager** in most settings is the front-line role accountable to the organization, the nursing staff, and the patients on the unit. This role is similar to the first-line manager role of the 1970s, 1980s, and early 1990s. The shift manager "is where the action is" and deals with the realities of nursing care delivery (Stevens, 1983). This role is accountable for the shift period and is often a staff member with additional human, conceptual, and diagnostic skills who formally or informally serves as the nurse in charge. The first-line manager is directly responsible for production of nursing services and uses the management skills of planning, organizing, directing, and controlling in concert with care coordination, communication, and counseling. The role lends itself to overinvolvement in immediate problems (Stevens, 1983), yet is expected to perform short-term planning and thinking ahead regarding shift needs. Nurses new to the role quickly find that a tentative shift plan is better than no plan at all. The short-term plans usually address the staff assignment and the distribution of admissions, handling of unexpected occurrences, and facilitation of necessary resources for work flow during the shift.

Shift Responsibilities

The shift manager is overall a resource to others throughout the shift. Specific duties generally include devising the shift assignment, communicating with other disciplines, serving as a resource to nurses and assistants, and providing input into performance evaluations.

The **shift assignment** is how the total work of the unit is distributed among the present staff members on a given shift (Stevens, 1983). The assignment is important to the care of the patients and is created with careful consideration to several factors. An accurate shift assignment considers:

- the census (number of patients on the unit)
- patient acuity (care complexity)
- known or anticipated discharges or admissions
- staffing guidelines for the unit
- the staff actually available to do the required work (RNs, NAs, and other support roles)

The **staffing guidelines** are used in many hospitals as a predetermined range of patients and care providers dependent upon the variations in census. Refer to Chapter 3 for a discussion of development and validation of patient care standards and staffing guidelines. The guidelines are a mechanism to ensure adequate staffing of licensed and unlicensed staff while controlling costs on the unit. For example, a unit with a census of 28 patients may use 6 RNs and 2 NAs on the day shift. If the census drops to 23 patients by 2:00 p.m., the evening shift guidelines may expect 4 RNs and 2 NAs, particularly if admissions are not expected. The guidelines are relative to the type of patients each unit cares for and the known fluctuations in care or census throughout the day. If the number of patients drops to the next guideline level during the shift, staff may also need to flex (i.e., a staff member may be sent home early).

It is the shift manager's responsibility to distribute the assignment as evenly as possible at the start of the shift. As changes in patient mix or census occur, the shift manager assigns patients and may redistribute the numbers as appropriate. Many hospitals have found cross-training of staff (with flexibility in care providers' specific duties) to be an effective means to get patient care done as patient census changes and unit needs fluctuate. Cross-training means that staff, such as NAs, are trained to do more than one role and can perform different parts of the role as needs arise on the unit. It is imperative that the shift manager be well versed on the roles that the caregivers are trained to do and make use of their skills throughout the shift to maximize quality and efficient patient care.

Communication with Other Disciplines

The shift manager **communicates** with other disciplines in the management of patients on the unit. The shift manager has collateral relationships with heads of supportive staff services, physicians and other health professionals, and patients and families (Stevens, 1983). The shift manager serves as the spokesperson for both unit needs and patient needs. It is important to use negotiation skills in this role facet. Generally, the shift manager negotiates with multiple services that come to the patient care unit (such as laboratory, pharmacy, dietary staff, etc.) but are not part of the unit in the traditional, more centralized systems. In the decentralized settings, where a patient focus situates services on the unit (Brider, 1992), the shift manager may be more of an overseer of the care goals and the individuals or care teams on the unit.

How the shift manager is expected to communicate with other disciplines in a given hospital depends greatly on the extent of decentralization present and the patient care model in place on the given units. The management skills of negotiation and communication are essential regardless of the care model in place when one is working with professionals, patients, and families.

Resource to Staff Nurses and Assistants

As the nurse who holds an overall view of the unit or shift, the shift manager must keep in mind the goal of positively balancing nursing actions as the means and patient outcomes as the end (Stevens, 1983). As a resource, the shift manager is able to anticipate problems and is ready to facilitate timely resolution. This role manages the staff by directing staff via the shift assignment, consulting with staff on problems or questions, and making follow-up calls to other disciplines or services as needed. The shift manager applies advanced technical, human, conceptual, and diagnostic skills in virtually every role aspect. These skills enable the shift manager to be an adept extra set of eyes, ears, or hands for a variety of patient care situations.

Unit Manager

The **unit manager** in many settings may be considered a middle management role and may in fact coordinate the activities of several nursing units with a broad overall perspective and related strategies. The unit manager has 24-hour accountability and is primarily responsible for production of the desired product, which in nursing is positive patient health outcomes and conditions during illness and adjustment (Stevens, 1983). The unit manager manages staff, materials, and systems and is accountable for:

- providing staff resources necessary to do the work of the unit(s)
- providing materials, through budgetary management, to ensure that equipment, supplies, educational materials, and so forth are available
- managing systems (e.g., staffing patterns, staff numbers needed, application of goals and objectives to the unit, interfacing with others to produce positive work flows)
- supporting shared governance models (in many hospital settings)

The overall accountability of the unit manager remains to the patients and the organization; the specific aspects often are charted by the management method in place, whether a traditional or a staff empowerment model. In shared governance, the manager moves from a narrowly defined, fixed role to a much broader role (Porter-O'Grady, 1991). The manager's role also changes from a controlling role to a supporting and facilitating role as the staff take an active role in nursing practice decisions (Porter-O'Grady, 1991).

Role Responsibilities

Regardless of the management model in practice, the unit manager uses some form of manager influence—motivation, power, leadership, or behavior modification—in achieving organizational objectives. In staff empowerment models, the nurse manager involves staff in the management process and key skills of planning, organizing, staffing, leading, communicating, and decision making. Chapter 6 provides details on the unit manager role in organizational management. From a patient care management perspective, the unit manager oversees budgetary issues, staffing and scheduling, and hiring and retention practices and communicates with multiple disciplines to promote most effectively the care, cure, and comfort provided by the nursing staff to the patients.

Staffing and Scheduling

Perhaps one of the key managerial responsibilities that affects staff nurses directly on a daily basis is staffing and scheduling. Staffing refers to the creation of a plan to determine how many nursing personnel, and of what classifications, will be needed for a given unit on each shift, or placing the right people in the right jobs (Douglass, 1992; Stevens, 1983). Scheduling refers to the ongoing filling of the staffing pattern. In most decentralized nursing settings, the unit staff take a personal role in helping the front-line manager complete the 4-week schedule by requesting preferred days off or on within predetermined guidelines. The shift manager then assigns staff to work on the shift based upon the completed schedule. Nursing staff at all levels are keenly aware of how well or poorly the work of the unit gets done when they function with enough staff or insufficient staff on a given shift.

The staffing and scheduling process takes considerable insight, planning, and a view to the future to meet effectively the needs of the nursing unit. A large portion of planning for staffing needs involves the budget allocated for the particular staff mix (numbers and levels of licensed and nonlicensed caregivers) and the personnel practices of recruitment and retention for the unit.

KEY CONCEPTS

- *Professional nurse:* an RN who successfully completed undergraduate education; role conception associated with principles and standards of the profession, strong patient care values, and application of the process of critical thinking
- *Comparison of patient manager roles*
  1. Staff nurse
     — *Accountability:* to the organization in meeting its needs in quality patient care; to patients in providing quality care
     — *Responsibility:* managing self, managing others, utilizing the nursing process, providing care to assigned patients
  2. Shift manager
     — *Accountability:* to the organization, the nursing staff, and the patients on the unit in terms of leadership of the designated shift period
     — *Responsibility:* production of nursing services during the shift, devising the shift assignment, interfacing with other disciplines, serving as a resource to nurses and assistants, providing input to performance evaluation
  3. Unit manager
     — *Accountability:* 24-hour; primarily accountable for production of desired product, providing staff resources, providing materials, managing systems, and supporting shared governance
     — *Responsibility:* budgetary issues, staffing and scheduling, hiring and retention practices, interfacing with multiple disciplines

LEARNING   Determine primary responsibilities for patient care management for the shift
CHALLENGE   manager and staff nurse in a clinical/management laboratory setting and
discuss with peers in conference. How are the roles similar or different?
Which role is accountable to the patients and why?

KEY PATIENT CARE MANAGEMENT SKILLS

Communication

Interpersonal **communication** is the process whereby a message is
passed from a sender to a receiver with the hope that the information
exchanged will be understood as the sender intended. Organizational communication is a formal process of using channels to receive and relay information. "Leadership and management are achieved through effective communication" (Douglass, 1992, p. 151). In the management of patient care,
effective communication at all levels is vital. Communication channels are
vital links in the management function and cannot be left to chance
(Stevens, 1983).

It is helpful for new nurses to understand the basic aspects of communication theory because role functions are carried out while the nurse is constantly interacting and communicating with others. Several purposes for
communicating have been identified. Some common goals may be to inform, entertain, inquire, persuade, or command (Stevens, 1983). Table 5–4
gives examples of common purposes of communication. The effectiveness
or ineffectiveness of communication is judged by the response received to
the question or message sent. Nurses send information through talking and
interacting and receive information from patients and others in interactions.

Table 5–4 Examples of Common Purposes of Communication in a Nursing Setting

Communication Goal	Example
Inform	"The next meeting will be Wednesday at 2:00 p.m."
Entertain	"Let's have a potluck to celebrate our new nurses."
Inquire	"Who will volunteer for the charting task force?"
Persuade	"You'll agree this intravenous monitor is superior to the old model."
Command	"Get the crash cart! Mr. B in 702 is doing poorly!"

Learning how to be a good communicator takes practice and is more than simply knowing what effective communication entails. Receiving the intended communication requires effective listening skills. Several fundamental **listening skills** are suggested by Raudsepp (1990). The first skill is to take time to listen; use eye contact, and ask questions for clarification. Second, teach yourself to concentrate, pace your thinking with the speaker's rate of speech, and try not to let your mind wander. While listening, do not interrupt the speaker, but listen to what the person is saying, not how he or she is saying it. You need to catch the content of the message and not jump to a conclusion. In addition, suspend judgment, and listen to the entire message before deciding that you have heard the whole message, especially if the ideas presented are contrary to your personal beliefs. Last, listen between the lines, and listen with your eyes (i.e., what is the sender really trying to say?). Facial expressions and body stance sometimes tell more about what the sender is trying to get across. Nurses apply these skills in interactions with other professionals but particularly in the one-to-one relationship with the patient and family members. With practice, listening skills become easier to perform. Schwartz (1992) summarizes active listening, in which one is perceptive to what the speaker says and accepts the information discussed, in four simple steps:

1. listen (to the full message)
2. think (form an initial opinion)
3. respond (reflect the message back to the sender, and stay with it until it is clear)
4. comprehend

The sender can transmit communication by several methods: verbally, nonverbally, in writing, by showing, and with various media. The form used will depend upon for whom the message is intended and how formal the message is. A common problem with communication is that the sender/speaker is often not clear in the message sent to others. Often a combination of talking (in person), displaying nonverbal cues, and following up with written words transmits the message most clearly. This combination enables the listener to use many senses to hear, see, and read the message sent.

In patient care, it is essential that caregivers understand all messages relayed to provide safe, effective nursing care. Medication errors and missed treatments occur when communication has not been clear or occurs in the midst of too many distractions. A physician communicates the patient medical plan and new orders via the chart and in one-to-one communication with the patient's nurse. The nursing care plan is the key communication tool for nursing. In addition, critical paths or pathways, which document important patient outcomes on a predetermined time line, are being utilized in many hospitals.

The nurse communicates the patient's response to care and changes in the plan of care and records other care notes through documentation in the patient's chart and by interaction with other caregivers. Face-to-face and written communication are useful when follow-up or other actions are needed, particularly in patient care. The nurse communicates the nursing plans, treatments, and information about tests or therapies through patient education in both informal and formal ways. An alert patient is receptive to both what the caregiver is saying and how it is said (tone of voice used). Nonverbal cues often say more to patients and families as care is being provided than words spoken. Touch and facial expressions are noted by the patient as vital signs and assessments are performed and treatments are provided. The professional nurse who understands the importance of both spoken and nonverbal messages learns to rely on effective communication processes and skills.

The nurse is pivotal in managing the communication among the patient, caregivers, and others in the system. Figure 5–3 represents the pivotal role of the nurse in sending and receiving communication in patient care. The nurse is involved in communication with the patient, family, physician(s), and ancillary providers of care throughout the day. It is important to realize that the communication is about and for the patient and plan of care, even though the family may have needs that are far different from those of the pharmacist, who needs to know whether the patient received a timed dose of an antibiotic, for example. Also, the nurse as sender of communication needs to understand that messages need to be tailored to the person and circumstances

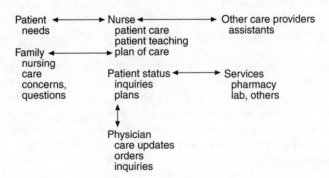

Figure 5–3 Pivotal role of the nurse in sending and receiving communication in patient care management.

involved. The nurse may keep the following concepts in mind to help send messages as clearly as possible (Douglass, 1992):

- Words mean different things to different people. For example, the patient and family who overhear the nurse and physician discussing the "low H&H" and the need for "2 U of washed PRCs" may be confused and fearful unless the terms are clarified for them.
- The message should be put in the simplest terms. For example, "Mr. Smith, the results of your morning lab test show that your red blood cells are low, which helps explain why you're feeling weak."
- If complex, the message should be expressed in several ways. Clarify terms, and say the same thing several different ways to ensure that you have been understood (utilize visual aids and reading materials).
- The language used should reflect the personality, culture, and values of the receiver. Approach the interaction based on your knowledge of the person with whom you are speaking.

Nurses make use of varied tools in the communication process in patient management. The patient's chart is the primary tool used in patient care communication. Nurses review the plan, treatments, and medications to be given and then document care provided as well as patient education performed so that others can review the nursing notes and follow up on and continue care as indicated. Other written tools are patient education forms and materials. In many settings, computers are a regular part of care planning and documentation and serve as a tangible communication method for caregivers. Time-saving flowsheets, in which the nurse simply marks a box to indicate patient status in a specific category based on a keyed code, are also common. Verbal messages are perhaps the quickest form of communication during care and may be one to one or in groups (such as during a patient care conference). Verbal communication should be followed by written documentation, particularly when care decisions have been made or follow-up is necessary.

In summary, the nurse maintains a professional demeanor in each transaction, whether it is with the patient, family, physician, or other caregivers and whether it is in person or on the phone. Communication skills of listening and sending clear messages are important in patient care, and the nurse is in a pivotal role in managing patient care communication. With experience and patience, good communication may become a comfortable process for the new graduate nurse in any setting.

KEY CONCEPTS
- Effective communication requires active listening and related skills.
- Active listening can be promoted by remembering four simple steps: listen, think, respond, and comprehend.

- The nurse has a pivotal role in communication with others in the management of patient care. The nurse interacts with the patient and family, the physician(s), and other care providers in the coordination and management of care.
- Communication with the patient consists of both verbal and nonverbal messages in patient care.

LEARNING CHALLENGE
Use the four basic steps of active listening to role play the following situations with a partner. Take turns role playing as the patient and the nurse. Document notes for each step. Respond to the sender (patient) until the message is clear and both of you agree that you have reached step 4 in listening.

1. Mrs. A is anxious about her diagnosis and afraid to ask questions, yet she tries to get nurses to tell her "what they know." You are her nurse today, and she is prodding you to tell her why she feels so "tired and awful" so much of the time and why she can't go home. One student is to role play Mrs. A, and one is to be her nurse. Have a dialogue in which the nurse uses active listening to clarify Mrs. A's concerns.
2. Mrs. Y has been in the hospital for 1 week, slowly recovering from trauma. Mr. Y complains about his wife's care and has told the nurse "No one gives her a bath, and she is in so much pain. Do something!" How do you approach Mr. Y to listen to his concerns?
3. You are Mr. R's nurse and need to explain a detailed nursing treatment and education plan regarding wound care. Is this a complex or simple message? Does this plan need to be expressed in more than one way? Document and then discuss ways to clarify the message for Mr. R.

Coordination

Coordination in patient care, in the broadest sense, means that all support services and caregivers provide their part in patient care at the right time and place for each patient. In health care facilities, there is "a great dependence and interdependence on forces that meet the many needs of the consumer" (Douglass, 1992, p. 130). Coordination of services is even more important in decentralized settings, where various departments must rely on each other to meet patients' needs. The patient is located on the nursing unit, and departments such as pharmacy, dietary, social services, and others must have a way of knowing what the patient's particular needs are. Coordination occurs through communication links and methods (Stevens, 1983). Physician order records and progress notes, nursing documentation, computer entries, and phone calls are examples of communication methods in care coordination. Coordination is less complicated on nursing units that have adopted a patient-focused design, in which personnel from formerly separate support departments are a part of the care unit and work side by side with the nurses during the course of the day (Brider, 1992). When there is no off-unit department to call or send orders to, the coordination of care is less complex.

Regardless of the delivery model in place, the nurse in charge of the patient coordinates care, people, and information. The nurse coordinates care by ensuring that identified patient needs are achieved (Cohen & Cesta, 1993). The nurse collaborates with the patient, the physician, and other professionals in the planning and coordinating of care and treatments. The nurse is responsible for reviewing the patient chart (medical and nursing notes) and ensuring that appropriate care is completed, whether it is provided directly by the nurse or by another staff member. An example of care coordination is timing the patient's day so that nursing therapies and the services provided by the physical therapist and respiratory therapist do not conflict with planned tests on or off the unit and the patient's need for rest between activities. The nurse collaborates with physical therapy and respiratory therapy to ensure that the times are a cohesive part of the overall patient plan of care for the shift.

The nurse coordinates people while coordinating care. In addition to balancing the timing of support service providers, the nurse directs care provided by assistants or technical staff. For example, in communicating care goals to staff, the nurse may say to the NA, "Mary, Mr. Brown in 609 needs to ambulate one more time today. I would like you to assist him in ambulating for at least 10 minutes, after dinner." The nurse acts on behalf of the patient and ensures that members of the care team understand their role in caring for a particular patient during the shift. The nurse coordinates the needs of the patient and family by also handling questions and concerns about care and following up on issues raised.

Coordination of information is associated with the communication process. Early in the shift, the nurse sorts through a variety of sources of information about each assigned patient. Valuable information can be collected from the history and physical, progress notes, laboratory results and test reports, and the nursing history and notes in the patient's chart. It is the nurse's responsibility to determine what amount of information to review during the shift to get to know the patient well enough to provide individualized care.

On most busy nursing units, the nurse has information coming from many directions during the shift. Patient test results may be accessed via computer printout, reports are sent, consulting physicians call for patient information, and so on. The nurse also sends information in response to requests from callers or to obtain necessary information from others or orders from the physician.

New nurses will find that others see them as the "expert" information source for the patients to whom they are assigned, whether they have cared for the patients for 1 hour or 1 week. Physicians making rounds ask for updated assessment data, the social worker will ask about family or visitors and the patient's response, and the physical therapist may ask how well the patient tolerated crutch-walking today. Although the nurse may not have all the facts up front, he or she should know where to obtain the data readily. Patient charts are usually organized so that specific information can be found in separate sections, such as the vital signs flowsheet and the nurse's notes and assessment section.

KEY CONCEPT
- Nurses coordinate care, people, and information for the benefit of the patient.

Consultation

Caplan in 1970 defined consultation as "a process of communication between professionals which can be systematically taught, applied, and analyzed" (Barron, 1989, p. 126). In the consultation process, the consultee identifies a problem that a consultant with specialized expertise may be able to solve. In nursing, the problems are commonly directly related to the care and treatment plans of patients. Four types, or purposes, of consultation are found in health care settings (Barron, 1989):

1. client-centered case consultation (for the patient care plan)
2. consultee-centered case consultation (related to lack of knowledge, skill, confidence, or professional objectives)
3. program-centered administrative consultation (for planning and administration)
4. consultee-centered administrative consultation (dealing with the client's problems that interfere with the objectives of the organization)

Nursing staff usually request consultation because they identify a problem with patient care and need help dealing with problem resolution. According to Barron (1989), client-centered and consultee-centered case consultation are common in patient care. Pure or formal consultation generally follows a four-step process once the nurse has requested a consultation:

1. assessment of the consultation problem
2. consultation report
3. implementation recommendations
4. follow-up

Staff Nurse Role in Consultation

The staff nurse plays a key role in consultation. The nurse identifies a problem or need and becomes the consultee when calling for a consultation with a more experienced bedside RN, a clinical nurse specialist (CNS), or other qualified care provider. Figure 5–4 represents staff nurse responsibilities in patient care consultation. The staff nurse does not give up the problem during consultation but retains responsibility in assisting with assessing the problem, choosing the best interventions, and ensuring that the interventions are indeed carried out. The staff nurse also discusses issues with the consultant during follow-up and evaluation of the interventions and the process.

Peer Consultation

A formal consultation process is not necessary for all patient care–related problems. A new graduate nurse consults with other staff or a CNS for help with patient problems, because of a personal lack of skill or knowledge, and to ask care questions on a less formal basis. Staff peers also consult with one

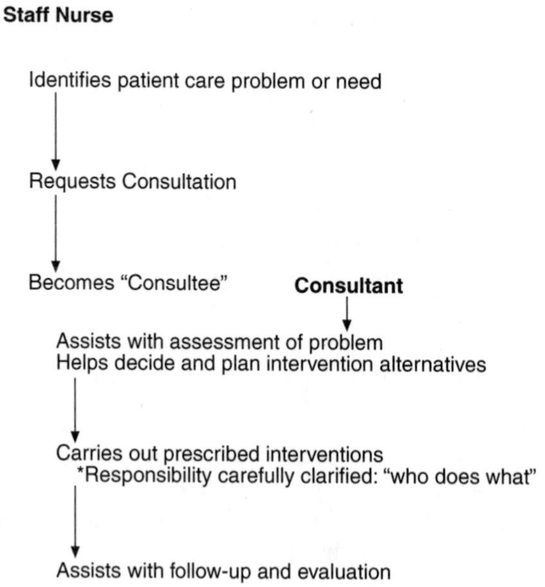

Figure 5–4 Staff nurse role in patient care consultation. *Source:* Adapted from A. Barron, *The Clinical Nurse Specialist in Theory and Practice,* 2nd ed., A. Hamric & J. Spross, eds., pp. 127–128, with permission of W.B. Saunders, © 1989.

another in approaching complex patient care to arrive at the best outcomes. **Peer consultation** is an important process in the development of critical thinking skills in the new graduate nurse. Consultation also serves to increase skill attainment in specific areas for the development of the new graduate nurse.

In today's complex and dynamic health care environment, development of employees is not a luxury. Staff training and development are necessary for growth of the organization and represent an ongoing, continuous process, not a one-time event. Training is improving the current job performance of an employee, and development is providing opportunities for the employee to learn and develop skills (Douglass, 1992). The new nurse especially needs opportunities to improve skills in a wide range of patient care activities, including consultation. The more skilled staff become, the more they experience success (Schwartz, 1992). New nurses work with more experienced staff, whereby their specific training needs are identified, and the experienced RN secures additional training or resources, whether as peer, preceptor, or formal consultant.

KEY CONCEPTS

- Types of consultation are client-centered case, consultee-centered case, program-centered administrative, and consultee-centered administrative consultation. The first two are most common in patient care.
- Steps of the consultation process are assessment of the problem, preparation of a consultation report, implementation of recommendations, and follow-up.
- The staff nurse role in the consultation process is as follows: identify the problem, request consultation, assess the problem, choose interventions, carry out interventions, and conduct follow-up and evaluation with the consultant.

LEARNING CHALLENGE

1. Kelly is a new graduate nurse on the medical floor and is taking care of a new type II diabetic. The patient is in need of extensive patient education, and Kelly has many questions as to the approach to use, how to determine the amount of diabetic information to include, and her particular role in the patient's teaching needs. Kelly has determined that she should consult with a more experienced nurse to handle this problem. Your task is to identify the type of consultation represented and why, outline the steps that Kelly will use in requesting the consultation and her role in the consultation process, and discuss your responses and how you would handle this type of care problem in your own practice with a peer or group.

2. David has just completed his second week as a new graduate nurse on a busy surgical unit. During the past week, David has been overwhelmed by the variety of intravenous (IV) lines and the many types of solutions administered. Some IVs are monitored on pumps or controllers; others drip by gravity. IV antibiotics, which require figuring of drip rates, are given to almost all the postoperative patients, and many receive blood products or some form of IV hyperalimentation. Today, David had three patients receiving multiple IV medications and infusions, and he was late giving most of the medications until another staff nurse stepped in to help. David feels that he takes too long to figure out drip rates, proper routes and lines to use, and compatibility of solutions for each patient. Your challenge is to develop a plan to increase David's proficiency with patients on IV therapy. Specify the type of consultation this problem requires, who may be consulted in this problem, how the problem will be assessed, specific interventions (examples) to address the problem, and how follow-up will be arranged and by whom. Compare your responses with your peer or group.

Coaching

Coaching, in the formal sense, is "on the job training by which a manager teaches or helps employees improve their job-related skills and performance" (Schwartz, 1992, p. 71). Coaching is also a "day by day, hands-on process that helps employees to recognize opportunities and ways to improve their performance and capabilities" (Douglass, 1992, p. 213). Coaching is also part of the professional nurse's role in patient and family teaching and, like employee coaching, is done in both formal and day-by-day approaches. As a coach, the nurse cultivates a climate of trust and mutual respect in approaching patient learning needs, self-care skill attainment, and changes in patient self-care practices. People (patients) must feel valued and understood for effective coaching (Schwartz, 1992). The nurse displays appreciation for the patient's individual style and need to learn through the use of a coaching process and skills. Skills needed by the RN include working with the patient/family to plan mutually acceptable actions and teaching goals, creating a supportive and helping climate, and influencing the patient to change or modify behaviors that are detrimental to health goals.

Coaching Process

In the nurse–patient relationship, coaching is intended to improve the patient's knowledge and skill in self-care and thus enhance overall wellness. Coaching involves both the patient and family/significant others who will take an active role in the patient's environment after discharge from the care setting.

Patients are expected to take an active role in their own care and health maintenance, and many are quite willing and eager to do so. This is particularly important in the reality of short lengths of stay and the need for self-care abilities at home. Common technical skills that patients often need to learn are self-administration of medications, blood glucose monitoring, wound and dressing care, care of special central IV lines, and others.

Once the particular skill or need is identified, there are important assessment questions to consider before the nurse approaches patient and family teaching and coaching in the learning process. The nurse needs to ask the following questions: What does the patient and family need to know to provide self-care after discharge? What specific skills are needed, and are they familiar to the patient or new skills? How can the patient's learning needs be met most effectively? Are there resources available in the home or community to support the patient's and family's learning? The nurse can use these types of questions to interview the patient and family in assessing their specific needs and to articulate a clear teaching and coaching plan.

Coaching Steps

Patient teaching begins as soon as needs have been assessed and learning needs identified. There are five basic steps in coaching that represent an ongoing process when done correctly (Schwartz, 1992). While coaching the patient/family in patient education, the nurse is responsible for:

- explaining why the skill being taught/coached is important to the patient
- answering any questions regarding the skill
- explaining how to do the skill/procedure
- demonstrating how to do the skill/procedure
- giving patient and/or family member an opportunity to practice the skill or procedure as many times as needed to do it safely
- giving constructive feedback, both positive and negative

Both the nurse and the patient help set the framework for positive coaching. The patient who shows interest in and concern for the teaching and skills needed helps establish a climate of trust and respect. If patients or family members express fear, resistance, or anger, the nurse needs to help them be willing to examine and discuss perceived problems and feelings before continuing with the coaching process.

Both formal teaching and informal teaching occur in patient coaching. Formal teaching involves following a plan to explain specific learning needs step by step and coaching the patient in learning them. Most standardized care plans and teaching aids provide steps to teach key points to patients and family members. Informal teaching occurs throughout the nurse–patient interaction. The nurse talks with the patient throughout the shift; these interactions may serve to teach, explain, assess, or offer comfort or support in trying situations and circumstances. For example, as the nurse gives medications, he or she reviews drug names and purposes and has the patient verbalize understanding in his or her own words. While family members visit, the nurse may take the opportunity to have them observe particular treatments that they may need to provide at home and discusses why and how he or she is doing a particular skill. As the family members observe, they can increase their comfort level and identify how much they need to learn as they prepare for formal teaching with the nurse.

In summary, in most instances, when the five steps of coaching are followed, the learner is quite capable of attaining the skill correctly with a minimum of confusion. The nurse explains any equipment, the process, and the steps of each skill so that the learner knows the what and how of the necessary skill. As patients or family members demonstrate the particular skill, the nurse gives immediate feedback on how they have done and any adjustments needed.

KEY CONCEPT
- Patient coaching entails the following five steps:
  1. Explain why the skill is important to the patient.
  2. Explain how to do the skill.
  3. Demonstrate how to do the skill.
  4. Give the patient/family time to practice the skill.
  5. Give constructive feedback.
- Repeat steps 2 through 5 until the learner has attained the skill at a safe and satisfactory level.

LEARNING CHALLENGE
Read the following patient teaching vignette and respond to the questions that follow. Keep the coaching steps and the nurse's role in mind as you proceed with the situation.

Mr. L has had two nephrostomy tubes placed for treatment of renal calculi. He will be going home with tubes in place to straight drainage. While he has been in the hospital, the nurses have irrigated the tubes every 4 hours with 5 mL of sterile normal saline. Mr. L is in a weakened state because of his illness and currently is unable to provide significant self-care. In addition, he speaks limited English. His wife and two English-speaking sons, ages 16 and 19, visit with him. The 19-year-old son goes to a nearby college, and the wife and the other son live at home. Discharge plans include continued irrigation and maintenance of the tubes with follow-up at the urologist 1 week after discharge. The nurse creates a supportive climate in approaching patient and family teaching.

Your challenge, as Mr. L's nurse, is to develop a coaching plan to teach the necessary skill to the family.

1. Utilizing the five steps in coaching, draw up a teaching plan.
2. Present the plan to your laboratory partner and discuss it. Compare plans.
3. How would your plan be different if Mr. L was able to directly learn the skill for self-care directly?

Delegation

Delegation is a tool that helps organizations run smoothly; after all, a manager or staff member cannot do everything alone. Work on the unit is best accomplished by delegation and cooperation among all levels of staff. "To delegate effectively is to manage effectively" (Schwartz, 1992, p. 2). In patient care management, working through others implies delegating and directing (Stevens, 1983). Failure to delegate can lead to the feeling of overwork and the "I thought it was done" syndrome. "Delegation is the entrusting of a specific task or project by one individual to another" (Schwartz, 1992, p. 8).

Delegation is usually a temporary procedure, and within the organization it can occur in any direction, as shown in Figure 5–5. Delegation is downward from manager to staff, laterally from peer to peer, and upward from staff to manager (Schwartz, 1992). In most traditional, hierarchical organizations, downward delegation is common; in collaborative practice settings, delegation truly occurs in all directions. In health care, delegation also occurs between nursing staff and assistants on the unit. This is the most significant aspect of delegation for the professional staff nurse.

There are many reasons to use delegation in any health care setting. In nursing organizations, to be truly effective an employee must have the authority to perform his or her own duties and to decide to delegate functions to others as appropriate. Organizations support this view from a staffpower, cost-savings perspective when they encourage delegation. An organization supports delegation to ensure optimal utilization of various skill levels; an employee is encouraged to take part in delegation to develop skills and enhance professional growth. A staff nurse also delegates to get work accomplished in a timely manner.

Figure 5–5 Directions of delegation in patient care management.

Key Terms in Delegation

When any employee delegates a task to another person, it is helpful to remember the two Ts: trust and time (Schwartz, 1992). Trust promotes self-confidence, and time is important because the delegatee needs time to complete the task and time from the delegator to receive feedback on the actions taken. Basic terms important in **delegation** include the following (Schwartz, 1992):

- delegator—the person who does the delegating
- delegatee—the recipient of the delegation
- responsibility—the delegator retains ultimate responsibility for successful task completion; the delegatee meets interim goals
- authority—having power to achieve an end; authority must be given to enable the delegatee to meet objectives
- accountability—the delegatee is held accountable for the established goals and must understand how his or her performance will be judged

Accountability and authority are important concepts in delegating work to any level of employee.

Process of Delegating

What to delegate. Professional nurses may often wonder just what gets delegated. In every work setting, there is a difference between permanent and temporary delegation. A position description includes elements of permanently delegated functions, tasks, and responsibilities (Stevens, 1983). The person holding a particular job or role is expected to perform permanently delegated functions on an ongoing basis. The number of tasks decreases and the number of responsibilities increases as one moves from lower-level to higher-level position descriptions. Temporary delegation occurs on a day-to-day interim basis and is the type of delegation that is important to the nurse in patient care management. Repetitive tasks or problems can be delegated to a lower-level employee, such as an NA, whereas unique problems are delegated to a higher-level employee. Position descriptions serve as a good general guide for what can be delegated to whom, but specific patient needs may change the person who does the task. For example, an NA normally does the vital signs, but Mrs. N needs the RN to do the vital signs because she must be monitored closely.

Beyond referring to particular job descriptions, the delegator needs to ask several questions to determine what to delegate (Schwartz, 1992). What is the purpose of the delegation? Should this task be delegated? What exactly do I want done? A professional nurse managing a particular patient caseload will generally recognize three categories of tasks in delegation: tasks the RN can delegate, tasks delegated during crises, and tasks the RN should not delegate.

The tasks the staff nurse can delegate are, as previously stated, the routine patient care–related tasks. To delegate a task and supervise task completion, a staff nurse needs to know his or her own job well and aspects of the NA's role. Is the given task within the NA's realm and not requiring an RN's skill?

During a crisis, a nurse may need to delegate tasks to an NA, but more often tasks will have to be delegated to a peer. When a patient's status suddenly deteriorates, the nurse needs to focus attention on amelioration of the problem and have another nurse assist with those tasks that must be completed on other patients at the same time. The peer may take care of other patients or handle phone calls so the nurse can remain with the patient in crisis. Delegation during a crisis occurs quickly, with staff members pitching in to help maintain a calm milieu for other patients on the unit. If a shift manager is available, the staff nurse can expect this person to help with tasks or details of the crisis, and the staff nurse can delegate many items.

Tasks that should not be delegated are most often those aspects of an assignment that staff nurses must complete themselves, such as charting assessments, patient and family teaching, or monitoring IV fluids. Although another nurse may be qualified to do these tasks, the nurse would delegate certain items to a peer only in a crisis or during a break, not as a routine part of his or her role.

Choosing a delegatee. In addition to knowing what tasks assistant roles can handle, it is helpful to know individual abilities of staff (assistants or peers) to determine who is the right person for the delegation. In general, delegation should be a gradual process, allowing the employee to assume responsibilities and authority for the tasks at a comfortable pace (Schwartz, 1992). When the nurse is deciding on a delegatee, as much of a single task as possible should be delegated to one person.

Selecting the right person—a person who is both able and willing to be a delegatee—is not always easy in busy hospital settings or any health care setting but can be made simpler by keeping five rules of delegation in mind (Schwartz, 1992):

1. The employee must be available for the assignment.
2. Match skills to demands of the task.
3. Spread several delegations or tasks among employees; do not overwhelm one person.
4. Avoid delegating tasks during the first 3 months of the person's employment (let staff get comfortable in their jobs before adding new responsibilities).
5. If the task is complex or time consuming, you may need to assign the task to two or more people.

The staff nurse generally delegates tasks in a downward direction to various assistants on the unit. If only one assistant role is available to a nurse, the options for choosing a delegatee are limited. This does not mean that the nurse must relent and do all the tasks himself or herself. Rather, it means that the nurse must become an efficient delegator to know what needs to be done, what can be delegated, and who should do it. This process is often a difficult task for the new graduate nurse, who may not be accustomed to overseeing others but rather to doing everything alone.

The How-To Components of Delegation

The formal process of assigning and delegating work to another person generally occurs in five sequential steps: goal setting, communication, motivation, supervision, and evaluation (Schwartz, 1992). The more serious or complex the delegated task, the more in-depth attention one must pay to each of the steps. Simple, routine tasks can be assigned quickly and require little if any supervision and minor evaluation.

In goal setting, the delegator works with the employee to determine expectations and goals. The nurse needs to be clear about whether he or she is delegating a decision or an action in patient care. Communication occurs initially and during the delegation and is a two-way process. It is the responsibility of the nurse to tell the assistant what task to do and to be clear as to any time constraints or limitations. The delegatee needs to ask questions to clarify responsibility or aspects of the task and communicate any problems that occur once the task is begun. Motivation to do an assigned task comes from recognition by the delegator and enhanced self-esteem. Most delegatees will perform positively when they feel motivation and recognition and have the necessary time and tools to do the work. Supervising the delegation is from a supportive stance, not just checking to see that the employee completed the work. The nurse who delegates knowingly and with thought can loosen his or her grip and be available as a resource, help foresee any difficulties, or review necessary resources with the delegatee.

The last step, evaluation, should occur in every type of delegation. Without follow-up, the nurse does not know how well he or she delegated or communicated or whether the task was indeed completed. In addition, without evaluation the delegatee does not receive feedback or learn from the delegation. With clear goal setting and communication, most delegatees perform tasks as well as they can. All employees need recognition for good work, particularly newer employees, who need input on their actions and skill attainment. Poor task performance usually is not due to a lack of education but more often is related to too heavy an assignment, a low-priority task, or unfamiliarity with the task or skill (Stevens, 1983). The assistant or nurse who already has a full assignment may not have enough time to do all the tasks, especially additional ones, as well as usual. The delegator and delegatee need to talk over perceived problems with the workload and prioritize what tasks come first. If the delegatee feels that the delegated task is a low priority, more time may be spent on needs of perceived higher priority. Communication is key to clarifying the importance of delegated tasks and to holding off on delegating low-priority tasks if the delegatee is already overwhelmed. Unfamiliarity with the delegated task also can lead to poor performance, as can hurrying through a task with which one is fairly familiar.

Evaluation of performance, particularly poor performance, requires identifying the probable cause(s) of the problem. The delegator and delegatee (e.g., the nurse and assistant) need to identify the cause and discuss how to improve performance. In the case of task unfamiliarity, evaluation provides a means for the delegatee to improve the skill and learn from mistakes or omissions. One of the key things for a nurse who supervises assistants to keep in mind during delegation is to guide the employee without taking over the job or the task (Schwartz, 1992).

Summary of Delegation

Delegation is a skill that staff nurses and managers use to promote timely completion of patient care and organization goals. The process of delegation involves five steps and can be applied in any setting. Learning the process of effective delegation, what tasks can be delegated, and to whom to delegate is an important skill for the new professional nurse.

**KEY
CONCEPTS**

- The three categories of task delegation are:

  1. tasks the nurse can delegate
  2. tasks delegated during a crisis
  3. tasks the nurse should not delegate

- The five steps of effective delegation are:

  1. goal setting
  2. communication
  3. motivation
  4. supervision
  5. evaluation

**LEARNING
CHALLENGE**

June is a staff nurse on the unit for which you have recently been hired. You have noticed that June delegates tasks to the NA by attaching notes written on small pieces of paper to the NA's clipboard soon after the shift begins. June goes about her own work without apparently following up with the NA. You are working with the same NA today, and when you ask her to help with a particularly heavy task she states, "Just leave me a note and I'll try to get to it."

1. Do you agree with this method of communicating and delegating tasks to assistants? Explain.
2. How are the sequential steps of the delegation process being used or misused?
3. Share and compare your responses with your laboratory partner(s).

GROUP DYNAMICS

Groups, and the unique characteristics of groups, are important in the management of patient care. Nurses and other health care providers are involved in many different types of groups in health care settings. "There is no instance where health care is delivered by a single individual. There is always a minimum of two—a patient and a care giver; and if in the hospital, there are many more individuals involved" (Sovie, 1992, p. 95). Groups are important to nurses and nurse managers for a variety of reasons. Groups serve a formal function in that they serve as the focal point of social life (a means for understanding social values and norms); satisfy individual needs for belonging, status, and security; and provide a major mechanism for the achievement of organizational goals (Douglass, 1992).

In health care agencies, groups are usually involved in the realization of organization- or work-related goals. Groups are sometimes referred to as teams. "A team is two or more persons who depend on one another to accomplish a common task" (Fairbanks, 1991, p. 3). Teams are not unique to health care settings but are seen in business as well. "Teams are everywhere. In business there are all sorts of teams for new products, quality, and projects" (Parker, 1990, p. 16).

For groups or teams to work together in goal achievement or tasks, interdependence of the individual members of the group is important. As Forsyth (1990) contends, interdependence among members is the hallmark of a group, but other characteristics are also true of groups. Some of the other characteristics essential to a true group include interaction, structure, size, goals, cohesiveness, and temporal change (Forsyth, 1990). Members influence one another's behavior through constant interaction. A group attains structure when stable patterns of relationships develop among the members. The relationships consider roles and status in most groups. Groups come in all shapes and sizes, but the average size is somewhere between 4 and 20 members, with many groups tending to be as small as 2 members. Goals are the reasons for the group's existence and what the members hold as common purposes. Enjoyment and satisfaction in the group as well as strengthened relationships characterize group unity or cohesiveness. The last common characteristic of groups is their tendency to change because of their complex nature, also known as temporal change.

Definitions

A **group** has been defined as "two or more individuals who influence one another through social interaction" (Forsyth, 1990, p. 6); a work group is a "collection of two or more who are interdependent and who interact with one another for the purpose of performing to achieve a common goal" (Douglass, 1992, p. 221). Parker (1990) contends that a group of people is not a team; rather, a team is "a group of people with a high degree of interdependence geared toward the achievement of a goal or completion of a task" (p. 16).

It would appear that the two terms *group* and *team* can actually be used interchangeably when one is referring to the nature of groups in a patient care setting. Nurses are inherently working together to achieve patient and organization goals through their actions as individuals and as members of a caregiving group. Nursing teams are goal directed and organized for the purpose of providing patient care; they are not just groups of people loosely congregating for a social event. Group structure and goals are evident as nurses provide quality care according to clearly defined standards (Douglass, 1992).

Nursing work groups also have varied reasons for forming to achieve different goals. Nurses group together to hear shift reports, receive assignments, conduct teaching or orientation sessions, or take part in councils, task forces, or committees to work on organizational or patient care–related problems. Teamwork is important in the work that nurses do as groups. Teamwork is "the working together of a group of people with a shared objective" (Parker, 1990, p. 16). *Teamwork* has become a buzzword in large businesses and organizations that are attempting to draw upon the strengths of individuals working together to solve major issues or create new approaches to doing business.

Group dynamics is a term that refers to powerful processes that occur within groups (Forsyth, 1990). Parker (1990) and Luft (1970) refer to group dynamics as a field of study of individuals interacting in small groups, or in other words group processes. Groups are by nature dynamic, as Forsyth (1990) asserts; they are powerful rather than weak, active rather than passive, fluid rather than static, and catalyzing rather than reifying.

Developmental Concepts

The dynamic nature of groups means that groups are not static, unchanging bodies of people who act in the same manner day in and day out. "All groups share an important feature: they change. Initial uncertainties give way to stable patterns of interaction, tensions between members wax and wane, old members are replaced by new ones, and levels of productivity fluctuate" (Forsyth, 1990, p. 76). The ability of group members to work well together develops over time. Group members must get to know and accept one another, agree on their purpose for meeting, and be willing to establish structure, rules, and procedures for accomplishing their goals (Douglass, 1992).

Stages of Group Development

Much like individuals, teams experience stages of development from early formation to a developed system (Parker, 1990). Patterns of growth and change occur in groups throughout their life cycle from formation to dissolution (Forsyth, 1990). Most theorists assume that groups pass through several phases, or stages, as they develop, and the number and name of the stages vary among theorists. In spite of their differences, many theories highlight certain interpersonal outcomes that must be achieved in any group that exists for a prolonged period of time. Most models include the first four stages listed in Table 5–5. Forsyth (1990) includes a fifth stage, dissolution.

The first stage, forming, is also known as the stage of dependence and initial group formation. This stage is a period of dependency in which members look to the leader, other team members, or existing rules for guidance.

Table 5–5 Five Stages of Group Development

Stage	Major Processes	Characteristics
Orientation (forming)	Exchange of information, increased interdependence, task exploration, identification of commonalities	Tentative interactions, polite discourse, concern over ambiguity, self-discourse
Conflict (storming)	Disagreement over procedure, expression of dissatisfaction, emotional responding, resistance	Criticism of ideas, poor attendance, hostility, polarization and coalition formation
Cohesion (norming)	Growth of cohesion and unity; establishment of roles, standards, and relationships	Agreement on procedures, reduction in role ambiguity, increased "we" feeling
Performance (performing)	Goal achievement, high task orientation, emphasis on performance and productivity	Decision making, problem solving, mutual cooperation
Dissolution (adjourning)	Termination of roles, completion of tasks, reduction of dependency	Disintegration and withdrawal, increased independence and emotionality, regret

Source: From *Group Dynamics*, 2nd edition, by D.R. Forsyth. Copyright © 1990 by Wadsworth, Inc. Reprinted by permission of Brooks/Cole Publishing Company, Pacific Grove, CA 93950.

Members "test the waters" to determine acceptable behaviors, tasks, and other expectations. During this forming stage, members often suffer through an orientation period marked by mild tension and guarded interchanges (Forsyth, 1990). As groups form, members must deal with people they hardly know and experience role uncertainty and fear of embarrassment. Eventually, members of the group begin to open up, and tasks are identified, patterns of communication are established, and a niche is set for each person (Carr, 1988). Members begin to "feel like one of the group."

The second stage of group development, storming, is characterized by conflict among team members and resistance to the task. Some of the conflicts are easy to resolve, whereas other issues may escalate and seriously disrupt the group's internal dynamics (Forsyth, 1990). Despite the negative connotations of conflict, disagreeing is a natural consequence of joining a group and is a reflection of the dynamic nature of a group. As the group confronts a problem or barrier, members need to refocus and move forward (Carr, 1988).

In the third stage of development, norming, a sense of group cohesion develops. Members show acceptance of the team and a willingness to make it work. The group develops team **norms**, which are standards of behavior that the team develops for guiding member interactions and for dealing with the task (Parker, 1990). A feeling of camaraderie and group unity develops. A "we-ness" emerges, and members share commonalities and goals (Forsyth, 1990). The group reaches stability—strong, group-level linkages and desire among the members to remain in the group—and satisfaction. The internal group dynamics becomes intense, with high levels of unity and cohesion and more pressure to conform. The increased intensity can become a negative force because groups sometimes become intolerant of any sort of disagreement (Forsyth, 1990). The group that keeps its original goals in mind is able to achieve cooperative problem solving, redefine particular roles, and accept diversity (Carr, 1988).

The fourth stage, performing, emphasizes group results. Interpersonal relationships have become stabilized, roles have been clarified in the previous stage, and the group has a structure, purpose, and role. Parker (1990) calls this the payoff stage. It takes time to get to the stage of group productivity. The group reorganizes and identifies problems clearly, and members participate openly in group activities (Carr, 1988).

The stages of group development are played out in different ways and on different levels throughout the life of a group. Forming can occur with a new group leader or when a new member arrives, because either is a change in team composition requiring reformation (Parker, 1990). Some groups do not go through the storming stage very well, or at all, because they fear the conflict, but groups need to go through each stage to work in a highly coordinated effort (Forsyth, 1990). Some groups go through a fifth stage, called adjourning, when goals are met (such as task force work) or when a member desires to leave. Although the entire group may not dissolve when one member leaves, the nature of the relationships of the remaining members shifts and needs to adjust or change to accommodate for the gap left by the lost member. Nursing units go through change when a manager leaves, when there is staff turnover, or when other changes occur in the team. Adjourning changes the unity and cohesiveness of the group and may be stressful for members, leading to emotions of grief and anger.

Group Socialization

Just as groups grow and change through group development stages, individuals within groups go through a **group socialization** process at the individual level. Nursing units experience changes in group composition quite often as a result of staff turnover or advancement. Whenever a new member joins an existing group, such as a nursing unit, two types of socialization occur. The new member evaluates the group, and the group evaluates and socializes the new member. The new member first evaluates the group, decides whether to make a commitment to this group, and finally makes a role transition to the group. During the evaluation of the group, the individual gets a sense of how this group functions and whether there is a fit between them. Before a commitment is made, the new person ponders any other alternatives available (e.g., is the job at the other hospital better?). Once the member decides that this is the group to join, time and energy are spent on gaining acceptance by the group. Role transition takes time and depends upon the member's previous experience and readiness to be an active group member. Role transition is particularly important to new graduate nurses as they join a group.

The second type of socialization occurs when the group latches onto the new member and tries to make a niche for that person. Table 5–6 lists the stages of socialization that groups go through when a new member joins. In the first stage, the group searches for more information about the new person and approaches the person cautiously and from a distance. Many a new nurse can remember being introduced to a new group of staff and receiving a formal, if not cool, reception. In the second stage, the group initiates the newcomer. The new member assimilates the rules and norms of the group, and the group accommodates its form and interpersonal relationships to accept the new member. In this second stage, the new member seeks acceptance into the group. A new staff nurse assimilates the expectations of the new group when he or she behaves as a team member during shift report and in working with assistants "the unit's way." The third stage, maintenance, involves negotiating the nature and quantity of the new member's contribution to the group (e.g., how does this nurse support the team's values, how does he or she help out others on the unit, and does he or she take a leadership role or only that of follower?). The fourth stage, resocialization, occurs when the

Table 5–6 Stages of Socialization into a Group

Stage	Actions
Investigation	Search for information about new member; use caution
Socialization	Initiation of new member, member assimilation of values, group accommodation; acceptance achieved
Maintenance	Negotiate nature and quantity of member's contribution to group, determine role
Resocialization	Refigure group roles when member leaves

Source: From *Group Dynamics,* 2nd edition, by D.R. Forsyth. Copyright © 1990 Wadsworth, Inc. Adapted by permission of Brooks/Cole Publishing Company, Pacific Grove, CA 93950.

member leaves the group to go to a new one. The whole process of socialization starts over again for the old group and for the new group.

In healthy, functioning teams, the process of socialization is made easier by clear communication among members early in the process. The team tells the new person things about the group, such as what the group is trying to achieve and key goals; who does what on the team (roles and skills); how the team works, makes decisions, and resolves conflicts; what is unique about the team and what might surprise the new member; and what the team members wish people had told them when they joined the team (Fairbanks, 1991). The new member imparts to the team the kind of work he or she likes and dislikes; what he or she would like to learn, the kind of relationships he or she would like to develop with others; how he or she decided to work here, and what an ideal workday is like for him or her (Fairbanks, 1991). Within the work of a nursing unit and group, a nurse holds an interpersonal role to relate well to others, an informational role to provide clear directions, and a decisional role to make sound decisions based on the nursing process (Douglass, 1992).

KEY CONCEPTS

- *Group development:* All working groups generally go through five stages of development:
  1. forming—group members must get oriented to one another
  2. storming—conflict evolves and a solution is sought to improve the group environment
  3. norming—norms and roles develop, behavior is regulated, and greater unity evolves
  4. performing—members work as a unit to achieve goals
  5. adjourning—the group disbands
- *Group socialization:* When a new member joins an existing group, the group puts the member through investigation, socialization, maintenance, and eventually resocialization.

Principles and Factors at Play in Groups

For groups to be most effective, they need to go comfortably through the stages of group development previously discussed and deal with issues of communication, trust, relationships, power, and how to be as effective as possible in achieving goals.

Communication, Trust, Relationships, and Power

Group members need to overcome negative behaviors, differing orientations, and distrust of others to develop a means to achieve outcomes. "Trust can affect the flow of information and decision making in a group" (Carr,

1988, p. 12). Although hierarchical organization structures tend to impede and restrict information flow, collaborative structures, such as shared governance, promote trust in leadership and the free flow of information with an increased likelihood of sound decision making. As Carr (1988) asserts, "there is a need to use direct, focused communication patterns in the work setting to develop trust" (p. 13). Fairbanks (1991) writes "One of the most influential power bases is the extent to which people can trust you" (p. 4). Old, traditional models impede trust and effectiveness because of the presence of negative power. Status in groups has often hampered the development of trust. Status is the social ranking of a member secondary to his or her position in the organization, seniority, or level of expertise. An overemphasis on status can decrease the frequency of interactions among members and the level of communication. Although power is not evenly distributed among individuals or groups, every individual has some degree of power in his or her ability to organize human, informational, or material resources to do a task.

The ability of group members to trust one another is promoted through development of positive group norms early in group development. A norm is a measure or standard of behavior or performance. Conformity is following and adhering to established norms. An example of conformity is the expectation that a staff nurse will not leave the unit for lunch break until checking on coverage and giving a report to his or her "buddy" nurse. Exhibit 5–1 lists examples of positive group norms that groups articulate in the norming phase of development. Effective groups or teams understand the importance of positive, communication-enhancing norms.

Effective Teams and Team Building

A good group has been defined as "one in which the atmosphere tends to be informal, comfortable, and relaxed; there is considerable discussion, in

Exhibit 5–1 Examples of Positive Group Norms or Expectations of Group Members

Group members agree to:
- be candid about ideas and feelings
- help others be candid
- be open
- begin the shift on time
- show commitment to the group
- accept and encourage individuality
- express concern for one another
- accept constructive criticism

which virtually everyone participates; the tasks or objectives of the group are well understood and accepted by the members" (Fairbanks, 1991, p. 2). Team building, in the formal sense, is an organizational development facilitative-tactical mode that is intended to make a group effective and to achieve unity of purpose (Fairbanks, 1991). Team building emphasizes interactive group processes, or the how of effective behavior, and focuses on developing work group maturity. It assumes that success in work groups results from a collaborative interdependence that develops through practice and improves effectiveness by building cohesion, clarifying structure, and reducing conflict (Forsyth, 1990).

Sovie (1992) asserts, "we need to teach our staff and clinicians how to be effective team players" (p. 95). Teamwork requires a reaching out and a movement toward sharing responsibilities and actions to get a quality job accomplished. In nursing, team building is often used to prepare groups of people to accomplish particular tasks. Teamwork at the unit level is also important and begins with staff members who are well prepared and competent in their jobs. Team members need to know the overall organizational goals as well as their unit's goals, and they need to identify with them as their own (Sovie, 1992). It also means that members need to understand the roles, functions, and responsibilities of each group member because they depend upon one another to perform their respective activities in a high-quality and consistent fashion.

Team building has been seen as an important management responsibility and needs to cover four areas: roles, activities, relationships, and environment (Sovie, 1992). The effective, mature team is accomplished in the four areas of group assessment and is characterized by many of the items listed in Exhibit 5–2. Effective teams exude a comfortable atmosphere and a high level of open participation by all members. An effective leadership style is often the basis for formation of an effective team.

Group Leadership Functions

Leadership is present in any group of people and may involve formal (appointed) or informal (chosen by peers) leaders. An effective team leader is an effective team player, uses good communication skills, and is committed to high-quality work (Parker, 1990). Effective team players support organization goals and do the work necessary to accomplish goals. An effective team is made up of a blend of people, each of whom contributes a special talent to the group. The leader imparts a vision to the group through clarification of organizational and unit goals and each member's unique role in carrying out his or her part in achieving the goals. The leader is also responsible for facilitating the functioning of the group in its day-to-day processes. The

Exhibit 5–2 Characteristics of Effective Nursing Groups or Teams

Comfortable atmosphere
Staff are involved and interested
No overt tensions
Goals and tasks are well understood by staff members
Members express feelings and ideas openly
Staff members listen to one another
Contributions by each level of staff are respected
Most unit/shift decisions are reached by consensus
Staff make their own patient care decisions and consult openly with others
The leader or charge nurse does not dominate the group
Assignments are perceived to be fair
Criticism is positive; no personal attacks

leader facilitates the work of the group through the appropriate wielding of the power and authority inherent in his or her role.

The patient care manager roles discussed earlier in this chapter each have a slightly different level of accountability and authority in terms of the type of group the manager is expected to lead. The staff nurse is a leader of his or her particular patient care module and assistants. The shift manager leads the work of the unit for the assigned shift, and the unit manager leads the entire unit in overall goal achievement on a long-term basis. Regardless of the group the nurse leads, attention is paid to the task(s) the group is expected to complete and to the processes involved (i.e., the way in which the group does the work).

LEARNING CHALLENGE   Utilizing your knowledge of the characteristics of the stages of group development, review the following vignette and answer the questions that follow.

As a result of recent changes in the patient mix and overall census in a large, acute care hospital, one nursing unit has been reclassified as a specialty unit, a unit that cares for patients with infectious diseases, and another unit has closed. Some of the staff from the unit that closed have been reassigned to the new unit, and others have been assigned to existing units. At the day shift staff meeting on the infectious disease unit, the following comments were made by several staff nurses: "The night nurses are always leaving unfinished admissions for us," "I disagree with our shift leader's decision to make us share lockers," and "I don't think everyone handles their fair share of the admits or paperwork on this floor."

1. What stage of group development is this unit in? Why?
2. What must the group do to move on to the next stage? Give examples.
3. What is the next stage this group will go through, and what will it experience in the next stage?
4. Compare your responses with your laboratory partner's.

Characteristic Problems of Groups or Teams

During the ongoing process of group development and socialization, it is not uncommon for groups to face barriers or impasses to effective teamwork. This may be particularly evident in nursing units that involve a variety of team players, such as full-time, part-time, and flexible staff nurses and various assistant roles. Problems often stem from role dilemmas and conflict. Role ambiguity is due to a lack of necessary information related to a given position and can lead to conflict in the work of the group (Fairbanks, 1991). Role conflict arises when two or more sets of expectations occur together and lead to tension and anxiety in an employee. Problems with members' roles are less likely to become serious when communication and role clarification occur during member and group socialization, as previously discussed.

Conflict

"Conflict is an inevitable by-product of interpersonal dealings" (Douglass, 1992, p. 169). Conflict is characterized by an inner or outer struggle that occurs regarding ideas, feelings, or actions. Most health care organizations experience a substantial amount of conflict, primarily because a complex organizational structure requires its members to engage in numerous and varied interdependent relationships (Douglass, 1992). Although many may recoil at the thought of conflict, conflict itself is neither beneficial nor harmful. What is important is how the conflict—its source and areas of friction— are handled. "Low levels of conflict usually mean members are uninvolved, unmotivated, and bored" (Forsyth, 1990, p. 80). Healthily dealing with group conflict enables the group to continue in a forward, growing direction. Most managers in collaborative structures consider conflict normal and a means to search for solutions for greater effectiveness.

Two types of conflict that may occur in nursing teams are intragroup (within the group) and intergroup (between groups). Conflict often arises when group members compete for desired goals and resources rather than cooperate for group success (Forsyth, 1990). When members compete for goals, coalitions may develop. Coalitions involve participants who disagree on enough of the fundamental issues essentially to form a subgroup. They form to try to reach certain outcomes, tend to be adversarial in their intent, and also tend to be temporary, dissolving after goals are met or resolved. Conflict between groups can also occur between various nursing shifts (e.g., day shift and night shift disagreements).

Conflict Resolution

When staff learn to manage and deal with conflict, positive consequences can be achieved, such as the following (Douglass, 1992):

- issues are recognized and brought into the open
- group cohesion and performance increase
- constructive results accrue
- other leaders arise in the group through hearing of all views

Conflict can be resolved via negative modes, such as imposing or forcing a position, taking no action or avoiding the issue, yielding or smoothing over the issue, or compromising principles (Forsyth, 1990). The most positive mode for conflict resolution is collaborative problem solving, in which the group identifies the source of the conflict openly and honestly and agrees on a solution to the problem. Collaborative problem solving increases the members' sense of responsibility and commitment to the success of the group. "How nurses approach workplace conflicts is an example of how they approach all other organization and leadership functions" (Douglass, 1992, p. 179).

Summary

Groups can expect to experience some level of conflict during each stage of development and in day-to-day operations. Disagreeing is a natural consequence of joining a group and leads to negative outcomes when conflicts are not resolved. A collaborative problem-solving process is a valuable tool for groups and enables groups to manage conflict rather than try to get rid of it altogether.

Assessment of Group Functions

As discussed in the preceding section, groups naturally change and evolve over time as members' roles change and goals and expectations are reformatted. As old members leave, new members arrive to take their place, as often occurs on a nursing unit. How well the group or team can adjust to the changes is a reflection of the overall health and professionalism of the members and the entire group. From time to time it is important for group members to take a conscious look at how well they are performing as a team and what factors are affecting their work together. Assessment of group functions can be accomplished both formally and informally; there is a different rationale for each approach used.

Evaluation Purposes

Specific reasons to assess group processes include group maintenance and improving team effectiveness. In group maintenance, members evaluate how well goals are achieved and whether any changes are necessary based on group evaluation (Parker, 1990). Some group questions might be "Is everyone being heard at staff meetings?" "Are there any underlying unit tensions or concerns we need to discuss?" and other types of questions. A group leader, such as a shift manager or unit manager, often is expected to initiate group self-evaluation. A staff nurse also performs group evaluation when he or she discusses care plans with peers and assistants and how well the team members are working toward meeting outcomes. Group evaluation is also aimed at measuring group progress and success and at celebrating successes. This form of evaluation is also referred to as team building, as previously discussed. The overall goal is to strengthen the team and its effectiveness as a cohesive work group. Some key areas that this form of group evaluation addresses are as follows (Fairbanks, 1991):

- How well is each member's role understood?
- Do we need better understanding of team purpose?
- How effective is our communication about issues?
- Do members need more support?
- Do we need more understanding of group process?
- Are we using conflict in a positive rather than a negative way?
- How well do we work with other groups?

Evaluation Methods

Common tools or methods to use in evaluation of staff work groups are staff meetings designated for evaluation purposes, worksheets to be completed by members and tallied by a manager or staff member, and one-to-one meetings with staff members followed by group meetings to discuss themes. In general, formal evaluation is chosen when a concerted effort is needed to build the team or celebrate wins. Formal assessment, because of the time involved and the impact on all staff, should be done less frequently than informal assessment. For example, a manager and staff member may decide to assess group functioning each September as part of annual goals and to do less formal assessments during the year, at monthly or semimonthly staff meetings. Groups that regularly assess their functioning find clearer understanding of roles, activities, and relationships (Sovie, 1992). The team that forgets to assess its functioning often finds itself in trouble, with no clear knowledge as to the nature of the problem (Parker, 1990).

Communication Patterns in Groups/Teams

The effectiveness with which members are able to work together depends to a large extent on the effectiveness of their communication. Functional or dysfunctional communication can be noted in the nature of the internal group dynamics. A **functional style** of communication, according to Parker (1990), is characterized by relaxed working relationships, confidence and trust among group members, values and goals being met satisfactorily, members being highly motivated to abide by the major group values and to achieve important goals, and a supportive atmosphere for interactions and problem solving. The effective team is eager to help each member develop to his or her full potential and is highly motivated to communicate, display openness, and support all members.

A **dysfunctional communication** style displays behaviors that are the opposite of those of the functional style and is often an outcome of poorly navigated group development processes. Internal team dynamics in a dysfunctional communication style might include an uncomfortable atmosphere, failure of members to listen to one another's issues, an overpowering leader who often sends mixed messages, and fear of conflict to the point of allowing disagreements to escalate to destructive conflicts. Groups tend to have difficulty reaching positive group goals and may see an unusually high rate of member turnover if the problems are not eventually addressed. Assessment of group functions is particularly important for groups that have difficulties with group processes and communication.

KEY CONCEPTS

- Functional communication is characterized by openness to new ideas and options, a comfortable group atmosphere, healthy disagreements, constructive criticism, clear assignments, and a sense of working well together.
- Dysfunctional communication is characterized by an uncomfortable group atmosphere, mixed communication messages, a low level of

interaction, tenseness in communication styles, difficulty in reaching objectives, unclear assignments, and a sense of unfair assignments.

LEARNING CHALLENGE   Utilize the concepts you have learned about group conflict and group communication in responding to the following vignettes.

1. The evening nurse feels rushed at the beginning of her shift because she needs to provide final discharge teaching and paperwork for two patients being discharged home within the next hour. During shift report, the offgoing nurse says "I know you're not that busy on evening shift" as she tells the oncoming nurse about the two discharged patients. What type of communication has occurred between these two nurses? How might the offgoing nurse have reworded her report? Is this interchange a healthy sign or an unhealthy sign of group process? If the oncoming nurse is new to the unit, what stage of socialization is represented in the vignette?

2. It is the start of the shift, and as you enter one patient's room he greets you with the complaint "I'm always left alone when I'm up in this chair. How do you expect me to stay here and care for myself?" You find out that an NA helped the patient to his chair more than 2 hours ago and is preparing to leave the unit. How would you approach this situation? If getting the patient to the chair is a delegated NA task, who has follow-up on the outcome or needs to follow up? Discuss the situation with a peer, and decide how to reach a positive outcome in a nonthreatening manner.

Group Stressors

No group that works together for a period of time can expect to remain unchanged or unaffected by internal or external events. As work groups, nursing teams need to be able to adapt to changes in health care and within the organization. Groups that have become overly cohesive, or adhere to a high level of conformity, will be intolerant of change and exhibit signs of stress (Forsyth, 1990). Signs of group stress may be inflexibility or a hesitancy to question "the way we do things," little evidence of individuality, and poor tolerance of new ideas or issues. A negative use of power or authority can also lead to group stress, particularly if it has developed over time.

In stressful groups, dysfunctional communication may be exhibited, and it may be difficult to define role relationships, activities, and responsibilities. Trust is often low, which leads to low openness among group members, with "a lot of talk but no communication" (Parker, 1990). Because of a desire for unity, the team may be overloaded with people who have the same team player style, with diversity in technical expertise but too much similarity in their group approach. Conflict is often about interpersonal, emotional issues, and disagreements are aired in private, with frequent gossiping. These signs of trouble are often allowed to boil in a group that forgets to assess its functioning on a regular basis.

Stress Adaptation

A group can move beyond negative and dysfunctional communication, particularly if enough members become conscious of the group's functioning. During the group socialization process when a new nurse is hired, the group is expected to share its norms and expectations with the new member, and it does so consciously and unconsciously. It soon becomes evident to both the new member and the group that behaviors or nonverbal messages do not match the declared norms or goals of the unit. Team members can use this time to reevaluate their effectiveness and roles and to move on to the performing stage of group development.

Team Building

At times, it is necessary to bring in an outside group facilitator to help the group in team building. The facilitator works as a consultant and can offer a more objective view of the group's process. Team building is important for groups charged with achievement of significant goals and tasks. Team building is intended to make a group effective and to achieve unity of purpose (Fairbanks, 1991).

Group adaptation is noted in an increase in openness, a capacity to extend the scope of the group's obligations beyond current boundaries, a capacity to alter norms and values, and the ability to accommodate new information and relationships (Luft, 1970). Groups adapt to stressors and move beyond negative patterns of behavior and communication. As mentioned previously, groups are dynamic entities in their ability to change and do not remain static (Forsyth, 1990).

Summary

Groups, as dynamic systems, change continually. Group development, or growth and change, occurs across the group's life span and operates at the group level. Group socialization, in contrast, is an individual process; over time the relationships among individuals in the group and the group itself change (Forsyth, 1990).

RESEARCH Taunton, R.L., & Otteman, D. (1986). The multiple dimensions of staff nurse
FOUNDATION role conception. *Journal of Nursing Administration, 16* (10), 31–37.

This research study looked at defining the staff nurse role conception, which is the expectations that staff nurses in hospitals hold for their own behavior and the behavior of other staff nurses in providing services to clients. The role conception includes personal and professional role expectations. Role concept is important to staff satisfaction, turnover, and retention.

The study was conducted in eight midwestern hospitals. Staff nurses ($N = 581$) responded to a questionnaire comprising 137 items on a Likert-type scale. Results were reviewed carefully to identify the most significant clusters. Results indicated seven major components of staff nurses' role conception: professional boundaries, job boundaries, direct patient services, authority relationships, autonomy, ethics, and billing and costs.

Findings from this study confirm the complexity of the staff nurse role conception. There is evidence that bureaucratic–professional role conflicts remain potential sources of stress for today's staff nurses and that operational definitions and instruments used by previous researchers do not reflect the real diversity of expectations among staff nurses. Data from this study can provide helpful information for nurse executives and nursing leaders to elucidate the dynamics of the hospital work environment for staff nurses. This research study is important to the new professional nurse who is developing a personal and professional concept of his or her role in any nursing organization.

REFERENCES

Barron, A. (1989). The clinical nurse specialist as consultant. In A. Hamric & J. Spross (Eds.), *The clinical nurse specialist in theory and practice* (2nd ed., pp. 126–128). Philadelphia: Saunders.

Brider, P. (1992). The move to patient-focused care. *American Journal of Nursing, 92* (9), 26–33.

Buckenham, M.A. (1988). Student nurse perception of the staff nurse role. *Journal of Advanced Nursing, 13*, 662–670.

Campbell, C.C. (1992). Redesigning the nursing organization. In T. Porter-O'Grady (Ed.), *Implementing shared governance* (pp. 53–57). St. Louis: Mosby–Year Book.

Carpenito, L.J. (1992). *Nursing diagnosis: Application to clinical practice* (4th ed.). Philadelphia: Lippincott.

Carr, N. (1988). Trust relationships. In S. Pinkerton & P. Schroeder (Eds.), *Commitment to excellence* (pp. 10–16). Gaithersburg, MD: Aspen.

Chaska, N.L. (1992). The staff nurse role. *Annual Review of Nursing Research, 10*, 185–203.

Cohen, E.L., & Cesta, T.G. (1993). *Nursing case management: From concept to evaluation.* St. Louis: Mosby–Year Book.

Douglass, L.M. (1992). *The effective nurse: Leader and manager* (4th ed.). St. Louis: Mosby–Year Book.

Fairbanks, J. (1991, June). *Team building: Essential to thriving in chaos.* Presented at the workshop for nursing managers, San Diego, CA.

Forsyth, D.R. (1990). *Group dynamics* (2nd ed.). Pacific Grove, CA: Brooks/Cole.

Hayes, P.M. (1992). Using group dynamics to manage nursing aides. *Health Care Supervisor, 11* (1), 16–20.

Luft, J. (1970). *Group processes: An introduction to group dynamics.* Palo Alto, CA: National Press Books.

Parker, G.M. (1990). *Team players and teamwork: The new competitive business strategy.* San Francisco: Jossey-Bass.

Parkman, C.A., & Loveridge, C. (1994). From nursing service to professional practice. *Nursing Management, 25* (3), 63–68.

Pinkerton, S., & Schroeder, P. (Eds.). (1988). *Commitment to excellence.* Gaithersburg, MD: Aspen.

Porter-O'Grady, T. (1991). Shared governance for nursing. Part II: Putting the organization into action. *AORN Journal, 53* (3), 694–703.

Porter-O'Grady, T. (Ed.). (1992). *Implementing shared governance: Creating a professional organization.* St. Louis: Mosby–Year Book.

Raudsepp, E. (1990). 7 ways to cure communications breakdown. *Nursing '90, 90* (4), 132, 134, 137–138, 142.

Schwartz, A.E. (1992). *Delegating authority.* New York: Barron's Educational Series.

Sovie, M. (1992). Care and service teams: A new imperative. *Nursing Economics, 10* (2), 94–100.

Stevens, B.J. (1983). *First-line patient care management* (2nd ed.). Gaithersburg, MD: Aspen.

Stichler, J.F. (1992). A conceptual basis for shared governance. In T. Porter-O'Grady (Ed.), *Implementing shared governance: Creating a professional organization* (pp. 1–24). St. Louis: Mosby–Year Book.

Taunton, R.L., & Otteman, D. (1986). The multiple dimensions of staff nurse role conception. *Journal of Nursing Administration, 16* (10), 31–37.

SUGGESTED READING

Loomis, M.E. (1979). *Group process for nurses.* St. Louis: Mosby.

Sinnen, M.T., & Schifalacque, M. (1991). Coordinated care in a community hospital. *Nursing Management, 22* (3), 38–42.

Ward, M.J., & Price, S.A. (1991). *Issues in nursing administration.* St. Louis: Mosby–Year Book.

Warner, M., Ford-Gilboe, M., Laforet-Fliesser, Y., Olson, J., & Ward-Griffin, C. (1994). The teamwork project: A collaborative approach to learning to nurse families. *Journal of Nursing Education, 33* (1), 5–13.

CHAPTER 6

Role of the Professional Nurse: Organizational Management

Susan H. Cummings

CHAPTER OUTLINE	**Management Problem Solving**	**Communication, Coaching, Consultation, and Coordination**

CHAPTER OBJECTIVES

At the completion of this chapter, the beginning professional nurse will be able to:

1. identify similarities and differences between patient care management and organizational management
2. describe key management skills and strategies to facilitate entry-level professional nurse roles
3. examine principles of communication, coordination, coaching, and counseling as they relate to organizational management
4. analyze the application of the four Cs (communication, consultation, coaching, and coordination) as they relate to organizational management in health care settings

CRITICAL You have been elected to represent your fellow staff members on the clinical
THINKING practice council. There have been many complaints on your unit about the
CHALLENGE timely availability of intravenous solutions and medications for patient care.
Your unit expects you to resolve the issue. What is your role in the council?
What is the council's role in the organization? How do you proceed with the
issue?

This chapter discusses the foundation for understanding the
management of organizations. Every nurse is a manager. Nurses manage the
care of patients whenever they practice. The problem-solving process and
skills used to communicate, coordinate, consult, and coach in caring for patients are easily transferable to nurses (with development of additional
knowledge and skill sets) in beginning professional nurse positions who have
assumed or will assume responsibility for organizational management.

Patient care management and organizational management have many
similarities. Both are based on a problem-solving framework, and in both
multiple process activities can occur simultaneously. The nursing process
focuses on appropriately managing the care of patients whose health care
requirements are amenable to nursing intervention. The management process focuses on facilitating individual and organizational objectives through
others.

MANAGEMENT PROBLEM SOLVING

Every nurse, whether in an organizationally sanctioned management role
or not, will be using organizational management skills with peers and other
colleagues in the provision of health care services that result in effective, efficient patient and organizational outcomes. Beginning professional nursing
positions are extremely divergent in both structure and responsibilities, but
problem-solving skills and their application are universal. **Problem solving**
in both patient and organizational management settings can be defined as a
process used when a gap is perceived between an existing state (what is) and
a desired state (what should be). It involves searching for information that
clarifies the problem and can be used to suggest alternative courses of action.
These alternatives are carefully evaluated, and an implementation strategy is
chosen. Once implemented, the solution is evaluated over time to determine
its effectiveness. If desired outcomes have not been reached and maintained,
some or all of the problem-solving processes are repeated.

The management problem-solving process follows traditional problem-
solving and nursing process steps, but the content of the questions that a
beginning professional nurse asks is modified to focus on organizational man-

agement issues. The problem definition must be within the scope of the beginning professional nurse's role responsibilities. Problems solved by beginning professional nurses often require immediate action, with solutions being guided by the framework of organizational policies and procedures. Questions to ask during problem solving fall into the following categories:

- Problem definition
  1. Do I have the authority to do something about this problem?
  2. What are the benefits of problem resolution?
- Information gathering
  1. Have I collected information systematically?
  2. Do I have enough information?
  3. Have I ignored or deleted extraneous information?
- Information analysis
  1. Can I categorize this information in terms of its reliability, importance, time sequence, and cause and effect relationships for this situation?
- Solution development
  1. Have I used data/information analysis in the generation of alternative courses of action?
  2. Have I involved participants in generating solutions if it would facilitate problem resolution?
- Decision making
  1. Have I considered the most feasible solution with the least perceived undesirable consequences?
- Implementation
  1. How will/have I involved staff?
  2. How can I facilitate change or overcome resistance to change?
- Evaluation of the solution
  1. How will outcomes be evaluated?
  2. How have I planned to ensure continued compliance with the implemented solutions?

Strategies utilized in management problem solving may be:

- trial and error, which involves trying one solution after another until a problem is resolved
- experimentation, which is often used with a new project when little is known about a problem or situation

- past experience, which involves repeating previous successes in similar situations but may ignore the use of negative past experiences that could be successfully adapted
- self-solution, which lets the problem run its course or uses the manager as a resource to facilitate participant solutions

ADJUNCTS TO PROBLEM SOLVING: POLICIES, PROCEDURES, AND STANDARDS

Policies, procedures, and standards assist professional nurses not only in clinical problem solving but in issues related to organizational management. **Policies** can be defined as statements that denote required actions for staff, and **procedures** describe practical steps to be taken for a specified action or purpose. **Nursing standards** are a "valid definition of the quality of nursing care that includes the criteria by which the effectiveness of care can be evaluated" (Mason, 1984, p. 2). Standards include process standards, which define quality related to implementation of care; content standards, which define nursing care's substance; and outcome standards, which define the expected changes in patients and the environment after nursing interventions take place. Internally defined standards can be used within a health care organization not only to guide nursing practice but in quality improvement, staff education, and research processes. External standards developed by professional organizations, such as nursing specialty associations, and accrediting bodies, such as the Joint Commission on Accreditation of Healthcare Organizations, can support both individual and organizational problem solving and positively affect quality. Refer to Chapter 9 for additional information about standards of care and standards of practice.

Policies, procedures, and institutional standards must be readily available for staff use on patient care units if they are to serve their purpose to promote standardization, positively support quality, and reduce risk liability. Effective policies, procedures, and institutional standards are reviewed periodically to ensure their relevance and currency. Clinical staff nurses should be involved in the development and review processes. Many organizations, especially those with staff empowerment models, have markedly reduced the number of policies and procedures to those required by accrediting agencies and regulatory bodies. These organizations have utilized current professional textbooks as references for standards of care and procedural information.

BORROWING IDEAS FROM INDUSTRY

Management ideas from industry can be helpful in organizational problem solving. If they are used indiscriminately, however, they could be a detriment to health care organizations. Peters (1987) encourages creative swiping of ideas, but those in beginning leadership positions must evaluate whether the ideas can be adapted to fit in their organization. Key questions to ask include the following:

- Will the ideas support the mission, values, and philosophy of the organization?
- Are the ideas compatible with organizational resources?
- Will the ideas facilitate individual patient and organizational outcomes and service satisfaction levels as perceived by key stakeholders, those individuals or groups who have a unique perspective of and a vested interest in the issue (i.e., staff, patients, families, physicians, third party payers, and the community)?

LEARNING CHALLENGE   One of the challenges in today's health care organizations is to determine how institutional goals are accomplished in an organization. Determine who or what group has responsibility for the accomplishment of organizational goals on the unit where you are assigned for clinical or management laboratory experience. Validate your findings with a peer or your instructor.

RISK MANAGEMENT

Risk management focuses on organizational activities aimed at preventing loss and thereby conserving institutional financial resources. These activities focus on risk financing through liability insurance, loss reduction when untoward events occur, and prevention of patient and employee injury. Risk management, like problem solving, includes risk identification, analysis, implementation activities, and evaluation. Risk identification is accomplished by review of the organization's previous claims, incident or occurrence reporting and screening, and the linkages with patient representative and quality assessment and utilization review activities inherent in integrated quality management programs in health care settings. Data analysis is facilitated by collection of meaningful data and their transformation into information through review by clinical and managerial experts. In-depth analysis of individual events as well as trended data and occurrences is imperative. Confidentiality of data is of the utmost concern to those charged with responsibilities for risk management activities in an organization. Data collection and analysis can be facilitated by information support and integration of data collection into already performed activities. Implementation of risk management activities focuses on:

- loss prevention or remedial actions to decrease the frequency of potential/actual losses (e.g., sponge, needle, and instrument counts in operating rooms)
- reduction of financial losses through effective claims management
- risk avoidance through nonperformance of high-risk procedures
- risk financing through self-insurance or commercial general and professional liability insurance
- evaluation, including frequency of reporting of risks and currency/applicability of policies and procedures
- ongoing education and communication for all staff in the health care organization as well as for the medical staff

The governing body of a health care organization must provide both resources and support for risk management activities. Although it is not an expectation of the beginning professional nurse in most health care settings to orchestrate risk management activities, it is imperative that beginning professional nurses understand potential areas for risk management and their responsibilities in preventing or reporting potential risk management occurrences. Risk management activities in most organizations focus on:

- the physical plant and equipment
- workers' compensation/employee benefits
- general and professional liability
- risk financing and claims management

Beginning professional nurses can assume responsibility for participation in educational activities that identify actual or potential sources of patient injury as well as strategies to decrease or eradicate potential sources of adverse occurrences. Nurses' routine daily activities in clinical practice, such as documentation, compliance with standards of practice (including safety and infection control standards), and prompt reporting of events that may place the individual practitioner or the organization at risk, are imperative links in a successful risk management program.

Confidentiality of patient information is becoming a growing concern from a liability risk management perspective as increasing numbers of institutions automate the medical record and develop interfacility systemwide databases of patient information. The beginning professional nurse with organizational management responsibilities must ensure that established policies and procedures related to access codes, protection of patient information, and release of information to internal and external sources are available and followed by those who are providing and supporting the provision of patient care. Nurses with responsibilities for organizational management should participate in the organizational development of policies and procedures that focus on access codes for job roles that differentiate functions such as data entry, deletion, viewing, and modification; acquisition and deletion of access codes or passwords; disciplinary action for noncompliance; authorization and methods for release of information; and prevention of unauthorized use or modification of data or the system (Gobis, 1994). Risk is increased with an automated medical record through the potential for unauthorized or accidental disclosure of information, document alteration, or entry of inaccurate information. Nurses in partnership with all systems users and vendors can protect patient information and create automated clinical records that are credible and integrated.

Maintaining one's own competency, participating in peer review, and facilitating the competency of other caregivers are important responsibilities of the beginning professional nurse. When the beginning professional nurse moves into a role with responsibility for organizational management, he or she must recognize that the primary source of potential liability for the nurse manager is staff selection and ongoing development of staff (Pelle, 1988). Individual professional nurses have a responsibility to be competent and actively participate in peer review.

Staff also are an invaluable asset in identifying risks and opportunities to reduce them because they are directly responsible for the provision of care. Parks (1994) encourages nurse managers not only to learn about risk management and practice strategies to avoid litigation but to also develop strategies to manage future exposures if untoward situations or outcomes occur. Although risk management involves total organizational involvement, nurse managers at the point of service or care delivery can learn to assess and manage risk as an adjunct to organizational mandates to provide quality, cost-efficient care.

LEGAL ISSUES IN NURSING

Laws provide protection for both patients and nurses. Law is defined by Creighton (1986) as those standards of human conduct that are established and enforced by the authority of an organized society through its government. Law originates from statutes enacted by legislative bodies, common or decisional law generated from judicial decisions, and administrative law created by administrative agencies that determine rules and regulations that have the force of law. Laws governing nursing focus on topics such as licensure, patients and physicians, responsibilities to the public, and responsibilities for documentation and reporting.

All states require nurses to be licensed. The licensure process facilitates minimum standards of practice, which aid in protecting the public from harm. One of the functions of nurses with responsibility for organizational management is ensuring that all nursing employees are currently licensed. Nurse practice acts delineate the definition of nursing, roles, responsibilities, and activities that may be performed within the scope of the nursing license. Specific questions regarding nursing practice and licensure requirements in a particular state should be addressed to the regulatory agency responsible for nursing licensure. State regulatory agencies are also responsible for disciplinary actions related to licensees and ongoing performance of individual nurses.

Nurses with responsibility for organizational management functions must also be aware of civil rights acts that forbid discrimination in employment practices; refer to Chapter 10 for further discussion. Compliance with Occupational Safety and Health Act requirements (Public Law 91-596) and workers' compensation laws (Creighton, 1986) as well as control of nursing care quality are additional responsibilities of nurses. Workers' compensation policies should be reviewed so that the beginning professional nurse can initiate the reporting process for work-related injuries.

Nurses with responsibility for organizational management must also be cognizant of requirements imposed by the Occupational Safety and Health Administration (OSHA; Department of Health and Human Services, 1988) as well as state health licensing boards. OSHA is responsible for communicating and enforcing standards related to work environments that are aimed at positively affecting occupational safety and reducing or controlling workplace hazards that might result in worker injury or harm. OSHA has the authority to inspect workplaces, give citations, and levy fines for noncompliance. OSHA also provides free consultation to facilitate healthier workplaces. The designated safety officer in a health care organization can be a resource to the beginning professional nurse with organizational management responsibilities related to issues concerning occupational safety.

Another area of concern for beginning professional nurses with organizational management responsibility is a recent decision by the U.S. Supreme Court that calls into question which nurses can be viewed legally as supervisors, an issue in patient care delivery models where nurses delegate care activities to others. The Supreme Court decision questions the eligibility of nurses to participate in collective bargaining units if they are involved in delegation of patient care tasks to nursing team members (DiMotto, 1994). This issue is best referred to the health care organization's legal counsel for discussion and recommendations.

Nursing's legal responsibilities to patients, physicians, and the public are multiple. Nurses' legal responsibilities to patients include avoidance of negligent care, avoidance of unlawful restraint, protection of the patient from injury, obtaining informed consent, maintaining confidentiality of information and the right to privacy, prompt assessment of patients, and appropriate reporting and documentation of the patient's condition. The beginning professional nurse with responsibilities for organizational management is encouraged to review information related to patient rights and informed consent in the state where he or she is practicing. Maintaining confidentiality of information must also be addressed in this age of computerization and electronic transmission of data, a topic discussed previously in this chapter. Health care organizations must also establish policies related to electronic transmission of information. Some health care organizations have included permission to fax information in their conditions of admission. Standing orders, needle and sponge counts in the operating room, verbal orders, and protection of patients from incompetent physicians are areas commonly addressed in discussions of legal responsibilities related to nursing's relationship to physicians. In addition, nurses must protect the community from dangerous patients, especially those eloping from psychiatric facilities. Nurses are also responsible for reporting specific types of information to public health agencies, such as communicable diseases and child or elder abuse.

The purpose of this discussion is not to provide specific information about legal aspects of nursing and risk management but to enhance awareness so that nurses with organizational management responsibilities can identify and utilize appropriate human and material resources to control risk liability and enhance quality care. Ongoing education for nurses in organizational settings is imperative to enhance their knowledge and understanding of legal and risk management issues that affect nursing practice. Laws and legislation related to health care and nursing are changing rapidly. Nurses in leadership/management roles must also keep abreast of changes affecting health care and nursing practice and participate in activities that have a positive impact on legislative outcomes related to improvement of health care.

DELEGATION

Concepts related to delegation are discussed in Chapter 5. This information is equally applicable to nurses who are delegating tasks or projects related to organizational management activities within the health care organization.

Delegation of organizational management activities is effective when the delegator has time to instruct or coach the delegatee, when there is a margin for error, and when the delegated activity is part of a staff member's development plan or a clearly stated job expectation of the delegatee. Tasks and projects should not be delegated just to get rid of unpleasant jobs, if the time allotted for completion is not long enough for successful completion of the project by the delegatee, if the task is clearly the delegator's role, or if lack of clarity precludes a clear explanation to the delegatee. Just as with patient care activities, effective delegation of organizational management activities is a useful time management activity, allows more work to be completed effectively and efficiently, and can be a proactive developmental experience for the delegatee.

The meaning of delegation in a bureaucratic organization and in an empowered organization requires an understanding of the processes used in both types of organizations.

COMPARISON OF OLD PARADIGM (BUREAUCRACY) AND NEW PARADIGM (EMPOWERED ORGANIZATION)

Old Paradigm (Bureaucracy)

Organizations throughout the United States, including those in health care, are in a transitional period as society passes from an industrial to a sociotechnological information age. Management leadership activities have used problem solving within a traditional framework, identified by Fayol (1925), of planning, organizing, commanding, coordinating, and controlling that has been modified to planning, organizing, staffing, directing, and controlling. Many organizations today are still organized around Weber's (1947) beliefs that a bureaucratic organization with centralized control maximizes efficiency. Bureaucratic organizations, with their many layers and hierarchies of control (see Chapter 1), function based on clearly defined sets of policies and procedures, and communication is vertical within the hierarchy. Policymaking, goal setting, and other organizational mandates are created at the top of the organization; managers at other levels of the organization see that the rules, regulations, policies, and procedures are carried out.

The beginning professional nurse's role in this structure has been to follow directions and contribute to the development of policies by committees. Within a bureaucratic organization, the professional nurse can expect the manager's role to focus on directing, controlling, finding problems, and supervising subordinates' behavior at the unit level. The role focus has been to process information up and down the organization, make operational decisions, and be a content expert and giver of orders.

New Paradigm (Empowered Organization)

Professional nurses' needs create a dichotomy in most health care organizations. In response to this need, empowered organizations in nursing have been structured through either shared governance models or self-directed work teams. Shared governance models (Smith, 1992) are accountability-based governance systems that share power, control, and decision making with the professional nurse. In these models, both managers and professional nurses have power and share decision making to facilitate attainment of clinical and organizational outcomes. The professional nurse is responsible for operationalizing the clinical accountabilities of the profession (i.e., practice, competency, quality, and research), and the manager is responsible for the professional accountability of resource management (i.e., coordination, facilitation, and integration of human, material, fiscal, service, and support resources). The nurse executive is responsible for ensuring that the organizational needs for nursing services are met.

Within a clinical decision-making framework, the professional nurse takes responsibility, exercises initiative, is accountable, and has the power to implement decisions in his or her clinical area related to practice, quality, competence, and research. The manager's role in a staff empowerment model is to coordinate, integrate, and facilitate human, fiscal, material, support, and system resources and to participate in decision-making forums for issues that support practice. The nurse executive's role is to create the organizational climate that supports empowerment, act as a facilitator and integrator, and participate in executive management of the hospital. Within this framework, the nurse manager's and nurse executive's role implementation focuses on systems issues, professional nurses as colleagues and peers, interactive problem solving, and coaching to enhance performance and attainment of outcomes.

Self-directed work teams are groups of employees who are fully responsible for completing a segment of work (Orsburn et al., 1990). Usually, membership on self-directed work teams includes all the staff providing or supporting patient care in a particular organizational setting (e.g., patient care unit, clinic, home health agency, etc.). Within this framework, the staff gradually assume roles and make decisions that previously were carried out by a manager. These functions usually include, but are not limited to, managing personnel issues, including hiring and performance evaluations, and production and service delivery processes on the patient care unit (Wellins, Byhom, & Wilson, 1991). The manager in this model is a resource and coach and provides linkages to the organization as a whole.

These new models support clinical and organization outcomes and radically change the structure of the organization, administrative and management roles, and how the work gets done. New paradigm (empowered) organizations have a flat administrative structure with one or two management roles between the staff nurse and nurse executive. Empowered organizations, both in health care and in other organizations in the United States, are structured around groups, not individuals, with rewards and recognition being focused on team as well as individual outcomes. Team members are often multiskilled and function within limited numbers of job categories with flexible, ever-evolving roles. Information flows in all directions throughout the organization, not in the traditional organization's top-down fashion. Information in empowered organizations is available to employees at the point of production or service so that they can more effectively manage processes and outcomes.

KEY CONCEPT   Key characteristics of staff empowerment models are:

- an environment that supports staff decision making
- activities that focus on common goals
- activities that focus on quality, cost, service, and satisfaction outcomes

Shared governance and self-directed work teams are examples of transitional structures that will support the societal movement from the industrial age to the information age. As the transition continues, nurses need to be cognizant that forums are available in the organization for them to voice their concerns and to operationalize the professional accountabilities of nursing (practice, competency, quality, resource management, and research) for both staff and managers.

COMMUNICATION, COACHING, CONSULTATION, AND COORDINATION

Communication, coaching, consultation, and coordination are key skills for the success of those performing entry-level management functions in all organizational environments. For the purpose of this discussion, the following definitions have been selected:

- communication—the exchange of ideas and information
- coaching—interactive processes to facilitate improvement of employee performance (Orth, Wilkinson, & Benfari, 1990)
- consultation—interactional process among professions to solve workplace problems and to enhance the ability to transfer skills to similar situations (Caplan, 1970)
- coordination—synchronization of activities toward established goals (Rowland & Rowland, 1992)

Communication

Effective **communication** is a key success factor in organizational management. The goal of communication is to increase understanding, not necessarily to facilitate agreement with the originator of the communication. The beginning professional nurse can implement communication strategies that enhance effective interactions and self-esteem and support individual and organizational development and outcome attainment. Principles and effective strategies for communication are discussed in Chapter 5 as they relate to the role of the beginning professional nurse in management of patient care. This discussion focuses on various communication skills within the context of organizational management activities that may be carried out by the beginning professional nurse.

Active Listening

Become a compulsive listener. Successful leaders who engage others in their cause do it by listening, not by talking and giving orders (Peters, 1987). Listening to those who work with you as well as patients will provide invaluable information about the stumbling blocks to enhancing quality and service satisfaction. This information can provide insights for the beginning professional nurse about organizational management strategies to improve consumer service and organizational outcomes. The beginning professional nurse can ask basic questions, such as "Why do we need three copies of a form for ordering lab tests when two are thrown away?" "Can the cross-trained health care team member who delivers and collects food trays also record oral intake and output?" "Can the housekeeper be unit based and make all the unoccupied beds on the unit?" and "What one thing would enhance a patient's service satisfaction level?" Refer to Chapter 5 for further discussion of active listening techniques.

Psychiatric mental health nursing textbooks as well as business communication texts can also provide interested readers with additional information and strategies to sharpen listening skills. The same listening skills used in patient care management are applicable when one is engaging in organizational management activities.

Speaking, Telephone, and Presentation Skills

Well-developed speaking skills are also vital to the beginning professional nurse as organizational management responsibilities are assumed. Listen carefully, and then send direct, specific messages that are verbally and nonverbally congruent. Present clear, concise information that is tailored to the audience. Engage in discussion and dialogue so that others can express their ideas. Allow time and opportunities for others to ask questions, and be sure that you ask questions to gather information or suggestions, emphasize a point, elicit support for a project, or encourage a change in behavior.

Written Communication

The beginning professional nurse may send written communication through electronic mail as well as correspondence formatted as minutes of meetings, memos, letters, reports, or project proposals. Written communication is often used in conjunction with verbal interactions. Writing puts one's expressions or thoughts in a permanent form. Effective written communication is clear and concise and reflects the culture of the organization. Considering the questions who, what, how, when, and where often provides the basic structure for written communication composed by the beginning professional nurse carrying out organizational management responsibilities. If replies to correspondence are required, the nurse should make certain that this expectation is communicated in the correspondence.

KEY CONCEPT

Written communication in organizational management:
- clear
- concise
- reflects organizational outcomes

LEARNING CHALLENGE

1. Play the game of telephone. Compare the content of the message repeated multiple times with the original message. Identify three strategies to facilitate clear communication and enhance active listening when one is carrying out organizational management functions. Share your experiences and strategies with your peers.
2. As a beginning professional nurse with organizational management responsibilities, you have just concluded a staff meeting where the staff's perpetual lateness has been discussed. You have agreed to prepare a memo summarizing the discussion and proposed solutions. The memo will be distributed to both the nursing staff and the patient care unit supervisor. Using the framework for written communication (clear, concise, and reflecting organizational outcomes), write the memo focusing on the questions who, what, when, where, and how. Critique your memo with a peer.

Communication in Organizations

Communication in new paradigm organizations may be predominantly horizontal and across departments or teams as opposed to the more formal, often vertical communication that occurs in organizational structures of a more traditional organization. Employees in new paradigm organizations must receive information about organizational performance, including operating results, competitor performance, and quality indicator and benchmark data to manage patient care effectively and facilitate the attainment of organizational outcomes. "Just in time" communication about how to use information is crucial to broaden employees' knowledge, skills, and problem-solving capabilities. For example, "just in time" communication about how to interpret budget reports would occur at the beginning of the staff meeting when monthly budget reports will first be reviewed by the staff. Employees who have the necessary information to make data-based decisions will influence the direction and performance of the organization both at the time health care services are provided and through their participation in self-managed work teams and quality forums (Bowen & Lawlor, 1992).

It is often helpful to understand the communication that occurs within the organization's "grapevine" and to learn who the reliable sources of information are within the context of this informal, ever-changing communication chain, which has no relationship to the formal organizational structure. The beginning professional nurse with organizational management responsibilities should become aware of formal and informal communication channels and networks within the framework of the organizational structure and the culture of the employing organization because they can have a favorable impact on the effectiveness and efficiency of communication.

Gender Issues in Communication

Cultural distinctions between genders reflect a society's beliefs and perceptions about what is male and female. Goffman (1979) tells us that gender is "one of the most deeply seated traits of man. We create masculinity and femininity in our ways of behaving, all the while believing we are simply acting normally" (p. 7). Because these perceptions have been accepted as the cultural norm, there are numerous implications for communications between the sexes in the workplace. Nursing is predominantly a female profession. Nurses, irrespective of their role in the organization, work in an environment where they continually interact with men. Men in leadership positions in nursing and health care must also interact in ways that are sensitive to gender differences in communication in the workplace. Peters (1990) asserts, "gone are the days of women succeeding by learning to play men's games. Instead the time has come for men to move to learn to play women's games" (p. 142).

Tannen (1990) views male and female differences from the perspective of gender differences in communication styles. If women, who tend to speak and hear a language of connection and intimacy, and men, who tend to speak and hear a language of status and independence, notice that interactions between them are difficult to understand, it is because they are speaking different "genderlects."

Supporting effective cross-gender communication focuses on accepting differences without placing blame, opening the lines of communication, and changing one's style when one decides to match the style of the opposite gender. As you already have learned, successful communication is predicated on assessing the goals and processes of communication, that is, focusing on the sender, the message, the receiver, and the interpretation of the message. When communicating, men are often more effective at addressing and attending to the task goal of communication, whereas women are often more focused on the interaction itself.

Nurse–Physician Communication

Effective nurse–physician communication is imperative to nursing's success. Stein (1967), in his classic article "The Doctor Nurse Game," reviews patterns of physician–nurse communication and their impact on effective communication. The game focuses on communication that avoids open conflict between nurses and physicians. Nurses ask questions and convey subtle hints rather than directly making suggestions to physicians about concerns that affect a patient's care. The game preserves the notion of the omniscient physician and the concept that nurses can and should contribute information to physicians. Stein concludes that, although the game has been supported by medical and nursing educational models as well as sexually stereotyped roles of the dominant male and passive female in our society, it is anti-intellectual and inhibits open communication. He further states, "The game is a transactional neurosis and both professions would enhance themselves by taking steps to change the attitudes which breed the game" (p. 703). Although the game was first described in relation to physician-nurse communication in patient situations, it has often been played in nurse–physician interactions related to issues of organizational management that affect patient care.

Strategies for successful communication with physicians include the following:

- Consider yourself and the physician partners on the health care team.
- Focus on the task or issue, not personal differences.
- Maintain improvement of patient care as the goal for the interaction.
- Establish clear roles for the physician, staff, and yourself.
- Communicate assertively.

Assertive Communication

All of us can be passive, aggressive, or assertive depending on our communication skills, the situation, our role, our mood, and our level of self-actualization. Assertive behaviors can be defined simply as standing up for oneself without violating the rights of others. Assertive communication involves direct, considerate, nonmanipulative, creative interpersonal interactions. Passive and aggressive behaviors are often viewed as manifestations of low self-esteem and demonstrate one's need to control others, whether it be their behavior, perceptions, or feelings. In the work setting these behaviors are burdened with blame, resentment, withdrawal, anger, retaliation, and decreased trust and communication. In addition, nonassertive, passive, or aggressive behaviors usually affect the work group, as evidenced by decreased productivity, motivation, and cooperation. Review of these communication patterns and effective nonverbal and verbal communication strategies can be found in psychiatric mental health textbooks. Beginning professional nurses can use assertive behavior in situations where their role includes involvement in organizational management, such as giving compliments, receiving compliments, giving criticism, and setting boundaries.

Constructive Feedback

Feedback is given to help others change their behavior or to enhance or reinforce performance that meets or exceeds standards. Be sure that feedback, whether it is positive or in the form of constructive criticism, is planned, is specific and criterion referenced, is given with empathy, offers suggestions or alternatives, and elicits commitment to change or continued behaviors.

When confronting others or offering constructive criticism, it is important for the beginning professional nurse to realize that the criticism will usually not be viewed as constructive by the person receiving it. Find an appropriate time and a private location for giving constructive feedback. Confrontation and giving constructive feedback are easier and more effective if you, as a beginning professional nurse, have developed trust and respect and have given the individual or group positive feedback in the past. Let the health care team member know that you allow mistakes and at the same time encourage excellence. Avoid value judgments such as "You're rude," indirect feedback such as "Someone isn't completing the work," or a lecture such as "How could you have forgotten to have that medication checked?" Instead, use the following framework for giving direct, constructive criticism:

1. Describe the situation.
2. Describe how you felt.

3. Describe the consequences.
4. Tell the other person what you want done about it.

Stated differently, you can phrase your comments as follows:

When you _____
I feel _____
And then _____
So would you please _____

Beginning professional nurses and other health care team members should invite feedback, listen to understand, and ask for examples. It is helpful to separate the information from the person giving the feedback and to paraphrase what you think has been said to clarify understanding. Thank the person for giving the feedback. Feedback from others is received as information. If the feedback is uncomfortable, respond with a neutral comment such as "I'll think about it." The last step in receiving feedback is to set behavioral goals for improvement. Remember, constructive feedback should motivate the receiver to continue or develop effective behaviors or to decrease negative behavior.

Beginning professional nurses may find themselves participating in or facilitating discussion of team performance. Once performance standards have been established for the team (see Chapter 5), team members should discuss their performance regularly within the context of determining what is facilitating success and opportunities for improvement. When one is verbalizing feedback about team performance, statements such as "Our self-scheduling of staff has improved. For the last month we have maintained our quality standards and have staffed within the dollars allotted for staffing. We should continue tracking our standards and staffing costs daily" are more helpful than "Things aren't going well. We are making too many mistakes."

Team performance should be discussed by team members periodically and when opportunities to improve have been identified by the group or a member of the group. It is important to plan time for these discussions, which should focus on the group, not clinical or organizational issues. Newly developed work teams often schedule daily performance checks, often at the change of shift.

Responses to Perceived Negative Communication

Confrontation, although sometimes perceived as negative, often simply involves a face-to-face meeting to look at a problem. The beginning professional nurse, when faced with confrontational situations, can respond by pointing out behaviors and eliciting assistance in the problem-solving process. When a health care team member states "This is the most unfair assignment I've ever had. Jane has one difficult patient and I have six," the beginning professional nurse can respond by asking "What would you like to see done differently?" or "Are you aware that _____. My expectation is _____." Both responses by the beginning professional nurse can facilitate the problem-solving process and provide opportunities to state expectations, make requests, and set boundaries when communicating with health care team members.

KEY CONCEPTS   Key characteristics of successful performance feedback include the following:

- It is planned.
- It is specific and criterion referenced.
- It is given with empathy.
- It offers suggestions and alternatives.
- It elicits commitment to effective behaviors.

Key behaviors for receiving performance feedback are as follows:

- Invite feedback.
- Listen with understanding.
- Ask for examples to clarify understanding.
- Treat feedback as information.
- Set behavioral goals for improvement.

LEARNING CHALLENGE   Think about a time when you received performance feedback that was helpful. Describe it. Think about performance feedback that was not helpful. How would you characterize it? Discuss your thoughts with your peers, and identify key characteristics of helpful and unhelpful feedback that can be applied in the health care setting by the beginning professional nurse carrying out operational management functions.

Conflict Resolution

Beginning professional nurses often must facilitate the resolution of conflict between health care team members. Conflict in the health care setting can be caused by competition for control of resources, the need to belong or the need for recognition, or differences in values. In addition, beginning professional nurses must also cope with organizational conflict. Individual conflict almost always involves a high level of emotion. Bolton (1986) offers a useful template for facilitating conflict resolution:

1. Respect the other person. Listen until the other's point of view is understood.
2. Paraphrase what has been said.
3. State your own issues, feelings, and needs.
4. Ask yourself "What have I learned from the situation?"

Most interpersonal conflicts between health team members can be resolved by the members themselves. When emotions are heightened, however, the beginning professional nurse may need to facilitate or mediate the conflict resolution process. Conflict resolution is really about problem solving and attaining resolution to a struggle about ideas, feelings, or actions.

KEY CONCEPT Helpful strategies for the beginning professional nurse to facilitate conflict resolution include the following:

- Protect each person's self-respect.
- Focus on issues, not personalities.
- Do not blame participants for the problem.
- Encourage open and complete discussion of the issues.
- Allow equal time for all parties to participate.
- Encourage expression of both positive and negative feelings.
- Encourage active listening and understanding among all parties.
- Summarize key themes in the discussion.
- Assist in the development of alternative solutions.
- At a later point in time:
  1. Follow up on progress in resolution of the conflict.
  2. Give positive feedback related to problem-solving styles.

The beginning professional nurse may actively participate in the process of mediation, in which those involved in a dispute meet with a neutral third party (the beginning professional nurse), who assists in resolving their conflict. Mediators help disputing people attempt to resolve their differences by:

- seeking commonly shared interests and striving for a gain–gain situation, not a win–win situation
- listening to both sides of the story to determine what the parties really want
- asking questions about what happened to clarify statements
- remaining neutral and impartial and not offering personal opinions
- guiding those involved away from placing blame and toward emphasizing future behaviors

- offering suggestions, choices, options, and alternatives
- reframing information in a form that can lead to a satisfactory solution
- maintaining a balance of power between those involved
- providing access to resources
- modeling open, nondefensive behavior and direct, courteous communication

When the beginning professional nurse is involved in assisting others to resolve their conflicts, it is important to realize that those involved in a conflict have the ability to resolve it. Assisting them to utilize their own resources to reach a solution will increase the likelihood of their supporting an agreement. Participating in successful conflict resolutions will also benefit the participants' learning related to resolution of conflict in the future.

LEARNING CHALLENGE You are a member of the patient care unit scheduling committee. It has come to the committee's attention that more than 50% of the staff have scheduled their vacations during August and that several of the staff have purchased nonrefundable tickets for travel. No one is willing to change vacation plans. Describe the committee's proposal for resolution of this conflict. What factors will affect the committee's decision? Discuss your thoughts about this situation with your peers.

Organizational Conflict

Although the beginning professional nurse will probably not be actively involved in the resolution of organizational conflict, understanding symptoms, causes, and strategies to resolve conflict will assist the beginning professional nurse in coping with it.

Symptoms of organizational conflict usually involve the following (Handy, 1993):

- inadequate communication laterally and vertically within an organization (this phenomenon can happen in both traditional and empowered organizations if two groups are working at cross-purposes)
- intergroup hostility and jealousy and interpersonal friction that results in focusing on people and personalities, not issues
- escalation of the level of conflict from a unit to an organizational issue
- proliferation of policies, procedures, rules, and regulations that paralyze independent action without approval
- decreased morale due to lack of ability to take action

Effective conflict management in an organization must look at determining the root causes of the conflict before strategies are implemented to resolve it. Organizational conflict is usually related to goals and ideologies or territorial issues (Handy, 1993). Goals and ideologies lead to conflict when work groups have divergent goals that adversely affect the groups, when roles are ambiguous, or when roles change and are subsequently perceived as less important. Organizational conflict caused by territorial issues should be viewed from a psychological prospective. If one's job role is questioned or taken away, conflict will develop. Functional issues also emerge in organizations after structural realignments because individuals must explore and define their new positions. Conflict in organizations can also result from territorial jealousy related to perceived status symbols (e.g., space) and access to information that is not readily available. Organizational conflict usually results in distorted information, imposition of additional rules and regulations, and control of rewards.

Conflict is often managed by reframing the conflict as competition or attempting to control it. Creating environments that support collaborative interaction can be used to manage conflict successfully if the organization has clear goals, a vision, and action plans. In these environments, information must be available about progress toward goal attainment and risk taking, and failure must be accepted.

Conflict can also be controlled in an organization by trying to resolve it at the lowest point in the organization, that is, closest to where the service is provided or the product is produced. Other conflict resolution strategies can include negotiating rules and procedures, creating an organizational role to resolve conflict, separating the conflicting parties (which is a temporary solution), and ignoring the conflict (which can impede productivity or role negotiation).

Role Clarification

Role concerns usually are related to ambiguity (expectations are not clearly defined), which is becoming more common in today's organizations, where change constantly alters roles (Neubauer, 1994). Questions in role negotiation include the following (Rubin, Fry, & Ploonick, 1976):

- What do I want/need from you?
- What do you want/need from me?
- What am I willing to do to help your success?
- What are you willing to do to aid my success?

Once these questions have been answered, other questions that focus on what behaviors should be continued, discontinued, or increased facilitate additional role clarification.

The beginning professional nurse may use these role negotiation questions as a tool to clarify and manage conflict arising from role ambiguity within the patient care work group, with other services or departments, and with physicians. Role clarification does not cause role conflict to disappear; it does, however, allow for discussion and negotiation.

Negotiation

Negotiation occurs when two or more people or groups with conflicting interests come together to discuss options for the purpose of reaching an agreement. Negotiation usually involves three critical elements (Cohen, 1980):

1. *Information*—It is key to ask questions to clarify the solution being negotiated.
2. *Time*—Patience is required in negotiation because many negotiations occur at the last possible moment.
3. *Power*—The other side's power is usually perceived to be greater than your own. Power is based on perceptions, however, so if you perceive that you have power, you do.

In the final analysis, negotiation really is about finding out what the other side wants, showing the other side how to get it, and at the same time getting what you want. Four strategies are key to successful negotiation (Fisher & Ury, 1981):

1. *Separate the people from the problem.* Negotiation is really a problem-solving strategy. The beginning professional nurse should focus on the problem or issue rather than on the people, who as a result of their intense emotions during the period of conflict may not be communicating effectively.
2. *Focus on interests not positions.* Focusing on people's interests rather than their positions (e.g., discussing how 12-hour shifts are more efficient in providing care than 8-hour shifts rather than participants' positions on the issue) frees the participants to look at commonalities, which may facilitate an agreement that meets their underlying interests related to more effective patient care.
3. *Invent options for mutual gain.* Pressure from both time constraints and the desire to seek a solution often inhibits generation of multiple alternatives for an optimal solution. Plan time for developing multiple solutions that focus on shared interests.
4. *Insist on using objective criteria.* Using a fair standard, an expert opinion, an industry standard, or a law facilitates decisions that are based on objective criteria.

Negotiation involves both parties stating their own interests and respecting the other's in an attempt to reach a mutually agreeable solution that is perceived as a gain–gain outcome.

LEARNING You have been asked to complete policies and procedures related to the
CHALLENGE disposal of hazardous waste of chemotherapy, and you have not been able to find time to complete them because of your patient care responsibilities. Negotiate with your manager strategies to facilitate their completion by the next clinical practice council meeting, which is 3 days away. Role play this situation with a peer. Ask an observer to validate your utilization of negotiation strategies.

Coaching

Coaching is effective in supporting professional development, giving recognition, and facilitating improvement in clinical performance. Coaching involves two distinct processes: short-term coaching, to assist with socialization and learning of new skills, and long-term coaching, to cope with corrective behavioral situations. Both types of coaching not only can result in performance improvements but can be strategies that increase retention and productivity or appropriate turnover of staff.

Short-Term Coaching for Developmental Opportunities

The beginning professional nurse observes opportunities to expand a health team member's experiences or skills and engages in the interactive process of coaching. Successful beginning professional nurses who use this technique view the educational process as important and helpful and as a developmental opportunity, not as an opportunity for evaluation or criticism. Using the same strategies as a sports coach, the nurse identifies opportunities for employees to develop new skills or enhance their performance. The coach guides the interactive problem-solving process and uses constructive feedback to develop or improve effective behavior, facilitate problem solving, and enhance individual effectiveness.

Key questions to consider when one is contemplating the use of a coaching strategy include the following:

- What do the staff need to know or do to enhance their ability to provide quality, cost-effective patient care that also results in customer and staff satisfaction?
- What resources, internal and external, are available to support the staff's development?
- How can those in staff support roles (e.g., educators and advanced practice nurses) work with me to develop staff?

- How can I utilize my superior to facilitate my own and the staff's development?

The role of the beginning staff nurse can also be to participate in coaching to facilitate the development of empowered forums within a shared governance model. Coaching is also critical in the implementation of shared governance or self-directed work teams. The coach spontaneously assists the team members in development and apprises them of their progress. Teams develop and pass through similar stages as groups in their maturation. For further information, see Chapter 5. Coaching teams is facilitated by "just in time" education, which is teaching a new skill or providing information about a process for which the team is responsible as close as possible to the time when the members will need it, and facilitation of interactive problem solving, which is delivered at the appropriate point in the team's development.

Long-Term Coaching To Correct Performance Deficiencies

Quick (1985) views coaching as a process that incorporates:

- data gathering through behavioral observations, evaluation of past work, educational experiences, and employee input
- determination of what is possible for individual employees or groups in terms of attainment of their human potential
- the coaching interview, which supports employee growth and development

It is helpful to determine and recognize whether the deficient behavior or opportunity to improve is related to performance or motivational deficits. Key questions to ask are the following:

- Is the deficiency creating a performance or outcome problem?
- Will it disappear if ignored?
- Is it due to lack of skill or compliance (motivation)?

If past performance has been at an acceptable standard, the problem may be one of motivation. If past performance has not been acceptable, the problem may be one of skill. Regardless of the cause, the beginning professional nurse's coaching activities focus on performance improvement. If unacceptable performance is related to lack of skill, coaching activities may include training, bedside coaching, or process simplification. If unacceptable performance is related to motivation, desired performance should be recognized with rewards that are valued by employees (Fournies, 1978).

Coaching to correct a performance deficiency is usually focused on a specific behavior and is planned, not spontaneous. Orth et al. (1990) reinforce this concept by stating that coaching to correct performance involves assisting employees over time to improve behavior to the level of their potential. Coaching models are based on interactive problem solving.

Before a formal coaching session, it is vital for the coach to identify the desired outcome of the session. Performance standards must be clearly articulated, and the employee must be given accurate feedback about current performance and opportunities for improvement. Effective developmental plans are best created with the employee. Progress is monitored once both the coach and the employee have agreed to the plan and it has been implemented. Both positive and corrective feedback should be provided during the coaching process. Appropriate recognition should be given based on performance outcomes. Coaching is documented according to organizational policies and may be incorporated as a step in documenting disciplinary action if the employee is unable to attain the mutually agreed upon performance objectives.

Professional nurses assuming beginning management roles should always consult with their superior before initiating coaching for performance deficiencies of other health team members. Experienced managers often find it helpful to use peer consultation in preparation for this type of coaching situation as well. Refer to Chapter 10 for further information.

Summary

Peters (1987) tells us to "celebrate—informally and formally—the small wins that are indicative of the solid day-to-day performance turned in by more than 90% of your workforce" (p. 304). Peters also reminds us to celebrate what we want to see more of and to use recognition and rewards not only to celebrate but as teaching feedback mechanisms of the specifics that lead to achievement. Coaching is normally vested in a designated management role. As staff empowerment models mature, peers assume responsibility for coaching, recognition, and rewarding clinical excellence.

In summary, successful coaches:

- are committed to facilitating employee improvement
- understand job requirements and performance criteria
- recognize individual differences in development of effective developmental plans
- utilize constructive feedback to motivate and facilitate behavioral change
- provide coaching continually, not infrequently

KEY CONCEPTS

- Key behaviors for short-term developmental opportunities include the following:
  1. Make a plan based on mutually agreed upon opportunities.
  2. Seize spontaneous opportunities.
  3. Utilize interactive problem solving.
  4. Challenge critical thinking/transfer to new situations (e.g., "what-ifs").
  5. Provide constructive feedback and reinforcement opportunities.
- Key behaviors for corrective coaching are as follows:
  1. Always prepare before the meeting.
  2. Tie the problem to the function of the organization and the person's self-interest.
  3. Let the employee know your expectations and the identified performance gap.
  4. Try to bring the reason for the problem into the open.
  5. Ask the employee for suggestions, and discuss his or her ideas about how to solve the problem.
  6. Listen openly.
  7. Agree on steps that each of you will take to solve the problem. Write them down.
  8. Assist the employee in plan implementation.
  9. Plan and record a specific follow-up date.
  10. Reward results attained.

LEARNING CHALLENGE

How would you, as a beginning professional nurse, interact with the employees in the following scenarios? Write or role play each situation, and discuss/validate it with a peer. Which principles could you apply that would be effective? What opportunities can you identify for your own growth?
1. A nursing assistant records vital signs but does not take them.
2. A staff nurse who never makes errors has given incorrect medications late for the last 2 days, which could adversely affect patients' clinical course.
3. A new graduate on the unit has never taken care of a patient on continuous ventilation.

Other Considerations in Coaching

Motivation

Motivation comes from within the individual. Motivation is described as the effort with which an individual applies his or her abilities to the job. One of the beginning professional nurse's roles in organizational management is to create an environment and implement strategies that facilitate the development of the human potential of the patient care work group. Each of us has needs and wants. Creating a work environment and implementing motivational strategies that support both organizational outcomes for effective, efficient patient care and individual outcomes for job satisfaction as well as personal and job growth can be facilitated by the behaviors of the beginning professional nurse.

Peters and Waterman (1982) stress that organizations must be designed to make individuals feel like winners. Motivation comes from within, but managers can influence motivation by providing effective feedback that supports growth and productivity. Managers and peers can give effective feedback using positive reenforcement by:

- giving specific and relevant examples of a positive performance (e.g., "I appreciate your helping care for Mr. Y today. Your assistance with his physical care really added to his comfort.")
- providing immediate and timely feedback and reinforcement
- setting achievable goals and celebrating small wins privately and publicly
- providing intermittent and unpredictable (spontaneous) reinforcement in recognition of the power of small rewards

Motivational theories may be characterized as content theories, based on human needs and motives, and process theories, based on how and why behaviors occur. Content theories include **Maslow's** (1943) **hierarchy of needs** and theory of motivation, which many nurses have utilized as a framework for planning patient care. Maslow's hierarchy of needs includes:

- physical needs (hunger, thirst, and physiological drives)
- safety needs (freedom from harm or danger; security)
- love and belonging needs (nurturing, acceptance, and respect)
- esteem needs (perceived self-worth)
- self-actualization needs (realization of one's potential)

Within Maslow's hierarchy, lower-level needs must be met before higher-level needs can influence human behavior. If the lower-level needs are not met continually, they will again become priority needs. For example, meeting physiological needs for food and rest will be more important to an individual than self-actualization needs if the individual has not eaten or slept for a prolonged period of time. Self-actualization can become a motivator if the environment is such that opportunities for individual development occur. These hypotheses are equally applicable to patients and health care team members.

Maslow's theory, although not empirical, has been widely used as a motivational theory.

Alderfer's (1962) **ERG needs–based motivational theory** focuses on three categories of need: existence, relatedness, and growth. Alderfer's theory is simpler than Maslow's in its taxonomy of needs, and it rejects Maslow's concepts by stating that multiple needs may be activated over a short period of time.

Probably the most controversial content theory of motivation is **Herzberg's** (1968) **two-factor theory**. This theory, also known as the **motivational hygiene theory**, is based on research involving engineers and accountants. Herzberg's premise is that hygiene factors keep employees from being dissatisfied but have little or no positive impact on motivation. These hygiene factors, also called extrinsic factors, include working conditions, salary, security, and interpersonal relations with workforce peers. Motivating factors that are inherent in the individual include job challenges, achievement, recognitions for accomplishments, opportunity for career growth, and responsibility. When these factors are not present, an individual may not be dissatisfied but on the other hand is not experiencing satisfaction. When motivator factors are present, Herzberg believes, individuals can be satisfied. Herzberg's implications are that motivation can be enhanced via job enrichment. In reality, hygiene factors must also be met before intrinsic motivator factors are operant.

Process theories of motivation include **Vroom's** (1964) **expectancy model**, which considers an individual's preferences or valences based on social values, which can be defined as positive, negative, or neutral; expectancy, or beliefs about actions and work outcomes; and instrumentality, the belief that personal consequences result from work performance. Stated differently, expectancy theory focuses on an individual's belief that performance affects results, consequences are linked to individual performance, and consequences are valued by the individual.

Adams (1963) focused on **equity as a process theory** of motivation with two dimensions. One is the perceived ratio of personal outcomes to work effort (input), and the second is the outcome–input ratio compared with that of individuals in the work group, that of similar groups, or industry standards. This theory influences motivation by causing individuals to seek to maintain equity and reduce actual or perceived gaps. Beginning professional nurses should not underestimate the power of comparison as a motivational factor for health care team members as well as themselves.

Motivation in Health Care Settings

Covey (1991) suggests that individuals are an organization's most valuable asset and that the "highest level of human motivation is a sense of contribution" (p. 70). Key to successful motivation of health care team members in empowered organizations is the identification of the overlap of both organizational needs and necessary outcomes and individual needs and goals. Agreements can then be created with team members that clearly define expectations related to outcomes, guidelines or boundaries, resources, accountabilities, and consequences. Beginning professional nurses can facilitate individual and group success by determining key success factors and using work group impact to modify processes and the environment to support positive outcomes. Clarifying objectives, outcomes, expected actions, and the coaching necessary to attain them, and providing both individuals and groups positive reinforcement or constructive feedback as appropriate, can improve motivation and performance. In health care settings, employees value recognition but often do not receive recognition or rewards for what they accomplish.

Supporting, Recognizing, and Rewarding Individuals and Groups

Rewards (Straka & O'Malley, 1994) should motivate employees toward higher levels of performance. Intrinsic rewards are associated with the job itself and include:

- a feeling of personal responsibility
- work outcomes that utilize skills and abilities
- perception of work as meaningful
- credible feedback regarding the amount and quality of work

Extrinsic rewards are supplied by the organization and include:

- monetary rewards
- professional or peer recognition
- career development and promotion
- compliments and recognition from supervisors

Recent studies of staff nurse perceptions of reward and recognition practices indicate that, although money is clearly motivating (Schuler & Huber, 1993), if salary is commensurate with responsibilities nurses value and desire personal feedback. Registered nurses in a recent study preferred to be rewarded for performance (Blegan et al., 1992), including private verbal feedback, written recognition of performance, assistance toward professional goals, and participation in unit planning and management activities.

Role Activities, Recognition, and Reward Strategies

The beginning professional nurse with responsibilities for organizational management functions with the patient care unit manager and advanced practice nurses, who have the responsibility to create an environment that maximizes human potential. By the nature of their roles, the beginning professional nurse, patient care unit manager, and advanced practice nurse act as role models and coaches, supporting staff in attaining individual and organizational outcomes and recognizing and rewarding successes.

Staff Accountability for Motivation in Empowered Health Care Settings

Behaviors that are critical to individual and group success must be developed within an empowered environment. **Job enlargement**, or increasing the scope of the job, and **job enrichment**, which involves the health care team member in planning, organizing, implementing, and evaluating work, are activities often accomplished by health care team members that positively influence motivation and also serve as a form of reward and recognition. Additional behaviors critical to success include taking responsibility for one's own and the group's development, developing personal mastery of the job, using one's judgment to respond to customers, enabling continuous improvement, and celebrating achievements. In addition, as peer processes are developed within the framework of empowerment models, accountability for selection of peers who are likely to be motivated in the setting, performance evaluation, peer recognition, and giving rewards will motivate the staff. In empowered settings, the beginning professional nurse should consider with work group members, in collaboration with the patient care unit manager, which rewards and recognition should be focused on individuals and which should reward team efforts.

KEY CONCEPTS

- Positive reinforcement is one of the most powerful motivators for staff.
- Successful motivation focuses on the individual as a person with specific needs and wants that can be influenced to enhance individual and group productivity, facilitate organizational outcomes, and positively affect individual development.
- In empowered models, consideration must be given to both individual and group motivation and to reward and recognition strategies.

LEARNING CHALLENGE

Reread the coaching learning challenge in this chapter, and review your responses to it. What fresh insights or different strategies would you incorporate into your interactions now that you understand basic concepts of motivational theories?

Consultation

Beginning professional nurses may be involved in peer **consultation** as they assume responsibility for case management of patient populations and also begin to assume role responsibility related to project development. In these roles, the beginning professional nurse may either seek or provide consultation. Consultation is defined by Caplan (1970) as "a process of interaction between two professionals—the consultant, who is a specialist, and the consultee, who invokes the consultant's help in regard to a current work problem with which she's having some difficulty and which she has decided is within the other's area of specialized competence" (p. 19).

According to Caplan (1970), this interactive communication process can be taught, applied, and analyzed. The dual outcomes of successful consultation are to improve the consultee's (health care team member's) skills in handling a work problem and to enhance the consultee's ability to address similar situations in the future. The consultative process and techniques parallel those of the nursing process and are similar among consultants. The content of consultation varies widely based on the expertise of the beginning professional nurse or other consultant and the individual needs of the health care team member.

The consultant must determine whether a nondirective approach (i.e., listening and asking questions) or a directive approach (i.e., directing the problem-solving process) would be most effective in a given situation. In contrast to coaching relationships, consultative relationships are voluntarily sought by the consultee and have a "take it or leave it" aspect in that the consultee is not obligated to implement the consultant's recommendations. If outcomes of patient care or organizational management could be adversely affected, however, the beginning professional nurse consultant should step back into a directive role. A nurse consultant who recognizes a potentially adverse situation must assume responsibility for intervening to ensure patient safety or favorable organizational outcomes.

Caplan (1970) has identified four types of consultation that are applicable in a health care setting: **client-centered case consultation, consultee-centered case consultation, program-centered administrative consultation**, and **consultee-centered administrative consultation**. The first two types are discussed in Chapter 5.

Program-centered administrative consultation involves planning and development of new programs or enhancement of current ones. An example of this type of consultation is planning an off-site outpatient chemotherapy center. In one health care organization, this project was orchestrated by an advanced practice nurse who used specialized expertise to facilitate the environmental assessment and offer plans for the development, implementation, and evaluation of the program. The consultees included a committee of members of the health care team on the inpatient oncology unit.

Consultee-centered administrative consultation focuses on problems that consultees may be having as they interface with the objectives of the organization. For example, a group of beginning professional nurses who are assuming responsibilities for the resource nurse role might seek consultation with a patient care unit manager to enhance their functioning in the resource nurse role.

Caplan (1970) conceptualizes the steps in consultation as follows:

1. problem assessment, initiated after the consultation request
2. preparation of a consultation report identifying planning/action steps
3. implementation of the consultant's recommendations
4. follow up on effectiveness

These steps can easily be equated with the steps of the nursing process. In most real-life situations, consultation does not proceed in discrete phases and is often circular in nature. Consultation provided by beginning professional nurses usually focuses on both client-centered case consultation and consultee-centered case consultation.

Phases of the Consultative Process

During the assessment step of consultation the consultant clarifies the following:

- What is the problem?
- Why is it a problem?
- How is the problem affecting achievement of outcomes?

Often, both the health care team member and the consultant will decide that assessment data are not complete and that they do not have a clear enough understanding of the problem to proceed. The process of gathering additional assessment data may include both the consultant and the consultee in jointly assessing the patient or organizational problem. Consultant–consultee assessment enables the consultant to teach and role model skills that may be helpful to the consultee in future situations. In addition to data that are gathered, it is important for the consultant to consider the health care team member's experience and feelings in relation to the problem. Organizational assessment data only provide part of the necessary information to arrive at a diagnosis that delineates the specific problem and describes the conditions underlying it. Other activities to be completed during this phase include discussing mutual expectations, realistic goals to be achieved, and a tentative time schedule.

Planning involves determining the interventions or activities that are most likely to alleviate the problem and facilitate attainment of the desired outcome based on the descriptive integration of data collected during the assessment phase. Often, the consultant will initiate a meeting to use collective problem solving. This activity may enhance the effectiveness of the planning process. Consultants can effectively utilize consultative processes to focus on the developmental needs of the health care team member or group as well. Planning is completed when a mutually agreed upon plan with clear alternatives, outcomes, goals, and responsibilities has been outlined.

Intervention, the next phase of the consultative relationship, is usually the sole responsibility of the consultee, who is free to accept or reject the consultant's recommendations. It is often helpful for the beginning consultant to role play or discuss how the health care team member or group might implement the identified plan.

Evaluation and closure, the last phases of the consultative process, begin in the planning phase when the consultant and consultee decide how the objectives and effectiveness of the interventions will be measured. If objectives are not met, the evaluation phase of the consultative process offers the opportunity to determine the reason why they were not attained and to modify interventions. Closure, the last phase of the consultative process, allows both the consultant and the consultee to review the process and content of the consultation. The closure point is often chosen during the initiation of the consultative relationship.

Through this feedback process, both the consultant and the consultee(s) can make improvements in their work relationship. Although most consultation provided by internal consultants within an organization will be verbal, if documentation of the consultation is desired or required, the consultant should refer to a book describing the consultative process for information about how to write consultation reports.

Perceived Ineffective Consultation

This discussion of the consultative process would not be complete without considering the issue of rejected recommendations. A principle of consultation is that the consultee who seeks help is free to accept or reject the consultant's recommendations if patient or organizational outcomes are not adversely affected. If consultative recommendations are not accepted, the consultant must accept this fact. The consultant may wish to review with the health care team member or group the reasons for nonimplementation. This review, as well as a discussion of the experience with a trusted peer, can facilitate the development of the consultant. Consultation is a complex, interactive process that can create opportunities to support mutual, creative problem solving and growth.

KEY
CONCEPT

• Elaborated steps in the consultation process are:
 1. initiation
 2. assessment
 3. problem clarification
 4. planned actions
 5. recommendations
 6. implementation
 7. evaluation and closure

LEARNING
CHALLENGE

Role play or write a process recording of the consultation between a beginning professional nurse and a supervisor. The beginning professional nurse is having difficulty getting timely responses from a home health agency to referrals for clients before discharge from the hospital.

Coordination

Coordination can be defined as synchronizing of activities to facilitate attainment of identified goals (Rowland & Rowland, 1992). Every organized human activity involves the division of labor into distinct tasks and coordination of these tasks to accomplish the activity. Organizations use five primary coordination mechanisms (Mintzberg, 1989):

1. mutual adjustment
2. direct supervision
3. standardization of work processes
4. standardization of work outputs
5. standardization of skills

Mutual adjustment creates coordination by informal communication and is effective in simple organizations (e.g., between two people) and complex organizations where multiple specialists complete all types of specific tasks and the next steps become obvious only as the project unfolds. Direct supervision creates coordination by having one individual take responsibility for others. Sports teams are an example of this type of coordination. Various tasks or roles are delegated to team members, who interact to produce outcomes. Refer to Chapter 5 for more information about delegation. Standardization of the work itself, work outputs, and skills are also effective coordinating mechanisms used in organizational management if everyone shares the same set of beliefs. A health care example of standardization of work is use of policies and procedures to complete identified patient care activities. Standardization of outputs is evidenced by quarterly profit or growth levels that reflect the results of the work completed on a particular unit. Standardization of skills is a coordinative mechanism when the kind of training required to perform the work is routine and specified (e.g., when the registered nurse and the clinical care partner both know what each other's responsibilities are when providing care for a group of patients).

As organizational work becomes more complex, coordination shifts from mutual adjustment to direct supervision to standardization and then back to mutual adjustment, which is most effective in both simple and complex situations. Most organizations mix the five coordinating mechanisms. Coordination in most organizations always includes mutual adjustment and direct supervision regardless of the degree of reliance on standardization for coordination. Standardization is effective when minimal interdependence is required. Sequential processes result in increased complexity, requiring mutual adjustment for coordination. In some instances, coordination shifts from a primarily internal process to one that involves changed relationships and coordination of activities between internal customers and external suppliers.

Coordination has changed in health care organizations as older paradigms have evolved into newer paradigms. In an older paradigm, meal trays for patients who were scheduled for measurement of fasting blood sugar levels were obtained by calling the kitchen, which often did not respond in a timely fashion. The kitchen was called again, then the nursing supervisor was notified, who then called the dietary supervisor, who called the kitchen, whereupon the meal tray was assembled and delivered. In the new paradigm, the entry of "fasting blood sugar" into the information system triggers a message in the food and nutrition department, which alerts the dietary personnel to assemble the appropriate tray and see that it is delivered to the patient by robot.

Coordination in Empowered Organizations

It is important to understand the role of organizational coordination not only from the perspective of getting the work of the organization accomplished but also from the perspective of the role of the nursing executive, nurse manager, coordinating body, and professional nursing staff as a whole. Within an empowered setting, and using a councilor model of shared governance as an example, it is important to coordinate and integrate the direction and goals of the councils, unit-based activities, and nursing division activities with organizational systems.

Successful organizational management in an empowered model mandates that all are responsible for coordination and integration. Staff members are responsible for activities between patient care units and nursing service councils, managers assist with the coordination and integration of the nursing department with other departments, the nursing executive ensures coordination and integration of nursing councils and committees with hospitalwide forums and systems, and the executive or coordinating council orchestrates coordination of activities among councils and committees. For example, coordination related to the implementation of performance evaluations by peer review within nursing would proceed as follows:

1. The practice council would determine practice standards.
2. The quality improvement council would determine the format and process for peer review.
3. The education council would provide communication and education to staff about the system.
4. The management council would determine and facilitate implementation of the redefined performance evaluation system with emphasis on resource management.
5. The executive or coordinating council would facilitate the timing and fit of individual council activities to ensure a coordinated, integrated whole.

Coordination in organizational models that are currently being developed will probably be accomplished differently than it is today. As cross-functional, self-managed work teams become responsible for a core process with multiple functions from conception to completion, much of the coordination performed in today's organizations will be accomplished within the framework of the team's activities during development and production of the product or service. In reality, in some health care organizations teams already coordinate many of the functions previously performed by management, including responsibility for work planning, setting goals, making assignments, monitoring care being performed, and evaluating the quality, cost, service, and satisfaction levels of customers or those who are involved in the development of the product or delivery of the service. The team also identifies opportunities to improve performance and accepts responsibility for correcting its daily operational performance. In these settings, direct supervision is no longer an effective coordination mechanism; the manager's role as a facilitator, resource, and coach, however, is imperative to facilitate organizational outcomes.

KEY
CONCEPTS

- Coordination facilitates harmony and is necessary to accomplish the work of an organization.
- Coordination includes five mechanisms: mutual adjustment, direct supervision, standardization of work processes, standardization of work outputs, and standardization of skills.
- Managers' responsibilities for coordination will continue to transition to the individuals and teams who produce the product or provide the service as organizational roles change.

LEARNING
CHALLENGE

Select a core process for delivering patient care, such as medication administration or availability of equipment and materials, that involves the division of labor for the completion of multiple, distinct tasks, and describe how these tasks are coordinated to accomplish the activity. Compare and contrast your answer with your postulations about coordination in old paradigm (bureaucratic) and new paradigm (empowered) organizations. Validate your thoughts with a peer.

Project Management

Project management is an important skill for beginning professional nurses who have assumed organizational management responsibilities. This skill is requisite to success within staff empowerment models. Examples of organizational management projects in which beginning professional nurses might be involved include:

- defining standards of practice and standards of care for the nursing service
- developing a unit-based educational program
- devising a quality improvement project to reduce noise on the patient care unit
- creating a charting by exception documentation system
- evaluating the effectiveness of various infusion pumps before product selection
- implementing peer review of professional nursing staff

Irrespective of the content, project completion is contingent on using problem-solving and group skills both within and between groups. For example, when peer review is being implemented within a councilor model of shared governance, the clinical practice council would determine performance standards, the evaluation council would determine the format and processes for clinical nursing staff peer review, the education council would orient the staff to the process, the management council would assume responsibility for fiscal resource management related to the program, and the nurse executive would facilitate support and approval of human resources. In empowered models, project management requires clear definition and identification of ownership for specific professional accountabilities as well as the development of cooperation and interdependence among councils during the problem-solving and goal-attainment processes.

Actual projects are completed using a set of discrete but somewhat circular steps. In most organizational projects, goals and measurable outcomes that signify whether the project has been a success are defined before the project's initiation. Information that can serve as a foundation for planning is gathered and analyzed. Information from literature, the organization, competitors, and others who have expertise or have successfully implemented similar projects are a few of the initial resources that can be studied. A project plan, including time frames, action steps, responsibilities for project activities, and available and needed resources, is developed. After initial discussion and approval of the project at appropriate decision-making forums within the organization (e.g., the coordinating or executive council within a councilor model of shared governance), the design and build phase begins. During this phase, models or systems are developed after careful analysis of multiple courses of action. Once the various jobs and tasks identified as necessary to complete the project have been developed, implementation steps can be defined and the project pilot tested or implemented throughout the organization. Implementation steps focus on:

- resource allocation (human, material, fiscal, support, and system)
- scope of responsibility, authority, accountability of those involved with or affected by project implementation
- contingency plans if some aspect of the project is not as effective as planned

Communication and education are critical to a project's success from inception until completion. These activities occur throughout the organization as well as with individuals with new job responsibilities. Lack of communication and inadequate education of those assuming new or redefined roles can derail a project.

Responsibility for ongoing coordination of the project should be defined before implementation. Coordination is a critical success factor in assisting those involved in integrating their efforts toward the project's success.

Evaluation, one of the last steps of project management, focuses on measuring the identified project outcomes that signify whether the project development and implementation have been successful and also identifies opportunities for ongoing development and improvement. In an era of rapid change in health care, most projects are undergoing continual development and refinement as health care workers continue to identify opportunities to enhance both clinical and organizational outcomes.

KEY CONCEPTS

- Project management steps are:
  1. goal setting and outcome measurement identification
  2. assessment
  3. project plan development
  4. design and build phase
  5. implementation
  6. evaluation
  7. ongoing refinement/development
- Inadequate education and communication can derail a project.

Time Management

Readers of this book have already had experience with managing their time during clinical laboratory experiences. The time management principles applied to clinical practice can be adopted by the beginning professional nurse and applied to organizational management activities.

Our perceptions and use of time, which are certainly evident in our time-conscious society, are affected by individual personalities, culture, and the environment. In Western cultures, time is often viewed as linear; once a particular point in time has passed, the opportunity it presented will never be repeated. Time in Eastern cultures is often perceived as circular and measured in seasons, which are continuous and constantly repeating.

Time management is really about goal setting and goal achievement. Before one can manage time, personal and professional goals must be determined, which can then be used to guide one's use of time. For example, a beginning professional nurse aspiring to a supervisory role and one aspiring to a clinical nurse specialist role within 5 years would spend their time developing a career in different ways. Goal setting is about outcome identification, determination of action steps, and up-front identification of outcome measures. It is important for beginning professional nurses to look at a balance of goals related to life, including mental, physical, and social/emotional goals and activities (Covey, 1989), as they set goals for their own personal and professional development.

One of the initial steps in time management is to determine how you are spending your time. Record your activities in 15- or 30-minute increments throughout the day, and then compare your time expenditures with your identified goals for yourself, your patients, your unit, the organization, and your significant others. Time logs can also help identify time wasters, which can be obstacles to effectiveness.

Planning is the next step in proactive time management. Whether providing patient care or engaging in organizational management activities, the beginning professional nurse can enhance effectiveness by proactive management, including priority setting. Multiple strategies for priority setting have been developed, including ranking activities as A, B, C; must, should, could; important, not important; or urgent, not urgent. Covey (1989) reminds us that most of us, especially those of us in roles of organizational management, do not spend enough time on important but not urgent activities, which are critical to our future success as individuals and organizations. The Pareto principle, or the 20/80 rule, a commonly accepted time management principle, states that 20% of activity produces 80% of results.

Successful strategies for beginning professional nurses assuming responsibility for organizational management activities include the following:

- Develop "to-do" lists and prioritize them.
- Go public—Let those around you know your priorities and plans to meet them.
- Work only on one task at a time, but schedule several tasks simultaneously.
- Be assertive—Know when to say *no*.
- Don't procrastinate—Move beyond indecision.
- "Swiss cheese" tasks—Break down large projects into small pieces.
- Handle crisis interruptions only—Schedule time to handle noncrisis interruptions.
- Match tasks with your energy level—Accomplish routine tasks when energy is low.
- Streamline work—Ask what you can do differently and what you can help staff do differently.
- Ask continuously "Is this the best use of my time? Am I wasting others' time?"

In summary, effective time management is learning about where your time goes, what your goals are, and your plans for achieving your goals.

KEY
CONCEPT

• Successful time managers plan their work and work their plan.

LEARNING
CHALLENGE

Identify one time waster in your personal or professional life, and describe strategies you might use to reduce or eliminate it. Note how you will act, feel, and think if you use these strategies the next time you are faced with the time waster. Discuss your action plan with a peer.

CONCLUSION

In the future, the beginning professional nurse will be involved in organizational management more so than has been the practice in the past. This involvement will include individual professional development as well as contributing to organizational operations. Development of management skill sets described in this chapter will be essential for the success of the professional nurse regardless of the practice setting in which the nurse is employed.

RESEARCH
FOUNDATION

Porter-O'Grady, T., & Tornebeni, J. (1993). Outcomes of shared governance: Impact on the organization. *Seminars for Nurse Managers, 1* (2), 63-79.

Program evaluation techniques were used to measure longitudinal changes in structure, function, and fiscal outcomes that reflected the effectiveness of shared governance in an organization. Empowerment and enhanced responsibility for operationalizing professional accountabilities have long been valued and frequently discussed in the literature. Information about the effectiveness of shared governance in an organization has only recently been discussed. Mercy Medical Center, a 523-bed tertiary care facility in San Diego, California, identified the following as concerns before implementation of shared governance:

- high operating costs
- high nursing administration costs
- low nursing satisfaction with concomitant high turnover rates and registry use
- low staff morale

A broad database was tracked over 5 years that clearly documented accomplishments and results during the implementation of shared governance. Findings included the following:

- Nursing turnover rates decreased from 28% in 1988 to 9% in 1992, coupled with an associated decrease in registry usage as reflected in registry/traveler expenses of $2.9 million in fiscal year (FY) 1987–88 and registry/traveler expenses of $536,575 in FY 1991–92.
- Nursing staff satisfaction increased.
- Nursing administrative salary expense dropped from $2.25 million in 1987 to $1.17 million in 1992.
- Nursing salary as a percentage of total hospital salaries was reduced in spite of an increase in the case mix index during this period.
- Nursing productivity increased from 79.5% in FY 1986–87 to 97.5% in FY 1991–92.
- Patient satisfaction increased from 84 to 88 points on the Press Ganey Patient Satisfaction Survey.

This project showed that staff involvement in the design, implementation, and evaluation of change that reflect partnerships through establishment of shared governance can result in a dramatic impact on the outcomes of an organization. This project also provides a framework for others who wish to quantify the success of structural and organizational changes involving the implementation of empowerment models in nursing organizations.

REFERENCES

Adams, J. (1963). Toward an understanding of inequity. *Journal of Abnormal and Social Psychology, 67* (5), 422–436.

Alderfer, C. (1962). *Existence, relatedness and growth.* New York: Free Press.

Blegan, M., Goode, C., Johnson, M., Maas, M., McCloskey, J.C., & Moorhead, S. (1992). Recognizing staff nurse job performance and achievement. *Research in nursing and health, 15* (1), 57–67.

Bolton, L. (1986). *People skills: How to assert yourself, listen to others and resolve conflicts.* New York: Touchstone.

Bowen, D., & Lawlor, E., III. (1992). The empowerment of service workers: What, why and when. *Sloan Management Review, 33* (3), 31–39.

Caplan, G. (1970). *The theory and practice of mental health consultation.* New York: Basic Books.

Cohen, H. (1980). *You can negotiate anything.* Secaucas, NJ: Ballinger.

Covey, S. (1989). *7 habits of highly effective people.* New York: Simon & Schuster.

Covey, S. (1991). *Principle centered leadership.* New York: Fireside.

Creighton, H. (1986). *Law every nurse should know.* Philadelphia: Saunders.

Department of Health and Human Services (DHHS). (1988). *NIOSH guidelines for protecting the safety of health care workers* (DHHS NIOSH Publication No. 88–119). Washington, DC: Author.

DiMotto, J. (1994). Are all nurses supervisors? *Aspen's advisor for nurse executives, 10* (1), 6–7.

Fayol, H. (1925). *General and industrial management.* London: Pittman.

Fisher, R., & Ury, W. (1981). *Getting to yes: Negotiating agreement without giving in.* New York: Penguin.

Fournies, F. (1978). *Coaching for improved work performance.* New York: Van Nostrand Reinhold.

Gobis, L. (1994). Computerized patient records: Start preparing now. *Journal of Nursing Administration, 21* (9), 15–16, 60.

Goffman, E. (1979). *Gender displays in gender advertisements.* New York: Harper & Row.

Handy, C. (1993). *Understanding organizations.* New York: Oxford University Press.

Herzberg, F. (1968). One more time, how do you motivate employees? *Harvard Business Review, 46* (1), 53–62.

Maslow, A. (1943). A theory of human motivation. *Psychological Review, 50,* 370–396.

Mason, E. (1984). *How to write meaningful nursing standards* (2nd ed.). New York: Wiley.

Mintzberg, H. (1989). *Mintzberg on management.* New York: Free Press.

Neubauer, J. (1994). Building your team. In R. Spitzer-Lehmann (Ed.), *Nursing management desk reference* (pp. 108–121). Philadelphia: Saunders.

Orsburn, J., Moran, L., Musselwhite, E., & Zenger, J. (1990). *Self directed work teams.* Homewood, IL: Business One Irwin.

Orth, C., Wilkinson, H., & Benfari, R. (1990). The manager's role as a coach and mentor. *Journal of Nursing Administration, 20* (9), 11–15.

Parks, S. (1994). Risk management. In R. Spitzer-Lehmann (Ed.), *Nursing management desk reference* (pp. 594–608). Philadelphia: Saunders.

Pelle, D. (1988). Risk management. In M. Stull & S. Pinkerton (Eds.), *Current strategies for nurse administrators* (pp. 115–128). Gaithersburg, MD: Aspen.

Peters, T. (1987). *Thriving on chaos.* New York: Harper & Row.

Peters, T. (1990). The best new managers will listen, motivate, support. Isn't that just like a woman? *Working Woman,* 142–143.

Peters, T., & Waterman, R. (1982). *In search of excellence.* New York: Warner.

Porter-O'Grady, T. (Ed.). (1992). *Implementing shared governance: Creating a professional organization.* St. Louis: Mosby–Year Book.

Porter-O'Grady, T., & Tornebeni, J. (1993). Outcomes of shared governance: Impact on the organization. *Seminars for Nurse Managers, 1* (2), 63–79.

Quick, T.L. (1985). *The manager's motivation deskbook.* New York: Wiley.

Rowland, H., & Rowland, B. (1992). *Nursing administration handbook* (3rd ed.) Gaithersburg, MD: Aspen.

Rubin, I., Fry, R., & Ploonick, M. (1976). *Improving coordination of care: A program for health team development.* Cambridge, MA: Ballinger.

Shuler, R.S., & Huber, V.L. (1993). *Personnel and human resource management* (5th ed.). St. Paul, MN: West.

Smith, S. (1992). Nursing staff roles in unfolding shared governance. In T. Porter-O'Grady (Ed.), *Implementing shared governance: Creating a professional organization* (pp. 111–140).

St. Louis: Mosby–Year Book.

Stein, L.I. (1967). The doctor nurse game. *Archives of General Psychiatry, 16*, 699–703.

Straka, D., & O'Malley, J. (1994). A professional development model: Rewarding excellence in nursing practice. *Seminars for Nurse Managers, 2* (3), 167–174.

Tannen, D. (1990). *You just don't understand.* New York: Ballantine.

Vroom, V. (1964). *Work and motivation.* New York: Wiley.

Weber, M. (1947). *The theory of social and economic organizations.* Translated by A. Henderson and T. Parsons. New York: Free Press.

Wellins, R., Byham, W., & Wilson, J. (1991). *Empowered teams.* San Francisco, CA: Jossey-Bass.

SUGGESTED READING

American Organization of Nurse Executives. (1993). *Nursing leadership: Preparing for the 21st century.* Chicago: American Hospital.

del Bueno, D. (1993). Delegation and the dilemma of the democratic ideal. *Journal of Nursing Administration, 23* (3), 20–21, 25.

Duffield, C. (1994). Nursing unit managers. *Nursing Management, 25* (4), 63–67.

Finsk, J. (1993). Legal aspects of standards of care Part 1. *Nursing Management, 24* (7), 30–32.

Finsk, J. (1993). Legal aspects of standards of care Part 2. *Nursing Management, 24* (8), 16–17.

Flarey, D. (1993). The changing role of the nurse manager: Redesigns for the 1990's and beyond. *Seminars for Nurse Managers, 1* (1), 41–48.

Hammer, M., & Champy, J. (1993). *Reengineering the corporation.* New York: Harper Collins.

Horvath, K., et al. (1994). Uncovering the knowledge embedded in clinical nurse manager practice. *Journal of Nursing Administration, 24* (7–8), 39–44.

Jones, K. (1993). Confrontation methods and skills. *Nursing Management, 24* (5), 68–70.

Kim, D. (1993). The link between individual and organizational learning. *Sloan Management Review, 35* (1), 37–49.

Kerfoot, K. (1993). From vertical to horizontal nursing management. *Nursing Economics, 11* (1), 49–51.

McCloskey, J., et al. (1994). Nursing management innovations: A need for systematic evaluation. *Nursing Economics, 12* (1), 35–43.

Mintzberg, H. (1994). Managing as blended care. *Journal of Nursing Administration, 24* (9), 29–36.

Porter-O'Grady, T. (1994). Of myth spinners and map makers: 21st century managers. *Nursing Management, 25* (4), 52–55.

Rovin, S., & Ginsberg, L. (1991). *Managing hospitals.* San Francisco, CA: Jossey-Bass.

Sovie, M. (1994). Nurse manager: A key role in clinical outcomes. *Nursing Management, 25* (3), 30–34.

PART II

The Business of Health Care

CHAPTER 7

Health Care Economics

Robert L. Seidman

CHAPTER OUTLINE

Important Economic Terms and Concepts
Resource Scarcity
Consumer and Firm Decision Behavior
Unusual Characteristics of Health Care
Private versus Social Perspectives
Measuring Productivity and Efficiency

Production of Health Supply and Demand for Medical Care and Insurance
Equilibrium Price and Quantity
Elasticity of Demand
Time Price of Medical Care
Insurance and Adverse Selection
Cost-Benefit and Cost-Effectiveness Analysis
Conclusion
Research Foundation

CHAPTER OBJECTIVES

At the completion of this chapter, the beginning professional nurse will be able to:

1. identify and define important basic economic terms and concepts and describe how they apply to the health care industry
2. discuss how resource scarcity affects economic decisions
3. understand the basic principles of supply and demand and how these forces influence outcomes in the health care sector
4. discuss how economic incentives influence decisions that are made in the health care industry
5. understand the importance and usefulness of marginal analysis in health care decision making
6. explain the difference between cost-benefit and cost-effectiveness analysis and describe the advantages and disadvantages of each
7. understand how a health production function may be used to allocate resources to achieve the maximum possible improvement in health

CRITICAL THINKING CHALLENGE

Although not useful in every situation, economic theory may provide a useful framework for analyzing many issues in the health care sector. A few examples of questions that may be addressed using standard economic concepts include the following:

- Why have health expenditures increased more rapidly than those of other goods and services during the last 30 years?
- What factors influence the amount of medical care that people receive?

- How do we measure the efficiency with which medical care is provided?
- How do we determine the most efficient mix of physicians, nurses, and allied health staffing? Does this vary across different practice settings?
- Can health be improved by redistributing some resources to prevention activities and away from acute medical care?
- What impact does an increase in wages have on the demand for, and supply of, nurses and other health care professionals?
- How will physicians respond to implementation of the Medicare fee schedule, which generally reduces payments for procedure-oriented services that are provided to Medicare beneficiaries? Will this change in reimbursement affect the quality of services and access to care by this population?

Why study economics? What can economic theory contribute to an industry such as health care, where the primary goal is often considered providing high-quality patient care to alleviate or prevent pain and suffering? Many people believe that economic factors should have no impact on which medical services are provided and who receives care.

There are several answers to these questions that suggest that economic factors have played and will continue to play an important role in the health care sector. First, even in an industry that is dominated by nonprofit institutions and may be less concerned with the bottom line than traditional for-profit business, economic principles may help guide decision makers to the best possible outcome, whether that is measured by increasing patients' health, maximizing profit, or achieving some other objective. This concerns whether the best allocation of scarce resources is being used.

Second, the relative importance of the health care sector in the overall economy has increased dramatically in the past 35 years, from 5% of the Gross Domestic Product (GDP) in 1960 to almost 15% in 1994. This greater economic presence has led to profound changes in the way medical services are organized, financed, and delivered. Whereas costs of providing care to patients with no insurance coverage formerly were shifted to other payers, and higher costs could be passed on to insurance companies, which would often pay the total bill, third party payers now negotiate reduced fees with providers and often scrutinize all medical services delivered for their appropriateness, resulting in less capacity by providers to absorb unreimbursed care. The reduction in resource availability has forced providers, insurance companies, and patients to make more difficult choices regarding what services are provided and even who receives them. Economic theory may provide a useful framework to evaluate existing standards regarding use of resources and to minimize the cost of providing a given level of care.

A primary focus of economics is the identification and analysis of factors that influence people's decisions. One of the basic presumptions is that individuals will respond to economic and other incentives in trying to achieve their desired objective. Variations in any of these incentives are likely to prompt these individuals to adjust their decisions. To study this, economists develop theories of how individuals or business firms behave based on a set of assumptions reflecting expectations of their objectives and key factors that influence their decisions. These theories provide a simplification or generalization of the relationships among complex factors that influence behavior in reality. Economic models are developed that include assumptions about what motivates the decision maker, the relevant variables, and theories about how these variables interact.

Business firms are viewed as hiring different inputs (e.g., labor, capital, etc.) and using these to produce finished goods and services. Individuals, on the other hand, sell their labor to firms and earn income with which to purchase these goods and services. Economic models may be used to examine the efficiency and equity of decisions regarding what types of and how many goods and services individual consumers will purchase, how much output firms will produce, and what combination of inputs they should use. These models also predict how these decisions about consumption and production will vary when important factors change (e.g., an increase in insurance coverage, a tax reduction, a technological improvement, a wage increase, etc.). Unfortunately, as with any unobservable phenomenon, assumptions about the important "facts" in a theory may vary considerably. This may explain why economists often predict different decisions by the same group of individuals. Thus accurate and realistic assumptions about individuals and characteristics of the environment in which they make decisions are crucial for formulation of a model that accurately predicts real-world behavior.

This chapter provides an introduction to selected economic concepts and issues that will be useful to both clinical and administrative nursing professionals. A more thorough understanding of economic principles and their application to health care may be obtained by reading a health economics text (e.g., Feldstein, 1993; Phelps, 1992) and additional references listed at the end of this chapter.

IMPORTANT ECONOMIC TERMS AND CONCEPTS

Resource Scarcity

The primary focus of economics is how to make the best decisions using scarce resources. Making decisions about what goods you wish to purchase, what types of services should be provided to patients, or how much of different inputs to use in producing those services would not be necessary if people had infinite incomes and inputs were available in endless supply. In other words, if economic resources were not scarce, decisions about how to allocate these resources would be unnecessary. Available resources are inadequate to satisfy the wants of all consumers and producers, however. This limits the amounts of goods and services that may be produced or purchased. Indeed, resource scarcity forces us to make choices. In doing so, we weigh the trade-off of any decision by comparing the benefits and the costs of that decision.

Figure 7–1 provides a simple illustration of the choices that are often faced in deciding what goods and services to produce and the cost of making these choices. The curve, typically referred to as a production possibilities frontier, shows all possible combinations of goods and services that may be produced by society given the available resources and assuming that all resources are being used to produce either medical care or other (nonmedical) goods and services. Points that lie farther down the curve toward the medical care axis correspond to greater production of medical care and lower amounts of nonmedical goods and services produced.

Production of all goods and services requires inputs, and no input may be used simultaneously to produce both medical care and nonmedical goods and services. This curve is downward sloping, indicating that greater production of one type of good requires a *reduction* in the amount of the other good that may be produced. When all available resources are being used in production, the decision to commit additional resources to produce more medical care requires withdrawing resources from nonmedical goods and services, resulting in lower levels of production. Thus with full employment of all available resources, society faces a choice. Because it cannot increase production of all goods and services simultaneously, a decision must be made regarding which goods and services will receive more resources than others.

The cost of choosing to devote more resources to producing medical care is given by the (foregone) potential production of nonmedical goods and services that would have occurred if those resources had instead been channeled into these sectors of the economy instead of toward health care. This sacrifice in potential output of nonmedical goods and services is referred to as the **opportunity cost** of producing additional medical care. For example, if the available resources may be used to produce either 100 units of medical care and 2,000 units of other goods and services or 200 units of medical care and 1,750 units of other goods and services, the opportunity cost of increasing production of medical care from 100 to 200 units is the 250 units of the other goods and services that must be foregone because resources are withdrawn from their production.

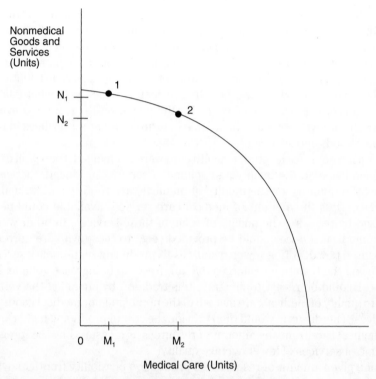

Figure 7–1 Production of medical care and other goods and services.

Whether the production possibilities frontier in Figure 7–1 is flat or curved reflects the degree to which resources are equally well suited for producing medical care and nonmedical goods and services (Stiglitz, 1993). For example, RNs are probably better suited to producing patient care and less well suited to producing clerical services compared with secretaries, and vice versa. Although the traditional bowed-out shape of this frontier is shown, even a straighter line would require a sacrifice of one type of good to produce additional amounts of the other (although the amount of foregone output would be different).

Suppose society is currently at point 1 on the curve, where M_1 units of medical care and N_1 units of nonmedical goods and services are being produced. If society desires that a greater amount of medical care be made available (e.g., to provide a minimum standard of care to those who are currently uninsured), this will entail moving from point 1 to a point such as 2, where more medical care (M_2) but less nonmedical care (N_1) is produced. This opportunity cost of increasing the amount of medical care available contributes useful information to evaluating whether the value to society of additional medical care outweighs the foregone production of nonmedical goods and services that would result, which provides justification for redistributing existing resources toward the health care sector. Indeed, this redistribution of scarce resources toward the health care sector is precisely what has occurred during the last 40 to 50 years. Further increases in resources devoted to health care will come at a high price in terms of greater sacrifices in nonmedical goods and services.

Even if resources devoted to health care were unchanged, there still exists a choice between the quality and volume of services produced. Increasing either the quantity or the quality of medical care requires additional resources. Thus the amount of medical care services available could be increased by reducing the quality of some of these services. In other words, more medical services could be provided (e.g., to those who are currently uninsured) by devoting fewer resources to producing high-quality services and using the resulting resources that are freed up to increase volume. Figure 7–1 could be recast to illustrate this trade-off by changing the vertical axis to quality of medical care instead of the number of nonmedical goods and services. This diagram would then provide the cost of producing higher-quality medical care from any amount of resources as measured by the foregone volume of services of lower average quality.

For a given amount of resources, a production possibility frontier such as that in Figure 7–1 illustrates the different amounts of medical and nonmedical goods and services that may be produced or the different quantity–quality combinations possible and shows what the opportunity cost would be for any change in these production levels. It does not indicate which combination would represent the most efficient or desired allocation of resources. This would require some representation of the value that society places on alternative decisions regarding production of all possible goods and services.

LEARNING CHALLENGE

1. What does the production possibilities frontier shown in Figure 7–1 imply about the opportunity cost of increasing production of medical services? In other words, as you increase production of medical care continuously by the same amount each time, starting at point 1 and moving down the curve, how does the decrease in nonmedical goods and services produced change? Would the same conclusion result if the production possibilities frontier were a straight line instead of the bowed-out shape shown in Figure 7–1?

2. Using Figure 7–1, show what would happen to society's production possibilities if there is a sudden increase in available resources.

Consumer and Firm Decision Behavior

A major element of economic theory is the assumption regarding what motivates people to make decisions. In other words, what objectives are decision makers trying to achieve, and how do they respond to economic and other incentives? Traditional economic theory of consumer behavior involves the assumption that individuals purchase goods and services to maximize their satisfaction, whereas business firms produce and sell goods and services to maximize profit. Although these are not the only possible assumptions of consumer and firm behavior, they usually predict observed economic activity in the U.S. economy more accurately than other plausible assumptions.

Consider the economic theory of consumer behavior. When was the last time you purchased goods and services that exhausted your list of wants and desires before you exhausted your income? If you are like most people, you ran out of money before all your wants were satisfied. This suggests that your income or wealth constrained your ability to satisfy all your needs and wants, and you were forced to make choices about which goods and services to purchase as a result. You probably made those choices by considering the value of all possible expenditures and comparing it with the cost of achieving that benefit. Economists view individuals as spending their limited income (and time) on goods and services in such a way as to maximize their satisfaction, which is called utility. If all goods and services cost the same, you would want to purchase more of those that provide you with greater utility because these would provide a better value for your money (i.e., greater contribution to utility at the same cost). By the same reasoning, commodities that have higher prices will have to provide you with greater utility to be as desired as those goods with lower prices.

Business firms face different motives and decisions. Producers of goods and services (e.g., hospitals and physicians produce patient care) are viewed as being motivated by the prospect of earning profits. A firm then hires inputs that will produce the desired level of output at the lowest possible cost (thereby maximizing profit). In making this decision, firms consider the amount of output that each input produces and the cost of hiring that input. If inputs imposed different costs but produced the same additional amount of output, firms would be interested in hiring more of the less expensive inputs because this would produce the desired level of output at the lowest possible cost. Profit maximization also implies that firms will use more costly inputs only if they also produce more output. Otherwise, these inputs would not provide a good value compared with less expensive inputs and would actually reduce the profits that could be earned.

Rather than comparing the total costs and total benefits of different feasible outcomes, it is useful to view consumers and firms as making decisions by considering how changes in costs and benefits will affect their desired objective. This comparison of the additional benefit of any decision with the corresponding additional cost forms the cornerstone of marginal economic analysis. Consumers weigh the marginal utility (additional satisfaction) and the marginal cost of different affordable bundles of goods and services in trying to maximize utility, whereas firms compare the marginal product (additional output) of another unit of input with the marginal cost of hiring that input in their pursuit of maximum profits. This process continues until no further change will yield a more desirable outcome. The result is the combination of goods and services that will maximize a person's utility, given available income, or the input combination that will maximize profit for a given expenditure on inputs.

This trade-off between marginal cost and marginal benefit is illustrated in Figure 7–2. The marginal cost increases with the number of units while the marginal benefit of additional units declines. Although this pattern for marginal cost and marginal benefit need not apply to all circumstances, it may be particularly appropriate for many situations in health care. For example, con-

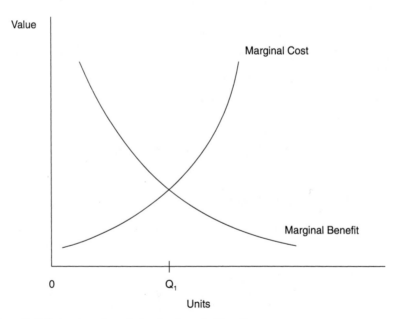

Figure 7–2 Comparison of marginal cost and marginal benefit.

sider some type of screening test (e.g., mammography or cervical cancer screening). For any group of women, reducing the time period between screenings may still identify positive cases (e.g., new positive or previous false-negative tests), although fewer new cases will probably occur as the screening frequency increases. Extending screening from high-risk to low-risk populations also leads to a decline in marginal benefit. Providing mammograms to women older than 50 years or screening for cervical cancer among women who are identified as having early sexual activity or multiple partners is expected to yield much greater benefit than when mammography is provided to women 40 to 50 years of age and women at lower risk for cervical cancer are screened. The marginal cost of additional screening may also be increasing. For example, expanding testing to reach a greater percentage of those at high risk may require increased advertising or hiring of additional staff to attract or locate these individuals.

This same pattern of increasing marginal cost and decreasing marginal benefit probably applies to other types of medical goods and services, including hospital days and physician visits. The decision maker has an incentive to increase the units of service provided so long as the marginal benefit exceeds the marginal cost (i.e., there is a net gain from each additional service). Conversely, there is an incentive to reduce the volume of services if marginal cost exceeds marginal benefit. The optimal level of services is at Q_1 in Figure 7–2, where the marginal cost exactly offsets the marginal benefit. This result will occur regardless of the precise shapes of the marginal cost and marginal benefit curves, so long as they have the same slopes as shown in Figure 7–2.

LEARNING CHALLENGE   Think about a local hospital or physician practice where patients receive medical care. Provide a few specific examples of patient diagnoses or treatments where it might be reasonable to expect that marginal cost increases and marginal benefit decreases with additional intensity or volume of services.

Unusual Characteristics of Health Care

There are several special characteristics of health and medical services that provide different incentives to decision makers and may lead to deviations from normal economic propositions about market behavior. For example, traditional economic theory presumes that consumers and producers have complete information about factors relevant to the decisions they make. All but those who are trained as health care professionals, however, have at best limited knowledge with which to make informed and efficient decisions about how many and what types of medical services to purchase. As a result, consumers play a limited role in the decision to purchase medical care and rely instead on their physician or other health care professional to evaluate alternative diagnoses or treatments and to provide appropriate care.

Perhaps the most important departure from traditional economic characteristics is the unusual way in which medical care is financed. The cost of most ordinary consumer goods is paid totally and directly from a consumer's income. For example, most people bear responsibility for the full cost when they eat at a restaurant, purchase clothing, take a taxi across town, go to a movie, and so forth. Most medical care today, however, is financed at least in part by public or private insurance companies and other third party payers. This has the effect of subsidizing purchases of medical care, reducing the out-of-pocket price paid by patients. Because patients make decisions about the volume and type of medical care to receive based on the cost they bear rather than on the price charged by providers, the availability of insurance and the resulting price subsidy influence the amount of medical care that people demand.

Individuals generally do not even pay most of the premium of their insurance policy. Instead, the policy is given to them by their employer as part of their total benefits package. Moreover, under current law, the insurance premium their employer pays is exempt from an employee's personal income tax. There is some evidence, however, that employer-provided insurance may decrease the wages received by workers and may limit their ability to change jobs (Cooper & Monheit, 1993; Gruber, 1994; Summers, 1989). This nontaxability of employer-provided insurance resulted in an estimated loss in tax revenue of more than $60 billion in 1990 (Feldstein, 1993). In addition to the foregone revenue, this tax exemption subsidizes insurance and provides individuals with incentives to buy a more comprehensive insurance policy than they would otherwise, reducing their out-of-pocket price for medical care to significantly less than what it would be if this nonwage benefit were taxed. The effect of this on the demand for medical care is discussed below. How long this tax exemption will continue in the face of federal budget deficits is unclear.

Private versus Social Perspectives

Economic decisions made by individual consumers and firms are based on a comparison of marginal costs and marginal benefits that they experience personally. Any costs incurred or benefits derived by others are typically not considered when they make decisions. In other words, individuals normally do not internalize any costs or benefits that do not affect them directly. Because scarce resources are not free, however, society should consider all costs and benefits in deciding on the best allocation of resources. When individual consumers or firms do not bear all costs of resources used in providing medical care (e.g., some costs are paid by others through taxes or higher premiums), they face a different set of incentives and trade-offs than society, and the private decision about the amount and types of medical care to receive or provide may not be socially optimal. This is an example of what economists call externalities (Stiglitz, 1993).

Economic evaluation of proposed programs represents an analysis where conclusions about efficient resource allocation may vary according to whether a private or social perspective is adopted. A work site prevention program or activity may provide long-term health benefits to individual participants, although the firm may consider only whether reduced operating costs will offset the cost of the program. Consequently, this program may be rejected even though the overall reduction in production costs and future medical costs as well as the value of improved quality of life far outweigh the cost of implementing the program.

Another example of different conclusions based on different analytic perspectives occurs when one perspective values the cost of work loss due to illness while the other does not. Lieu et al. (1994), estimated that a routine varicella vaccination program for children would cost health care payers more in vaccine and administrative costs than it would save in reduced medical expenditures due to prevented cases of chickenpox. If the insurer evaluated this vaccination program strictly from the standpoint of net medical expenditures, it would not be viewed favorably. From a societal perspective, however, which also takes account of costs associated with lost work, such a program was estimated to save more than $5 for every dollar invested. Thus in evaluating decisions about which programs to implement and the resulting implications for resource allocation, it is important to identify which among several alternative analytic perspectives is being used.

Measuring Productivity and Efficiency

Most providers in the health care sector are interested in improving productivity and efficiency, although there is often confusion about how these concepts should be measured. There are several different notions of efficiency in economics. They vary according to whether production costs are considered rather than the relationship between inputs and output (where both are measured in physical units), which perspective is used (i.e., private or social), and whether health care is viewed as a final output or as an input in the production of health. Technical efficiency refers to the relationship between a firm's inputs and the amount of output produced. Technical efficiency is achieved when reducing the amount of one input that is used would decrease the amount of output produced, holding all other inputs constant. For example, using five registered nurses (RNs) and four nursing assistants (NAs) would not be a technically efficient method of providing care to a given number of hospital patients if an identical number of NAs and only four RNs could provide the same care. This concept does not preclude the possibility of substitution between RNs and licensed vocational nurses (LVNs). It is possible that three RNs and six LVNs could also satisfy technical efficiency in providing the same level of patient care. In fact, there could be many different technically efficient input combinations that would produce the same amount of output, although probably at different costs.

When most people talk about efficiency, they are referring to what economists call economic efficiency, which involves producing a given level of output at the lowest possible cost. Although there may be many technically efficient input combinations, there is generally only one combination of inputs that is economically efficient for any output level. We view firms as substituting among these different technically efficient input combinations, each of which produces the desired output level, until the lowest cost is obtained. For example, suppose five RNs and five NAs or four RNs and seven NAs could provide hospital care for 20 patients per day, given other available inputs. If the first combination of RNs and NAs costs more than the second combination, hospitals would have an incentive to substitute NAs for RNs (although not necessarily one for one) to reduce the cost of providing this level of patient care. Moreover, if a health care provider is currently producing a given level of medical goods or patient care using an input combination that satisfies economic efficiency (i.e., minimizing cost) and there is a sudden increase in the cost of one input, this will generally prompt that provider to substitute away from this input toward other inputs to minimize its costs.

Both technical efficiency and economic efficiency apply to the situation where medical care is an output that is produced by combining labor, equipment, and other inputs. The focus is then on the efficiency with which these inputs are combined in producing medical services. An alternative view is that the appropriate output of the production process is health or healthy days, and medical services represent one input that individuals use to produce health. This approach gives rise to a third definition of efficiency. We say that allocative efficiency is satisfied if production of health is maximized given the amount of resources (including medical care) available. This implies that health status could not be improved by using more of one input and less of another, given the available resources. For example, some analysts have contended that too many resources are devoted to medical services and that the amount of health produced would increase if resources were redistributed away from medical services toward programs that increase nutrition, housing, and life style factors (Fuchs, 1974). This evaluation of how much health is produced from medical care and other resources is discussed below.

KEY CONCEPTS

- Resource scarcity forces individual consumers and business firms to make decisions. Economic principles provide guidelines for making efficient decisions.
- A production possibilities frontier, like that shown in Figure 7–1, depicts the possible combinations of different goods and services that may be produced using all available resources and given the technology that exists. The slope of this frontier provides the opportunity cost of increasing production of a particular good and is measured by the potential output of the other good that must be sacrificed to make available adequate resources to increase production of that good.
- Consumers are assumed to make decisions in an attempt to maximize their utility, whereas producer decisions are based on profit maximization. Both evaluate the trade-off between marginal costs and marginal benefits in deciding whether any action is desirable. The value of the outcome that achieves their desired objective will be where marginal cost and marginal benefit are equal.
- Insurance policies subsidize the purchase of medical care, reducing the out-of-pocket price paid by patients. The tax exemption of employer-provided health insurance also provides consumers with incentives to obtain a more comprehensive insurance policy, and thus face a lower out-of-pocket price for medical care than they would otherwise.
- Economic evaluations of proposed programs may yield markedly different conclusions and recommendations, depending on whether all costs and benefits are included or whether the analysis includes only those experienced directly by the decision maker.
- Technical efficiency, economic efficiency, and allocative efficiency represent three different measures by which to evaluate the allocation of resources in production. Technical efficiency and economic efficiency are appropriate when medical care is the final output that is produced by combining labor, equipment, and other inputs. In contrast, allocative efficiency applies to the situation where medical care is an input in the production of health.

LEARNING CHALLENGE

Consider a local community hospital that provides a broad range of patient services.

1. How would inputs used in providing emergency department services differ from those used to treat patients in the medical ward, the intensive care unit, or the outpatient clinic?

2. Is it possible to have a particular combination of RNs, LVNs, physicians, and allied health personnel that satisfies economic efficiency but
   not technical efficiency?

3. Some inputs may be used to provide care to distinctly different types of
   patients and in different settings (e.g., radiologic equipment may serve
   both inpatients and outpatients). How should we allocate costs in
   identifying the least costly input combination for providing only
   inpatient services?

4. Current data suggest that almost all health expenditures are for acute
   medical care, with a small percentage of total health expenditures being
   spent on prevention. Do you think this allocation of health care inputs
   satisfies allocative efficiency?

PRODUCTION OF HEALTH

Firms generally receive benefits from using more inputs because this produces greater output that can be sold, resulting in higher profit levels. One
important question involves the rate at which output increases as more of
any input is used. According to the traditional theory of firm behavior, the
total output produced by any firm is eventually presumed to increase by suc-
cessively smaller amounts with each additional unit of input used (at least
when production occurs over such a short period of time that some of the
inputs, such as the firm's capital stock, cannot be changed). Because the additional output produced by using one more unit of any input is called the
marginal product of that input, this is referred to as the principle of diminishing marginal product.

This same concept may be applied to evaluate the most efficient allocation
of resources that affect health status using a health production function approach. This presumes that health is produced from medical care and other
inputs. The focus is on medical goods and services as an input that is used to
improve health. Other inputs may include such factors as a person's life style
(e.g., diet, smoking, or alcohol consumption), education (including knowledge of prevention), and environmental factors (e.g., pollution). Because
genetic factors are not easily observed, they are omitted from the analysis
(i.e., they are assumed to be the same across all individuals) despite the fact
that they play a potentially important role in influencing health.

Figure 7–3 shows the probable relationship between medical expenditures
and health levels. The curve depicts how total health produced will increase
as more is spent on medical care, assuming that all other inputs do not
change. The upward-sloping curve indicates that additional medical care will

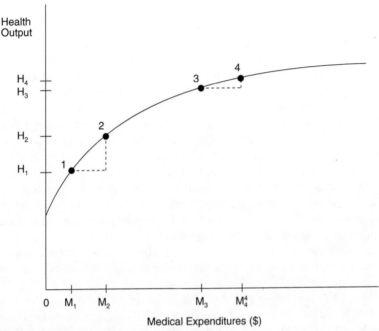

Figure 7-3 Production of health.

result in a greater amount of health produced. However, the rate at which health increases with medical expenditures is not constant. This has important implications for efficient resource allocation. Even though the total production of health increases with medical expenditures, the marginal product (the additional health produced) decreases because the curve becomes flatter as more medical care is used.

This is easily seen by considering two identical increases in medical expenditures starting at different initial levels of this input. An increase from M_1 to M_2, beginning at a relatively small initial amount of medical expenditures, will result in a larger increase in the amount of health produced (from H_1 to H_2) compared with the increase in health (from H_3 to H_4) that would occur for the same increase in medical expenditures starting at the higher initial level of M_3. If production of health is characterized by diminishing marginal product of medical care, each $100 increase in medical expenditures will contribute less to the amount of health produced than the previous increase in expenditures. Stated differently, health production increases at a decreasing rate with medical expenditures. This same relationship of diminishing marginal product is also presumed to hold for other inputs used to produce health.

The marginal products of all inputs in the health production function may be estimated using multivariate regression analysis, provided that enough data are available. If all estimates are statistically significant, we may estimate the contribution to health per dollar spent on each input. Redistributing resources toward inputs with higher contributions to health per dollar spent will increase the amount of health produced from a given expenditure on inputs. Even though there is just one overall health production function that includes all determinants of health, we may be able to draw a curve resembling Figure 7–3 for each input. This shows the relationship between that input and the amount of health produced, assuming that all other factors affecting health remain unchanged. After observing how much is spent on each input, we may identify the current location on the corresponding health production curve and estimate that input's marginal product. Following reasoning similar to that in Figure 7–2, in which the optimal production or consumption of medical care occurs where marginal cost equals marginal benefit, the allocation of resources that achieves the greatest health possible from available resources will occur when the last dollar spent on all inputs contributes the same amount to the production of health.

Suppose the number of healthy days per year is used to measure health and that, given existing expenditures on medical care and other factors that affect health, an additional medical expenditure of $10,000 will result in 30 additional healthy days whereas $10,000 spent on behavior modification programs, such as weight reduction or smoking cessation, is estimated to yield 50 additional healthy days. We may then conclude that these education programs produce healthy days at a lower cost than expenditure on medical care. An efficient allocation of resources would require devoting more resources to these behavior modification programs and fewer resources to medical care because these programs contribute more to health per dollar spent than medical care. Of course, this example considers aggregate medical expenditures instead of expenditures on specific types of medical care. Although the marginal product of some medical goods and services may be much greater than that of others (e.g., at point 1 instead of point 3 in Figure 7–3), including the health contributions of different types of medical care would clearly require more detailed data.

Most health production studies in the United States have concluded that we are near the "flat of the curve" (i.e., near point 4 in Figure 7–3) in medical expenditures, receiving a fairly small marginal contribution of medical care toward health, but that there exists substantial potential to improve health through nonmedical expenditures (Brook et al., 1983; Fuchs, 1974; Hadley, 1982). The low marginal product of medical expenditures does not necessarily mean that we should drastically reduce expenditures on all types of medical care. Instead, the empirical evidence suggests that the sacrifice in health status if society spent a little less on medical care (i.e., moved down the health production curve toward points 2 or 3) would be more than offset by the increased health status if these resources could be redirected toward programs that improve an individual's life style or other factors that may contribute much more to production of health. A more detailed analysis that allows for separate measures of preventive and acute care may also find significantly different marginal contributions of each to health.

KEY CONCEPTS

- A health production function approach may be used to evaluate the contribution of medical care, education, life style factors, and other determinants to a population's level of health. The decreasing marginal product of each input in this production function indicates that greater expenditure on any input results in smaller improvements in health.
- Redistributing resources toward inputs with relatively higher marginal products (i.e., contributions to health) per dollar spent will increase the total amount of health produced from a particular expenditure on inputs. This will also result in greater allocative efficiency in using scarce resources.

LEARNING CHALLENGE

Your local health department is considering how to spend an additional $10 million on medical care and existing public health programs. Its objective is to use these funds to achieve the greatest improvement possible in health status.

1. Provide two alternative ways to measure the health status of the population.
2. What are the most important inputs in the health production function (i.e., what public health programs, types of medical care, and other factors influence health)?
3. Using a health production function approach, explain what criteria you would use to decide on the best allocation of these funds. Show your result graphically (i.e., use a diagram similar to Figure 7–3 to show the marginal contribution to health of each input in the health production function).
4. How would your recommendations on resource allocation change if expenditure on several of the inputs was twice the level you originally thought?
5. How would your measure of health status and program recommendations change if the target population was just infants?

SUPPLY AND DEMAND FOR MEDICAL CARE AND INSURANCE

Traditional economic theory focuses on how individuals in different markets make decisions about how to allocate scarce resources. A **market** is a setting in which buyers and sellers interact and exchange inputs or finished goods and services for money based on prices. The **demand** for a good or service is the amount that a person is willing and able to purchase at a given price. Factors that are generally presumed to influence the demand for any good or service include the price of that good, prices of other related goods (i.e., complements and substitutes), the person's income, the value of that good to an individual (called tastes or preferences), and expectations about future prices. For any good or service, we may consider the demand by one person, a household, or even a large geographical area (e.g., demand by all consumers in a county or state).

The focus of demand theory is the relationship between the price of a good and the demand for that same good. As the price of any good or service changes, we usually expect to observe a change in the amount demanded. For example, as the price of a good increases, people have an incentive to substitute toward purchases of other goods and services that satisfy roughly the same need or want but are now relatively less expensive because their prices did not change. As a result, less is demanded of the good whose price increased. This inverse relationship between price and quantity demanded is referred to as the law of demand and is illustrated by the downward-sloping demand curve in Figure 7-4.

The **supply** of goods and services that sellers make available in the market is also influenced by price. Selling any good or service becomes more profitable as its price increases, other things being equal, and firms will devote additional resources to produce a larger quantity. Thus in contrast to the inverse relationship that characterizes demand by consumers, sellers will increase the amount they wish to sell at higher prices. This direct, or positive, relationship between price and the quantity supplied by producers is shown in Figure 7–4 by the upward-sloping supply curve. Other factors that influence production costs, such as technology and input prices (e.g., wages), will also influence the amount of any good that producers want to supply.

Equilibrium Price and Quantity

The curves in Figure 7–4 show the quantities that will be demanded by consumers and supplied by producers at different prices. In a free market with no outside interference, the actual price and quantity exchanged will be at their equilibrium values (i.e., P_1 and Q_1), where the demand and supply

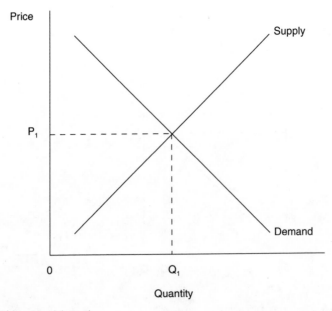

Figure 7–4 Supply and demand.

curves intersect. If the price should be either above or below P_1 (resulting in a different amount demanded than is supplied at that price), it will automatically adjust back to P_1. The term "equilibrium" indicates that the price and quantity will remain at P_1 and Q_1, respectively, unless there is a change in one of the determinants of demand or supply other than price (e.g., income, prices of other goods, or production costs). This would then generally lead to an entirely new relationship between price and quantity demanded or quantity supplied at any price and is shown graphically by a shift in the corresponding curve. Such a shift in the demand and/or supply curve(s) will result in a new intersection and generally a different equilibrium price and quantity.

For example, suppose more people in a particular area are offered health insurance. This would be expected to increase the market demand for medical care and is shown by a shift to the right of the demand curve, from D to D' in Figure 7–5. The inverse relationship between price and quantity demanded still holds because the amount of medical care demanded falls at higher prices as you move up D'. A larger amount of medical care, however, is now demanded at any price. The impact of this increase in demand on equilibrium price and quantity is given by comparing the original values with those at the intersection of the supply curve and the new demand curve (i.e.,

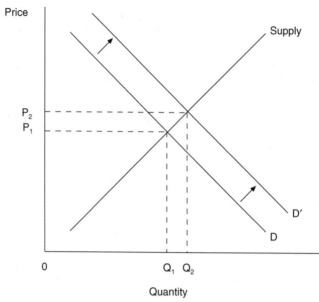

Figure 7–5 Change in equilibrium price and quantity.

S and D'). Greater insurance coverage is shown to increase both the equilibrium price and the equilibrium quantity of medical care (to P_2 and Q_2, respectively). A similar analysis could be done for changes in factors that shift the supply curve. For example, higher wages would increase production costs, and suppliers would now require a higher selling price for the same number of units. This would shift the supply curve up, causing an increase in the equilibrium price of medical care but a decline in equilibrium quantity.

Although representing a simplification of reality, this supply–demand interaction provides a powerful conceptual framework that accurately explains how prices and quantities are determined in many unregulated markets. Price plays a critical role in rationing scarce resources by excluding those who are unwilling or unable to pay for goods and services and limiting the use of costly inputs in the production process. Unlike the situation with markets for most other goods and services, however, consumers often play a minor role in the decision to purchase medical care because of their lack of information, as discussed above. For this reason, physicians (one supplier of medical care) generally decide which resources will be used in diagnosing and treating illness. As a result, the amount of medical care demanded by individuals may depend largely on incentives and constraints faced by the very individuals who supply this care (e.g., reimbursement and malpractice considerations may influence the amount or type of medical care provided). Moreover, until recently, higher costs of medical care could generally be passed on to insurers. Thus, the traditional theoretical approach to analyzing the interaction of demand and supply forces may be less successful in predicting the operation of health care markets than those for other goods and services.

In addition to these limitations, many health care policymakers believe that medical care should be provided based on need rather than demand. From a health production standpoint, this may indeed result in greater overall health improvement achieved from a given allocation of medical care resources. There are several problems in using this concept as the basis for allocating medical resources, however. First, rather than being observed (as is demand), need is a subjective assessment of the medical care required to improve a person's health to a particular level. Objective standards often do not exist regarding what this minimum level of health should be or possibly the best way to attain it. Second, even if agreement on appropriate standards were possible, significant financial and physical access barriers to receiving this medical care may exist. Individuals with more significant health problems and in the greatest need of medical care often reside in areas with relatively few hospitals and physicians per capita and have low incomes and limited health insurance.

Elasticity of Demand

We know that a decrease in the out-of-pocket price of medical care will lead to an increase in the quantity demanded if the demand curve is downward sloping as in Figures 7–4 and 7–5. Nevertheless, it is often useful to know the precise amount by which demand is expected to increase. For example, if an insurance company reduces patient cost sharing from 20% to 10%, how much more medical care will be demanded, and what will be the increase in benefit payouts by the insurer?

Elasticity of demand provides a measure of consumer responsiveness in the quantity demanded of any good to changes in its price. Demand is said to be inelastic if the percentage change in quantity demanded is smaller than the percentage change in price. A consumer is then judged to be fairly unresponsive to a change in price. For example, if the price of a physician office visit doubled but the number of visits made by a group of people during the next year was observed to fall by just 20% on average, we would conclude that the demand for office visits is inelastic and that these individuals are not very sensitive to a change in price. Conversely, elastic demand indicates that consumers are quite responsive to a change in price and occurs when the quantity demanded changes by a larger percentage than price.

Elasticity of demand may provide useful information to suppliers in deciding whether to change the price of medical care. If the demand curve for a particular type of medical care is downward sloping, any increase in price will lead to a smaller amount of medical care demanded, as shown above. The effect on revenues collected by the provider, however, depends on the elasticity of demand for this good or service. If demand is elastic, the increase in price will lead to a substantial decline in purchases, and revenue will fall. In contrast, the same price increase would lead to higher revenues when demand is inelastic because consumers are fairly unresponsive to price changes and thus will not decrease their purchases substantially. Numerical values for the elasticity of demand can be estimated statistically if enough consumer data are available.

Time Price of Medical Care

To receive medical care, an individual generally must travel to the provider's office and wait to be seen. In addition to any money paid to the provider for medical services (i.e., the out-of-pocket price), the value of the time spent consuming medical care is an important component of its overall cost to the person. In contrast to most goods and services, this time price of medical care may be much larger than its money price for most individuals because they have fairly comprehensive insurance that reduces the price they pay by as much as 80% to 100%. There is no insurance policy or other mechanism to share the cost of spending time receiving medical care, however. The full time price is borne by the patient. The value of the time spent in any activity is given by its opportunity cost. This is often measured simply by an individual's wage rate because that person theoretically could have been working and earning additional income instead of devoting time to consuming medical care.

Several studies have found that individuals respond similarly to changes in the time price of medical care as they do to changes in the corresponding money price (i.e., they reduce the amount they demand as either price increases). The response to a change in either price measure, however, has generally been estimated to be quite small (Feldstein, 1993). Using the terminology developed above, this small responsiveness to price changes suggests that individuals tend to have very inelastic demand for medical care with respect to either money or time price. One aspect of insurance and the way it is purchased in the United States may obscure the true responsiveness of individuals to changes in money and time prices, as discussed below.

Insurance and Adverse Selection

Suppose an uninsured patient must pay the full charge of $50 for a physician office visit. After receiving an insurance policy that pays 80% of any charge, this same individual now must pay only $10 for each visit. As with most goods and services whose prices fall, the average person would respond by demanding more office visits because they are now more affordable and represent a greater value (utility) per dollar spent. Thus insurance subsidizes the purchase of medical care by reducing a person's out-of-pocket price, resulting in a larger quantity demanded.

Individuals purchase insurance policies, often choosing among many different policies that vary according to cost sharing provisions. Even if their employer provides insurance as a fringe benefit, there may be several policies with varying coverage from which to choose, and employees may be required to contribute if they select more comprehensive, and more costly, policies. Whether the insurance policy chosen features limited or comprehensive coverage of medical expenses, and thus whether a person faces a high or low out-of-pocket price of medical care, is influenced partly by current and expected health status. A simple example illustrates how this choice of insurance policy influences the demand for medical care and may obscure the true responsiveness of consumer demand to price changes.

Suppose you had a chronic illness that allowed you to pursue normal employment opportunities but required frequent physician visits and testing to monitor your condition, continuous medication, and even occasional hospitalization. After changing jobs, your new employer offers to provide your choice of two insurance policies that have different copayments. Policy A is with a health maintenance organization (HMO) that features no copayment or deductible, and policy B involves traditional fee-for-service coverage with a high deductible and 20% copayment. Your employer will pay the entire premium of the less comprehensive policy A, but the more comprehensive policy B will cost you $25 per month. Which do you choose?

Because you expect to have fairly high medical expenditures during the next year, you have an incentive to select policy B. Even though you pay a small portion of its premium each month, you anticipate that this more comprehensive policy will result in lower total out-of-pocket payments for insurance and medical care during the year. Based on your expected amount of illness, the difference in insurance coverage, and the amount you pay each month for the more comprehensive policy, you are essentially choosing between an expected reduction in your disposable income of $300 (your contribution to the insurance premium) plus modest copayments for physician visits and medication at the HMO and a decrease of a much greater amount (attributed to hospital and medical deductibles as well as 20% copayments of expenditures that exceed these deductibles) if you select the fee-for-service policy. If you were in good health, had a pattern of relatively little consumption of medical care, and had no expectation that this pattern would change during the next year, you would have an incentive to select the less comprehensive insurance policy A. This choice of insurance policies based on their coverage and a person's expected future medical expenses is called adverse selection.

During the next year, your medical expenses were high, as expected, and you received a large amount of medical services. In contrast, people who expected to experience little illness and selected the less comprehensive policy, resulting in a higher out-of-pocket price, were observed to receive a relatively small amount of medical care. The potential adverse selection problem obscures the cause of these differences in the demand for medical care and prevents economists from attributing all the increase in medical care consumption to the lower out-of-pocket price. That is, some of the greater demand for medical care at lower prices may be due to the fact that sicker people have an incentive to select the lower out-of-pocket price by choosing the more comprehensive insurance policy. Thus the true demand elasticity for medical care may not be what is estimated from actual expenditure data because changes in demand for medical care may combine responses to differences in out-of-pocket price and illness expectations.

This potential adverse selection problem, and the desire to estimate a reliable demand elasticity that is independent of illness expectations, were the motivations for the RAND Health Insurance Experiment during the 1970s. This was a large social experiment that randomly assigned insurance policies with varying degrees of insurance coverage. These groups were similar in other respects, so that differences in medical care utilization and expenditures were attributed to the fact that individuals with different insurance policies faced different out-of-pocket prices. The results of this study indicated that total expenditure on medical care by those who paid 25 cents of every dollar was almost 20% lower than the corresponding expenditure by those who received free care and that expenditure by those who paid 50% of all medical costs was one third less than that by the free care group (Feldstein, 1993; Manning, Newhouse, Duan, Keeler, Leibowitz, & Marquis, 1987). Increasing a patient's copayment from 0% to 25% also appeared to reduce the likelihood of a hospital admission. Thus once the potential adverse selection problem is controlled, people do appear to be fairly responsive to differences in the out-of-pocket prices of medical care.

KEY CONCEPTS

- The interaction of demand and supply forces determines the equilibrium price and quantity in an unregulated market. These values occur where the demand and supply curves intersect. Variation in any determinant of the demand or supply of a particular good (other than its own price) will generally shift the corresponding curve, resulting in a new intersection between the demand and supply curves and a new equilibrium price and quantity.

- Prices play a critical role in rationing scarce resources by limiting the use of relatively costly inputs in production of goods and services and allocating these to consumers for whom they have the highest value.
- The price elasticity of demand measures the sensitivity of a consumer to changes in the price of a good or service. We say that demand is elastic (or inelastic) if a small percentage change in price leads to a larger (or smaller) percentage change in quantity demanded. This provides information about how a price change will affect total expenditure by consumers and total revenue received by sellers.
- It is important to consider the time price of medical care in analyzing the demand for medical care. This price will probably be greater than the money price for individuals with comprehensive insurance policies. Consumers will respond similarly in their demand for medical care to a change in either price measure.
- People who expect large future medical expenses have an incentive to purchase or select a more comprehensive insurance policy, reducing their out-of-pocket costs. This adverse selection may limit our ability to observe a person's true responsiveness to changes in the price of medical care. The RAND Health Insurance Experiment found that average medical expenditure declined with increased patient cost sharing after controlling for adverse selection.

LEARNING CHALLENGE

1. Implementation of Medicare and Medicaid in 1965 resulted in a significant increase in the number of people with some form of insurance coverage. Using supply and demand analysis, and assuming that supply remained unchanged in the short term, show and explain what you would expect the result of this policy change to be on the equilibrium price and quantity of inpatient hospital services.
2. Consider different types of medical services (e.g., inpatient care, outpatient care, preventive versus acute ambulatory care, etc.). How would you expect the money and time price elasticities of demand to vary across these different services? It may be helpful to focus on the necessity of each type of medical care.

COST-BENEFIT AND COST-EFFECTIVENESS ANALYSIS

Economic evaluation of treatment decisions, prevention programs, and new medical technologies is becoming increasingly important as resources devoted to preventing and treating illness are scrutinized more carefully. Cost-benefit analysis and cost-effectiveness analysis are two common approaches that have been used to compare the costs and benefits of different proposed expenditures. Both techniques are designed to guide decision makers in achieving the greatest benefit from existing resources. These evaluation tools may provide information with which to determine whether investment in a new technology is worthwhile or to decide on the best expenditure among alternative programs that reduce morbidity or mortality. Several cost-benefit and cost-effectiveness studies affecting nursing practice have been performed, such as evaluations of introducing computer systems in nursing practice (Zielstorff, 1985), staffing prenatal clinics with clinical nurse specialists (Graveley & Littlefield, 1992), and using advanced practice nurses to deliver primary care services to nursing home patients (Kane, Garrard, Buchanan, Rosenfield, Skay, & McDermott, 1991). A recent comprehensive listing of health studies that have relied on these evaluation methods may be found in Elixhauser, Luce, Taylor, and Reblando (1993).

Both cost-benefit analysis and cost-effectiveness analysis require that the monetary costs associated with any decision be identified and estimated. These approaches differ in how benefits are measured, however. Cost-benefit analysis measures all outcomes in monetary terms (e.g., dollars). This permits a direct comparison of costs and benefits because both are measured in the same units. A decision may then be made regarding whether any proposed program or action is desirable in the sense that its benefits are predicted to be greater than its costs, resulting in a positive net benefit. Because a common objective of health services and programs is to reduce mortality by preventing illness, cost-benefit analysis requires that we value saving a life in monetary units. Many analysts have been troubled by the ethical implications of such a valuation, and the technique that is often used to make these estimates has serious shortcomings (Eisenberg, 1989; Hodgson, 1983; Max, Rice, & MacKenzie, 1990).

Cost-effectiveness analysis avoids this problem by measuring the benefits of alternative programs in nonmonetary units related to their effectiveness in achieving desirable objectives, such as additional years of life gained or disability days avoided. This approach yields a ranking of different possible actions according to which achieves the desired result at the lowest cost. Thus we could decide whether to allocate additional resources to general health education classes, hypertension or cancer screening programs, diet modification workshops, or direct provision of medical services based on which of these are estimated to increase life expectancy at the lowest cost. Unlike cost-benefit analysis, however, cost-effectiveness analysis does not provide explicit evidence that the outcome of any program at least offsets its costs. Moreover, it is not appropriate to conclude that any one program is cost effective by itself. Instead, a program is said to be more cost effective than alternative expenditures that attempt to achieve the same objective (e.g., increase years of life).

A refinement of cost-effectiveness analysis involves an adjustment of the nonmonetary measure of program effectiveness to capture the estimated quality of additional years of life instead of simply the total number of life years gained from a particular program. Effectiveness is then defined by the increase in quality-adjusted life years (QALYs) or years of perfect health. Several health status indices exist that incorporate this type of quality adjustment (Patrick, 1993). They generally involve weighting each year of life gained by values people attach to being in the corresponding state of health in that year. For example, suppose people assign a value of 1.0 to being perfectly healthy and that having some chronic condition is given a value of 0.7. The effect of a program that prevents this chronic condition in 100 people who are otherwise healthy would then be measured as a gain of 30 well-years. One advantage of this type of "cost-utility analysis" is that it permits comparison of alternative programs that have different objectives because the same measure of effectiveness is used.

The differences among these three methods may be illustrated by considering evaluations of prenatal care and other programs to improve birth outcomes. The focus of cost-benefit analysis would be whether any program yields a positive payoff (i.e., reducing costs by more dollars than it costs to implement and operate the program). Several studies have estimated that cost savings from fewer low–birth-weight infants exceed the costs of providing prenatal care by as much as 240%, depending on the population studied (Gorsky & Colby, 1989; Institute of Medicine, 1985; Schramm, 1992). Huntington and Connell (1994), however, list several potential methodological problems with these studies that may limit the reliability of their results. Cost-benefit studies have also been performed for programs such as smoking cessation (Ershoff, Quinn, Mullen, & Lairson, 1990; Shipp, Croughan-Minihane, Petitti, & Washington, 1992) and management of prepregnancy diabetes (Elixhauser, Weschler, et al., 1993; Scheffler, Feuchtbaum, & Phibbs, 1992), with results also suggesting that the costs of these programs are much lower than the cost savings due to reduction in low–birth-weight infants.

Several cost-effectiveness and cost-utility studies of prenatal care and other programs to improve birth outcomes have been performed, including estimations of cost per high-risk pregnancy identified from cystic fibrosis screening (Lieu, Watson, & Washington, 1994) and the cost per well year resulting from cervical cytologic examinations (Carter, Coburn, & Luszczak, 1993). Another recent study examined the cost of reducing infant mortality that would result from such diverse activities as teenage family planning; neonatal intensive care; abortion; the Women, Infants, and Children program; and prenatal care (Joyce, Corman, & Grossman, 1988). The investigators found that early initiation of prenatal care was the most cost effective of all methods considered in reducing neonatal mortality rates. Not surprisingly, neonatal intensive care was found to be the most effective among these strategies in reducing mortality but one of the least cost effective because of the high costs involved.

Many economic evaluations include comparisons of alternative programs or treatment strategies that involve different units or intensities of service. In deciding which program or treatment option represents the best use of resources, it is important to focus on the change in both costs and benefits. For example, reducing the time interval between screenings for breast or cervical cancer will probably identify a few additional cancer cases and may appear to be desirable. The small additional benefit, however, may be more than offset by the large increase in the cost of pursuing the more aggressive and more intensive screening strategy. Brown and Burrows (1990) report results from an earlier study that found it cost $2,451 per year of life saved when six fecal occult blood tests were administered but that it cost more than $47 million per additional life year to administer the sixth test after the costs and effects of the first five tests were considered. A similar conclusion may apply to expanding asymptomatic screening beyond a known high-risk population. In each case, a comparison of increased benefits and costs may provide more useful information with which to choose between two alternative programs than the (average) cost effectiveness of either one.

Many costs and benefits occur in the future (e.g., the cost savings from preventing illness). The value of future costs or cost savings will probably be higher than the value in the current year because of inflation. For example, a person may pay $105 next year for the identical good or service that costs $100 this year. Failure to adjust for increased costs due to pure price changes would inflate the true cost impact associated with any program. Even after inflation is taken into account, however, the total costs and benefits over time may not reflect their true value. Most people will place a different value on something if it is realized today compared with the value they would place on the same amount in the future. This occurs because people would prefer to consume goods and services today rather than postpone that consumption to some future time. Thus, to induce an individual to postpone receiving a good or service until next year, its value must be larger than it is in the current year (i.e., it is worth waiting to receive something of greater value). This may explain why few people would place money in a savings account with a financial institution if they received the same amount the following year. As a result, even though costs or cost savings are higher in future time periods, they may not have a larger value to an individual than if they occurred this year. Failure to adjust for this time preference would also overstate the actual economic impact of any program where costs or benefits occur over time.

Because the decision to implement a program or provide certain services must be made today, even though costs and benefits often occur in the future, all costs (and possibly health effects) must be **discounted** to reflect their present values. The process of discounting future values involves dividing a dollar amount in any year by $(1+r)^k$, where r is the discount rate and k is the number of years beyond the current one. The estimated costs of the program or activity being evaluated will then be lower than they would by simply summing the corresponding values in the current and future time periods. The appropriate discount rate to use is often unclear, however (Hodgson, 1983; Krahn & Gafni, 1993). Most analysts apply a 5% discount rate to future inflation-adjusted dollar values. Thus if $100 in cost (after inflation) is expected to occur next year and the discount rate is 5%, the discounted present value would be $100/(1.05)^1 = 95.24. The discounted value of the same cost occurring in 2 years would be $100/(1.05)^2$, or $90.70. Thus for any discount rate, costs occurring farther in the future will have smaller discounted present values. Using a higher discount rate, which reflects a stronger preference for current consumption over future consumption, will also decrease the discounted present value of any future cost.

Discounting is one of many factors that play an important role in evaluating prevention and other programs in which beneficial health effects are often delayed many years. Suppose we are deciding whether to offer a screening program that costs $100 per person. Roughly 10% of all individuals who are screened will be identified as having the targeted disease. Early detection and prevention of this disease will result in a one-time reduction in (inflation-adjusted) illness costs of $2,000 occurring in exactly 10 years. Following the cost-benefit methodology outlined above, should this program be offered? Ignoring any subsequent treatment costs, and assuming a 5% discount rate, the discounted present value of future illness costs avoided if this disease is prevented equals $2,000/(1.05)^{10}$, or $1,227.83. Because only 1 of every 10 individuals screened will experience this cost savings, the average discounted cost reduction per person screened equals $122.78. It appears that this program will result in a net cost reduction of $22.78 per person. If the same cost savings occurred just 5 years later, however, the average discounted value would fall to $(0.1)($2,000)/(1.05)^{15}$, or $96.20 per person, and we would decide against offering the program.

Thus the longer the elapsed time until cost savings occur or the lower the percentage of the targeted population that benefits, the less attractive any prevention or health promotion program will appear. Other factors that may influence cost-benefit or cost-effectiveness results include an individual's gender, age when the illness is detected, the initial level of risk, patient compliance with and possible side effects of drug regimens or other treatments, false-positive and false-negative test results, and changes in the effectiveness of continued therapy over time. The study by Weinstein and Stason (1976) of the cost effectiveness of hypertension detection and treatment provides an excellent example of how these and other factors may influence the results of an economic evaluation.

In performing cost-benefit analysis, it is important to value all costs of illness that a proposed program is designed to prevent as well as the costs of implementing and operating the program. Economists have developed a cost of illness framework for identifying and estimating different components of illness costs (Hodgson, 1983; Max et al., 1990; Rice, Hodgson, Sinsheimer, Browner, & Kopstein, 1986). **Direct** costs are expenditures for medical goods and services, such as hospital care, physician services, drugs, diagnostic tests, and laboratory services. Direct costs also include nonmedical expenditures, such as transportation, food, and other expenses that are directly related to illness. **Indirect** costs reflect the economic impact of morbidity and mortality that result from illness. For example, following the human capital approach, morbidity costs are the reduced earnings over a person's entire lifetime that result when illness causes unavoidable absence from work, reduced productivity, or perhaps lost promotion opportunities and unwanted job changes. Mortality costs are measured by the earnings that would have been expected but did not occur because illness led to premature death. These definitions of direct and indirect costs differ from those that apply to health care organizations, as described in Chapter 8. A third cost category includes the pain and suffering related to illness. These **intangible** costs, or psychosocial costs, are also difficult to quantify and are frequently omitted from economic evaluations. All measurable costs of illness must be discounted to reflect their present values.

Because the true values of many factors presumed to influence costs or outcomes may be unknown, analysts are often forced to rely on assumptions or estimates derived from existing data. As a result, it is important to perform **sensitivity analysis** after any cost-benefit or cost-effectiveness analysis. This involves repeating the analysis using different values of key variables (e.g., the discount rate, disease incidence rates, treatment costs, etc.) to determine whether the original results are sensitive to the assumptions or values used. If the same conclusions emerge when these values are varied, we may be fairly confident in the original result despite the use of assumptions or estimates for important variables.

Interpretation of economic evaluations is often not straightforward. Results from cost-benefit and cost-effectiveness studies may vary according to a program's objectives and how its outcomes are measured (e.g., are the effects defined as cost reductions, increased life expectancy, or additional QALYs?). In addition, differences in data used, populations studied, and assumptions about unknown variables may lead to different conclusions about the relative merits of any program or decision. It is important to consider these factors that may affect the results of cost-benefit and cost-effectiveness analyses when one is comparing conclusions from different studies or judging the validity and applicability of any one evaluation.

Other issues may also limit the interpretation and generalizability of the results from economic evaluations. First, it may be important to the decision maker to identify which individuals benefit from proposed programs and which ones bear most of the costs. Some programs may appear to be worthwhile based on cost-benefit or cost-effectiveness results, but they either do not benefit the desired population subgroup or impose an unwanted financial burden. For example, society may choose not to select a program that benefits primarily wealthy individuals even though it is cost effective compared with other alternatives. Second, although health effects and costs are often discounted, some analysts have questioned whether it is appropriate to discount future outcomes that are not defined in monetary terms (Krahn & Gafni, 1993). Most researchers discount both costs and health effects by the same rate to avoid asymmetry when comparing discounted present value streams of costs and outcomes. Third, as discussed in a previous section, whether a particular program or option is judged to be cost effective may depend on the perspective of the decision maker. A private organization or individual may focus on just those benefits or costs that accrue directly, whereas society would include all benefits or costs regardless of who experiences them. Finally, it is unclear whether medical expenses associated with illness that occurs in additional years of life gained should be included in the analysis. This would increase total program costs and may actually bias decisions away from programs that increase life expectancy. Russell (1987) has suggested that it is inappropriate to include this component unless the objective of the evaluation is to determine how future medical expenditures will change.

KEY CONCEPTS

- Cost-benefit and cost-effectiveness analyses are different methods of economic evaluation that assist decision makers in maximizing the benefit derived from limited resources. Both approaches rely on estimates of monetary costs but differ in how benefits are measured. Cost-benefit analysis measures benefits in monetary units, whereas the outcome in cost-effectiveness analysis is defined in nonmonetary units, such as years of life saved.
- Cost-benefit analysis permits a direct conclusion about whether a program is worthwhile in the sense that cost savings outweigh costs. This generally requires estimating the value of saving a life, however.

Cost-effectiveness analysis produces a ranking of programs according to the cost of achieving the stated objective. Although this evaluation method does not require value of life estimates, it also does not provide explicit information about whether a program results in net cost savings.

- A modification of cost-effectiveness analysis involves adjusting the outcome for quality. This is often measured as quality-adjusted life-years (QALYs).

- Several different components of illness costs are considered in estimations of the impact of preventing future illness. Direct costs are expenditures for medical and nonmedical goods and services. Indirect costs are estimates of the economic impact of morbidity and mortality and are often measured by the reduction in a person's lifetime earnings due to illness. Intangible costs capture the pain and suffering associated with illness. Indirect costs, and especially intangible costs, are difficult to quantify.

- It is important to adjust future costs and benefits to estimate their values in the current year, when the decision about implementing a program is made. The discounted present value of costs or benefits will decline as the discount rate increases or as costs or benefits are delayed.

- Results of cost-benefit and cost-effectiveness studies may vary as a result of differences in how objectives are defined and program effects are measured (e.g., are the effects defined as cost reductions, increased life expectancy, or additional QALYs?), what data are used, which populations are studied, and what assumptions are made about important unknown variables. Performing sensitivity analysis reveals how the results will change if key assumptions are varied.

LEARNING CHALLENGE

1. Using the cost of illness framework, discuss how the proportion of total cost of illness attributed to direct, morbidity, and mortality costs would be expected to vary for diseases such as stroke, acquired immunodeficiency syndrome (AIDS), breast cancer, and gunshot injuries. What factors explain these differences (i.e., why don't these different components account for the same percentage of total costs)?

2. The study by Weinstein and Stason (1976) found that the relationship between age and the cost effectiveness of hypertension detection and treatment was different for men and women. In other words, detection and treatment were estimated to be more cost effective (i.e., costing less per additional year of life expectancy) for women as age increased but less cost effective (higher cost per additional life year) as men became older. What factors might account for this difference?

3. Discuss why an individual health plan and society may reach different conclusions about the desirability of offering a program to prevent illness for which benefits are not expected to occur for at least 20 years. How do disease incidence rates, changes over time in a person's choice of insurance policy or health plan, and discounted present values of costs and benefits influence evaluations by these decision makers?

CONCLUSION

The question posed at the beginning of this chapter was: Why study economics? It is hoped that a few of the ways in which economics may contribute to solving problems are now evident, even in an industry such as health care where traditional economic assumptions may not apply. Individual consumers, business firms, and others make decisions every day that involve how scarce resources are allocated. It is in their best interest to allocate these resources as efficiently as possible. This requires producing goods and services at the lowest possible cost and identifying the combinations of goods and services that provide the greatest satisfaction given the limited resources available. In making these choices, decision makers will respond to economic and other incentives they face while attempting to achieve their objective(s). Economics provides a useful framework in which to analyze, explain, and predict what decisions are made.

Information about decision behavior may be especially valuable in considering the types of incentives included in new programs or changing incentives in existing programs to achieve a more efficient allocation of resources. Previous empirical studies have provided ample evidence that reimbursement incentives do influence hospital and physician decisions, such as clinical treatment patterns, radiology and specialty referrals, adoption of new technology, and hospital length of stay (Freiman, Ellis, & McGuire, 1989; Hillman, Joseph, Mabry, Sunshine, Kennedy, & Noether, 1990; Hillman, Pauly, & Kerstein, 1989; Kane & Manoukian, 1989; Lave & Frank, 1988; Wenneker, Weissman, & Epstein, 1990). The RAND Health Insurance Experiment also demonstrated that patients will respond to changes in insurance coverage by adjusting their demand for medical care (Manning et al., 1987).

Although the current status of health care reform is unclear, the continued increase in resources being devoted to the health care sector suggests that some type of reform is inevitable. Many of the economic principles discussed in this chapter may be useful in predicting how the demand for medical care utilization and expenditures would change if individuals who are currently uninsured are provided some form of insurance or how hospitals and physicians might respond to continued reductions in reimbursement rates. Any structural changes in health care markets that affect the competition that hospitals and physicians face may also influence the cost of providing services and employment conditions of nurses (Buerhaus, 1994; Melnick & Zwanziger, 1988; Robinson, 1988). As managed care continues to play a greater role in the delivery of health care, there will be greater pressure to provide medical services at lower costs and quite possibly new opportunities for advanced practice nurses to participate in the delivery of medical services. Although much uncertainty surrounds the future of health care financing and delivery, we can be certain that economic considerations will figure prominently in any outcome after health care reform.

RESEARCH FOUNDATION   Zwerling, C., Ryan, J., & Orav, E.J. (1992). Costs and benefits of pre-employment drug screening. *Journal of the American Medical Association, 267* (1), 91–93.

Greater emphasis is being given in industry to drug awareness, and activities to ensure a drug-free work environment are being considered or implemented. In general, this would be expected to confer benefits to a firm, such as increased productivity and lower absenteeism, turnover, accidents, injuries, and training costs. All these factors will increase profits by reducing labor costs associated with producing a given level of output (e.g., providing hospital care to a given patient population).

Despite these cost advantages to a firm, is it always cost effective to implement a program to detect drug abuse among prospective or current employees? Implementing a drug screening program certainly involves additional costs. Clearly, the cost savings described above from detecting drug abuse must more than offset the additional expenses of the program for the firm to experience a net reduction in costs.

The recent study by Zwerling, Ryan, and Orav (1992) compared the costs and benefits associated with preemployment drug screening of U.S. Postal Service employees in Boston. The cost of implementing the screening program included the cost of collecting and processing urine samples and the cost of recruiting and hiring a new applicant to replace one who had been screened out. The urine collection and processing costs depended on the prevalence of positives because any positives detected using an enzyme-multiplied immunoassay technique were confirmed by the more expensive gas chromatography–mass spectrometry test.

Estimates of cost reductions (i.e., benefits from drug screening) were based on average cost data for postal workers in Boston, and statistical techniques were used to estimate separate probabilities of accidents, injuries, and turnover for drug-negative and drug-positive groups. Estimates of differences in probabilities between individuals in these two groups, multiplied by the corresponding costs associated with accidents, medical expenses, and wage replacement for injuries and turnover, gave an estimate of the reduced cost attributed to screening out a prospective employee who tested positive for one of the targeted drugs. All estimates of costs and benefits were measured in 1990 dollars. The prevalence of positive results on urine test samples was 0.122 (i.e., 12.2% of all urine samples tested positive).

The results suggest that drug screening would have yielded a net cost reduction, saving the Postal Service $162 per applicant hired based on the assumptions of the analysis. Lower absenteeism accounted for more than two thirds of the benefits resulting from drug testing, and almost 25% of the cost savings were attributed to fewer injuries. As expected, this study also demonstrated that screening costs of urine samples and prevalence of drug use in the tested population are important parameters in determining whether drug screening will yield cost savings for a firm. The additional costs associated with this drug screening program were estimated to exceed the benefits at low prevalence rates that may characterize areas with relatively little drug use (i.e., ≤1%). Moreover, doubling the cost per urine sample screened did not result in net cost savings even at a fairly high prevalence rate of 9%. Of course, this analysis was a strict cost-benefit analysis and included only those costs and benefits of screening that were experienced by the employer. It is unclear whether the same conclusions would emerge from a more comprehensive analysis that adopted a social perspective and considered all costs and benefits related to the screening program.

REFERENCES

Brook, R.H., Ware, J.E. Jr., Rogers, W.H., Keeler, E.B., Davies, A.R., Donald, C.A., Goldberg, G.A., Lohr, K.N., Masthay, P.C., Newhouse, J.P. (1983). Does free care improve adults' health? Results from a randomized controlled trial. *New England Journal of Medicine, 309* (23), 1426–1434.

Brown, K., & Burrows, C. (1990). The sixth stool guaiac test: $47 million that never was. *Journal of Health Economics, 9* (4), 429–445.

Buerhaus, P.I. (1994). Economics of managed competition and consequences to nurses: Part II. *Nursing Economics, 12* (2), 75–106.

Carter, P.M., Coburn, T.C., & Luszczak, M. (1993). Cost-effectiveness of cervical cytologic examination during pregnancy. *Journal of the American Board of Family Practice, 6* (6), 537–545.

Cooper, P.F., & Monheit, A.C. (1993). Does employment-related health insurance inhibit job mobility? *Inquiry, 30* (4), 400–416.

Eisenberg, J.M. (1989). Clinical economics: A guide to the economic analysis of clinical practices. *Journal of the American Medical Association, 262* (20), 2879–2886.

Elixhauser, A., Luce, B.R., Taylor, W.R., & Reblando, J. (1993). Health care CBA/CEA: An update on the growth and composition of the literature. *Medical Care, 31* (7), JS1–11, JS18–138.

Elixhauser, A., Weschler, J.M., Kitzmiller, J.L., Marks, J.S., Bennert, H.W. Jr., Coustan, D.R., Gabbe, S.G., Herman, W.H., Kaufmann, R.C., & Ogata, E.S. (1993). Cost-benefit analysis of preconception care for women with established diabetes mellitus. *Diabetes Care, 16* (8), 1146–1157.

Ershoff, D.H., Quinn, V.P., Mullen, P.D., & Lairson, D.R. (1990). Pregnancy and medical cost outcomes of a self-help prenatal smoking cessation program in an HMO. *Public Health Reports, 105* (4), 340–347.

Feldstein, P.F. (1993). *Health care economics* (4th ed.). Albany, NY: Delmar.

Freiman, M.P., Ellis, R.P., & McGuire, T.G. (1989). Provider response to Medicare's PPS: Reductions in length of stay for psychiatric patients treated in scatter beds. *Inquiry, 26* (2), 192–201.

Fuchs, V. (1974). *Who shall live?* New York: Basic Books.

Gorsky, R.D., & Colby, J.P. Jr. (1989). The cost effectiveness of prenatal care in reducing low birth weight in New Hampshire. *Health Services Research, 24* (5), 583–598.

Graveley, E.A., & Littlefield, J.H. (1992). A cost-effectiveness analysis of three staffing models for the delivery of low-risk prenatal care. *American Journal of Public Health, 82* (2), 180–184 .

Gruber, J. (1994). The incidence of mandated maternity benefits. *American Economic Review, 84* (3), 622–641.

Hadley, J. (1982). *More medical care, better health?* Washington, DC: Urban Institute.

Hillman, A., Pauly, M.V., & Kerstein, J.J. (1989). How do financial incentives affect physicians' clinical decisions and the financial performance of health maintenance organizations? *New England Journal of Medicine, 321* (2), 86–92.

Hillman, B.J., Joseph, C.A., Mabry, M.R., Sunshine, J.H., Kennedy, S.D., & Noether, M. (1990). Frequency and costs of diagnostic imaging in office practice—A comparison of self-referring and radiologist-referring physicians. *New England Journal of Medicine, 232* (23), 1604–1608.

Hodgson, T.A. (1983). The state of the art of cost-of-illness estimates. In R. Scheffler & L. Rossiter (Eds.), *Advances in health economics and health services research* (pp. 129–164). Greenwich, CT: JAI Press.

Huntington, J., & Connell, F.A. (1994). For every dollar spent—The cost-savings argument for prenatal care. *New England Journal of Medicine, 331* (19), 1303–1307.

Institute of Medicine. (1985). *Preventing low birthweight.* Washington, DC: National Academy Press.

Joyce, T., Corman, H., & Grossman, M. (1988). A cost-effectiveness analysis of strategies to reduce infant mortality. *Medical Care, 26* (4), 348–360.

Kane, N.M., & Manoukian, P.D. (1989). The effect of the Medicare prospective payment system on the adoption of new technology: The case of cochlear implants. *New England Journal of Medicine, 321* (20), 1378–1383.

Kane, R.L., Garrard, J., Buchanan, J.L., Rosenfeld, A., Skay, C., & McDermott, S. (1991). Improving primary care in nursing homes. *Journal of the American Geriatric Society, 39* (4), 359–367 .

Krahn, M., & Gafni, A. (1993). Discounting in the economic evaluation of health care interventions. *Medical Care, 31* (5), 403–418.

Lave, J.R., & Frank, R.G. (1988). Factors affecting Medicaid patients' length of stay in psychiatric units. *Health Care Financing Review, 10* (2), 57–66.

Lieu, T.A., Cochi, S.L., Black, S.B., Halloran, M.E., Shinefield, H.R., Holmes, S.J., Wharton, M., & Washington, A.E. (1994). Cost-effectiveness of a routine varicella vaccination program for U.S. children. *Journal of the American Medical Association, 271* (5), 375–381.

Lieu, T.A., Watson, S.E., & Washington, A.E. (1994). The cost-effectiveness of prenatal carrier screening for cystic fibrosis. *Obstetrics and Gynecology, 84* (6), 903–912.

Manning, W.G., Newhouse, J.P., Duan, N., Keeler, E.B., Leibowitz, A., & Marquis, S. (1987). Health insurance and the demand for medical care: Evidence from a random experiment. *American Economic Review, 77* (3), 251–277.

Max, W., Rice, D.P., & MacKenzie, E.J. (1990). The lifetime cost of injury. *Inquiry, 27* (4), 332–343.

Melnick, G.A., & Zwanziger, J. (1988). Hospital behavior under competition and cost-containment policies: The California experience, 1980–1985. *Journal of the American Medical Association, 260* (18), 2669–2675.

Patrick, D.L. (1993). *Health status and health policy: Quality of life in health care evaluation and resource allocation.* New York: Oxford University Press.

Phelps, C.E. (1992). *Health economics.* New York: HarperCollins.

Rice, D.P., Hodgson, T.A., Sinsheimer, P., Browner, W., & Kopstein, A.N. (1986). The economic costs of the health effects of smoking. *Milbank Quarterly, 64* (4), 489–547.

Robinson, J.C. (1988). Hospital competition and hospital nursing. *Nursing Economics, 6* (3), 116–124.

Russell, L.B. (1987). *Evaluating preventive care: Report on a workshop.* Washington, DC: Brookings Institution.

Scheffler, R.M., Feuchtbaum, L.B., & Phibbs, C.S. (1992). Prevention: The cost-effectiveness of the California Diabetes and Pregnancy Program. *American Journal of Public Health, 82* (2), 168–175.

Schramm, W.F. (1992). Weighing costs and benefits of adequate prenatal care for 12, 023 births in Missouri's Medicaid program, 1988. *Public Health Reports, 107* (6), 647–652.

Shipp, M., Croughan-Minihane, M.S., Petitti, D.B., & Washington, A.E. (1992). Estimation of the break-even point for smoking cessation programs in pregnancy. *American Journal of Public Health, 82* (3), 383–390.

Stiglitz, J.E. (1993). *Economics.* New York: Norton.

Summers, L.H. (1989). Some simple economics of mandated benefits. *American Economic Review, 79* (2), 177–183.

Weinstein, M., & Stason, W. (1976). *Hypertension: A policy perspective.* Cambridge, MA: Harvard University Press.

Wenneker, M.B., Weissman, J.S., & Epstein, A.M. (1990). The association of payer with utilization of cardiac procedures in Massachusetts. *Journal of the American Medical Association, 264* (10), 1255–1260.

Zielstorff, R.D. (1985). Cost effectiveness of computerization in nursing practice and administration. *Journal of Nursing Administration, 15* (2), 22–26.

CHAPTER 8

Budgeting and Management of Health Care Finances

Maryann Cone

CHAPTER OBJECTIVES

At the completion of this chapter, the beginning professional nurse will be able to:

1. define basic managerial cost accounting and financial terminology
2. calculate the total direct departmental costs per unit of service
3. outline the basic process of budgeting within a health care institution
4. define basic productivity terminology and principles for the management of human resources
5. identify specific strategies to manage a unit budget in a proactive manner
6. differentiate between productive and nonproductive time and budget for both
7. identify fixed costs and variable costs for a department

8. identify the components of a variance report and explain specific variations between budgeted and actual figures
9. determine the impact of volume of expense per unit of service
10. identify and understand the income statement

CRITICAL THINKING CHALLENGE The present practice in hospitals is to define costs in terms of patient days. There is a movement toward the development of costs per case mix. Discuss the types of issues encountered in the use of these concepts.

The spiraling cost of health care has contributed to the greatest change in health care reimbursement in the past several decades in the United States since the advent of Medicare and Medicaid. In 1981, total medical costs were $286 billion, and in 1991 they soared to $750 billion. The total medical dollars were divided between physicians, who received 20%, and hospitals, which received 40%. The remainder was spent on research, construction, equipment purchases, and other health-related expenditures (Aaron, 1991; Curtin, 1993b). In an attempt to control the cost of health care, federal and state governments as well as third party payers have moved from a fee-for-service reimbursement method toward paying a predetermined fixed rate per case. This change has significantly affected health care delivery and the role of health care managers. To be successful, present-day managers must have an excellent understanding of the budgetary process in health care institutions. To maintain staffing ratios and efficiently manage finite resources, the manager must understand and use financial information when relating to hospital administrators and financial officers. The nurse manager's success in budgeting and fiscal management becomes important in ensuring that necessary resources are available to deliver quality patient care. This chapter provides information to help the beginning professional nurse with management responsibilities to understand and monitor financial reports.

THE IMPACT OF MANAGED CARE ON HEALTH CARE

In the past, the majority of payers for health care, such as Prudential, Blue Cross/Blue Shield, Medicare, and Medicaid, reimbursed hospitals based on either the itemized patient bill or the full cost of services. This was called **fee-for-service payment**. These reimbursement methods provide incentives to physicians and hospital providers to perform multiple procedures, diagnostic tests, and services because the more they did, the greater the profit. These methods also encouraged hospitals to organize around individual services as well as to keep patients for longer lengths of stay (LOS). The costs of these longer LOS were passed along to the consumer in the form of increased insurance rates. Hospitals, physicians, and patients were aware that most bills would be paid by insurance companies rather than by patients. This loss of personal accountability for decision making contributed to exorbitant medical costs.

The uncontrolled inflation of costs in the medical care system, which at times doubled and even tripled the general inflation factor, has been ascribed to a number of factors (Goldsmith, 1989). Supply and demand for health care services have changed with the increase in life expectancy and advances in technology. Increasing numbers of people now seek medical care, particularly growing numbers of older people. Although people older than 65 years constitute only 13% of the population, they use more than 25% of all services (Moore, 1992). In addition, greater use of diagnostic tests, such as magnetic resonance imaging (MRI), nuclear scanning, and computerized tomography, has driven the cost of health care upward.

The federal Health Care Financing Administration (HCFA) is the single largest payer of health care costs, financing about 60% of all personal health care spending (Strasen, 1987). The HCFA is responsible for the Medicare and Medicaid programs, which pay for about one in every five persons' health care services. Medicare is the federal health care program for the aged, the disabled, and those with end-stage renal failure. Medicaid is a joint federal and state program for low-income persons and their families. The increased involvement of the government in paying for medical care means that more and more tax money must be appropriated for health care costs, and thus the cost issue has become a chief target for federal legislation.

In 1983, the federal government passed the Social Security amendments, which included a change in medical care reimbursement to diagnosis-related groups (DRGs). Whereas previously the health care industry had been reimbursed retrospectively (i.e., after the service was provided), this legislation moved the health care system to a prospective payment system.

Prospective Reimbursement

Prospective reimbursement is a payment plan that is defined before specified services are actually rendered. In a prospective reimbursement system, a hospital knows on admission the amount of money that will be reimbursed for a patient before the services are delivered. There are two different forms of prospective reimbursement that currently affect health care: Medicare's per discharge DRG reimbursement, and a per diem reimbursement that is a flat, per day rate. The purpose of the prospective payment system is to control the patient's LOS and the amount of money paid for each DRG (Pass, 1987). Hospitals now have an incentive to save costs by moving patients out of the hospital as soon as possible and by using resources wisely.

Managed Competition

As health care systems transition to an environment of **managed competition**, there are strong financial incentives to work in a cost-effective manner. The theory of managed competition asserts that it is possible to create a marketplace in which health care plans will work to improve utilization of health care resources and thereby reduce cost (Wilson, 1993). Health plans that do not manage resources well will lose members to other health plans that offer services at a cheaper cost. Managed competition will transform the health insurance industry into an active purchaser of health care. The motto "compete on cost, win on quality" will create an environment rewarding those provider groups that offer high-quality, economical care.

Capitation

Capitation is a method for reimbursing health care providers and physicians that is gaining more popularity as economic drivers are changing health care. Capitation involves paying the physician and other health care providers a fixed dollar amount per person per unit of time without regard to the volume of services provided. The physician agrees to be responsible for a group of patients and provides services to those patients for whatever is necessary within the previously agreed upon range of services (Williams & Torrens, 1980). The capitated method uses the concept of a gatekeeper, who controls access to services. Using this method of control, the primary care physician has the ability to assess the patient and determine whether referral to a physician specialist or hospitalization is necessary.

Because the physician's income is determined by the number of patients or enrollees who are contracted for care, there is an incentive to keep the patients healthy, thereby reducing physician and diagnostic services. Under such a system, patients choose their physician from a medical group roster. This system changes the health care paradigm from illness to health promotion. Under a capitated arrangement that includes hospital care, it is more desirable to keep the patient out of the hospital and the hospital beds unfilled. The hospitals will get an agreed upon amount of money per enrollee whether the enrollee is in the hospital or not. Once a patient is admitted to a hospital, it is typically more expensive to provide services.

KEY
CONCEPTS

- Health care costs have escalated for several reasons: inflation, overutilization of diagnostic tests, technology, an aging patient population, increased staffpower costs, and inefficiencies of too many hospitals.
- The government instituted new health care payment plans that include the prospective payment system, DRGs, capitation, and managed care.

Financial Organization of the Hospital

The organizational structure of the hospital can either benefit or detract from efficiency and flexibility when providing services. Hospitals are organized in many fashions, but most are either centralized or decentralized. Many hospital organizations are recognizing the benefits and value of having the individuals who are responsible for the implementation of decisions participate in the decision-making process. This holds true for the budgetary process as well, so that the budgets are prepared by those who will implement and monitor them.

During the strategic planning process, the core goals of the organization are identified, and methods for achieving them are established. The organizational goals will set the course for action for the next year and establish the financial objectives to accomplish the goals. These goals are established by the top executive team in the organization, and responsibility is then moved to the middle-level manager, who must become actively involved in the planning and budgeting process.

A decentralized budgeting approach has four advantages:

1. Department managers have more intimate knowledge of their departments' business.
2. The manager has the ability to respond more rapidly to changes in market conditions or volume fluctuations.
3. A decentralized structure allows for increased dialogue between staff and management regarding resource needs and utilization.
4. Morale and satisfaction are higher when individuals have the opportunity to participate in decision making that affects them.

In the current decade, health care organizations are reorganizing for financial and operational reasons. A decentralized structure lends itself to improved market sensitivity and the ability to make rapid changes.

BASIC FINANCIAL CONCEPTS AND TERMINOLOGY

Historically, nurse managers were not expected to develop, monitor, or analyze budgets. As health care continues to evolve in an ever-changing market, however, it is essential that nurse managers have the skills to assist the organization in maintaining a strong financial position. The size of the nursing department and the associated payroll dollars dictate that nurse managers possess the skills to develop and monitor a budget. Also important is the ability to articulate budgetary issues to the bedside nurse so that services can be produced with the highest quality at the lowest cost possible.

An increased understanding of cost and cost relationships can improve the quality and effectiveness of management control in health care organizations. It can lead to improved efficiency and better cost control. Managers who obtain and use information about the behavior of hospital costs can improve their efforts to achieve cost containment without sacrificing quality of care.

Direct and Indirect Costs

The basic elements of hospital costs are personnel, materials, supplies, and administrative services (typically overhead or support costs). These elements are usually expressed as direct or indirect costs. **Direct costs** are generally defined as those costs that can be specifically traced to or identified with the service or product. Two examples of direct costs are the nurse's salary and benefits (in that the nurse actually provided the care to the patient) and the cost of monitoring equipment in the intensive care unit. In most hospitals, this is referred to as the major operating expense. Also included would be items such as supplies and medical materials used for the patient.

Indirect costs are those costs that cannot be specifically traced to an individual service or procedure. Indirect costs will continue even if a specific service is no longer provided. An example of an indirect cost is the utilities purchased by the hospital, which represent a cost for doing business but are not directly related to a specific procedure or service.

The full cost of providing services is called the **total cost**. The total cost includes both direct and indirect costs. Additional examples of direct and indirect costs are shown in Table 8–1.

Table 8–1 Typical Cost Categories on a Nursing Unit

Direct Costs	Indirect Costs
Nurses' salaries	Secretaries' salaries
Medical supplies	Administrative supplies
Depreciation of equipment	Office supplies
Linen services	Financial/billing

Cost/Volume Relationships

One key to effective cost accounting management is understanding the relationship of cost to volume. How does the number of patients affect the cost of a procedure? If more laboratory tests are performed, does the price of the tests remain the same?

Generally, costs can be divided into two categories: fixed and variable. **Variable costs** are those that vary directly and proportionally with changes in volume, whereas **fixed costs** are those that do not vary with changes in volume.

Examples of fixed costs for a nursing unit include the salary for the nurse manager, the salaries for the minimum required staff on a unit, and the cost for the infection control nurse. Examples of fixed costs for the entire hospital include the salaries for employees in the billing department, the financial department, and administration; the cost for insurance; and the cost of depreciation. Figure 8–1 displays how fixed costs are represented on a graph that includes cost and/or revenue in relationship to volume, such as patient days or number of procedures.

Variable costs change with volume or patient days in a nursing unit. Variable costs are over and above the fixed costs. Some examples of variable costs include those for nursing staff above the minimal requirement, medical supplies, food, and linen. Figure 8–2 displays variable costs and the relationship between total costs and volume.

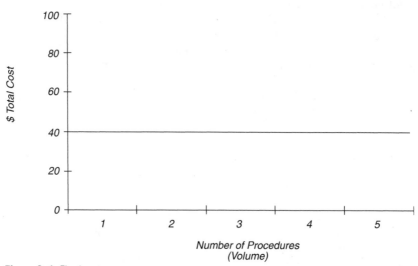

Figure 8–1 Fixed costs.

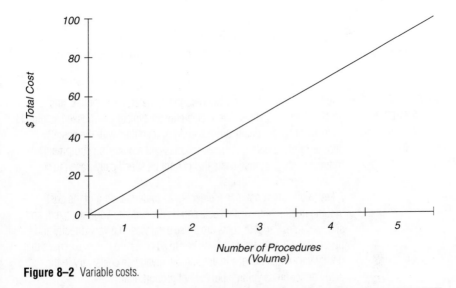

Figure 8–2 Variable costs.

The third type of cost is **semivariable cost**. These costs vary in the same direction as volume but are not proportional. For example, if the number of procedures increases by 10%, cost in the semivariable category would increase but would be less than 10%. Nursing costs can fall into this category, as shown in Figure 8–3.

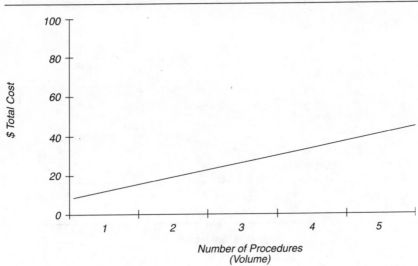

Figure 8–3 Semivariable costs.

Standard cost accounting is a managerial cost accounting method that identifies the total or standard cost for each hospital procedure, as displayed in Figure 8–4. The standard/total costs for a procedure include those listed in Table 8–2.

KEY CONCEPTS

- The basic elements of cost are personnel, materials, supplies, and administrative services. These elements are typically expressed as direct costs that can be specifically traced to or identified with the actual service or product (e.g., nurses' salaries and monitoring equipment). Indirect costs are those costs that cannot be specifically traced to a service or product (utilities).
- A key to effective cost management is an understanding of the cost/volume relationship. Total costs can be divided into variable, fixed, and semivariable. Variable costs are those expenses that vary directly and proportionally with volume, whereas fixed costs are those expenses that do not vary with changes in volume. Semivariable costs vary in the same direction as volume but are not proportional.

Productivity Index

Productivity measures how efficiently labor resources are utilized in producing a good or service. In nursing, productivity is defined as how efficiently human resources are used to deliver care to patients. The productivity per-

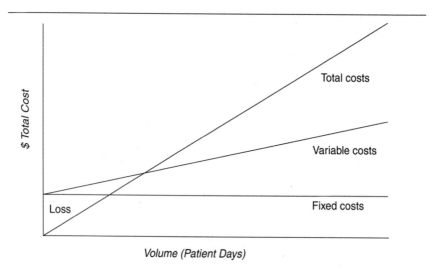

Volume (Patient Days)

Figure 8–4 Total costs.

Table 8–2 Standard/Total Costs for a Laboratory Procedure

Standard/Total Cost	Example
Fixed overhead	Department overhead: supervisor, depreciation of equipment, biller; hospital overhead: electricity
Fixed labor costs	Medical technologists/pathologists
Variable labor costs	Laboratory blood drawer
Variable supply costs	Supplies for procedure: needles, gloves, test tubes, alcohol wipes
Variable overhead	Laboratory requisition forms, computer software

centage or index is measured against a work standard. A **work standard** is a quantifiable amount of time to accomplish the work. On a nursing unit, the nursing productivity standard is usually defined as hours per patient day (HPPD).

Jelinek and Dennis (1976) applied an open system model to analyze nursing productivity. They discussed the relationships among inputs, processes, and outputs. Input includes the number and type of nursing personnel used, output represents the product resulting from the input and processes, and processes include all activities required to convert inputs to output (Figure 8–5):

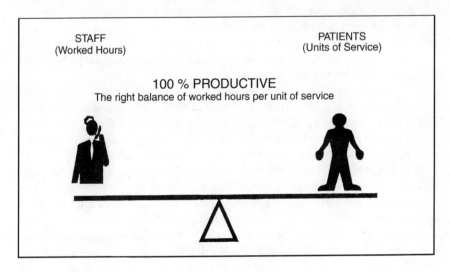

STAFF
(Worked Hours)

PATIENTS
(Units of Service)

100 % PRODUCTIVE
The right balance of worked hours per unit of service

Figure 8–5 Productivity.

$$\frac{\text{Output (patient days)}}{\text{Input (worked hours)}} = \text{Productivity percentage}$$

The higher the percentage, the greater the productivity or efficiency in the particular unit. Nurse managers need to be acutely aware of the productivity in each individual area of responsibility because:

- human resources are the greatest expense in any hospital; personnel represent 60% or more of the hospital's total budget
- high productivity maximizes personnel usage, thereby reducing costs
- productivity assists in ensuring that the organization has a competitive edge in producing the service in a high-quality way at lower costs

It is helpful to have a staffing productivity report developed to assist in managing human resources in the most cost-conscious way possible. In the recent literature, an emphasis on improving the productivity percentage in hospitals has been represented as a critical factor in ensuring hospital survival in heavily managed care or capitated environments. The purpose of a staffing productivity report is to help determine the level of staff necessary for a given amount of work defined by the units of service (UOS).

Traditionally, the only comparison a department was able to make in a budget was the budgeted amount of full-time equivalents (FTEs) and its actual FTEs. This approach works great for departments that do not need to vary the staff based on volumes or for departments that can control volume. For example, a physician's clinic that operates with one nurse, one receptionist, and one scheduler/biller can predict the volume of patients the next week. In contrast, a hospital-based nursing unit cannot control the volume of patients in any given day. Some days the patient census may be higher than budgeted, and other days it may be lower.

To determine the budgeted or established productivity index on a nursing unit, the number of patient days or units of service is multiplied by the established work standard for that unit. The manager must continually assess the operative work standard to ensure accurate reflection of need(s) (Figure 8–6). Exhibit 8–1 shows a sample productivity index calculation.

The most important strategy to increase productivity is to involve the staff in a partnership to achieve the goal. The staff working in individual departments have the most in-depth understanding of the unit's work flow and ways to improve performance on the unit. Placing certain services and/or technologies in the right place can improve the work design on a unit. Additionally, when one is considering different job designs on a unit, it is important to remember to use the right people for the right job. Sometimes using support personnel (i.e., ancillary or nonprofessional staff) is a more efficient way to accomplish the work than using higher paid individuals.

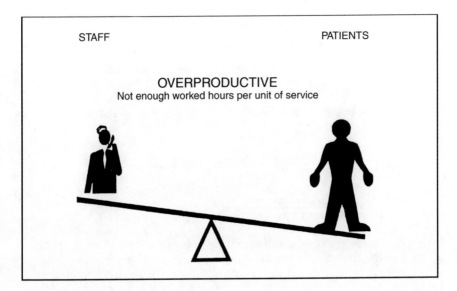

STAFF   PATIENTS

OVERPRODUCTIVE
Not enough worked hours per unit of service

Figure 8–6 Overproductive (105%).

Support services contribute directly to the work flow in nursing departments. Ensuring that patient supplies, dietary trays, patient medications, and transportation services are readily available reduces the amount of time a nurse is away from the patient and can improve nursing productivity.

Another area to assess is documentation standards and the amount of duplication in charting that can be reduced. It has been reported that bedside computers can reduce the amount of time a nurse spends in patient documentation. Curtin (1993a) reported that as much as 25% of nurses' time is expended on developing the facts, details, and database upon which health care providers, payer systems, and government organizations depend.

KEY CONCEPT
- Increasing the productivity in the health care organization can result in significant cost savings. Productivity is defined as the efficiency in producing a product or delivering a service. All hospital departments should have productivity standards. Nursing departments need to staff to actual need as determined by the work standard rather than to the amount of care provided.

BUDGET

Nurse managers at all levels of the organization need to be skilled in and understand the budget process. Every health care organization has slight

Exhibit 8–1 Sample Calculation of Productivity Index

Patient days × unit standard = projected work hours
350 patient days × 6.0 HPPD = 2,100 work hours

To determine the productivity index, divide the projected work hours by the actual hours worked.

$$\frac{\text{Projected hours worked}}{\text{Actual hours worked}} = \text{Productivity Index}$$

$$\frac{2,100 \text{ hours required}}{2,000 \text{ actual worked}} = 105\% \text{ productivity}$$

In this example, the nursing staff were 105% productive. The staff worked with 5% fewer staff to care for the patients than the patient classification recommended.

variations and differences in budgeting forms and procedures, but the concepts and principles are universal.

A **budget** can be defined as the statement or plan of operation for the upcoming year expressed in quantifiable fiscal terms. A budget is utilized to predict the goods or services that the organization will deliver. Budgets help coordinate and identify the resources that the organization will expend, by whom, where, when, and for what purposes. The budget is a powerful tool because it serves as a guide for nursing care activities and allocation of resources, supplies, support services, and facilities.

In health care institutions, the business is determined by the needs of the community and projections for growth in the market. The business volume that a health care system delivers is categorized by the broad term of units of service. A **unit of service** is the specific unit of health care service that a department delivers to its customers. UOS are generally projected based on the previous year's actual services delivered.

At the individual unit level, identifying and tracking the cost per UOS is of paramount importance. Cost per UOS is the cost to produce the product or identified service and is discussed later. Examples of UOS for other hospital and ambulatory departments are shown in Table 8–3.

Types of Budgets

The budget types that nurse managers most commonly develop and manage in hospital institutions are operating budgets, capital expenditure bud-

Table 8–3 Examples of UOS for Health Care

Department	Units of Service
Nursing unit	Patient days
Emergency department	Patient visits
Surgery	Anesthesia minutes
Radiology	Procedures
Dietary	Meals
Home health	Home visits

gets, and personnel budgets. An **operating budget** includes services to be provided and goods that the unit expects to use during the budget year. For a nursing unit, this will cover the cost of supplies, small equipment, paper supplies, and miscellaneous items. A **capital expenditure budget** consists of an itemized list of current capital assets (usually items valued at more than $500) with an estimated life longer than 1 year. Capital may be either equipment or remodeling costs and can be depreciated. Depreciation is a reduction in the value of fixed assets, buildings, or equipment based on the assumption that they lose value and usefulness over time. Depreciation is the financial tracking of this loss of value. The **personnel budget** consists of the number of various nursing and support personnel required to operate a nursing unit and the monies allocated for those personnel. Table 8–4 lists examples of items that are usually included in the different budget types.

Budget Methods

There are four different budgeting methods that hospitals have used to calculate the annual operating budget:

1. historical, trended, or incremental increase budget
2. planning/programming budget

Table 8–4 Items Usually Included in a Nursing Operating, Capital, and Personnel Budget

Operating Budget	Capital Budget	Personnel Budget
Supplies	Large equipment	All categories of nursing
Materials	(usually > $500)	personnel
Small equipment	Remodeling costs	Salaries and benefits
Paper supplies	Multiple smaller items that add	
Services	to > $500	
Miscellaneous items		

3. zero-based budget (ZBB)

4. appropriations or fixed budget

Because all these methods have been used in the past and are used in various hospital settings currently, it is important that a nurse manager have an understanding of each method. Most hospitals use several methods depending upon the specific service or program.

The historical, trended, and incremental methods are all variations on a projected budget based on the data and information from the current year. For example, a **historical or trended budget** takes the current budget and compares that information with the actual activity. The upcoming budget for a department is then easily developed by annualizing the current year to date (YTD) expenses. An **incremental increase budget** is developed in the exact manner as described for the trended or historical budget (Exhibit 8–2). The next year's budget is based on this year's information; it is annualized, and then a certain percentage increase is applied to the projected expense. This method is most often used in times of high inflation, and the percentage increase is usually the same as the consumer price index.

Budgeting by these methods is simple and quick. If there are no expected changes in services, then this is the preferable method. The trended or historical approach is the most effective for calculating the relationship between volume and costs. The limitation of these methods is that they are not sensitive to changes in the acuity of patients.

The second method is the planning/programming budget method. It was first introduced during President Johnson's administration (Sullivan & Decker, 1988). The principles of the **planning/programming budget** use a system of developing objectives to determine which programs and/or services are financially supported by the organization and will be included in the budget. This method allows for the identification of a smaller budget within a budget. The planning/programming budget is useful in comparing options for programs, especially if they cross two or more different departments.

The third method, **zero-based budgeting**, was first developed by Pyhrr at Texas Instruments in the 1970s (Pyhrr, 1970). **ZBB** uses an analysis of alternative programs and services on three different levels: the minimum ob-

---

Exhibit 8–2 Calculation of an Incremental Increase Budget

Salary expense YTD × annualizing factor = annualized salary expense

Annualized salary expense × percentage increase = budgeted salary expense next year

jective level, the current or expected level, and the improvement objective level. Once all program budgets are developed, they are ranked in order of importance to the organization. ZBB places new programs on the same level as existing programs and thereby provides a systematic basis for allocating resources by means of the budgetary process. A major advantage of ZBB is that it forces the organization to set priorities and justify resources. It is a time-consuming process, however.

The last method is the **appropriations or fixed budget**. The government currently uses this method in Veterans Administration hospitals. The budget is developed from what the expected expenses will be for the quarter based on prior usage; a projection is then made on what will be used in the future. This method determines spending amounts that cannot be exceeded without additional review.

Budget Cycle

All organizations identify a budgeting cycle to precede their fiscal year (FY). The **FY** defines the time period for which the business will evaluate and compare the budgeted figures with the actual figures. These comparisons are done on a pay period, monthly, quarterly, and a year to date basis. There are 26 pay periods, 12 months, and 4 quarters in an FY. An FY typically starts on January 1, July 1, or October 1. An example of an FY that starts on July 1 is shown in Table 8–5.

BUDGET PROCESS

Before the actual budget packets are prepared, the organization's leadership team will assess and analyze the external environment to establish future goals and objectives. Environmental factors usually cannot be changed, so that the organization will need to base its strategies on the factors as they present themselves. This should include consideration of the economic, social, and political forces that will affect the hospital or health care organization. Examples of such forces are government laws and regulations, local industry trends, the financial future of business in the area, and the payer status of the community served.

Table 8–5 Example of July FY

Quarter	Months
First quarter	July, August, September
Second quarter	October, November, December
Third quarter	January, February, March
Fourth quarter	April, May, June

The planning process can be separated into two related aspects: strategic and operations. The strategic aspect focuses the planning process on the future direction of the organization. The operational aspect of the planning process deals with the preparation of the budget. It consists of organizing the hospital resources to accomplish the strategic plan and projecting capital needs in the future. It is essential for the organization to have a clear vision so that strategic goals and the capital necessary to accomplish the goals are planned into the operational budget.

KEY CONCEPTS	• There are four budget methodologies that are utilized to develop the budget: trended, historical, or incremental; planning/programming; ZBB; and appropriations/fixed budgeting. • A budget is a statement or plan of operation for the upcoming year expressed in quantitative terms. Budgets can help coordinate and identify the resources that the organization will expend. There are three types of budgets: personnel, capital, and operating. • The health care organization's business is determined by the community and projections for growth in the market. The business volume that a health care system delivers is categorized by the broad term unit of service (UOS). A UOS is a specific unit of health care service that a department delivers to its customers. On a nursing unit, the UOS may be defined as a patient day. • All organizations identify a budgeting cycle to set their FY. The FY determines how the business will evaluate and compare the budgeted figures with the actual figures.

Steps To Create an Operational Budget

The first step in creating a budget is the preparation of the budget manuals. This is the responsibility of the financial department and the chief financial officer of the institution. The budget manual should explain in detail how the budgeting system works. It should contain deadlines for completion of individual steps, the approval process, sample forms and instructions for completing the forms, and a glossary of terms. Meetings to discuss and answer specific questions about the budgeting process can greatly assist in the successful completion of the budget.

The next step is the actual projection of UOS based on assumptions about the future business projections. The department directors should approve the projected UOS based on their knowledge of the business they control. The primary units of service (which are considered patient days) will drive the secondary units for all supporting services.

Preparing the Revenue Budget

After statistical worksheets are developed and approved, revenue and expense worksheets are prepared. Revenue projections for health care organizations are determined by predicting service volumes according to payer types. Various payer types reimburse different amounts for similar services. For example, some payers reimburse all billed charges, whereas others receive discounts, fixed prospective rates, or capitated dollars. Because there are so many different types of contractual arrangements, the estimation of a hospital's revenue is extremely critical to the revenue budget.

There are two types of patient revenue: inpatient revenue and outpatient revenue. Often the focus has been inpatient revenue, but as more patients shift to an outpatient status the ability to bill and collect for outpatient services will greatly assist in the success of hospitals in the future. The increase in outpatient services will only add to the complexity of estimating revenue for the hospital, but it is important to estimate as accurately as possible.

Some hospitals prepare the revenue and expense budget at the same time. The revenue budget is projected first based on the last year's charges and reimbursement. These revenue projections are compared with the expense projections for the same volume of activity, and adjustments are made. In other hospitals revenues are projected first, and guidelines are then given to the department managers to help them establish their expenses. Under prospective reimbursement, this may be the most logical method if expenses are to be based on total authorized revenues.

Preparing the Personnel Budget

After receiving the approved UOS, the department managers are responsible for completing their specific department's annual expense budget, which consists of the salary (personnel) and operating budgets. When computing the personnel budget, one should take into consideration the following factors:

- work standards (mix in patient acuity)
- fixed and variable staffing
- productive and nonproductive time
- staffing patterns
- salary differentials
- benefits

Work standards/productivity standards. Nursing uses productivity measures in the form of acuity systems or patient classification systems for several reasons. **Patient classification systems** provide a method to classify patients according to a specific group of tasks, acuity of illness, degree of nursing dependency, and/or risks and to predict the amount of nursing time that will be required to care for the patients on the unit (see Chapter 3 for a more detailed discussion of patient classification systems). A nurse manager can predict the staffing needs fairly accurately with a subjective assessment, but it is essential to have objective data to support staffing and budgetary needs. It is important to assign staff based on the actual need rather than on the amount of care actually provided. There are many different types of patient classification systems that are being utilized today, but what is most important is that whatever system is used must demonstrate validity and reliability in accurately predicting nursing care hours.

All areas in health care need to have a work standard. This is just as important for the outpatient care areas. The same general concepts of efficiency and best use of resources need to guide staffing decisions. In the field of industrial engineering, work has been done to establish actual time for specific nursing tasks that are implemented routinely. These efforts, using time and motion studies, accurately measure many procedures, including documentation time. After the general flow of the unit is determined, a specific work standard is developed.

On nursing units, the most common work measurement is HPPD. The first step in calculating the HPPD is to use the patient classification system and to categorize the patients. This information can be prospective by having the staff gather the information from the patients. Exhibit 8–3 shows how to calculate HPPD.

Full-time equivalent. An **FTE** is a time equivalent of 2,080 hours paid during a year. This 2,080 hours per year includes all the paid hours for one FTE. Paid hours include actual worked time, or productive time, as well as all nonproductive time, which includes vacation, holiday, jury duty, education time, ill time, and any other codes that are hospital approved. Table 8–6 lists the different percentages of FTEs and the number of hours paid per year for a typical staffing pattern.

Fixed and variable staffing. There are two types of worker FTE categories: fixed and variable. **Fixed FTEs** are defined as FTEs that are not replaced, do not flex with changes in volume, and do not contribute directly to the department UOS. **Variable FTEs** are defined as FTEs that are flexed with volume, are replaced as needed, and contribute directly to the UOS.

Productive and nonproductive time. Salary expense for a health care organization includes productive time or actual time worked and nonproduc-

Exhibit 8–3 Prospective HPPD Calculation

Step 1: Patient Categorization by Patient Classification System

Level of Care	Number of Patients
I	8
II	19
III	15
IV	4

Step 2: Hours of Nursing Care for Patient Mix

Level of Care	HPPD
I	4.8
II	6.2
III	8.0
IV	12.0

Step 3: Daily Hours of Nursing Care Required

Level of Care	Number of Patients/Day		HPPD		Hours of Care/24 Hours
I	8	×	4.8	=	38.4
II	19		6.2		117.8
III	15		8.0		120.0
IV	4		12.0		48.0
Total	46				324.2

Step 4: Calculation of HPPD

$$\frac{324.2 \text{ hours of care/24 hours}}{46 \text{ patients}} = 7.04 \text{ HPPD}$$

---

tive time or benefit time. The division between productive and nonproductive time is an important management decision. Small changes can lead to significant labor expense or cost savings. Once the total labor hours and FTE budgets are prepared, salary dollars can then be computed.

Productive salaries in nursing can be divided into direct care hours and indirect care hours. **Direct patient care salary hours** are the time given directly to the care of patients. **Indirect patient care salary hours** include the cost for the nurse manager, unit secretaries, staffing office, committee work, and off-shift supervisors. There may be other staff who also fit into this description based on the specific needs of the organization.

Table 8–6 Percentages of FTEs and Number of Hours Paid

FTE	Hours per 2-Week Pay Period	Total Annual Paid Hours
1.0	80	2,080
0.9	72	1,872
0.8	64	1,664
0.7	56	1,456
0.6	48	1,248
0.5	40	1,040

Staffing patterns. Using the recommended hours of care, nurse managers can work with the staff to plan how the hours of care are best distributed over all shifts. Other factors that should be considered are the skill mix, hours of work (e.g., Monday through Friday or 7 days per week), distribution of workload, and the type of delivery method.

Assessing the actual work on the unit will identify the skill mix [registered nurses (RNs), licensed vocational nurses (LVNs), and nursing assistants (NAs)] recommended for the patient acuity. Many hospital departments use a mixture of 8-, 10-, and 12-hour staffing patterns to match the work flow and to assist with staff satisfaction. Each of these staffing patterns requires a different replacement factor to account for days off. The **replacement factor** is the percentage of time that the organization pays an employee for not actually working. The replacement factor can account for only the days off based on staffing patterns or can be combined as a larger percentage with other employee benefits (e.g., sick time, paid time off, and holidays).

Salary differentials. There are a variety of salary differentials and overtime payment or reimbursement options. Staff who work the evening or night shift usually earn a shift differential. Additionally, many hospitals pay for working on holidays at a premium rate, usually 1.5 times the regular pay for working, which may be up to 12 holidays in some institutions. The manager needs to take into consideration the amount spent on differentials, overtime, and on-call hours to ensure that the budget accurately reflects the true salary costs.

Benefits. Employee benefits are figured as a percentage of the salary dollars. Employee benefits include workers' compensation, state disability, tuition reimbursement, and health care insurance. The definition of what is included in benefits varies from institution to institution. Employee benefits are costly to any organization because they are considered fixed overhead and average about 20% to 25% of total personnel salary dollars. The financial department will usually apply the percentage to the budget at the predetermined amount.

KEY CONCEPTS
- The two types of worked FTE categories are fixed and variable. Fixed FTEs are not replaced, do not flex with changes in volume, and do not contribute directly to the department's UOS. Variable FTEs are flexed with changes in volume, are replaced as needed, and contribute directly to the UOS.
- An FTE is a unit of time that is equal to 40 hours of work per week, 80 hours of work per pay period, and 2,080 hours per year.
- A manager should have an understanding of the following factors that affect the hospital's operations:
  1. patient census
  2. productivity
  3. physician practice patterns
  4. community economics
  5. reimbursement plans
  6. supply usage
  7. hospital programs and services
  8. competition

Building a Salary Budget

The labor hours and FTE projections are significant cost projections because most hospital departments are labor intensive and salary dollars are usually the single largest line item. Some hospitals use average hourly salary cost per job category of staff to build a salary budget. A simple method for calculating salary expense for a nursing unit with a standard of 10 HPPD for direct and indirect patient care hours is shown in Exhibit 8–4.

Exhibit 8–4 Calculating Salary Expense

Total projected patient days = 10,000
Nursing work standard = 10 HPPD

Patient days × HPPD = total productive paid hours
10,000 × 10 HPPD = 100,000 total hours of care

$$\frac{100,000 \text{ total hours of care}}{2,080 \text{ productive hours per FTE}} = 48.076 \text{ FTEs}$$

48.076 FTEs × 1.16 nonproductive (replacement) time* = 55.768 total FTEs

55.768 × 2,080 = 115,998 hours

115,998 hours × $20 (average hourly rate) = $2,319,948

The total salary expense to care for 10,000 patient days, giving each patient 10 HPPD at an average salary rate of $20/hour, is $2,319,960.
*Replacement percentage

Exhibit 8–5 Sample Position Control List

Cost Center	7000
Position Number	1934
Job Title	RN
Assign Hours	80
Position FTE	1.0
Employee Number	20
Employee Name	Doe, John
Current Base Rate	$20.00
Annual Salary	$41,600

Other institutions project the salary costs using a position control list that accounts for each individual employee and his or her specific salary. The **position control list** is the approved list of positions in a department. The position list displays the individual positions by category of personnel, the amount of hours worked, and the salary rate. Exhibit 8–5 shows an example of the position control list.

What do you do if you are budgeting for a department that uses a mix of 8- and 12-hour staff? It will be necessary to break the hours and employees down into the actual percentage of staff that work 8 hours and the percentage of staff that work 12 hours. The first step is to identify all fixed FTEs. These positions are not replaced, so that the total fixed FTEs multiplied by the hourly salary rate equals the salary costs for fixed FTEs. Figure 8–7 shows a worksheet to determine fixed salary costs.

The next step is to determine variable staffing costs. The worksheet shown in Figure 8–8 provides a step-by-step method to determine the salary dollars when a mix of staffing hours is used. In the instructions that follow, the numbers in parentheses are keyed to numbered areas on the worksheet.

1. Enter the facility, department, cost center, and manager name on the top of the worksheet. Next, enter the budgeted UOS (1) and the work standard (2). *Example:* UOS, 7,300 patient days; work standard, 8.0 HPPD.

2. Divide the total UOS by 365 days in a year (3). *Example:* 7,300 patient days (UOS)/365 days per year = 20 patients (average daily census).

3. Establish daily staffing hours needed to care for patients in the department (4). *Example:* 8.0 HPPD (work standard) × 20 patients = 160 hours.

4. Determine the unit's staffing patterns (8-,10-, and 12-hour shifts or a combination). If the staff are on a combination of hours, determine the

Facility:
Department:
Cost Center:
Manager:

Fixed Salary Budget
FY _____

Sub-Account Number	Position	Composite Hourly Rate (1)	Scheduled Paid Hours (Max: 2080) (2)	Gross Annual Salaries (1 × 2)
	Management and Supervision			
	Clerical and Other Administrative			
	Environmental and Food Service			
	Other Salaries and Wages			
	TOTAL			

FTEs (Column 2 Total Divided by 2080) (2 Decimals) _____

Figure 8–7 Fixed FTE budget.

Facility:
Department:
Cost Center:
Manager:

(1) Budgeted Units of Service (UOS)

(2) Work Standard per UOS	(3) AVG Daily UOS (1)/365	(4) Daily Hours Required (2) ∞ (3)	(5) Daily Staff (4)/8, 10 or 12

FTE Coverage Ratio

	Days not worked			(7) Worked Days 365 / (6)	(8) FTE Ratio 365/(7)
	Weekend Days	VAC HOL SK Taken	(6) Total		
8 Hr Shift	104	26	130	235	1.55
10 Hr Shift	156	26	182	183	1.99
12 Hr Shift	208	17	225	140	2.61

Personnel Classification	Daily Staffing Positions			Daily Staff Total (5)	FTE Ratio (8)	Needed Staff	Hours Per Shift	Total Daily Hours	Composite Rate	Daily Staffing Expense	Calendar Days Staffed (7)	Budgeted Salary Expense
	Day	Evening	Night									
RN – Shift 8												
– Shift 10												
– Shift 12												
LVN – Shift 8												
– Shift 10												
– Shift 12												
Aides and Order Med Practice												
Total												

Figure 8–8 Worksheet to determine salary dollars for a mix of staffing hours.

percentage of staff in each category. Break the staff up into their job classifications (RNs, LVNs, and NAs). *Example:* all RN staff, 50% on 8-hour shifts, 50% on 12-hour shifts; 160 hours × 0.50 = 80 hours of staff time on both 8- and 12-hour shifts.

5. Calculate the number of staff needed by staffing hours for each day (5). *Example:* 80 hours/8 hours = 10 FTEs working 8-hour shifts; 80 hours/12 hours = 6.66 FTEs working 12-hour shifts.

6. Distribute the hours required over all shifts. Include the total number of days not worked (e.g., weekends, vacation, sick time, and holidays) (6) and the total number of days worked (365 days – days not worked) (7).

7. Identify the FTE replacement ratio (productive hours to nonproductive hours) for each shift category (8). For an 8-hour shift, the replacement ratio is 1.55, and for a 10-hour shift it is 1.99. For 12-hour shifts, you need the hospital's assessment of the replacement ratio. A ratio of 2.61 is often used (this appears to be overstated, however, and a more appropriate replacement ratio may be 2.0).

8. Multiply the total number of staff by the appropriate replacement ratio. *Example:* 10 FTEs × 1.55 = 15.5 FTEs needed for 8-hour shifts; 6.66 FTEs × 2.0 = 13.32 FTEs needed for 12-hour shifts.

9. Add up the number of FTEs needed to provide care to the budgeted number of patients 24 hours per day, 365 days per year. *Example:* 15.5 FTEs + 13.32 FTEs = 28.82 total flexible FTEs.

10. Multiply each classification of FTE by the hours per shift that the staff group works. The total is the daily staffing hours. *Example:* 15.5 FTEs × 8 hours = 124 total daily hours of 8-hour staff; 13.32 FTEs × 12 hours = 159.8 total daily hours of 12-hour staff.

11. Determine the composite rate for each job classification. This rate should include any overtime, shift differentials, holiday overtime pay, and the like. Using the actual payroll for the current FY will provide an accurate average salary rate. Multiply the average composite rate by the daily staffing hours for each job classification; this is the daily staffing expense. *Example:* 124 hours × $20/hour = $2,480 daily staffing expense for 8-hour staff, 159.8 hours × $24/hour = $3,835 daily staffing expense for 12-hour staff.

12. Multiply the daily staffing expense per job classification and shift worked by the number of calendar days staffed. For a 72-hour pay period, an 8-hour shift is 235 days worked, a 10-hour shift is 183 days worked, and a 12-hour shift is 140 days worked. *Example:* $2,480 × 235 days worked = $582,800 budgeted salary expense for 8-hour staff;

$3,835 \times 140$ days worked = $536,900 budgeted salary expense for 12-hour staff.

13. Add the salary expenses together to determine the total labor costs for the variable staffing component in the unit. Add this number to the fixed amount to determine the total salary costs for the department. *Example:* $582,800 + $536,900 = $1,119,700 total salary cost for variable staff (8- and 12-hour staff).

The worksheet in Figure 8–8 is a valuable tool to validate the budget dollars, particularly if there are any changes in the work standard or shift patterns. Exhibit 8–6 summarizes the steps in budget preparation.

KEY CONCEPTS

- As the inpatient census continues to drop, monitoring and control of the expense per UOS are the most important interventions for cost-effective management of resources.
- A unit personnel budget can be developed by predicting patient days by level of activity, determining the number of nursing hours required for the patient mix, distributing the nursing hours over all shifts, developing a staffing pattern that considers the staff mix, and converting hours of care to actual costs.
- In the health care industry, 50% to 70% of the annual operating budget is attributed to personnel salaries.

Exhibit 8–6 Summary of Budget Preparation

1. Obtain the budget manual developed by the financial department.
2. Predict the UOS (e.g., patient days).
3. Determine the hours of care required for the patient mix:
   - Fixed and variable staffing
   - Regulatory requirements
   - Support services / new delivery methods
4. Distribute the hours required over all shifts.
5. Develop a staffing pattern considering the personnel mix available.
6. Convert hours of care to actual costs:
   - Personnel salary expense
     — Productive time
     — Nonproductive time
   - Differentials and overtime
   - On-call pay
   - Promotional increases
   - Per diem staff

Preparing the Nonsalary Budget

The other significant line items are the supply costs in a nursing unit. The operating budget relies on the projected UOS or patient days. Most health care institutions provide managers with a list of medical supplies, linen supplies, maintenance contracts, printing supplies, medical equipment, books and journals, pharmacy supplies, and minor equipment. The expense categories are numerous, so that most organizations publish a list of expense codes for the users' reference. What is included in individual nursing department budgets varies by specific hospital.

The majority of health care organizations budget for supplies by annualizing the amount spent in the current year and then applying a percentage for inflation as necessary. This method takes last year's actual supply expense for each specific category, divides the expense per UOS, and then multiplies the expense per UOS by the projected units for the next FY.

As an example, a hospital has an FY that begins in October, and the budget preparation begins in May. The hospital uses April YTD expenses for a line item such as medical supplies and multiplies the actual YTD dollars by 1.7 to obtain the annualized amount. Annualized figures are approximate numbers based on what the total supply cost per category would be if the spending remained the same until the end of the FY. Annualized numbers can be obtained by multiplying the YTD number for the first 7 months (in this example, $20,000) by 1.7, giving $34,000 as the annualized cost of medical supplies. The annualized cost of medical supplies is then divided by the annualized UOS to establish the cost of medical supplies per patient day (patient days can be annualized in the same way that the medical supplies are annualized). The cost of medical supplies per patient day is then multiplied by the projected UOS (patient days) for the next FY. An inflation factor, if necessary, can then be applied.

This methodology can be used for all nonsalary budgets, such as nonmedical supplies, linen, dietary, and paper supplies. One weakness of this methodology is that it carries over inefficiencies from year to year. A sample worksheet to annualize operating costs is shown in Figure 8–9.

Approval of the Budget

Once the budgets are submitted to the financial department, the individual department budgets are added together to form an integrated hospital budget. If the budget is accepted by the finance department, it will be presented to the board of directors for final approval. The actual implementation of the budget begins at the start of the new FY.

Facility:
Department:
Cost Center:
Manager:

MEDICAL SUPPLIES

1. $\dfrac{\text{Actual Cost Medical Supplies}}{\text{Actual UOS}} = \text{Medical Supply Cost/UOS}$

2. $\dfrac{\text{Medical Cost/UOS}}{} \times \text{Budget UOS} \times \text{Inflation Factor} = \text{Next Year Medical Supply Budget}$

NONMEDICAL SUPPLIES

1. $\dfrac{\text{Actual Cost Nonmedical Supplies}}{\text{Actual UOS}} = \text{Nonmedical Supplies—Cost/UOS}$

2. $\dfrac{\text{Nonmedical Cost/UOS}}{} \times \text{Budgeted UOS} \times \text{Inflation Factor} = \text{Next Year Medical Supply Budget}$

LINEN

1. $\dfrac{\text{Actual Cost Linen}}{\text{Actual UOS}} = \text{Linen Cost/UOS}$

2. $\dfrac{\text{Linen Cost/UOS}}{} \times \text{Budgeted UOS} \times \text{Inflation Factor} = \text{Next Year Linen Budget}$

Figure 8–9 Nonsalary budget worksheet.

TECHNIQUES FOR ANALYZING MANAGEMENT REPORTS

The budget is both a planning tool and a control tool to manage expenditures by providing feedback to management. Control of the budget is accomplished through the monthly monitoring of the actual expenses compared with budgeted expenses. By comparing the actual and budgeted expenses and analyzing any variances, the nurse manager can make modifications and adjustments to operations to meet the monthly organizational goals. Management reports that are used to assess the budgetary performance of the hospital include the following:

- Hospital reports
  1. Income reports
  2. Statistical reports
- Department/unit reports
  1. Trend analysis
  2. Productivity reports
  3. Labor distribution
  4. Accounts payable
  5. Materials management
  6. General ledger

Income Reports

The **income report** is important to all levels of management. It is a record of all the revenues that are posted for the organization for the services provided and all the expenses that are incurred to provide those services. The income statement typically compares the current month's actual activity with the budgeted activity and last year's activity for the same time frame. The income statement is divided into three distinct categories: revenues, deductions from revenue, and operating expenses.

The hospital's revenue appears on the first section of the income report. On most hospital income statements, the first line is revenue from patient care services and is followed by revenue from ancillary services, such as radiology, laboratory, respiratory care, and so on. **Total gross income** is the amount of money that would be received if all bills were collected as billed. This does not occur, however, because of bad debt, charitable allowances, and contractual allowances. These allowances are subtracted from the gross revenue to form the **net patient revenue** (Figure 8–10).

The operating expenses include all the institution's expenses in providing patient care, such as salaries, employee benefits, medical supplies, nonmedi-

DESCRIPTION	MONTH			YEAR TO DATE			
	Actual	Budget	Variance	Last Year	Actual	Budget	Variance
GROSS PATIENT REVENUE							
Routine Services	$2,008	$2,164	($156)	$6,011	$5,664	$6,392	($728)
Ancillary Services—IP	4,994	5,250	(256)	14,237	13,932	15,478	(1,546)
Ancillary Services—OP	3,084	3,490	(406)	9,458	9,434	10,426	(992)
TOTAL PATIENT REVENUE	10,086	10,904	(818)	29,706	29,030	32,296	(3,266)
DEDUCTIONS FROM REVENUE							
Charity & Uncompensated Care	324	289	(35)	825	856	854	(2)
Medicare, Medi-Cal Allowance	4,180	4,361	181	11,469	11,730	12,909	1,179
Other Contractual Allowances	1,287	1,466	179	3,838	3,928	4,340	412
TOTAL DEDUCTIONS FROM REVENUE	5,791	6,116	325	16,132	16,514	18,103	1,589
NET REVENUE FROM PATIENTS	$4,295	$4,788	($493)	$13,574	$12,516	$14,193	($1,677)

Figure 8-10 Statement of revenues: December 1994 and the 3 months ended December 31, 1994 ($ × 1,000).

cal supplies, medical fees, purchased services, maintenance and utilities, and depreciation (Figure 8–11). The common term **bottom line** is the result of subtracting the total operating costs from the net patient revenues. Another meaning of *bottom line* is the net income from operations or profit. All organizations need a profit to purchase capital or invest in future growth. In the past, many not-for-profit hospitals operated with budgeted net incomes as low as 1% to 5% of total gross revenues, whereas for-profit organizations budget for operating margins at 10% to 15%. The major difference between for-profit and not-for-profit institutions is the use of the profits.

KEY CONCEPT	• The income report is divided into three major categories: revenue, deductions from revenue, and operating expenses. The income statement typically compares the current month's actual activity with the budgeted activity and the last year's activity for the same time period. The net profit or income is the difference between the revenue and the expense. All organizations need to produce a certain bottom line to finance capital and future growth.

Statistical Reports

All hospital organizations are required to produce reports that have statistical information about the actual services that are produced in the organization. These reports contain demographic information such as number of patient days, LOS, surgical procedures, births, and so on. These reports are important in assessing the actual level of activity in the hospital and in noting trends that may require further assessment.

Departmental Reports

Nurse managers are responsible for making necessary adjustments to the departmental operations for keeping the actual expenses close to the budgeted expenses based on the projected number of UOS. Figure 8–12 displays the flow of budget information and data to a trend report that is provided monthly. A **trend report** summarizes and displays the budget information, including the revenue and expense for a specific department. The revenue and expense will match the department's activity for a month and will include payroll, accounts payable (bills), supplies, materials, and other related expenses.

The most effective method of monitoring costs is the **variance report**, which breaks the budget into expenses per UOS (Figure 8–13). Cost per UOS

	MONTH		DESCRIPTION	YEAR TO DATE			
Actual	Budget	Variance		Last Year	Actual	Budget	Variance
$4,295	$4,788	($493)	NET REVENUE FROM PATIENTS	$13,574	$12,516	$14,193	($1,677)
96	104	(8)	OTHER OPERATING REVENUE	361	282	313	(31)
4,391	4,892	(501)	TOTAL NET REVENUE	13,935	12,798	14,506	(1,708)
			OPERATING EXPENSES				
1,918	2,054	136	Salaries and Wages	5,639	5,585	6,083	498
358	422	64	Employee Benefits	1,073	1,089	1,249	160
66	49	(17)	Registry Personnel	309	143	139	(4)
746	783	37	Supplies	2,256	2,201	2,337	136
143	143	—	Medical Fees	433	480	430	(50)
212	262	50	Purchased Services	889	598	768	170
232	222	(10)	Maint., Utilities & Rentals	667	689	669	(20)
61	69	8	Business Insurance	323	184	208	24
260	240	(20)	Depreciation & Amortization	691	737	718	(19)
71	79	8	Interest	304	214	235	21
62	82	20	Other	218	182	247	65
4,129	4,405	276	TOTAL OPERATING EXPENSES	12,802	12,102	13,083	981
$262	$487	($225)	TOTAL EXCESS REVENUES OVER EXPENSE	$1,133	$696	$1,423	($727)
-3.2%	1.8%		% OF NET PATIENT REVENUE	-0.0%	-4.0%	1.6%	

Figure 8–11 Statement of revenues and expenses: December 1994 and the 3 months ended December 31, 1994 ($ × 1,000).

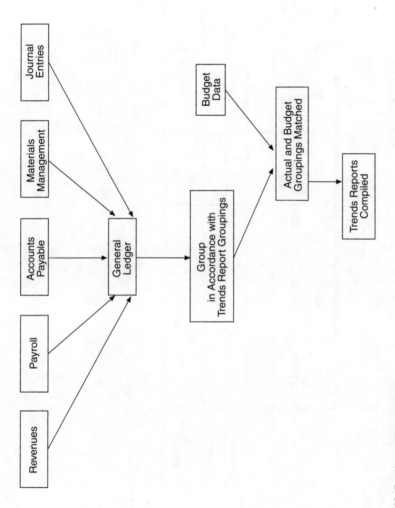

Figure 8–12 Trends report components.

UOS _____

(1) Actual YTD _____

(2) Budget YTD _____

YTD Through _____

Dept. _____

Budget Center # _____

	(3) ACTUAL EXPENSE	(4) BUDGET EXPENSE	(5) $ Variance (4) − (3)	(6) ACT. EXP. PER UNIT (3) − (1)	(7) BUDG. EXP. PER UNIT (4) − (2)	(8) % VARIANCE [(7) − (6) − (7)] ∞ 100
Salaries						
Benefits						
Registry						
TOTAL LABOR						

Figure 8–13 YTD expense variance report.

is calculated by dividing the total costs of a specific expense account by the number of UOS for a selected period of time. Cost per UOS calculations are the same for all types of UOS categories.

Cost per UOS becomes important when the hospital census becomes more unpredictable and the hospital revenue drops. If an institution is having census problems, it is increasingly important to keep the fixed costs as low as possible. As the volume of UOS declines, the expense per UOS increases unless the expenses have been reduced to accommodate the drop in census. To change the cost per UOS, the nurse manager must reduce expenses, move as many fixed costs into variable as possible, increase volume, or stop providing the service.

Listed below are the steps and questions that should be considered when a variance report is analyzed:

1. Compare actual results with the budget (analysis of variances). Is the line item over the budgeted amount or under the budgeted amount? How significant is the variance (usually institutions feel that 5% difference is the threshold for significance)? What are the reasons for the variance (e.g., were positions open or was overtime used)?

2. Monitor levels of fiscal performance by comparing expenses per UOS over time. Did the volume of patients change? Did the department business increase? If so, was this an isolated event, or are there trends to establish a pattern?

3. Analyze payer mix in hospital and department revenue reports. Has the type of patient changed? Did the hospital get a new contract that has a different payer status? Monitor legislation for changes in federal and state regulations that may affect availability of resources and specific services.

4. Monitor actual productivity and staffing levels versus predetermined standards. Is the unit staff working more productively? Did the acuity of patients change (e.g., the unit provided care for five transplant patients this month and the budgeted number was two patients)?

5. Monitor changes in the medical staff that may alter service demands. Did the physicians overutilize expensive diagnostic tests? Ordering expensive diagnostic tests can increase the expense per case. The development of critical pathways can assist in planning a course of care for individual DRGs, thereby managing the cost per case.

6. Monitor changes in the economy that may affect the demand and availability of each of the services.

7. Monitor changes in the services offered by other hospitals that may affect the demand (competition). Did the hospital down the street

open a new heart catheterization laboratory that changed the admitting patterns of the cardiologists?

8. Monitor inventory and supply price increases. For example, did the price of a thrombolytic agent increase by 20%, thereby increasing costs?

9. Evaluate capital equipment, its condition, and future projected needs. What is the age of the facility? This will affect maintenance, utilities, and housekeeping.

The nurse manager must be keenly aware of changes in the business and access the customers on a daily basis to identify concerns and opportunities for improvement. The manager is expected to be able to identify strategies to improve the performance of the department and decrease costs to maintain the organization's viability.

KEY CONCEPT
- The variance report is an evaluation tool to monitor the budget. Actual numbers are compared with the budgeted numbers on a monthly and YTD basis to identify and modify operations as needed in managing a department or organization.

Health Care Budgeting Trends

Current health care budgeting methodologies have evolved from projected budgets based on doubling of the midyear's budget (incremental) in the 1960s and 1970s, to top-down in the 1980s, to product line budgeting in the 1990s. Top-down budgeting is based on the cost per patient day that the health care system can afford or on revenue that is necessary. As payment strategies change, hospital accounting needs to follow suit to account more accurately for projected revenue. Product line/service line budgeting is a viable alternative. Product line/service line budgeting refers to the cost per case (service), such as cardiology services. This method will necessitate the creation of new financial accounting systems. It is important to track patients' LOS, payer mix, expected reimbursement, direct costs, resource utilization, and profit/loss per case. Product line/service line budgeting appears to be the natural next phase in hospital budgeting.

CONCLUSION

Nurse managers are responsible for a significant portion of an institution's financial resources. These resources can be invested most wisely for the provision of quality health care by the manager who is knowledgeable about the department budget and can effectively articulate the need for resources. Effectively planning, implementing, and monitoring financial resources are essential skills for nurse managers today as well as in the future. In the decades ahead, cost-efficient, high-quality care will dominate the health care industry.

Numerous books have been written about finance in health care organizations and budgeting. This chapter has highlighted the key financial and budgeting concepts that are important for the nurse manager to understand for effective planning and monitoring of financial resources.

RESEARCH FOUNDATION Wiesehe, A., & Bantz, D. (1992). Economic awareness of registered nurses employed in hospitals. *Nursing Economics, 10*(6), 406–411.

The health care industry is in a period of rapid change and uncertainty. The federal government as well as the general public have realized that health care is a scarce resource and that no longer can people receive all the health care services they desire. The nursing profession is in the middle of this health care revolution and nurses must have the knowledge and understanding of health care economics to compete and survive.

Wiesehe and Bantz (1992) used a convenience sample of RNs employed in three different hospitals in the Midwest to describe the knowledge of economics in relationship to nursing care and practice. Four issues were examined that included economics of health care, ethics and economics, impact of economics on quality of care, and economic changes and service delivery.

The findings of the study suggest that the majority of nurses did not have basic knowledge of health care economics, nursing budgets, or how federal government dollars were spent for health care. Further analysis indicated that the majority of these respondents were knowledgeable about delivery of services as it related to DRGs, PPOs, and HMOs. Analysis of variance indicated that baccalaureate-prepared nurses were more likely to identify and understand the differences underlying philosophies of PPOs and HMOs than associate or diploma nurses.

A majority of the responding nurses stated that health care costs could be reduced by nurses' involvement in decision making related to health care delivery and by better collaboration between physicians and nurses. A majority also indicated that the quality of care was dependent upon the money spent on nursing staff. Concerning family avocation, the majority of the respondents believed the nurse should intervene for the family regarding its wishes for resuscitation because of high and, at times, prolonged costs.

This research identified that the study respondents lacked a basic understanding of economics yet had the desire to learn more about economic issues as related to nursing practice and health care. It is important that nurses have the education and information about budgeting and health care finances to support and preserve the necessary resources required for the provision of health care.

REFERENCES

Aaron, H.J. (1991). Serious and unstable condition: Financing America's health care. In *Academic American Encyclopedia*. Danbury, CT: Grolier.

Curtin, L. (1993a). Barbarians at the gate. *Nursing Management, 24* (12), 9–10.

Curtin, L. (1993b). Keepers of the keys: Economics, ethics, and nursing administrators. *Nursing Administration Quarterly, 17* (4), 1–10.

Goldsmith, J. (1989). A radical prescription for hospitals. *Harvard Business Review, 89* (3), 104–111.

Jelinek, R., & Dennis, L. (1976). *A review and evaluation of nursing productivity.* Bethesda, MD: Health Resources Administration.

Moore, R.B. (1992). Financial planning for hospitals. *Topics in Health Care Financing, 18* (3), 9–15.

Pass, T. (1987). Case-mix, severity systems provide DRG alternatives. *Healthcare Financial Management, 41* (7), 74–82.

Pyhrr, P. (1970). Zero based budgeting. *Harvard Business Review, 48* (6), 111–121.

Strasen, L. (1987). *Key business skills for nurse managers.* Philadelphia: Lippincott.

Sullivan, E., & Decker, P. (1988). *Effective management in nursing.* Menlo Park, CA: Addison-Wesley.

Williams, S.J., & Torrens, P.R. (Eds.). (1980). *Introduction to health services.* New York: Wiley.

Wilson, A. (1993). The cost and quality of patient outcomes: A look at managed competition. *Nursing Administration Quarterly, 17* (4), 11–16.

SUGGESTED READING

Ames, C., & Hlavacek, J. (1990). Vital truths about managing your costs. *Harvard Business Review, 68* (1).

Anthony, R., & Reece, J. (1989). *Accounting text and cases* (8th ed.). Homewood, IL: Irwin.

Cleverly, W.O. (1992). *Essentials of health care finance.* Gaithersburg, MD: Aspen.

Davis, K., Anderson, G.F., Rowland, D., & Steinberg, E.P. (1990). *Health care cost containment.* Baltimore: Johns Hopkins University Press.

Douglas, L.M. (1992). The effective nurse—Leader and manager (4th ed.). St. Louis: Mosby–Year Book.

Eckhart, J. (1993). Costing out nursing service: Examining the research. *Nursing Economics, 11* (2), 91–98.

Felteau, A. (1992). Budget variance analysis and justifications. *Nursing Management, 23* (2), 40–41.

Felteau, A. (1993). Tools and techniques to effect budget neutrality. *Nursing Administration Quarterly, 17* (4), 59–64.

Gillies, D.A. (1989). *Nursing management: A systems approach* (2nd ed.). Philadelphia: Saunders.

Hollander, S., Smith, M., & Barron, J. (1992). Cost reductions part I: An operations improvement process. *Nursing Economics, 10* (5), 325–364.

Kanss, V. (1993). Influencing the rising costs of health care: A staff nurse's perspective. *Nursing Economics, 11* (2), 83–86.

Kirsch, J. (Ed.). (1988). *The middle manager and the nursing organization.* Norwalk, CT: Appleton & Lange.

Marriner-Tomey, A. (1992). *Guide to nursing management* (4th ed.). St. Louis: Mosby-Year Book.

Naisbitt, J. (1984). *Megatrends.* New York: Warner Books.

Strasen, L. (1987). Standard costing/productivity model for nursing. *Nursing Economics, 5* (4), 158–161.

Suver, J., & Neumenn, B. (1985). *Management accounting for healthcare organizations.* Chicago: Pluribus Press.

Swansberg, R., & Sowell, R. (1992). A model for costing and pricing nursing services. *Nursing Management, 23* (2), 33–36.

Thomas, S., & Vaughan, R. (1986). Costing nursing services using RVUs. *Journal of Nursing Administration, 16* (12), 10–16.

Watson, P., Lower, M., Wells, S., Farrah, S., & Jarrell, C. (1991). Discovering what nurses do and what it costs. *Nursing Management, 22* (5).

Wiesehe, A., & Bantz, D. (1992). Economics awareness of registered nurses employed in hospitals. *Nursing Economics, 10* (6), 406–411.

Wilburn, D. (1992). Budget response to volume variability. *Nurse Management, 23* (2), 42–44.

Zembala, S. (1993). Managing the costs of nursing care delivery. *Nursing Administration Quarterly, 17* (4), 74–79.

CHAPTER 9

Quality Improvement

Jennifer Biggs

CHAPTER OBJECTIVES

At the completion of this chapter, the beginning professional nurse will be able to:

1. recall the history of quality improvement in industry and health care
2. describe the main concepts of quality improvement, including quality, customers, and work processes
3. list the fundamental principles for implementing quality improvement, including organizational commitment, process improvement, measurement, problem-solving methods and tools, and employee involvement and empowerment
4. describe how the Joint Commission on Accreditation of Healthcare Organizations' 10-Step Process may be utilized to assess and improve nursing care

300

5. list other components of a comprehensive quality improvement
   program including quality assurance, utilization management, peer
   review, program evaluation, and research utilization

CRITICAL   Identify, during your clinical experience, an aspect of nursing care or service
THINKING   that can be improved. Develop an indicator that will measure the selected
CHALLENGE   aspect of nursing care and service. Determine how the data will be collected,
                 including the development of a data collection tool. Finally, determine how
                 the data will be analyzed to produce meaningful results.

Quality is one of the most prevalent topics discussed in the
health care industry today. Health care organizations are being required to
improve the quality of services while consuming fewer resources. Organizational adoption of a total quality management (TQM) philosophy and successful implementation of quality improvement are key to organizational survival in the current, highly competitive health care market.

It is necessary for the beginning professional nurse to have an understanding of TQM and continuous quality improvement concepts. The beginning
professional nurse will be working in a quality-conscious environment. In this
type of environment, each employee is asked to participate in improving the
care and service provided to customers while conserving valuable resources.

The concept of TQM in relationship to health care was introduced in the
1980s. TQM is a management philosophy that implies an organizationwide
commitment to the improvement of quality (Master & Schmele, 1991).
According to the Joint Commission on Accreditation of Healthcare Organizations (Joint Commission, 1991), TQM "builds upon traditional quality assurance methods by emphasizing organization and systems (rather than individuals), the need for objective data with which to analyze and improve
processes, and the ideal that systems and performance can always improve
even when high standards appear to have been met"(chap. 2,p. 3). A simpler
definition of TQM is to do the right thing the first time, on time, all the time
and to strive always for improvement and customer satisfaction (Deming,
1982; Juran, Goyna, & Bingham, 1979).

HISTORY OF QUALITY IMPROVEMENT

Quality management in industry can be traced back to before the turn of
the century. At that time, quality management was based on the principles of
product inspection by customers and the craftsmanship concept, in which
buyers relied on the skill and reputation of trained, experienced craftsmen.
The development of factories in Europe during the Industrial Revolution

added additional strategies for quality review, including measurement and standardization. American industry adopted many of these strategies (Juran, 1989).

American industry during World War II was faced with the need to produce enormous quantities of military products. Manufacturing companies gave top priority to meeting delivery dates, and as a result the quality of manufactured products declined. In an effort to improve the quality of military goods, a War Production Board was created that sponsored courses in a new quality strategy called statistical quality control (SQC). Around this time, the American Society for Quality Control was established, and SQC techniques continued to proliferate. During the war, the results and cost effectiveness of these efforts were never evaluated. After the war, when the government discontinued subsidizing SQC programs, companies evaluated the cost effectiveness and results of SQC and found that the programs had failed (Juran, 1989).

The United States after World War II experienced a boom in industry, and the Japanese began a rebuilding process that had as its foundation product quality. To solve its quality problems, Japan started a massive effort to learn how to manage quality that included visiting other countries to learn different approaches and calling in quality experts from the United States to train management personnel. Learning from these experiences, Japanese management instituted quality strategies that relied heavily on upper management's involvement and direction. In addition, these strategies included total workforce training and participation in the quality improvement efforts (Juran, 1989).

In the early postwar period, American companies considered Japanese competition in price rather than quality. As the years unfolded, price competition declined, and quality competition increased (Juran, 1981). During the 1970s and 1980s, numerous Japanese manufacturers of electronics, automobiles, and steel and machine tools greatly increased their share of the American market. American industry today is now trying to respond to the quality competition (Juran, 1989).

Important figures in the movement toward quality improvement include W. Edwards Deming, Joseph M. Juran, Philip Crosby, Avedis Donabedian, and Donald M. Berwick. Deming is probably the most famous of the quality "gurus." During World War II, Deming was primarily responsible for training American engineers in improving the quality of military goods. He was also the principal figure in training Japanese management in the concepts of SQC. Deming is noted for his 14-point management philosophy. Deming's 14 points emphasize leadership, cultural change, training for all employees, elimination of barriers and fear, continuous improvement, and employee involvement (Walton, 1986).

Juran, like Deming, was instrumental in training Japanese managers in quality management concepts. Juran's contributions to the quality improvement effort included broadening the focus of quality improvement beyond production to include management functions and the institution of a project-by-project process of improvement (Bliersbach, 1991). The Juran trilogy (Juran, 1989) makes up the components of effective quality management. The Juran trilogy of interrelated processes includes quality planning, quality control, and quality improvement.

Crosby is most renowned for his "zero defects" concept and for defining quality as conformance to requirements (Bliersbach, 1991). Crosby (1979) articulated four quality absolutes and a 14-step quality improvement process. The four quality absolutes are as follows: The definition of quality is conformance to requirements, the system of quality is prevention, the performance standard is zero defects, and the measurement of quality is the price of nonconformance. Crosby's 14 steps emphasize management commitment, the use of quality improvement teams, measurement, training for all employees, goal setting, and employee involvement and recognition.

Donabedian and Berwick have taken quality management principles and applied them to health care. Donabedian (1986) is recognized for his suggestions on structure, process, and outcome criteria for quality assessment. This model emphasizes the importance of relating health care structures (e.g., qualifications of providers, technology, and facilities) and processes (e.g., diagnostics and therapeutics) to patient outcomes. Berwick (1989) compares older quality assurance (QA) methods to a "theory of bad apples." He indicates that the bad apple view assumes that people are lazy and the cause of problems. Inspection and discipline are the old QA solutions. Instead of the bad apple view, Berwick proposes a theory of continuous improvement. This theory states that quality can be managed and improved through understanding and revising production processes based upon data collected about the processes.

QUALITY IMPROVEMENT IN HEALTH CARE

A paradigm shift is occurring in the health care industry. The traditional medical paradigm is being challenged by consumers who expect health care providers to allow them to be more involved in decision making and to show greater concern for their needs and wants as individuals. In addition, government, business, the insurance industry, consumers, and other groups are pressuring health care institutions to provide quality, customer-oriented services at a reduced cost (Leming, 1991). These groups are seeking information from health care organizations about clinical performance and other dimensions of care quality.

The new health care quality paradigm has brought about intense competition among health care organizations vying for business. The application of TQM to health care has been touted as the key to survival in the current marketplace. Quality improvement assists health care organizations in providing quality, customer-oriented services at a competitive price.

The Joint Commission has been influential in bringing quality improvement to health care organizations. The Joint Commission launched a major developmental project in 1986 entitled the Agenda for Change. One goal of the Agenda for Change is to develop an outcome-oriented monitoring and evaluation process that will assist health care organizations in improving the quality of care they provide (Joint Commission, 1991).

The Joint Commission survey process will focus on clinical and organizational performance. Clinical and organizational excellence is an essential component of quality. The Joint Commission hopes to be able to help institutions answer the question "Does this organization provide quality health care?" To evaluate more accurately an organization's effectiveness in improving the quality of care provided, the Joint Commission is identifying and selecting clinical and organizational indicators and revising their standards. The revised standards emphasize a multidisciplinary approach to providing health care services. Appropriate disciplines are responsible for monitoring and evaluating care and service in 14 functional areas (Exhibit 9-1).

Exhibit 9-1 Important Functions as Defined by the Joint Commission

Care of patients
  Assessment of patients
  Treatment of patients
  Operative and other invasive procedures
  Education of patients and family
  Rights of patients and organizational ethics
  Entry to setting or service
  Nutritional care
  Coordination of care
Organizational functions
  Leadership
  Management of information
  Improving organizational performance
  Management of human resources
  Management of the environment of care
  Surveillance, prevention, and control of infection

Source: Copyright © 1993, Joint Commission on Accreditation of Healthcare Organizations, Oak Brook Terrace, Illinois. Adapted with permission from *The 1994 Accreditation Manual for Hospitals, Volume I: Standards,* p. xiv.

KEY
CONCEPTS

- Quality improvement in health care involves:
  1. a paradigm shift requiring health care to be customer oriented
  2. the provision of improved quality of care and service at reduced cost
  3. intensive competition among health care organizations for business
  4. the Joint Commission's Agenda for Change driving the application of quality improvement in health care organizations
- Quality, customers, and work processes are the focus of quality improvement in health care. The beginning professional nurse must understand these quality improvement concepts to work effectively in a quality improvement environment.

Defining Quality

Quality in the medical paradigm was defined as meeting professional standards or knowing intuitively that one provided quality care. If one asked a beginning professional nurse what quality care is, he or she might say "I don't know what it is, but I know it when I see it." In the new quality paradigm, quality in health care is defined as meeting or exceeding the customer's needs and fulfilling his or her expectations. The professional nurse's customer defines quality. Quality care for the customer may be different from what the nurse perceives as quality care.

The most influential factor in a customer's selection of a health care organization is service. Health care consumers know how to evaluate the service they receive even though they may not always be able to evaluate the quality of health care provided (Leebov & Scott, 1994). Patients may perceive quality care as having their call light answered quickly, having fresh drinking water available, and being treated with courtesy and respect. The professional nurse may perceive quality care as thoroughly conducting a head-to-toe assessment, providing patient education on medications, and collaborating with the physician on the patient's care. Even though these duties are important in the care of the patient, the patient has additional needs that must be fulfilled. Only then is the care perceived as quality care by the patient.

The Joint Commission expands the definition of quality to include positive patient outcomes. It describes quality as "the degree to which patient care services increase the probability of desired patient outcomes and reduce the probability of undesired outcomes, given the current state of knowledge" (1991, chap. 2, p. 3). Clinically, professional nurses and other health care providers must improve their practices to produce positive patient outcomes. Patient care standards and guidelines and critical pathways have been developed to describe, standardize, and improve practice to produce positive patient outcomes (Schroeder, 1994). Analysis of conformance to standards, guidelines, and/or critical pathways are one benchmark by which quality is measured (Katz & Green, 1992).

In quality improvement, quality must be quantified. Measurable and objective clinical, managerial, and governance indicators that reflect the mission of the health care organization must be developed. These indicators produce data that, when analyzed, reflect the performance of an organization. Only when data are collected and analyzed is the organization ready to make changes to improve care and service. Decisions must be based on fact, not on myth or intuition.

Customers

Customers define quality for professional nurses. In quality improvement, the term *customer* takes on a broader definition than traditionally understood by the beginning professional nurse. Nurses have customarily defined their customers as the patient and the physician. The definition of customer in quality improvement is anyone to whom the nurse provides information or who receives the nurse's product or service. The professional nurse is the supplier of information, a product, or a service. Customers can be people, departments, companies, or agencies. The professional nurse's customers may be internal or external to the organization. Internal customers of the professional nurse may include patients, families, physicians, pharmacy personnel, laboratory personnel, administration, finance, another patient care unit, peers, and so forth. External customers include third party payers, licensing and regulatory agencies, businesses, other health care organizations, and the like. The customer–supplier relationship is reciprocal. The nurse may be a supplier of information or service at one moment and a customer the next. For example, the nurse supplies the laboratory (the customer) with an order for stat electrolytes. The laboratory supplies the nurse (the customer) with the stat electrolyte results.

Processes

Frequently, when a problem is identified in health care, the provider is blamed for the problem. For example, if a stat laboratory result is not available within the 15-minute time frame identified as the standard for the organization, the physician blames the laboratory staff for not immediately running the test. According to Deming, 85% of time problems result from a breakdown in the process or system, not because of individual employee performance (Merry, 1990). In the example, the laboratory staff immediately ran the test when it was received, but it took 20 minutes to transport the specimen to the laboratory utilizing the current transportation system. The process of transporting the specimen is "broken." Quality improvement concepts emphasize that improvement will occur when we stop assigning blame and instead study and change the way the system works (Schroeder, 1994).

KEY CONCEPT   Quality improvement emphasizes the following:
- Quality is meeting or exceeding the customer's needs and expectations.
- Quality is the degree to which patient care and services increase the probability of desired patient outcomes.
- Quality is measurable.
- The customer is anyone who receives information, a product, or a service.
- Customers can be internal or external to the organization.
- The customer–supplier relationship is reciprocal.
- Problems occur 85% of the time as a result of a breakdown in the process or system, not because of individual performance.

LEARNING CHALLENGE   A beginning professional nurse is having difficulty obtaining a stat medication from the pharmacy. The nurse blames the pharmacist for not sending the medication in a timely fashion. The pharmacist states that he sent the medication more than 30 minutes ago and cannot understand why it has not been received.
1. Who is the customer in this scenario?
2. What is the customer's need or expectation?
3. Who or what is possibly the cause of this problem?

FUNDAMENTAL PRINCIPLES FOR IMPLEMENTING QUALITY IMPROVEMENT

The success of any quality improvement program rests on the use of several fundamental principles of quality improvement. Organizational commitment, process improvement, the use of a scientific approach, and employee involvement and empowerment are essential components in a quality improvement program.

Organizational Commitment

A health care organization's governing body holds the ultimate responsibility for quality care. The governing body delegates that responsibility to administrative leaders, such as the chief executive officer, senior management, and elected/appointed individuals who lead the medical staff. These leaders plan, direct, and coordinate efforts to improve health care services that are responsive to community and patient needs and improve patient care outcomes. These leaders accomplish these activities in consideration of the organization's mission and vision. An organizational mission refers to the purpose of the organization. An organizational vision describes the organization's future development (National Association for Healthcare Quality, 1994). "An organization's direction is built upon its mission, and guided by its vision" (National Association for Healthcare Quality, 1994, p. 13).

Progress toward customer satisfaction and quality improvement is driven by administrative leaders who explicitly communicate their commitment. They develop and lead the service strategy that moves the organization forward. Administrative leaders must create a clear vision of service excellence and communicate that direction to all staff (Leebov & Scott, 1994).

The beginning professional nurse should consider his or her organization's mission and vision during the workday. An understanding of the organization's mission and vision provides the beginning professional nurse with direction for the day and an image of the future, allowing him or her to become involved in and supportive of change. Refer to Chapter 1 for further discussion of organizational mission. Development of organizational vision is discussed in Chapter 12.

For quality improvement to be successful in an organization, key leaders and staff must be educated in quality improvement concepts, tools, and techniques. They must create an organizational structure to support quality improvement efforts in the organization. Also, appropriate resources must be made available, including staffpower, money, and time. It is not enough for administrative leaders to provide only tangible support, however. Administrative leaders must "walk the talk" and role model service excellence (Leebov & Scott, 1994).

Process Improvement

Health care is delivered via numerous work processes. Processes are a series or set of actions carried out to achieve a certain result (Schroeder, 1994). Completion of a process usually involves several departments and can be complex in nature. For example, the process of a patient obtaining a chest radiograph involves multiple steps and the participation of many staff. The physician must determine that a chest radiograph is medically indicated and write the order. The unit secretary transcribes the order and notifies the radiology department that a chest film has been ordered. The beginning professional nurse teaches the patient what to expect during the procedure and prepares the patient for transport. Transportation staff transport the patient to radiology. The radiology technician takes the chest radiograph and develops the film. The radiologist interprets the film. A secretary types the report. The beginning professional nurse will see that completion of what seems to be a simple work process can be complex. In health care, the kinds of processes carried out can be clinical (e.g., intravenous therapy), managerial (e.g., performance appraisal), or systems oriented (e.g., ordering laboratory tests; Katz & Green, 1992).

Variation in how a process is completed is common. Processes are carried out differently by different people, at different times of the day, or in different departments. According to Schroeder (1994):

> Some of the greatest opportunities to create improved care and service, as well as to increase efficiency and cost savings, is to understand and control (and ultimately decrease) process variation. Most quality improvement tools measure or study variation, and assist in identifying more effective ways to decrease variation when processes are carried out. (p. 7)

Organizations need to streamline work processes by eliminating duplication, waste, rework and non–value-added steps. Often by reducing the complexity of a process, productivity increases, resources are conserved, cost decreases, performance is enhanced, and positive outcomes are promoted (Masters & Masters, 1993; Schroeder, 1994). Improving quality of care and service is not limited to problem areas. Health care organizations should evaluate all their processes and systems to determine whether they can be improved.

As mentioned above, variation occurs in work processes. Variation can be related to the patient (e.g., unable to read), physicians and staff (e.g., not oriented to a specific procedure), and/or a system (e.g., inability to order needed supplies). There are two types of variation. The first is called **common cause variation**. Common cause variations are minor variations that occur no matter how well a system works. Common cause variation is often due to chance. Frequently, these variations are attributed to employee performance. Examples of common cause variation include a staff member's abilities, unclear instructions, or lack of equipment. Intensive employee training and hard work do not eliminate these variances. Common cause variations, are tolerated. **Tampering**, or trying to eliminate common cause variations results in organizations spending much time, effort, and money trying to fix something that is not "broken" (Katz & Green, 1992). To illustrate, the beginning professional nurse notices two experienced nurses changing a sterile wound dressing in slightly different ways. The patient's wound is healing, and no signs or symptoms of infection are present. It would not be beneficial to try to have both nurses perform the procedure identically because the patient outcome is favorable either way.

Special cause variation is the second type of variation. Special cause variation occurs when processes and systems break down. Possible reasons for process breakdowns include employee error, lack of knowledge, or failure of equipment. Special cause variation is easier to fix than common cause variation (Katz & Green, 1992). To illustrate special cause variation, consider the ordering of material supplies. The patient care unit requires a suction set-up to insert a chest tube emergently. The unit secretary orders the suction set-up from material supply, only to find out that the equipment is kept in an off-site warehouse and will not be available in the hospital for 1 hour. The system of ordering supplies is "broken" in this example and is considered a special cause variation.

The scientific method for distinguishing between common cause and special cause variation is called **statistical control** (Katz & Green, 1992). Statistical control is a simple concept. "Statistical control means that things are happening the way they were planned to happen" (Katz & Green, 1992, p. 145). A system that is in statistical control is not necessarily ideal or defect free. Rather, the system is stable, meaning that variation in the process falls within predetermined parameters established by the organization. When an organization's processes are in statistical control, the organization can be confident in its outcomes and begin to work toward quality improvement. When a process is in statistical control, improvement is achieved through a change in the system, not a change in individual workers. When a process is out of control, it must be stabilized before work toward quality improvement begins. Stability is achieved by investigating and correcting the special cause variations that are affecting the process (Katz & Green, 1992).

In health care, quality improvement activities are patient care focused and recognize that the processes of patient care are interdisciplinary and interdepartmental. Even though health care organizations are generally hierarchical structures, the majority of functions and processes cross the boundaries of disciplines and departments. The completion of even a simple task often depends on the actions of other people and the availability of resources. Changing and improving these functions and processes requires the input of all involved (Schroeder, 1994). Health care providers need to acknowledge that they are not isolated units but rather components of a system providing care. Problem solving becomes an interactive rather than reactive process (Masters & Masters, 1993).

Scientific Approach

Quality improvement methods are scientific. The scientific approach to improving care and service is a systematic, planned, organized method of problem solving that is understood and followed by all employees. Decisions are based on data rather than experience, intuition, and hunches. By utilizing a scientific approach to problem solving, organizations will determine the root causes of problems and fix them rather than implement an ineffective "quick fix" (Katz & Green, 1992).

A number of problem-solving methods are available for use in quality improvement. The plan, do, check, and act (PDCA) cycle (Schroeder, 1994; Walton, 1986) is one such method. The PDCA cycle entails the following (Schroeder, 1994, p. 8):

1. Plan
   - Identify one's customer groups.
   - Define their unique needs and the characteristics of quality they hold most dear.
   - Develop your product or service to meet these needs.
2. Do
   - Deliver your product or service.
3. Check
   - Continuously measure and analyze key aspects of quality.
   - Contrast these data to customer needs and expectations.
4. Act
   - Refine and improve the system and one's product or service.

Various other problem-solving methods may be utilized in quality improvement efforts, including the nursing process and the Joint Commission's 10-Step Process for Monitoring and Evaluation (Exhibit 9–2). Both these approaches use a logical thinking process that requires careful assessment, planning, the delivery of care and service, measurement and actions (Schroeder, 1994).

A number of problem analysis tools are available for use in quality improvement. All investigate variation and determine the root causes of problems. These tools are called statistical process control tools. A number of these tools exist, but the ones used most often in quality improvement include the flowchart, the cause-and-effect diagram, and the run chart. The beginning professional nurse participating in quality improvement efforts will become familiar with these tools during the improvement process.

A flowchart is a pictorial representation of the sequence of steps performed in a specific work process. A flowchart is used to identify the actual

Exhibit 9–2 The Joint Commission's 10-Step Monitoring Process

---

1. Assign responsibility
2. Delineate scope of care
3. Identify important aspects of care
4. Identify indicators
5. Establish thresholds for evaluation
6. Collect and organize data
7. Evaluate care
8. Take actions to solve identified problems
9. Assess actions and document improvement
10. Communicate relevant information to organizationwide quality program

Source: Copyright © 1991, Joint Commission on Accreditation of Healthcare Organizations, Oak Brook Terrace, Illinois. Adapted with permission from *Strategies for Quality Improvement in Nursing,* p. 6.

---

steps of a process to reveal duplication, inefficiencies, or misunderstandings; to identify the steps that the process should follow if everything is to work right; and to create a common understanding among individuals of how a process works (GOAL/QPC, 1988). Flowcharts are helpful in problem identification, problem analysis, and planning solutions. They use easily recognized symbols to represent the type of process being performed. Figure 9–1 is an example of a flowchart depicting the nurse administering a medication.

The cause-and-effect diagram represents the relationship between some effect and all possible causes influencing it. A well-detailed cause-and-effect diagram will take on the shape of fishbones, hence the alternative name *fishbone diagram*. Cause-and-effect diagrams are used for developing the big picture of a problem, for providing ideas for data collection and solutions, and as a starting point for determining the focus of improvement efforts. Cause-and-effect diagrams are useful in problem identification, problem analysis, and identification of causes of variation (GOAL/QPC, 1988). Figure 9–2 is an example of a cause-and-effect diagram representing the causes for a stat laboratory test not being completed within 15 minutes.

Run charts are used to represent data visually. Points are plotted on a graph in the order in which they become available over time. Run charts identify meaningful trends or shifts in data. They are used in data analysis and to monitor solutions (GOAL/QPC, 1988). Figure 9–3 is an example of a run chart showing the trend in one unit's patient falls over a 6-month period.

Employee Involvement and Empowerment

Quality improvement education and training for all members of the organization are key to a successful quality improvement program. Training should

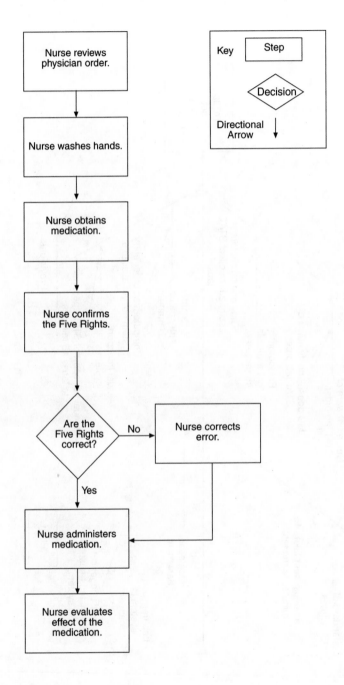

Figure 9–1 Flowchart.

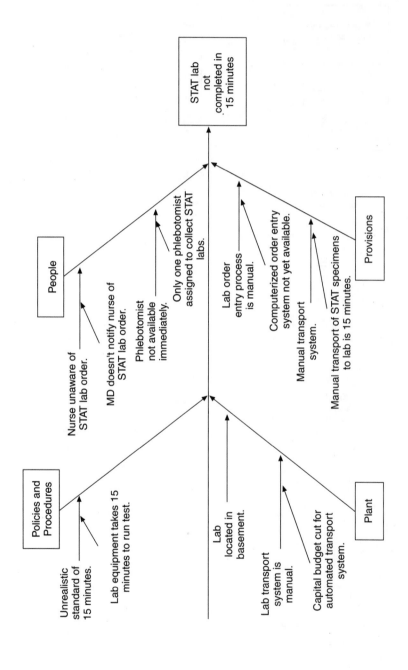

Figure 9–2 Cause-and-effect diagram.

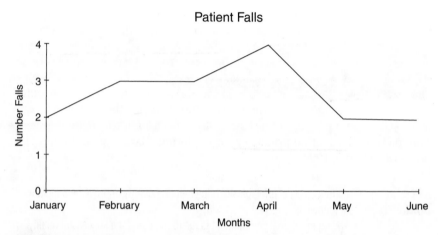

Figure 9–3 Run chart.

begin at the top of the organization and cascade down through the organization. Educational content will vary depending upon each staff member's level
of responsibility. All employees must understand their roles and responsibilities and what impact they have on quality improvement. Providing education
about quality improvement concepts is not enough; staff need to be encouraged to elevate constantly their level of skill and professional expertise (National Association for Healthcare Quality, 1994).

Employee involvement and empowerment are essential to improving the
quality of care and service. Employee involvement means employee participation in quality improvement. Participation in quality improvement might
entail participating on a team to design and improve a work process or to
improve upon how customers are served, determining ways to increase job
satisfaction, creating strategies for organizational improvement, and so
forth. Involvement and participation only lead to empowerment if leaders act
on employee/team input and suggestions. In addition, leaders must allow
employees the autonomy to act responsibly in meeting customers' needs
(Leebov & Scott, 1994). "Empowerment takes place when the employee's
level of authority matches the employee's level of responsibility" (Leebov &
Scott, 1994, p. 224). Solutions that come from the top down generally are met
with resistance and often do not work. When employees generate solutions,
all staff feel empowered. This feeling of empowerment spreads across the
organization, perpetuating a quality attitude. Not only does the quality of the
care and service provided increase, but productivity and job satisfaction increase as overall costs decrease.

The beginning professional nurse may be asked to participate on a quality improvement team. The use of teams in quality improvement is a powerful technique. Teams allow employees to own a process and take action to improve it. Team members become empowered while working on the team. Quality improvement teams consist of employees from within the organization who are expert in the process being studied. Team members are selected because they are involved in the process, not because they are in management. The responsibility of the team is to focus on improving one process. The team uses scientific principles for exploring, clarifying, and improving processes (Parisi, 1994).

KEY CONCEPT   The fundamental principles of implementing quality improvement include the following:

- Organizational commitment is the foundation for a successful quality improvement program.
- Health care is delivered via numerous work processes.
- Streamlining work processes to eliminate variation increases productivity and performance, decreases cost, and promotes positive patient outcomes.
- Two types of variation occur in work processes: common cause variation and special cause variation.
- The delivery of health care is an interdisciplinary/interdepartmental process. All health care providers must participate in quality improvement efforts.
- A scientific approach to problem solving is utilized in quality improvement.
- Tools frequently used in quality improvement include flowcharts, cause-and-effect diagrams, and run charts.
- Employee involvement and empowerment in quality improvement create a successful program.

LEARNING CHALLENGE   A beginning professional nurse has received training in the use of quality improvement methods and tools. During a staff meeting, the manager of the unit states that there is a problem with the delivery of meal trays to the patients. Currently, nutrition services brings a cart with the meals to the unit, and the unit staff are required to pass the trays. Unfortunately, trays are sometimes delivered to the patients 30 minutes after they arrive on the unit. The patients complain because the food is cold.

1. What tool might the nurse suggest be used to identify the actual steps in the process of delivering trays to the patients?
2. What tool might the nurse suggest be used to identify the reasons for trays not being delivered to patients in a timely manner?

ASSESSING AND IMPROVING NURSING CARE USING THE JOINT COMMISSION'S 10-STEP PROCESS

A primary responsibility of the division of nursing is to continuously assess and improve the nursing care and service provided to its customers. This responsibility is accomplished by developing a quality improvement plan, assessing care and service to determine areas for improvement, identifying customers' needs and expectations, utilizing indicators to measure care and service, evaluating the results, and taking action to improve processes.

The Joint Commission (1993a) specifies that every health care institution must have a plan to improve organizational performance. The organization's plan must demonstrate a systematic, organizationwide approach to designing, measuring, assessing, and improving performance. Depending on how the organization structures its quality improvement program, the division of nursing and/or a patient care unit may or may not have an individual quality improvement plan. Nevertheless, the division of nursing will be included in any organizational quality improvement plan. A comprehensive quality improvement plan will include the following elements (Joint Commission, 1993a):

- the organizational structure of the quality improvement program
- responsibility for the quality improvement program
- the process for assessing areas for improvement
- the process for determining customers' needs and expectations
- quality indicators used to measure care and service
- the process for evaluating care and service
- the process for improving care and service
- the process for communicating results organizationwide

The Joint Commission's 10-Step Process is useful in developing and implementing a quality improvement plan.

The beginning professional nurse should familiarize himself or herself with the organization's quality improvement plan and the division of nursing's and/or patient care unit's quality improvement plan, as appropriate. The quality improvement plan will assist the nurse in understanding his or her role in quality improvement, at both the patient care unit level and the organizational level.

Assign Responsibility for Quality Improvement

Quality improvement is the responsibility of every employee in an organization. Various levels of involvement are expected of employees based on their job responsibilities, however. Top administrators are responsible for developing a quality improvement plan and providing the necessary support for it to be successful. Middle managers are usually responsible for implementing the plan. Staff generally participate on quality improvement teams. The level of involvement in quality improvement is outlined in the employee's job description. The professional nurse may be expected to participate actively in quality improvement activities at the patient care unit level, the division level, or even the organizational level. By reviewing her or his job description, the beginning professional nurse will be able to determine the level of involvement expected of him or her in quality improvement activities.

Define Scope of Nursing Care and Service

After the responsibility for quality improvement is defined, the next step is to delineate the scope of nursing care and service. Katz and Green (1992) state that this step involves two distinct parts: the customer, and care and service. First customers are identified, and then the care or service that each customer receives is identified. Katz and Green (1992) define the customer by referencing clinical, professional, and administrative domains. Customers in the clinical domain include the patient and family. Customers in the professional domain include physicians, ancillary staff, and nursing staff. Administrative customers consist of administrators and managers. The division of nursing's and/or patient care unit's scope of care and service should reflect all three domains to monitor and evaluate care and service comprehensively. An example of nursing care provided in the clinical domain is the provision of patient and family education. A nursing service that is related to the professional domain is providing the physician with the patient's most current vital signs and physical assessment data. Nurses provide their administrative customers with information such as the types of equipment needed to care for patients.

Once customers are identified, the scope of care and service needs to be defined. The division of nursing and/or patient care unit should consider the types of patients it serves (e.g., age and diagnoses), the processes of care (e.g., assessment and education), and the types of diagnostic and therapeutic modalities it uses (e.g., procedures performed, medications used, and services provided).

For example, 5-North is a 30-bed cardiac telemetry unit. It receives adult patients in the acute phases of illness who require continuous cardiac monitoring. The most common types of diagnoses for which patients are admitted to the unit include cardiac disease (e.g., dysrhythmias, angina, myocardial infarction, sudden cardiac death, and congestive heart failure), cardiovascular surgery, and cardiac transplant. The nursing process, with emphasis on education and discharge planning, is carried out by registered nurses and licensed practical nurses. 5-North provides continuous cardiac monitoring, temporary pacing, and rapid defibrillation/cardioversion. Investigational medications used in the treatment of cardiac disease are administered on the unit. All support services are available to patients admitted to 5-North.

Define Important Aspects of Care

After defining the scope of care and service, the division or patient care unit needs to prioritize its most important aspects of care. Important aspects of care are those activities that are appropriate to the patient's condition and essential to achieving the desired results (Katz & Green, 1992). Determining important aspects of care requires knowing the customer's needs and expectations. Important aspects of care can be streamlined by deciding whether they are high-volume activities, high-risk activities, problem-prone activities, or high-cost activities (Katz & Green, 1992). Important aspects of care for 5-North, the example patient care unit, may include providing patient education regarding the use of sublingual nitroglycerin or facilitating home health referrals for patients requiring nursing care after discharge.

Identify Indicators

Indicators are defined as quantitative measures of an organization's performance of processes and outcomes (Joint Commission, 1993b). Indicators are useful in monitoring and evaluating the quality of care and service provided. Two general types of indicators exist: sentinel event and rate based (Lehman, 1989). A **sentinel event indicator** identifies a grave, untoward process or outcome of care (e.g., cardiopulmonary arrest). A **rate-based indicator** identifies processes of care or patient care outcomes that may require further assessment based on significant trending or variances over time (e.g., patient falls) (Williams, 1991). Indicators may be derived from standards of care and practice, infection control standards, safety standards, patient satisfaction surveys, accident and incident reports, utilization management activities, QA activities, and active problem identification by employees.

Nursing standards of care and standards of practice should be used in assessing and improving the quality of nursing care and service. "Standards of care are statements of patient expectations and/or patient outcomes, describing the kinds of care patients can expect to receive from health care providers" (National Association for Healthcare Quality, 1994, p. 28). Indicators addressing standards of care therefore are outcome oriented and focus on patient outcomes or meeting the patient's expectations. An example of a standard of care is "The patient will maintain a blood glucose level between 60 and 120 mg/dL." Standards of practice focus on the providers of care and describe what health care providers must do to meet the standard of care or patient expectations (National Association for Healthcare Quality, 1994). Indicators addressing standards of practice are process oriented and involve professional performance and accountability. An example of a standard of practice is "The nurse will monitor the patient's blood glucose level every 4 hours." Analysis of conformance to standards of care and practice is how quality is measured (Katz & Green, 1992).

Indicators must be written so that they are measurable. In addition, they must be reliable and valid. Reliability is the degree of consistency achieved in measuring the concept of interest over time (Burns & Grove, 1987). Validity is the extent to which the tool is measuring the characteristics sought (Burns & Grove, 1987). Williams (1991) proposes a seven-step process that facilitates the development of reliable and valid indicators:

1. Health care professionals need to discuss patient care and nursing practice issues to allow for the initial generation of indicator ideas.

2. Nursing standards of care and practice and the literature are reviewed to facilitate further development of the indicators.

3. The proposed indicators are written specifying methods of measurement, data collection, and so forth.

4. The indicators are reviewed by quality professionals.

5. The indicators undergo a final review by the authors.

6. The indicators are piloted. A pilot allows data collection and data analysis problems to be addressed.

7. The indicators are continuously refined over time.

Establish Threshold for Evaluation

During the process of developing quality indicators, a threshold for evaluation may be established. A threshold for evaluation is simply a trigger point at which further investigation into the issue is warranted. Thresholds may be parameters set by the organization that are applied to data. For example, the threshold for the number of postoperative infections is 4%. If recently collected data indicate that 5% of patients have developed infections postoperatively, the threshold has been exceeded. This result triggers further investigation into why there has been an increase in postoperative infections.

Health care organizations may use data from other health care institutions or agencies to compare performance and set a threshold for evaluation. This is called **benchmarking** and is discussed in more detail later in this chapter.

Collect and Organize Data

Internal and external sources of data for assessing and improving nursing care may be used. Internal sources of data may include QA activities, utilization management activities, committee reports, peer review, infection control reports, safety reports, incident/accident reports, medical records, patient care conferences, patient care audits, supervisory reports, and physician and staff input. External data sources include regulatory/licensing agency survey reports, community surveys, and reports from third party payers.

Data can be collected in a number of ways. Frequently, retrospective and concurrent medical record review is used to gather data. A check sheet is a simple tool that is often used to gather data from the medical record. Figure 9–4 is an example of a check sheet used to collect data regarding length of stay for patients undergoing exploratory laproscopy. Data may also be collected utilizing interviews, surveys, and observation.

Evaluate Nursing Care and Service

Data collected from a variety of internal and external sources must be analyzed to identify opportunities to improve care and service. Analysis of data is a crucial step in the quality improvement process. Solutions to problems based on uninterpreted data may result in poorly designed systems and undesirable outcomes. It is important that a systematic process be used in data analysis to identify significant trends and patterns in the data. Results of data analysis may reveal desirable or undesirable trends. If a desirable trend is revealed, the processes to achieve the outcome measured should be maintained. If an undesirable trend is revealed, an opportunity for improvement is identified. An example of a desirable trend in intravenous site complications is shown in Figure 9–5. The practice guidelines for intravenous therapy management have been shown to be effective in producing a positive outcome of few intravenous site complications. An example of an undesirable trend in the rate of urinary tract infections for patients with indwelling catheters is shown in Figure 9–6. The practice guidelines for care of these patients need to be reviewed.

Results of data analysis should be compared with current standards of care and standards of practice. Does the result of data analysis indicate that the

	24 hours	48 hours	72 hours	96 hours	120 hours
January	/	////	//		
February	//	///	/	/	
March		/////	//		/
April	///	//	/	/	
May	//	////		/	
June	/	/////	///		/

Figure 9–4 Check sheet: Length of stay for patients who have undergone exploratory laparoscopy.

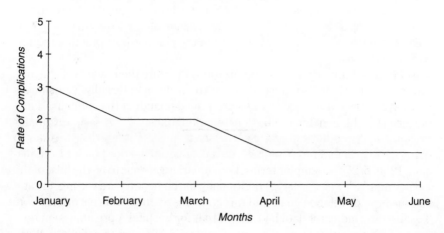

Figure 9–5 Desirable trend in data.

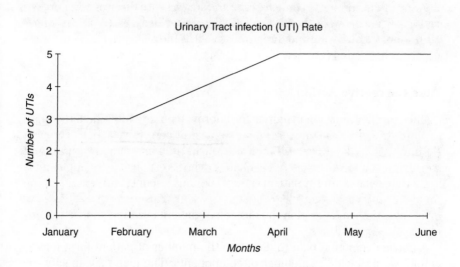

Figure 9–6 Undesirable trend in data.

current standards of care are producing positive patient outcomes? If the answer to this question is no, then the standards of care need to be reviewed and revised. Does the result of data analysis indicate that the current standards of practice are effective? If not, then the standards of practice require review and revision.

Not only is it important that organizations measure their own performance internally, but they also must measure themselves externally. Consumers and payers of health care services are now demanding that organizational performance be benchmarked. Benchmarking means "to measure a similar organization's product or service according to specified standards in order to compare it with and improve one's own product or service" (Joint Commission, 1993, p. 27). In simpler terms, benchmarking means to be the best of the best (Camp & Tweet, 1994). Traditionally in the health care setting, organizations have developed goals and direction based on an internal orientation. To illustrate, indicator data had shown that for hospital A preadmission testing for ambulatory surgery takes an average of 1.75 hours to complete. Without benchmarking, hospital A's leadership believed this length of time to be reasonable. Benchmarking, however, revealed that hospital B was able to complete preadmission testing in 1.25 hours. Hospital A set a goal of reducing preadmission testing time and studied the best practices at hospital B, which allowed hospital A to complete testing in a shorter time.

Benchmarking forces a continual focus on the external environment, thus allowing organizations to compare care and service with those of other organizations. Knowing what the best practices are provides a better means of organizational goal setting and direction as well as the ability to meet customer expectations better (Camp & Tweet, 1994).

Take Corrective Action

Once problems or opportunities for improvement are identified, the quality improvement team must formulate a plan for corrective action. The plan should be interdepartmental and/or interdisciplinary as appropriate and specify who or what is expected to change; who is responsible for implementing action; what is appropriate in view of the cause, scope, and severity of the problem; and when change is expected to occur. The corrective action plan must take into consideration the mission of the organization and customers' needs and expectations.

A corrective action plan to decrease the number of patient falls, for example, would include a number of components. The plan may specify the development of a fall risk assessment tool and a fall prevention protocol. The plan may include a staff education program. The education program's goals would be to heighten awareness regarding the impact of falls on both the patient and the institution, to discuss risk factors associated with falls, and to teach staff how to use the risk assessment tool and fall prevention protocol. Education can serve as a motivating factor for staff in improving patient care and service.

Evaluate Action Plan Results

After implementation of an action plan, the impact of the plan must be evaluated. Evaluation should include analysis of the impact on patient care and service and a cost-benefit analysis. Do the benefits obtained from the action plan outweigh the costs of the action plan? The first step is to determine the benefits derived from the action taken, both tangible and intangible. Are customers' needs and expectations being met? Are services efficient and cost effective? Second, the total costs of the action plan, both direct (e.g., salaries and materials) and indirect (e.g., facility maintenance), should be evaluated. If the benefits of the action plan outweigh the costs, the action plan was successful and should be continued. If the costs of the action plan outweigh the benefits, the action plan should be reevaluated.

Communicate Relevant Information Organizationwide

The final step in quality improvement is to communicate relevant information effectively to all involved employees. Communication is essential because it facilitates decision making at all levels, promotes understanding, and fosters organization and coordination. Communication requires planning in determining who is to receive the information, why they need to know it, how to deliver the information most effectively, and what is appropriate to communicate (Katz & Green, 1992).

KEY CONCEPT Assessing and improving nursing care using the Joint Commission's 10-Step Process involve the following actions:
- Assign responsibility for quality improvement.
- Define the scope of nursing care and service.
- Define important aspects of care.
- Identify indicators.
- Establish a threshold for evaluation.
- Collect and organize data.
- Evaluate nursing care and service.
- Take action to improve care and service.
- Evaluate action plan results.
- Communicate relevant information organizationwide.

LEARNING   A beginning professional nurse has been asked to participate on a task force
CHALLENGE   to prevent medication errors. The task force is currently developing an
indicator by which to measure medication errors and to establish a threshold
for evaluation.
1. What data must be collected to determine the extent of the problem?
2. The task force decides that two medication errors or fewer during a
quarter would be tolerated. If the data revealed that five medication
errors occurred during the last quarter, what is the next step that the
task force should take?

OTHER COMPONENTS OF A COMPREHENSIVE QUALITY IMPROVEMENT PROGRAM

A comprehensive quality improvement program has a number of other
components that facilitate the identification of issues and problems related
to providing quality care and service. These components include QA, utilization management, peer review, program evaluation, and research utilization.

Quality Assurance

The new quality improvement approach is grounded in past efforts of QA.
The major strengths of QA provide a foundation from which to develop a successful quality improvement program. According to Roberts and Schyve
(1990), QA:

- prompts attention to high-priority areas of clinical care
- prompts the development and use of relevant process and outcome indicators
- stimulates analysis of the appropriateness and effectiveness of clinical
  care
- serves as a basis for targeted education programming and other approaches to improvement
- stimulates needed improvement in clinical information systems
- expands individuals' knowledge about theory and methods of QA and
  quality improvement

QA's strengths should be preserved in the new quality improvement paradigm. QA's major weaknesses, however, have the potential to be corrected
with quality improvement (Table 9–1).

QA is still a component of any quality improvement program. Traditional
QA monitoring and evaluation must continue in an organization. QA results
feed into the quality improvement program. For example, an organization's

Table 9–1 Differences between QA and Quality Improvement

QA	Quality Improvement
Largely driven by external requirements	Driven by internal requirements
Focused primarily on clinical care	Focused on clinical, governance, managerial, and
Follows organizational structure	support services
Focuses on individuals	Follows the flow of patient care
Holds out unrealistic expectations of perfection	Focuses on processes
Departmentalized analysis of effectiveness and	Continuous quality improvement
efficiency	Intradepartmental and interdepartmental analysis

Source: Copyright © 1991, Joint Commission on Accreditation of Healthcare Organizations, Oak Brook Terrace, Illinois. Adapted with permission from *Strategies for Quality Improvement in Nursing*, p. 5.

QA activities monitor and evaluate the number of adverse drug reactions that occur over time. The results of these activities indicate a sharp rise in adverse drug reactions during the last quarter. This undesirable trend in adverse drug reactions prompts the organization's leadership to utilize the quality improvement approach to study and resolve this problem.

Utilization Management

Utilization management is an integral component of a quality improvement program. Utilization management facilitates efficient and effective use of resources in improving the quality of care and service. "Utilization Management is an organized comprehensive approach to analyze, direct and conserve organizational resources, while providing care which is both efficient and cost-effective" (National Association for Healthcare Quality, 1994, p. 145). Utilization management is taking on increasing importance in the current health care market. Health care institutions are required to function more and more as businesses, and actively managing resources is crucial to an organization's survival.

A utilization management program is a comprehensive, integrated, formal method of monitoring an organization's resources. The program is based upon the organization's mission and vision, its strategic plan, regulatory considerations, and the scope of authority/responsibility delegated to it by its governing board. The program may include the following components (National Association for Healthcare Quality, 1994):

- third party payer review and coordination
- discharge planning monitoring
- overutilization and underutilization surveillance

- identification of quality of care and liability problems
- financial issues
- physician and staff education

Third party payer review and coordination involve review of the medical record during a patient's hospitalization to facilitate appropriate reimbursement. Coordination may also include facilitating referrals (e.g., to home health, rehabilitation, or long-term care) for aftercare with the selected agencies of the third party (National Association for Healthcare Quality, 1994). The discharge planning and monitoring component facilitates appropriate, timely, and effective discharge planning. Discharge planning may actually be performed by nurses, social workers, case managers, or discharge planners. Utilization management professionals review cases for appropriate use of resources using criteria sets, clinical pathways, or practice guidelines. Surveillance facilitates the identification of underutilization or overutilization of resources. During the course of review, quality of care and risk/liability issues can be identified. Reporting of these issues to quality and risk management allows for timely corrective action. It is an integral part of an effective utilization program to obtain concurrent financial as well as clinical data on all cases. These data can educate providers about the cost of treating patients as well as provide administration with information regarding case mix, cost, length of stay, complications, and mortality. A goal of every effective utilization management program is the education of physicians and staff in managing resources.

Utilization management uses the process of utilization review (UR) to accomplish its stated purposes. UR activities are a source for identifying areas for improvement in care and service. It is a formalized mechanism of reviewing the appropriateness of health care services. Generally, an organization's quality department is responsible for UR. The following is an example of how UR may identify areas for quality improvement. The UR analyst has noted that, for all patients admitted to the intensive care unit after open heart surgery, a physician order is written for daily chest radiography. This order is not discontinued until the patient is discharged from the hospital. The UR analyst brings this issue to a clinical quality improvement team for study to determine whether it is an appropriate use of resources for this type of patient.

Peer Review

Peer review activities also provide a source for identifying areas of care and service to improve. According to the American Nurses Association (1988):

Peer review is an organized effort whereby practicing professionals review the quality and appropriateness of services ordered and performed by their professional peers. Peer review in nursing is the process by which practicing registered nurses systematically assess, monitor, and make judgments about the quality of nursing care provided by peers as measured against professional standards of practice. (p. 3)

Peer review is used to evaluate the quality and quantity of nursing care provided, determine the strengths and weaknesses of nursing care, provide data to support changes in nursing care standards and guidelines to improve patient outcomes, and identify areas where practice patterns indicate that more knowledge is needed (American Nurses Association, 1988). Refer to Chapter 10 for further discussion of peer review.

Program Evaluation

All quality improvement programs need to be evaluated regularly. The Joint Commission requires an annual appraisal of an organization's quality improvement program (Joint Commission, 1993a). The purpose of program evaluation is fourfold: to determine whether the organization's approach to quality improvement is planned, systematic, and organizationwide; to determine whether the organization's approach to quality improvement and its activities is carried out collaboratively; to determine whether the organization's quality improvement approach needs redesign; and to determine whether the program was effective in the improvement of care and service (National Association for Healthcare Quality, 1994).

Evaluation should occur in four areas of the quality improvement program: cost, productivity, processes, and satisfaction (Katz & Green, 1992). Quality and cost are inextricably linked. The benefits gained from quality improvement should outweigh the costs of quality improvement in an effectively managed program. Costs that need to be considered in making this determination include prevention costs, appraisal costs, and failure costs (Katz & Green, 1992). Prevention costs are those associated with activities designed to prevent problems in the development of a product or service (e.g., development of standards). Appraisal costs are incurred during the monitoring and evaluation phase and include the cost of staff hours of those participating in quality improvement. Failure costs are the costs of doing things incorrectly (e.g., the cost of repeating a radiograph that was not taken correctly the first time).

The effects of the quality improvement program on productivity need to be evaluated. Productivity is the relationship between the output of a system and its input. Inputs to the health care system include labor and materials; outputs are care and service. Measuring productivity allows documentation of progress in the improvement of goods and services, determines the efficiency and effectiveness of systems, and determines whether the resources used in producing the results were appropriate and cost effective (Katz & Green, 1992).

Process evaluation involves determining whether the quality improvement program is efficient and effective. The Joint Commission (1993a) asks organizations to assess the following program areas: program design, the process for data collection, the process to assess collected data, the approach to performance improvement, and collaboration among departments and disciplines.

The final aspect of quality improvement program evaluation is satisfaction. Analysis of the impact of the program on customer satisfaction is essential. Customers of the quality program, including patients, staff, physicians, administrators, and external agencies, should have the opportunity to provide information as to how well the quality improvement program has met their needs and expectations.

Research Utilization

Research and research utilization are important aspects of quality improvement. Quality improvement and research programs are not the same, however. Research is the process of discovering new methods of providing care or confirming existing practices. Quality improvement demonstrates that the expected standard and quality of care or service are provided (Thurston, Watson, & Reimer, 1993).

Aspects of the research process are frequently used in designing and implementing quality improvement activities. One example is establishing the reliability and validity of a data collection tool. Also, statistical tools used during the research process are used in the quality improvement process. For example, analysis of quality improvement data may require calculations of the mean, standard deviation, and level of significance.

Research is used in developing nursing standards of care and standards of practice. Research studies are helpful in determining the outcomes of patient care and service. Research can also help design processes more effectively.

KEY CONCEPT   Other components of a comprehensive quality improvement program are as follows:
- QA results feed into the quality improvement program.
- Utilization management facilitates efficient and effective use of resources in improving the quality of care and service.

- Peer review provides a means for identifying areas of concern regarding the delivery of health care.
- Program evaluation assists facilities in determining whether their approach is effective in improving patient care and service.
- Research concepts are used during the design and implementation of a quality improvement project.
- Reported research is useful in developing standards of care and practice.

LEARNING CHALLENGE   A beginning professional nurse is participating on a quality improvement team charged with the task of developing a skin care protocol. Current nursing standards of care and practice for skin care are outdated. How would the nurse utilize current research in developing this protocol?

CONCLUSION

Quality improvement is a useful methodology for improving nursing care and service. Health care organization survival is dependent upon the ability to improve care and service while reducing costs. The beginning professional nurse has an important role in quality improvement. He or she must understand the fundamental concepts of quality improvement, participate in quality improvement efforts at a level equal to his or her job responsibilities, and support the process of change.

RESEARCH FOUNDATION   Brady, R., Chester, F.R., Pierce, L.L., Salter, J.P., Schreck, S., & Radziewicz, R. (1993). Geriatric falls: Prevention strategies for the staff. *Journal of Gerontological Nursing, 19,* 26-32.

The literature contains many examples of how quality improvement efforts have improved outcomes for patients. Brady et al. (1993) undertook a quality improvement project to decrease the number of falls in the geriatric population in a rehabilitation center. A quality improvement team was assembled when statistics showed an increased rate of geriatric falls. In addition to claims for fall-related injuries, other expenses incurred included those for increased length of stay, diagnostic/treatment procedures, and emotional suffering of the patients, families, and the nursing staff.

The first step the team took was to perform a retrospective chart review to establish baseline data. Over a 10-month period, 71 falls occurred. The greatest incidence of falls occurred during the first (23%) and fifth (26%) weeks of hospitalization. The highest percentage of falls occurred during the day shift, with 6% occurring at 8:00 a.m. and 15% between 2:00 p.m. and 3:00

p.m. Eight percent of evening shift falls happened at 10:00 p.m. During the night shift, 8% of the falls occurred between 5:00 a.m. and 6:00 a.m. Activities in which the patients were engaging at the time of the falls included attempting to get to the bathroom, leaning forward in their chairs, and transferring in and out of bed.

The results of the chart review indicated that toileting, seeking rest, and obtaining nutrition and hydration were prevalent activities at peak fall times. The team designed a plan to provide proactive nursing interventions to reduce falls during the identified peak fall times. Thirty minutes before the beginning of the peak fall times, nursing staff asked each patient on the unit whether there was a need for toileting, assistance in or out of the bed or wheelchair, or fluids/nourishment.

The quality improvement team monitored 25 patients for 2 weeks after implementation of these proactive nursing interventions. Staff completed the interventions 86% of the time. Patient falls without injury decreased by 50% during this 2-week period.

This unit-based project was so successful that a housewide fall prevention program was developed. A nursing task force wrote a fall prevention protocol that outlined the nursing responsibilities for and management of a patient at risk for falls. Assessment, intervention, reportable conditions, patient/family instruction, and documentation were the areas addressed in the protocol. In addition, an awareness campaign was launched that targeted all individuals who had contact with patients during hospitalization. The awareness campaign was designed to heighten the consciousness of the staff and to introduce them to the fall prevention protocol.

This quality improvement effort was successful. The project reduced the rate of falls and minimized unsafe patient activity, thus providing an environment that was conducive to less restraint use, maintained autonomy and self-esteem in geriatric patients, facilitated time management by utilizing planned interventions, and reduced expenditures related to falls.

REFERENCES

American Nurses Association. (1988). *Peer review guidelines.* Kansas City, MO: Author.

Berwick, D.M. (1989). Sounding board: Continuous quality improvement as the ideal in health care. *New England Journal of Medicine, 320* (1), 53–56.

Bliersbach, C.M. (Ed). (1991). *National Association of Quality Assurance Professionals guide to healthcare quality management.* Skokie, IL: National Association of Quality Assurance Professionals.

Burns, N., & Grove, S.K. (1987). *The practice of nursing research. Conduct, critique and utilization.* Philadelphia: Saunders.

Camp, R.C., & Tweet, A.G. (1994). Benchmarking applied to health care. *Journal of Quality Improvement, 20*, 229–238.

Crosby, P.B. (1979). *Quality is free: The art of making quality certain.* New York: McGraw-Hill.

Deming, W.E. (1982). *Quality, productivity, and competitive position.* Cambridge: Massachusetts Institute of Technology Press.

Donabedian, A. (1986). Criteria and standards for quality assessment and monitoring. *Quality Review Bulletin, 3*, 99–108.

GOAL/QPC. (1988). *Memory jogger. A pocket guide of tools for continuous improvement* (2nd ed.). Methuen, MA: Author.

Joint Commission on Accreditation of Healthcare Organizations. (1991). *Strategies for quality improvement in nursing care.* Oakbrook Terrace, IL: Author.

Joint Commission on Accreditation of Healthcare Organizations. (1993a). *1994 accreditation manual for hospitals.* Oakbrook Terrace, IL: Author.

Joint Commission on Accreditation of Healthcare Organizations (1993b). *Measurement mandate. On the road to performance improvement in health care.* Oakbrook Terrace, IL: Author.

Juran, J.M. (1981). Product quality: A prescription for the West. Part I: Training and improvement programs. *Management Review, 70*, 8–14.

Juran, J.M. (1989). *Juran on leadership for quality: An executive handbook.* New York: Free Press.

Juran, J.M., Goyna, F.M., Jr., & Bingham, R.S., Jr. (Eds.). (1979). *Quality control handbook.* New York: McGraw-Hill.

Katz, J., & Green, E. (1992). *Managing quality. A guide to monitoring and evaluating nursing services.* St. Louis: Mosby.

Leebov, W., & Scott, G. (1994). *Service quality improvement. The customer satisfaction strategy for health care.* Chicago: American Hospital Publishing.

Lehman, R. (1989). Forum on clinical indicator development: A discussion of the use and development of indicators. *Quality Review Bulletin, 15* (7), 223–227.

Leming, T. (1991). Quality customer service: Nursing's new challenge. *Nursing Administration Quarterly, 15* (4), 6–12.

Master, F., & Schmele, J.A. (1991). Total quality management: An idea whose time has come. *Journal of Nursing Quality Assurance, 5*, 7–16.

Masters, M.L., & Masters, R.J. (1993). Building TQM into nursing management. *Nursing Economics, 11* (5), 274–291.

Merry, M.D. (1990). Total quality management for physicians. *Quality Review Bulletin, 16* (3), 101–105.

National Association for Healthcare Quality. (1994). *National Association for Healthcare Quality. Guide to quality management* (4th ed.). Skokie, IL: Author.

Parisi, L.L. (1994). Process improvement: Committee or team? *Nursing Quality Connection, 4* (2), 5.

Roberts, J.S., & Schyve, P.M. (1990, May). From QA to QI: The views and role of the Joint Commission. *Quality Letter*, pp. 9–12.

Schroeder, P. (1994). *Improving quality and performance. Concepts, programs and techniques.* St. Louis: Mosby.

Thurston, N.E., Watson, L.A., & Reimer, M.A. (1993). Research or quality improvement? Making the decision. *Journal of Nursing Administration, 23* (7/8), 46–49.

Walton, M. (1986). *The Deming management method.* New York: Putman.

Williams, A.D. (1991). Development and application of clinical indicators for nursing. *Journal of Nursing Care Quality, 6* (1), 1–5.

SUGGESTED READING

Bernstein, S.J., & Hilborne, L.H. (1993). Clinical indicators: The road to quality care? *Journal of Quality Improvement, 19* (11), 501–509.

Clafin, N. (1993). Nursing standards of patient care and standards of nursing practice—A practical approach. *Journal of Healthcare Quality, 15* (3), 25–33.

O'Leary, D.S. (1991). CQI—A step beyond QA. *Quality Review Bulletin, 17* (1), 4–5.

CHAPTER 10

Human Resource Management

Donna Fosbinder and Myrna Warnick

CHAPTER OUTLINE	**Framework of Human Resource Management**	Exit Interviews and Turnover Trending
	Philosophy	**Functions of the Nursing**
	Professional Beliefs	**Department in Human**
	Organizational Beliefs	**Resource Management**
	Functions of the Human	Interviewing
	Resources Department	Hiring
	Employee Assistance Programs (EAPs)	Position Descriptions
		Performance Appraisal Systems
	Forecasting Personnel Needs	Retention
	Job Analysis	Staff Development
	Recruitment	**Research Foundation**
	Diversity	

CHAPTER OBJECTIVES At the completion of this chapter, the beginning professional nurse will be able to:
1. describe and evaluate their values and beliefs, and their congruency with the organization's philosophy and beliefs
2. select and apply tools and techniques used in the interviewing process, performance appraisal, coaching and counseling, and exit interviews
3. assess the functions of the human resource department in its relationship to the management of personnel
4. gain knowledge in use of peer review, interviewing, and evaluation techniques utilized by the nursing department to manage its human resources

CRITICAL THINKING CHALLENGE You are a member of a shared governance council charged with responsibility for developing criteria to evaluate staff nurse competencies at the time of hiring. In addition, your council is to identify performance competencies to be used in the peer review process. What are the resources available to you in your organization that will assist your council in meeting its obligations?

Management of human resources is significant in health care organizations because effective use of human resources allows the organization to compete in the environment in both cost and quality. Executives and managers of employing agencies know that people are their most valuable resource. Health care organizations recognize that they are in the service or human care business. Thus for the organization to be successful, people working in the organization need to be the best qualified to perform the services needed by the clientele.

Because people are the most important asset in a service organization, a philosophy of how people are treated is basic to human resource planning. Creating a supportive work environment for employees will improve not only the quality of service available to individuals but the productivity of and profits to an organization. In researching high-performance companies, Peters & Waterman (1982) determined that such organizations had some common characteristics: "there was talk of organizational cultures, the family feeling, small is beautiful, simplicity rather than complexity, [and] hoopla associated with quality products. In short, we found the obvious, that the individual human being still counts" (p. xxiii). Therefore, it is clear that a service organization that is successful will have a human resource philosophy and culture that support the individual employees as they provide the service (see Chapter 1 for a detailed discussion of organizational culture).

FRAMEWORK OF HUMAN RESOURCE MANAGEMENT

Philosophy

A philosophy of managing human resources is governed by values and principles that determine how an organization will treat its employees. When an organization strives for excellence in human resource management, it is seeking high employee morale and high productivity. There is no ideal model to reach this goal, but there are some basic components:

- structures that utilize input from clinical staff into the decision-making process
- encouragement of the intellectual capabilities of professionals
- organizational tolerance for differences of opinion
- actions from the management team that demonstrate care for both the employee and the employee's environment
- recognition for excellence in practice

A company's human resource management philosophy needs to be clear to all employees. Clarity is promoted through printed and verbal messages as well as action. During orientation of new registered nurses, the philosophy of the nursing department will be presented. At that time, new employees can clarify the organization's philosophy and beliefs. Through dialogue with the nurse executive, new employees can gain understanding regarding significant issues, such as:

- role clarification
- the role of the patient in planning care
- support for patient care
- participation and autonomy
- evaluation processes
- responsibilities for committee work

Matching employee values and beliefs with the organization's values and beliefs is important to implementing the philosophy. When there is a discrepancy between two value systems, organizational problems are increased, and employee morale is affected. Haddon (1989) outlines a mutual belief system for professionals and organizations (Table 10–1). Every new employee could use Haddon's suggestion to "make a list of the organization's beliefs and compare them with your professional beliefs" (p. 182). This encourages nurses to explore thoughtfully what is, and is not, acceptable in a potential employer. When values are congruent, the organization's philosophy will be accomplished through highly motivated, productive employees. The resulting culture will find staff nurses who feel satisfied and fulfilled in their roles.

LEARNING CHALLENGE Use the matrix shown in Figure 10–1 to compare your beliefs with the organization's beliefs. To use this matrix, make a list of criteria that are important to you as you practice nursing. Next, prioritize your list according to those areas that are the most important. Finally, as you make comparisons, use the matrix to capture a picture of the congruency between your beliefs and the organization's beliefs.

Professional Beliefs

The new nurse identifies his or her professional beliefs by examining attitudes toward:
- the individual worth of both patients and coworkers
- teamwork
- flexibility
- roles and responsibility
- lifelong learning
- rewards and recognition
- input into decision making

Table 10–1 A Mutual Belief System for Professionals and Organizations

Organizational Beliefs	Professional Beliefs
Being the best	Being the best. Being given all the necessary tools and resources to accomplish positive patient care outcomes. Autonomy in practice. Credentialing.
Importance of the details of execution	Being able to provide nursing care with the ability to delegate nonnursing activities to nonnursing personnel. Use of "detail" tools (e.g., care plans, flowsheets, etc.). Having time to provide the details of nursing care.
Importance of people as individuals	Humans are unique and require personalized and individualized care. The differentiation of nurses by skill level, education, experience, and performance. Each should be treated accordingly.
Superior quality and service	Providing quality service, theoretically and scientifically based, through a reasonable caseload whereby patients can be developed as partners in care.
Organizational members as innovators with support for failure	Creative approaches to health care delivery, risk taking, and experimentation. Failure used as a learning tool to achieve higher aims.
Informality in communication	Communication used as a therapeutic milieu designed to resolve conflict and come to decisions. Communication used as a healthy outlet for fears and frustrations as well as new ideas.
Importance of economic growth	Organization profit making as a means to better self-economic status, provided that the profits are shared with the individuals who made the profits possible. Employee incentives and productivity rewards.

Source: Reprinted from R.M. Haddon, Nursing Resource Management, in *Changing Organizational Structures*, Series on Nursing Administration, Volume 2, Marion Johnson and Joanne McCloskey, series eds., Nancy Evans and Debra Hunter, issue eds., p. 184, with permission of Mosby-Year Book, © 1989.

Individual Worth

For an individual to feel valued and respected as an employee, there should be direct and immediate feedback regarding concerns, issues, and performance. Trust develops among coworkers when there is direct and hon-

Criteria	Personal Importance	Organization Response		
		Important	Meets Needs	Doesn't Meet Needs
Self-governance				
Continuing education support				
Job description				
Patient care system				
Evaluation process				
Autonomy				
Salary/benefits				
(List others)				

Figure 10–1 Matrix to compare employee and organization beliefs.

est communication. To have a healthy working environment, gamesmanship must be left behind; this includes hallway conversations after meetings and criticism of colleagues, both of which diminish relationships among peers. Trust is fragile but nevertheless is the most important ingredient in producing high morale and high productivity, signs of an excellent organization.

Valuing and respecting patients and their families require the nurse to include them in all decisions regarding their plan of care. Dialogue with patients needs to be encouraged so that the nurse can ensure understanding of the dilemmas faced by the patient. Thoughtful consideration should be given to all patient/family concerns. Fosbinder (1990) found that "friendliness and understanding helped the patient feel comfortable, and set the stage for trust to develop in the nurse–patient relationship" (p. 123). Clearly, individual worth is the element that builds trust between nurse and patient and among nurses.

Teamwork

Because an environment must be created that fosters teamwork, the new nurse must be comfortable working with groups of people. Patient needs are complex, requiring the use of multiple specialties. Respect for the contributions of each team member affects how the team performs. Delegation and coordination skills are imperative for the nurse to facilitate appropriate response to patient care needs. According to Katzenbach and Smith (1991):

> . . . teams and good performance are inseparable; you cannot have one without the other. But, people use the word team so loosely that it gets in the way of learning and applying the discipline that leads to good performance. . . . To understand how teams deliver extra performance, we must distinguish between teams and other forms of working groups. That distinction turns on performance results. A working group's performance is a function of what its members do as individuals. A team's performance includes both individual results and what we call "collective work-products." (p. 112)

The differences between a work group and a team are identified in Table 10–2.

Because patient care demands the use of multiple specialists to proceed effectively, each nurse must ensure strong multidisciplinary commitment to common goals and teamwork that produce appropriate patient care outcomes. The use of a plan of care that identifies standardized daily outcomes from all disciplines requires the nurse to coordinate care. The nurse who facilitates teamwork among the patient, physician, and other disciplines must

Table 10–2 Not All Groups Are Teams: How To Tell the Difference

Working Group	*Team*
Strong, clearly focused leader	Shared leadership roles
Individual accountability	Individual and mutual accountability
The group's purpose is the same as the broader organizational mission	Specific team purpose that the team itself delivers
Individual work products	Collective work products
Efficient meetings	Open-ended discussion and active problem-solving meetings
Effectiveness measured indirectly by influence on others (e.g., financial performance of the business)	Performance measured directly by assessing collective work products
Discusses, decides, and delegates	Discusses, decides, and does real work together

be articulate, respectful, thoughtful, and clinically sound. Mutual accountability is often difficult because of the need for trust among all members of the team. When the team becomes mutually accountable, the members make promises to each other to complete respective work and fit it into the total effort to achieve organizational goals.

KEY CONCEPTS
- Three key words for effective teams are **trust**, **commitment**, and **mutual accountability**.
- To create trust, a team member must complete work according to the time frames and accountabilities identified by the group. Whenever work is not complete, the group must be notified and new time frames established to hold trust and mutual accountability in place.

Flexibility

With the rapidity of change in today's health care system, the nurse who is flexible will survive in the current environment. Organizations that are alive and have a lot of vitality demand a highly educated workforce that can accommodate change easily. This requires nurses to give up things they enjoy doing when those things add little value to the organization. The cost of doing nonessential activities can no longer be sustained.

Often, new roles for nurses require expansion into areas that are currently unfamiliar. A professional nurse needs to have a moral compass to decide whether the decisions being made will jeopardize or augment patient care. As a professional, the nurse has a duty to speak out for a true quality concern, even if opposed by a majority. It is also the obligation of any professional, however, to be able to change and to move into the future to ensure cost-effective, quality care.

LEARNING CHALLENGE   Ask yourself these challenging questions: Am I intellectually capable? Am I open and willing to change? Can I see things differently so that the team can achieve its goals?

Roles and Responsibilities

Katzenbach and Smith (1991) state, "Agreeing on the specifics of work and how they fit together to integrate individual skills and advance team performance lies at the heart of shaping a common approach" (p.115). The role of the nurse must be clearly defined to understand the nurse's contribution to the team. If the agency uses differentiated practice, which focuses on the structuring of roles and functions of nurses according to education, experience, and competence, the role and expectation of each nurse staff member will be identified.

KEY CONCEPT   • If the organization uses multiskilled workers, know the role of each member and how the roles affect you. Will you participate in or be totally responsible for hiring, mentoring, evaluating, and recognizing the work performance of each worker under your direction?

Life-Long Learning

As a new graduate with your state board licensing completed, your education is just beginning. Learning is not a segmented experience; it is not like a feature film, where "The End" occurs. Rather, it is like a serial movie: never ending. Many new nurses entering the workforce seek stability and role clarification. Organizations, however, are seeking nurses who can embrace change and ambiguity. Nurses who will succeed are those who are conceptually grounded and willing to test new ideas and methods regarding quality and cost of care. Organizational resources are allocated for education to assist in these endeavors through tuition reimbursement and continuing education support. Managers can identify programs used in the organization to achieve the standards of certification or preparation needed for professional nurses. Managers also will identify expectations for new nurses regarding further education that nurses undertake on their own time and at their own expense.

Rewards and Recognition

Reward systems should have a strong link with valued outcomes. Most reward systems are centered on individual performance. Deming (1993), however, recommends giving rewards to teams and groups of people who achieve the organization's goals. He suggests that individual merit and ranking systems are counterproductive and that the organization pays a price in the long run for setting up internal competition among employees. Reward and recognition systems are generally categorized **extrinsic rewards**, **intrinsic rewards**, and **recognition**.

Extrinsic rewards. Extrinsic rewards include compensation (see Compensation Systems, below, and Chapter 6), bonus programs, employee incentive programs, contributions to tax-sheltered annuities and pension plans, health and dental programs, tuition incentives, and sick leave. A potential employee should be a good shopper when interviewing a potential employer. Extrinsic rewards, however, rarely make up for lack of intrinsic rewards. Most employees could get higher pay in another organization if they searched out the opportunity for more pay, so why do they stay with a company? It is because they receive satisfaction from the job they are doing.

Intrinsic rewards. Intrinsic rewards are those that individuals receive for themselves. They are largely a result of employees' satisfaction with their work. Nothing is more satisfying to the nurse than direct feedback from patients and families who are satisfied with their care and express that to the nurse. Deming (1993) states, "An award in the form of money for a job done for the sheer pleasure of doing it is demoralizing, overjustification. Merit awards and ranking are demoralizing. They generate conflict and dissatisfaction. Companies with wrong practices pay a penalty. The penalty cannot be measured. Rewards motivate people to work for rewards" (p. 116). A brief note that a person can keep is by far a higher reward than a monetary tip. Efforts to redesign work to increase personal worth to the employee will make the work more intrinsically rewarding by allowing nurses the opportunity to control the patient's environment for the good of the patient.

KEY CONCEPT
- A responsibility of the beginning professional nurse is to assist in fostering intrinsic rewards by becoming an effective member of the team.

Recognition. The philosophy of the executive team and the nurse executive will set the tone for the organization in terms of formal recognition programs. Whether these are "Employee of the Month" or "Nurse of the Year" programs, the criteria for selection should be consistent to prevent them from becoming a popularity contest. Programs that recognize certification and documentable outcomes have a positive effect on individual employees. Even more important is recognizing the work of teams if the organization relies on teams to achieve its goals. Case management programs are dependent on teams to achieve the cost and quality outcomes needed for designated patients. If the team is recognized for its work rather than just the case manager, trust and mutual accountabilty for work are reinforced. The nurse administrative team can set the stage for an informal recognition program by being role models. Commendation for risk taking and encouragement of the nurse to be fully accountable for patient outcomes will increase the pride of individual nurses. Verbal recognition of a job well done is available to all managers and all employees.

Input into Decision Making

The nurse with little experience can still make contributions based on recent education, prior clinical experiences, readings, and research. New nurses often are the most flexible members of the nursing staff because they do not have a history of providing care in a specified way. Organizations attempting to make extensive changes have set up mechanisms to receive input from those providing clinical care. This presupposes that employees will take the opportunity to contribute to the dialogue and will assume responsibility for their ideas. Katzenbach and Smith (1991) state, "Think about the difference between, 'the boss holds me accountable, and we hold ourselves accountable' " (p. 116). When employees accept accountability for their decisions, they take control over changes in practice and in the environment. This kind of accountability significantly changes the role of the manager, who becomes a facilitator for group decision making instead of a supervisor making decisions solo.

Organizational Beliefs

Organizations have beliefs and cultures that affect the professional nurse. Organizational beliefs set direction through the written mission and vision statements. The new nurse should look for the prominence of patient care and employee relationships in the mission and vision documents. The manager will describe how the organizational systems operationalize the mission and vision through the patient care delivery system, continuous quality monitoring, compensation systems, and evaluation systems.

Patient Care Delivery Systems

The recent emphasis on patient-focused care has taken many different avenues, from redesigning units, to improving patient comfort, to cross-training of staff, to decreasing the actual number of employees interfacing with a patient, to case management, to improving continuity of care, and finally to qualitative methods for eliciting patient perceptions of quality of care. All these methods have as their primary purpose the institution's ability to keep its current patient base and to function both efficiently and effectively in the present cost-constrained environment (for additional information, see Chapter 3). If new nurses have learned specific skills that are technical in scope, they will be limited to the delivery system in which they have had experience. If, however, nurses are grounded in critical thinking with patient outcomes as the focus of care, they will be able to provide care within any type of delivery system and in multiple settings.

Continuous Quality Monitoring

The organization should have an identified way to allow employees to improve services continuously, either through shared governance or through continuous quality improvement (CQI). Because the Joint Commission on Accreditation of Healthcare Organizations has changed its standards for monitoring quality on an ongoing basis, most hospitals have a distinct plan to improve processes affecting quality as well as the quality of care itself. The semantics of the differences between total quality management and CQI programs can be explored, but the underlying principles for nurses will be the same. The concepts in CQI are similar to those of the nursing process: Identify the problem with concrete data, analyze the data, state the problem, and change the plan with reevaluation to determine whether the problem has been solved. Data are then compared with set standards or benchmarks from outside entities or standards of professional organizations. No longer is monitoring an extraneous function. It is a part of everyday work and the responsibility of every team member. Part of nurses' evaluation is based on their participation in quality improvement (see Chapter 9).

Compensation Systems

Numerous federal and state laws apply to pay systems. Salaries are paid to those workers who are exempt from regulations of the Fair Labor Standards Act. Exempt status employees have supervisory responsibility or professional accountability for the outcomes of their clients. Exempt employees are generally paid a monthly or annual salary. Overtime is not paid to exempt employees. Nonexempt employees are paid an hourly wage for work performed for an employer and usually receive overtime compensation.

For those nurses who provide care across the continuum, appropriate compensation would best fit the exempt salary model. Many nurses are still receiving nonexempt or shift compensation, however. Donovan-Sierk (1994) presents some of the key benefits of exempt models. Rather than nurses being paid for time spent at work, they are paid for responsibilities and outcomes. Eubanks (1992) poses the question: Should performance be linked to customer expectations? She suggests that traditional pay systems do not support the transition to patient-centered care. Blouin (1992) states, "The values and goals inherent in the role of the nurse as a knowledge worker managing her own patients' care and supervising assistive staff support a professional compensation model" (p. 24).

Evaluation Systems

There are three basic systems for staff evaluation: self-evaluation, supervisor evaluation, and peer review. In addition, there may be a combination of two or all three in the process. Self-evaluation allows employees to assess their performance over a period of time and to identify strengths, weaknesses, and plans for growth. Within this evaluation, contributions to quality improvement, cost-effective use of resources, protocol development, or other clinical skills should be outlined and presented as the employee's contribution to patient care.

KEY CONCEPT

- To facilitate the self-evaluation, look at your position accountabilities and identify your expected and unique contributions. Use analysis and data to support your statements. In addition, compare yourself with outside professional benchmarks when possible.

Supervisor evaluation is a second method used to assess employee performance. This evaluation focuses on the supervisor's judgment of the employee's support to the organization, including use of resources, perceptions of clinical competence, interpersonal relationships, and patient satisfaction. Often, input from coworkers, staff who follow the individual being evaluated on the next shift, and the clinical educator is sought by the supervisor to provide an accurate evaluation of performance.

The dictionary defines *peer* as "a person who is equal to another in abilities, qualifications, etc." The word originates from the Latin word *par*, meaning "equal." Therefore, peer review is an evaluation by one's equals. The use of peer review in the evaluation process for staff nurses places the responsibility for judgment of clinical competence where it belongs: on the clinical nurse. Colleagues who work alongside one another are in the best position to evaluate the level of competence of the individual nurse. Peer rating is valid if members of the group have sufficient interaction with each other and if established criteria are used.

There is still controversy about peer review systems, especially as it relates to fairness in a "buddy system." There is also concern about the relationship of peer review to salary compensation. Although these concerns have some merit and should be discussed, strategies can be put in place to address them (see Performance Appraisal Systems, below).

No matter which of these systems or combination of systems is used to evaluate the staff nurse, the outcome is to assist the new nurse in his or her technical, interpersonal, and leadership development. Development goals can include personal growth, career guidance, continuing education, and clinical mentoring.

LEARNING CHALLENGE

1. If you are working in an organization that does not include the patient in establishing the plan of care, what do you do?
2. If data from the CQI program are not being shared with the staff, how do you get the organization and manager to respond to your need for information regarding patient care practices and processes?
3. If you are paid an hourly wage with overtime, how do you follow patients on the continuum of care, and into the home in a cost-effective manner?
4. If you were given the opportunity to do a self-evaluation or to participate in a peer evaluation of a colleague, what criteria or standards would you like to use?

FUNCTIONS OF THE HUMAN RESOURCES DEPARTMENT

The human resources department supports the nursing department in many ways, including employee assistance programs (EAPs), personnel need forecasting, job analysis, and recruitment. The department also conducts exit interviews and compiles turnover statistics. The department also acts as a resource for interpreting internal personnel policies and those of regulatory bodies. Advice on and interpretation of policies are available directly to individuals as well as to the management team.

Employee Assistance Programs

Most human resources departments have EAPs directly available to employees for personal or professional problems. The work of the EAP is confidential and often requires support from outside resources, such as mental health counselors or rehabilitation programs, to help the employee.

Impaired nurses (i.e., those with drug or alcohol problems) have found significant help using EAPs. In addition, most states have implemented laws that support the recovering impaired nurse by permitting the nurse to retain his or her license while undergoing treatment for substance abuse. Treatment is generally administered through the agency where the nurse is employed, under stringent guidelines and the supervision of the nurse executive. Nursing personnel are at high risk for substance abuse because of easy access to controlled substances and pressures of the workplace. When impaired nurses get help early rather than wait for colleagues to identify them, their chance for recovery is much better.

Forecasting Personnel Needs

The process of forecasting future personnel needs involves a close working relationship between the human resources department and the nurse administration team as they look at health care trends, future needs for each department, current resources, trends in turnover, and allocation of current and future resources. Once needs are predicted, the department assists with filling current openings through recruitment (see Recruitment, below). When the needs are in the future, human resources departments begin to plan strategies with managers to achieve desired employment levels.

Job Analysis

Job analysis performed by the human resources department identifies levels of autonomy, independence, critical thinking, skills, and interpersonal relationships of a job. The level of education and experience for each element dictates the salary level. From the job analysis and job qualifications, position descriptions are written (see Position Descriptions, below).

The dynamic nature of health care organizations brings into question the current methods of writing position descriptions. There are two approaches in doing this task. In the first approach, the assumption is that the job analyzed today will consist of the same set of duties and functions tomorrow. The problem with this approach is that environmental forces are bringing about job restructuring. Thus one could be recruiting, selecting, and training based on job requirements that are obsolete. For example, computerization and downsizing may alter substantially the nature of jobs and personal employee characteristics needed to meet new job requirements successfully.

A second approach is reducing the number of job titles and developing fewer but more generic job descriptions. This provides needed flexibility to manage change. With **generic job description**, the focus is not specific duties and tasks but rather the personal qualities necessary for an employee to function in a continuous improvement culture (e.g., flexibility, innovativeness, and the ability to work as part of a team).

KEY CONCEPT
• Personal characteristics (e.g., flexibility and communication skills) are significant parts of the job requirements because they are consistently important.

Recruitment

Recruiting is a process in which the needs of both the institution and the individual must be satisfied. Providing realistic job information for the beginning professional nurse can increase employee satisfaction. In addition, when potential employees are given accurate information about a position, they can self-select out of jobs that are not seen as offering opportunities they value. Curran (1991) states, "The essential values and skills must be honestly featured in nursing recruitment materials. We should attempt to match ourselves with employees who possess similar values and goals" (p. 231).

When a nurse is aware of anticipated job openings, an initial interview occurs in the human resources department. The personnel department should keep a record of the future work desires of employees for the purpose of identifying nurses who might be strong internal candidates to meet future needs of the institution.

Human Resource Considerations

The expense of recruitment is significant and includes costs related to the operation of the department, advertisements, travel expenses, brochure development, and search firm fees. Channels for recruiting nurses for employment include newspaper ads, journal ads, professional placement agencies, placement bureaus at universities, and special publications. Nurses seeking positions can obtain information at job fairs, career days, professional meetings, and conventions.

KEY CONCEPT
• Employment while one is a student nurse helps with placement after graduation. Many positions are filled through personal contacts.

Planning recruitment. There are two things to consider when one is planning recruitment for specific units: patient profile, and what types of personnel are needed to meet patient needs. The patient profile consists of medical diagnoses, nursing diagnoses, acuities, patient age ranges, and plans

of care. Because of the rapid changes occurring in health care, patient pro-
files may need to be reviewed each year. The recruitment of personnel is
based on preplanned staffing patterns developed according to the patient
profile. The plan can include registered nurses, licensed practical nurses,
nursing assistants, and other clinical and support personnel assigned to the
unit.

Diversity. In the recruitment plan, diversity strategies (racial, gender,
age, and disability) need to be addressed. The Equal Employment Opportunity Commission (EEOC) enforces the laws regarding hiring a diverse workforce. Guidelines for discrimination are outlined in Title VII of the Civil Rights
Act of 1964 as amended, the Age Discrimination Act of 1967 as amended, the
Equal Pay Act of 1963 as amended, and Title I of the Americans with Disabilities Act of 1990 as amended. An essential ingredient of a recruitment plan is
a nondiscriminatory employment policy that neither intentionally nor inadvertently screens out minorities or other protected groups. A company with
more than 15 or 20 employees must be able to show that it uses nondiscriminatory standards in selecting employees. The recruitment and screening process is the first place the EEOC looks for signs of discrimination.

Diversity focuses not only on cultural, ethnic, gender, and racial differences but also on unique individual differences. The beginning professional
nurse with organizational management responsibilities can facilitate the understanding of cultural and workforce diversity by supporting an organizational culture that values differences and uses them to attain positive outcomes within the work setting.

LEARNING CHALLENGE   We all notice differences in others without recognizing that we also are
different. Differences can be beneficial or can create barriers to individual or
group effectiveness. Consider how each of the following characteristics of
diversity is a benefit or a barrier to your personal or work group effectiveness: age, gender, ethnicity, beliefs, customs, interactional style, values,
attitudes, learning style, and work habits. Share one thing you have learned
about your diverse characteristics with a peer.

Initial screening of applicants. The recruiter's primary responsibility
is the initial contact with the potential employee. The recruiter is responsible
for finding the highest-qualified potential candidates and encouraging them
to seek positions in the organization through interviews with managers.
These initial interviews are usually done through the human resources department to ensure EEOC compliance as well as to establish and maintain a
database on hiring practices. Often, there will be multiple interviews for the

potential candidate. These interviews are generally held on different days and at different times. Recruiters are also responsible for ensuring that employees or potential employees are aware of internal and external employment opportunities.

Nursing Department Considerations

Nursing positions require specific skills, abilities, competencies, behaviors, education, and often experience. During recruiting, it is important to know whether there is a shortage cycle or only a few registered nurse vacancies. From the manager's perspective, when dealing with a few vacancies there are more candidates to interview, so that, although more time will be consumed, managers have an opportunity to choose from a stronger candidate pool. Employees, however, may accept positions when they suspect that there is not a good match between themselves and the organization, the manager, or the unit because there are fewer vacancies available. During a shortage cycle, from the manager's perspective there is a longer lag time to fill positions. The other consideration is that a manager may accept minimally qualified individuals. Employees, on the other hand, can choose the organization for which they wish to work and can change jobs frequently to upgrade their position.

Another recruitment issue is the ability to recruit diverse staff who can care for the diverse patient population that is present today in the health care system. Currently, minorities are not adequately represented to meet the needs of the population requiring care. The diverse patient population is projected to increase. Without a plan from the profession and the colleges of nursing to increase the number of candidates of diverse backgrounds entering nursing programs, nurses may be limited in providing culturally appropriate care in the future.

KEY CONCEPT • Be an active participant in bringing minorities into the profession.

Exit Interviews and Turnover Trending

An exit interview occurs when an employee terminates employment with an institution. Exit interviews are usually conducted in the human resources department to maintain confidentiality. A termination questionnaire can be helpful in tracking how many employees leave, from what units, and for what reasons. Group data are then shared with the nursing department.

There are many variables that contribute to nurses leaving their positions. Analyzing reasons for turnover can help management change practices to reduce turnover of current employees and can help in the selection of employees who are more likely to remain with the hospital. If the leave taking is a result of the organization's environment, steps need to be taken to implement appropriate policies to keep staff satisfied in their positions. A word of caution to the newly hired professional nurse: When you terminate from a first position, be honest in the exit interview about your feelings. If an exit interview has not been requested, ask for one. If you have had a good experience in the organization, give positive feedback. If you have not had a positive experience, it is equally important to share your concerns during the exit interview.

KEY CONCEPT
- Nurses who care about furthering their profession will take responsibility for the environments in which they work. It is no longer enough to say "I'm out of here," and not try to change the situation as you leave it.

Turnover is defined as the number of workers replaced in an organization during a specific period of time. It is a multistage process. The decision to stay at or leave an organization begins with a person's perception regarding how satisfied he or she is with the current position. The more satisfied people are, the less likely they are to leave the organization. Because turnover is a process, management can attempt to influence the employee's decision to stay or leave. In some instances, turnover actually may increase organizational effectiveness.

LEARNING CHALLENGE
1. Can general patient care environments accommodate all disabilities? If so, what kind of accommodations must be in place for the nurse to function?
2. In a community with limited minorities, how does one encourage minority employment?

FUNCTIONS OF THE NURSING DEPARTMENT IN HUMAN RESOURCE MANAGEMENT

Interviewing

Selection of staff is a major function of the nurse manager role. Nurse managers must hire individuals who will meet patient needs and function effectively as team members on the unit. In the past, hiring of staff for the unit was done exclusively by the nurse manager. Today, often staff members will interview and have significant input into the selection decision. The objective of the interview is to obtain input into the hiring process from the people who will be affected by the appointment.

The Potential Employee

When you prepare to interview for a position, begin by thinking about what questions you may be asked and how you will respond. Sample questions include the following:

- Why do you want to work here?
- Tell me about your strengths and weaknesses.
- What are your career goals?
- What are the challenges facing health care today? How will you meet those challenges?
- Tell me about any experience you have had working in teams.
- Give me an example of a recent change you were involved in and how you responded to the situation.
- Tell me about a problem you faced recently, and how you worked through that problem.
- What are your expectations should we hire you into this position?
- Why should we hire you? (If this question arises, be prepared to sell yourself.)

KEY
CONCEPTS
- Emphasize your strengths.
- Be honest, but discuss your limitations not as weaknesses but as areas for growth.
- Be clear about your enthusiasm for learning.
- Be articulate about your willingness to be flexible and your skills as a team player.

If possible, ask a friend about the institution and the person who may be doing the interview. In addition to thinking about what questions you may be asked in the interview, think about what you want to know about the organization. It is a two-way street. While the interviewer is ascertaining your qualifications for the job, you will want to decide whether you want to work for the organization and whether your values match theirs. Basic questions to ask the manager and/or staff include the following:

- What is your philosophy regarding patient care?
- What are your expectations of new staff?
- After orientation, where do I go for continued guidance in refining my nursing practice?

- What policies do you have in place to mentor new staff?
- How are unit decisions made, and will I have input into them?

Husted (1991) lists ethical questions that it is appropriate for you to ask, such as "Do the patient's wishes determine the disposition of their organs, or does the institution go along with the family's views if they are different from the patient's?" You can also ask about the organization's philosophy of nursing and what it values. Ask for a copy of the job description and the performance appraisal system. If you have not had a group interview with staff from the unit where you are going to be working, ask to meet and talk with the unit staff.

KEY CONCEPT

- There are four processes to consider when you are going for an interview:
  1. Think about the questions you may be asked in the interview.
  2. Gain information regarding your potential employer.
  3. Prepare a list of questions you want to ask.
  4. Meet as many of your potential coworkers as possible.

The Employer

Preparation for the interview is important. Familiarize yourself with the resume of the applicant so that you enter the interview with knowledge of his or her experience. During the interview process, be clear to the candidate what your expectations are. Questions should probe the candidate's ability to meet the needs of the patient population and the needs of the team providing patient care. Always ask open-ended questions, and ask the candidate to give you examples of real situations.

In preparing for the interview, an effective interviewer should:

- create an open communication atmosphere while maintaining control of the interview
- use an interview guide so that the same questions are asked consistently (There are many types of interview tools and scoring formats. When a group interview occurs, tools and scoring formats can be used by each group member. The group can then compare the scoring sheets, discuss each question and the candidate's answer, and reach a group consensus on the applicant.)
- not ask inappropriate questions (The EEOC has clear guidelines regarding personal questions that cannot be asked.)
- be a good listener and note taker
- appropriately interpret nonverbal cues

- ask good follow-up questions to evaluate the use of higher-level cognitive skills during routine patient care
- ask the candidate, toward the end of the interview, whether he or she has questions (Candidates should be as interested in whether they want to work with you as in whether you want them to work with you.)

Because managers are responsible for the success of their areas, the good manager will quickly assess the beliefs and goals of the individual in the interview process. If it is apparent that there are differences between the applicant and the current staff, the hire offer should not occur. When this happens, the manager should take the opportunity to provide career direction to the interviewee.

Group Interview

A group interview usually includes two or three staff members from the same shift but can include as many as five or six staff members with all shifts being represented. Frequently, staff are chosen by their peers to represent them at the interview and to present to the potential employee their expectations of new staff. Staff are a good judge of whether potential employees will meet the needs of the patients and the needs of the team on the unit.

There are many advantages to having unit staff members involved in the selection process. Because it is a serious responsibility, staff will feel accountable for the success of the new staff they have selected. They will want to become involved with helping new staff members succeed in their position. Another advantage of a group interview is that, while one person is asking the question and waiting for the answer, another person in the group can be watching the candidate for the nonverbal response to the question. Often the verbal and nonverbal answers are not congruent. This can then lead to an expansion of the previous question by the person witnessing the dichotomy.

Staff who are a part of the group interview need to understand their responsibility in the hiring process. If peer review is a significant part of the evaluation process on the unit, then it is appropriate to have staff make the hire decision. If the manager alone is responsible for the evaluation, the manager will take responsibility for hiring the individual. Allowing staff on the unit to make a hire decision fosters professional accountability. If staff want input into the hiring process, then they should have input into the evaluation process.

One disadvantage of a group interview is that the candidate may feel overwhelmed and become nervous. A group interview is stressful, but frequently so is the work of the staff nurse, so that it may be advantageous to see how the candidate responds to stress. Another caution with a group interview is that the candidate may not do enough talking. Sometimes a panel member helps the candidate phrase an answer to a question that has just been asked. For example, a panel member will tell the candidate what he or she expects from a new employee. This should only come at the end of the interview process. If it is done early on in the interview process, it is easy for the candidate to tell the group members what they want to hear.

KEY CONCEPT Important areas to consider when new employees are being hired include:
- using an interview tool
- determining who should be involved in the interviewing process
- determining who will make the final hire decision

Hiring

Before a candidate receives a hire offer, his or her references need to be checked. Reference letters that accompany an application or resume can be misleading. Sometimes what is not said is as important as what is said.

Although past work performance is key, the nurse manager should keep in mind that references are a reflection of one person's opinion. A poor reference may not be an accurate reflection of someone's work. There may not have been a good match in the candidate's last position. If this is an issue, it can be discussed during the interview by asking why the candidate left his or her last position. While the manager is interviewing the candidate, it is appropriate to ask for the names of three or four people with whom the candidate has worked recently who can be called for a verbal reference. Sometimes with a verbal exchange people will be more open, and one can ask specific questions pertaining to one's reason for wanting to hire the candidate.

If there is difficulty in making the selection, candidates can be brought back for a second interview. Additional questions may surface from the references, from the discussion with the staff who participated in the group interview, or from reviewing the candidate's file. It is appropriate to request a second interview for clarification purposes. After the hire decision is made and the person is verbally offered the position, a confirmation letter should follow (Exhibit 10–1).

It is important to communicate with the candidates who are not offered a position and to provide them with information about why they were not chosen. This communication serves two purposes. First, as professionals, we need to attend to the growth of our colleagues; second, we want to establish good public relations with our community of colleagues.

Exhibit 10–1 Sample Confirmation Letter

January 10, 1995

Dear Ms. Smith:

We're on the move at Salt Lake Regional Medical Center, and we're glad you've joined the effort. Health care today and tomorrow is being defined right here, and it's our hope that you'll be challenged by the environment and excited by its opportunities. Questioning past practices and routines, creating ways to "work smarter," and being willing to take risks are all parts of professional practice that we encourage.

We're dedicated to high-quality patient care, whether it be delivered on an outpatient or inpatient basis. As the Sisters of the Holy Cross believed when the hospital was born, our primary objective is the relief of suffering and the restoration of patients to the highest level of well-being possible within available resources. We do so in an environment that respects the dignity of each person while we seek to restore his or her physical, psychological, and spiritual health.

Tremendous personal challenge, exciting professional development, and hard work are promised. Our responsibility and pledge are to prepare, support, and orient you based on your individual needs and experiences. It is difficult to be new, and we understand that. If at any time you feel your orientation is not going as you had hoped and anticipated, call me at 555-1212. I want to know about it.

Best of wishes as you begin your work with us. I look forward to meeting you and working with you in building a dynamic, exciting health care organization prepared for the future.

Sincerely,

Alex Brown, B.S.N., M.A., R.N.
Vice President, Operations

Courtesy of Salt Lake City Regional Medical Center, Salt Lake City, Utah.

KEY CONCEPT

- If you were not hired and it is not clear why you were not selected, make a call to the hiring manager to ask for information about how you could have strengthened your application and interview. This information will be helpful as you continue your job search.

Position Descriptions

Position descriptions are written by the nursing department utilizing the job analysis and job qualification information provided by the human resources department. Excellent position descriptions are of value to both employee and employer and can be written in either an open or closed format (see Job Analysis, above). Position descriptions give direction to the employee. They identify an employee's role in the organization, and outline responsibilities and accountabilities. For the employer, they establish expectations of work from the individual employee as well as the employee's work within the group. They also establish management's right to take corrective action when the duties specified in the position description are not performed or are performed inappropriately.

There should be a close relationship between a position description and the performance evaluation. At one institution in Southern California, a tool was developed to serve both functions. This tool establishes standards for the desired quality of nursing care with clear expectations for professional practice defined by objective, quantifiable criteria (Figure 10–2). Evaluation is based on documentation of work performed, peer review, observation, and peer and health care team interactions. The review of the pilot project at this institution demonstrated positive results (Fosbinder & Vos, 1989).

Performance Appraisal Systems

Evaluation Tools and Techniques

Of interest recently has been the movement away from supervisor-dominated evaluation to participation of the person being evaluated and his or her peers in the evaluation process. Because the registered nurse is a professional and fully capable of self-evaluation, many managers request a self-evaluation. Employees can be asked to research their performance and its relationship to the work environment. They can make self-assessments against goals and expectations previously identified and analyze their progress. During the evaluation, employees can express their needs and seek assistance of the manager in meeting their goals and objectives. Many managers today use a peer review system as part of their evaluation process. Again, a hallmark of a profession is the ability of its members to review each other. The social contract with the public mandates that nurses review the professional work of their peers (Figure 10–3).

Using personnel effectively is the most significant contribution a nurse administrator makes to the organization. Mentoring, evaluating, and improving performance of the nursing staff are critical to the success of the agency.

Figure 10–2 Nurse practice expectations and evaluation: Clinical Nurse II.

Exceeds Expectations— Employee continually performs above the standard. Functions as "role model." Consistently goes beyond expectations. Requires little or no supervision.

Meets Expectations— Employee is viewed as performing skillfully on the standard. Requires normal amount of supervision.

Does Not Meet Expectations— Employee needs to improve performance on the standard. Requires more than normal supervision in this area of performance.

Check One

I. CLINICAL COMPONENT

Standard 1 Nursing Process
Develops, interprets, implements, evaluates, and documents a plan of care for each patient using the nursing process:

	Exceeds Expectations (ExE)	Meets Expectations (ME)	Does Not Meet Expectations (DNM)
A. Assesses patient and initiates patient admission database.			
B. Identifies problems and formulates plan of care within 24 hours. Care plan demonstrates use of nursing diagnosis, planned outcomes, and nursing judgment related to patient/family needs. Initiates discharge plan.			
C. As primary/associate nurse, demonstrates accountability and coordination of care by:			
1. Following through on less predictable problems.			
2. Referring to other appropriate disciplines.			
3. Updating care plans, reviewing target dates, and documenting progress of patient toward goals.			
4. Involving patient/family in care.			
5. Establishing teaching plans with patient/family.			
6. Coordinating discharge plan.			
7. Attending physician rounds on primary patients.			
D. Organizes and participates in patient care conferences; utilizes information to provide continuity of patient care.			
E. Identifies deviations from expected vital signs and lab tests. Documents, reports, and follows through on abnormal findings with physicians/nurses.			
F. Sets priorities. Demonstrates skill in problem solving and follows through with assigned functions.			
G. Demonstrates an understanding of the medical plan of care and ensures that physician orders are implemented promptly and accurately.			
H. Documents nursing assessments and interventions accurately, clearly, and concisely.			
I. Evaluates and documents patient response and outcome to nursing interventions.			

continues

Figure 10–2 continued

Measurement Method   *Meets*
Based on a minimum of 4 observations   Audit reveals
spread throughout the year. Peers   75% compliance

COMMENTS _____
_____
_____

Standard 2 Quality Assurance

Acts as advocate for providing safe delivery of patient care.
            (ONLY MARK IN MEET OR DOES NOT MEET)

	DNM	ME
A.* Satisfactorily completes 90% of skills checklist of specific unit.		
B.* Attends one session each year: (provides documentation of attendance at evaluation time)		
1. Fire Safety _____		
2. General Hospital Safety _____		
3. Infection Control _____		
4. Disaster _____		
C.* Maintains the following certifications		
1. Registered Nurse License _____		
2. CPR _____		
3. Other _____ (as designated on unit)		
D.** Medication		
1. Demonstrates knowledge of dosage, route, action, side effects, and contraindications of medications. Utilizes resources as necessary.		
2. Administers medication, narcotics, and IVs following hospital policies and procedures.		
3. Identifies drug interactions.		
4. Knows antidotes/treatment for medication overdose.		
5. Knows antidotes/treatment for medication infiltrations.		
6. Calculates all dosages accurately.		
7. Properly dilutes medications for individual dose.		
8. Documents appropriately.		

Measurement Method Meets
Supervisor/Charge Nurse   */**

COMMENTS _____
_____
_____

continues

Figure 10–2 continued

	DNM	ME	ExE
E. Demonstrates setup, operation, and trouble shooting of equipment on unit. Reports all damaged equipment.			
F. Keeps work area clean and neat. Replaces, removes, and returns equipment and supplies as appropriate.			
G. Follows procedures for body substance isolation system.			
H. Maintains a safe, therapeutic environment for patient/family.			
I. Demonstrates knowledge of unit response to a disaster situation and carries out employee responsibilities.			
J. Checks crash cart and completes other duties as directed.			
K. Is familiar with crash cart and acts as effective team member during emergency situations.			
L. Assists in data collection for nursing/medical research projects. May initiate ideas for research project.			
M. Contributes to unit quality assurance activities, i.e., unit QA committee, data collection for audits.			

Measurement Method   *Meets*
Supervisor/Charge Nurse observation   75%
Comments from peers/discussion

COMMENTS _____
_____
_____

TOTAL POINTS_____
OF CRITERIA_____

II. EDUCATIONAL COMPONENT

Standard 3 Education
Communicates knowledge formally and informally to meet needs of patient and staff.

	DNM	ME	ExE
A. Patients/Families			
1. Anticipates educational needs of patient and family; plans and imparts knowledge to meet the needs.			
2. Utilizes creative skills (e.g., CCIV) when instructing and adapts to patient/family's level of understanding. Provides written resource material.			
3. Documents instruction and patient/family response to educational activities. Updates nursing care plan based on analysis of patient's response to instruction.			
4. Collaborates with multidisciplines in planning patient education.			
5. Participates in discharge planning.			

continues

Figure 10–2 continued

Measurement Method	*Meets*
Based on a minimum of 4 observations spread throughout the year.	75%

COMMENTS _____

	DNM	ME	ExE

B. Staff

1. May act as preceptor. Participates in orientation of new employee and provides feedback to charge nurse or supervisor on employee performance.
2. Supports unit-related inservices, conferences, and meetings by active participation, encouraging staff and assisting with unit coverage.
3. Provides instruction and guidance to staff in a positive, constructive manner.
4. Assists in identifying staff learning needs.

C. Students
1. Provides opportunities for student involvement in patient care and procedures.
2. Demonstrates and supports professionalism in nursing practice.

Measurement Method	*Meets*
Unit Supervisor/Charge Nurse	≤ 2 Negative
Comments from peers	

COMMENTS _____

Standard 4 Professional Growth

Participates in educational programs and research that contribute to the improvement of nursing practice.

	DNM	ME	ExE

A. Nursing Education Programs
1. Takes responsibility for own educational needs to enhance area of practice.
2. Attends at least 60% of unit inservices and staff meetings. Participates and gives suggestions.
3. Takes responsibility for reading minutes of staff meetings and integrating information into practice.

B. Nursing Practice Improvement
1. Participates in one of the following: data collection, product evaluation, nursing committee, or writing of patient care procedures.
2. Communicates awareness of current issues in nursing and clinical practice.

continues

Figure 10–2 continued

Measurement Method	*Meets*
Observation and discussion with employee during evaluation process	Provide attendance records, discusses one issue and cites one example

COMMENTS _____

_____

_____

TOTAL POINTS_____

OF CRITERIA_____

III. MANAGEMENT COMPONENT

Standard 5 Responsibilities to the Medical Center Nursing Department

Fulfills professional responsibility to the institution by adherence to philosophy and policy guidelines. (ONLY MARK IN MEET OR DOES NOT MEET)

	DNM	ME	
A.** Demonstrates awareness of and functions within attendance requirements:			
1. Works weekend requirement.			
2. Follows correct schedule change procedure.			
3. Follows department sick time policy.			ExE
4. Is prepared to start promptly at beginning of shift.			
5. Follows policy and procedure as stated in contract regarding:			
a. overtime usage			
b. breaks			
c. vacation and comp time usage			
B. Accepts and demonstrates a positive attitude toward patient care assignments.			
C. Notifies charge nurse if patient assignment increases or acuity decreases; seeks help or offers unsolicited help to others.			
D. Accepts relief charge assignment, coordinating unit activities. Orients float personnel who are not unit career staff members.			

Measurement Method	*Meets*
Staffing and attendance records	90%
Feedback from other managers	

COMMENTS _____

_____

_____

continues

Figure 10–2 continued

Standard 6 Professional Image

Demonstrates a positive, constructive attitude that provides the patient/family with a sense of security.

	DNM	ME	ExE
A. Conducts professional practice as defined by the UCSD model of practice (Primary Nursing).			
B. Identifies self as Primary Nurse to patient and family.			
C. Personal appearance and self-presentation reflect cleanliness, neatness, moderation, and a professional image. Always wears name tag.			
D. Adheres to the principles of the guest relations standards. Recognizes a guest relations problem and develops a solution to improve the situation; refers to other resources when appropriate.			
E. Demonstrates a helpful responsive attitude to promote the smooth functioning of the unit.			

Measurement Method	*Meets*
Supervisor/Charge Nurse	75%
Patients/Peers	

COMMENTS _____

_____

_____

Standard 7 Professional Management

Demonstrates professional nursing management of patient care.

	DNM	ME	ExE
A. Sets priorities, organizes and completes care for assigned patients within shift. Demonstrates ability to reorganize and reprioritize workload to meet changes in unit activity.			
B. Independently makes decisions. Seeks assistance in critical, complex situations. Gives pertinent, accurate, concise, organized report: documents on record.			
C. Is cost conscious, i.e., efficiently uses supplies, adheres to patient chargeable billing system. Performs within staffing guidelines as defined by the classification system.			
D. Adapts behaviors based upon guidance of peer and charge nurse evaluations.			
E. Maintains confidentiality of patient related issues. Intervenes to protect patient confidentiality; reports errors in practice standards to nursing management.			
F. Is accountable to standards set forth in the California Nurse Practice Act.			

continues

Figure 10–2 continued

Measurement Method	*Meets*
Supervisor/Charge Nurse/Peers	75%

COMMENTS _____

_____

_____

TOTAL POINTS_____
OF CRITERIA_____

Clinical

	÷		=	x's 1.2 =
Total Points	÷	# of criteria	=	

Educational

	÷		=	x's 0.8 =
Total Points	÷	# of criteria	=	

Management

	÷		=	x's 1.0 =
Total Points	÷	# of criteria	=	

Did the employee receive a "does not meet" on any asterisk (*) statement?

Yes _____ No _____ If yes, drop evaluation one rating.

OVERALL EVALUATION	Please check appropriate box	COMMENTS
( ) Unsatisfactory	0.0–5.9	_____
( ) Improvement	6.0–8.0	_____
( ) Satisfactory	8.1–10.8	_____
( ) More than satisfactory	10.9–13.1	_____
( ) Superior	13.2–15.0	_____

FUTURE PLANS AND ACTION

Goal	Specific Steps	Review Date

FUTURE GOALS

continues

Figure 10–2 continued

EMPLOYEE COMMENTS

<u>Employee Signature</u>
Your signature indicates neither agreement
nor disagreement with the evaluation, but it
does indicate that you have read it.

Signature of Immediate Supervisor	Date

Signature of Endorsing Supervisor	Date	Signature	Date

Department Head Signature	Date

Courtesy of UCSD Medical Center, Department of Nursing, San Diego, California.

Designing an effective performance appraisal system requires input and ownership of the nursing staff, so that their outcomes of work reflect the mission, vision, and goals of the organization. A good performance appraisal system will include staff-designed, criteria-based behaviors that are measurable; a process for feedback; and guidelines for improvement of performance.

Performance appraisal systems provide a vehicle for distribution of promotions and assignments, selection for education, and increased pay. For employee performance needing improvement, effective evaluation provides a structure for goals to be written, action plans to be formulated, and follow-up to be implemented.

Problem Areas with Performance Appraisal/Evaluation

Surveys have revealed dissatisfaction with performance appraisal systems among both those who are evaluated and those who do the evaluation. Employee dissatisfaction can occur because the criteria for evaluation are not relevant and/or are biased; the system is poorly created to allow positive or negative halo effects to occur; managers may be either lenient or tough, creating great variance in value judgments; there is racial bias and a focus on longevity; or evaluation is given in a punitive manner to identify deficiencies in job performance rather than in a positive manner to identify areas for

Feedback on: _____ Position: _____ Date: _____

Return to Charge Nurse by: _____ Signature: _____

	Did Not Observe	Rarely	Often	Consis-tently
1. Utilizes assessment skills demonstrating appropriate knowledge of pathophysiology.				
2. Uses care plan to facilitate patient care outcomes.				
3. Sets priorities for patient care; problem solves effectively.				
4. Provides quality patient care.				
5. Follows through on patient care problems.				
6. Responds appropriately to educational and psychosocial patient needs.				
7. Documents accurately nursing assessments, interventions, and patient response.				
8. Maintains a safe, clean, patient environment.				
9. Shares knowledge by teaching fellow staff and students.				
10. Demonstrates a positive attitude toward patient care assignments.				
11. Functions as an effective team member to ensure completion of all patient care activities.				
12. Assumes professional responsibility; functions effectively in a group.				
13. Responds to guest relation problems appropriate to CN level.				
14. Maintains confidentiality of patient issues.				
15. Communicates constructively with patient, family, and health care team.				
Additional Comments:				

Figure 10–3 Peer review feedback form: Clinical nurse series.

growth. Employer dissatisfaction may occur because there is lack of preparation, the employer's own role models were often punitive, evaluation is time consuming, evaluation is of questionable value to the system, or salary increases are tied to the evaluation process. For a performance appraisal system to be successful, managers and employees must be a part of its development and embrace it as an organizational necessity for long-term survival.

A significant issue today is whether to separate annual performance appraisal from annual merit salary increases. This issue is key because qualifying for a merit increase means looking back at past performance. Appraisals done for performance improvement look ahead. Also, managers tend to rank all employees equally on the high side of the Bell curve to ensure a maximum merit increase to all employees.

KEY CONCEPT
- Be prepared to speak out about your own strengths and areas for development. This will allow both staff and the manager to plan for appropriate goals for the next year. At the time of hire, ask what criteria will be used for the evaluation.

Coaching

Coaching is defined in the evaluation process as informal counseling. One of its greatest strengths is that it eliminates surprises. Coaching can be brief, regular, frank, open, and factual and can include the employee's viewpoint. Coaching should be used to discuss perceptions of both the staff and the manager (see Chapter 6 for a more detailed discussion of coaching).

Counseling

Counseling is one of the most productive functions to improve employee performance. **Counseling** is a formalized session between the manager and the staff nurse in which either one can create the agenda. Counseling sessions are always held for substandard performance, but they are not always indicative of a performance problem. The employee can ask for help in working through problems with patients, physicians, or other employees. The manager may initiate the counseling session for the purpose of clarifying with the employee standards of patient care, unit responsibilities, or staff relationships. Before entering into a counseling session, it is important to prepare so that both manager and employee can set mutual goals at the end of the session.

Counseling works best when problem behaviors are responded to in a timely manner. This creates trust between the manager and employee that has a long-term impact on the performance of the employee. Before an effective strategy for addressing substandard employee performance can be developed, the cause of the problem behavior must be identified. Without an accurate understanding of the antecedents of the problem, inappropriate corrective strategies may be used. Although employee performance problems often result from lack of motivation, frequently poor performance is caused by lack of ability. It is important to distinguish the cause because the treatment will differ. The objective in determining an appropriate intervention should be improvement of the problem behavior rather than punishment. Specific steps to be used in the counseling session are as follows:

1. The problem is clearly stated.
2. The staff nurse explains his or her perception of the situation.
3. The manager states the rationale of why it is important to correct the problem.
4. The staff nurse makes suggestions about how to prevent the behavior from recurring.
5. Mutual expectations are set that are measurable and have time frames for compliance and reevaluation.

Counseling is used in two ways. One is to assist and support the employee to improve behaviors or skills, and the other is as disciplinary action when employees do not perform at the level desired. Although most employees cause little difficulty for the organization, employees who do perform poorly create significant problems.

KEY CONCEPTS
- To get the best results for an employee from the counseling session, the manager should anticipate how the employee will react so that an appropriate response can be formulated.
- Be cautious of the counseling session that is focused on proving inappropriate behavior rather than improving performance.

Termination

Counseling sessions are held over a period of time until performance improves. If performance does not improve, termination is the next step. According to Rajokovich (1987), "There comes a time when employees part from an organization. The policy, procedures, and environment surrounding this event determine the degree of goodwill created for the organization" (p. 205). Termination can be categorized into two categories: voluntary and involuntary. Voluntary termination occurs when the employee decides on his or her own to leave the organization. Involuntary terminations occur for performance and organizational purposes.

Voluntary termination. Voluntary terminations often follow the pattern of the economic status of the community. During a marketplace shortage, when opportunities are open and salaries are competitive, nurses may move from one organization to another for increased salaries and bonuses. This movement can detract from stable career and personal growth and create organizational instability. Although the movement is a fast track to better salary and bonus rewards, it is rarely a fast track to career development.

Voluntary termination can also occur because of spousal job transfers or for personal considerations. It is to the advantage of both the organization and the employee to maintain good relationships and ongoing contact. These are valuable employees who will lend their expertise to the profession and an organization wherever they are.

Involuntary termination. Involuntary termination generally comes after a series of counseling sessions with an employee. The termination occurs when there is unacceptable job performance, professional misconduct, or inability to work with the team. The human resources department has policies and procedures that must be followed explicitly during involuntary termination for performance reasons. Employees are given specific rights to be heard by the organization's bureaucracy before final determination of termination is made. This is called a grievance procedure in most organizations. It is instituted to ensure a fair hearing for the employee by someone other than the manager. The final arbitrator is usually the chief executive officer or the board of trustees.

Involuntary termination for organizational need can occur because of restructuring or downsizing of an organization. This is a difficult procedure because valuable, often senior people are lost to an organization. Employees going through this process need to understand that they are excellent practitioners and/or managers and must be prepared to move into the future. Often, outplacement services are available for the laid-off employees. An outplacement service will help employees seek other employment. They can provide help in several areas: updating of a curriculum vitae or resume to present highlights of past experiences, courses on resume writing, lists of available positions, and tips for successful job searches. They may also have support personnel available for counseling. The terminating employee needs to be aware that the "big D," depression, may occur. Personal lives are often closely linked with professional roles, and a reduction in force can cause an employee to question his or her personal worth and value. Colleagues need to give personal support to individuals as they seek new positions.

KEY CONCEPT

- When developing a performance appraisal system, there are three philosophical questions to be considered:
  1. Is the role of the supervisor one of directing, punishing, and controlling versus encouraging, creating opportunities, and removing obstacles?
  2. Should merit salary increases be tied to evaluation?

3. What is the role of peer review and self-evaluation? Do they facilitate self-improvement and individual accountability, and how do they relate to management evaluation?

Retention

Retention of staff is one of the hallmarks of a successful organization. The reason for retaining staff is to maintain a history of the organization and its culture. Senior staff understand community norms and their impact on patient expectations. They have knowledge of physician practices and protocols. They also are superb planners and can expedite patients through the continuum of care. These senior people understand the importance of collaboration with other disciplines and the creation of multidisciplinary teams to solve patient problems.

For an organization to be successful, it must provide for internal growth. Organizations want to promote from within if staff have the necessary skills and education for open positions. An effective organization will always have a majority of its practitioners as senior staff.

Past retention programs have focused on improving pay and benefits, providing tuition reimbursement, and establishing bonus programs. It is interesting to note, however, that staff satisfaction surveys generally indicate dissatisfaction with the environment in which staff work, management practices, and/or lack of autonomy, not pay and benefits. In today's environment, many of these issues continue. If there is little staff input into the restructured environment, staff will continue to feel a lack of autonomy or that their opinions are not valued (see Exit Interviews and Turnover Trending, above). Programs that have been implemented and have had some success in retaining employees include clinical ladders, shared governance, work restructuring, and differentiated practice.

Clinical Ladders

Clinical ladders provide a means to recognize and reward nurses who want to remain involved in direct patient care at the bedside. As the nurse moves up the ladder, there is an increase in responsibilities and accountabilities with a consequent pay increase. A nurse who has advanced on the clinical ladder typically provides highly skilled nursing care and acts as a coach and role model for less experienced nurses. The highest level of a clinical ladder is generally a specialist in planning and developing care for complex patients. Successful clinical ladders have in place objective, measurable criteria by which each staff nurse is evaluated.

Many institutions have implemented clinical ladders without significant success. This is due to lack of objective evaluation criteria, lack of budgetary support, and inability to measure interpersonal skills and interdepartmental/

intradepartmental collaboration. Also, some institutions do not have patient populations that require highly skilled nursing care, or roles are not defined to utilize the advanced skills of the nurse. Thus many nurses continue to have the same role function as before their advancement up the clinical ladder.

Shared Governance

Shared governance is defined in many ways. Successful shared governance models have these elements: an ability of the group members to move together on issues, honesty in communication among the group, trust, understanding of the boundaries of group decision making, and appropriate committee and hierarchy structures that assist and support implementation of change. An important factor in implementing shared governance is recognizing the time and expense needed. If the time and expense for a shared governance model are not offset by cost savings in quality improvement and patient care, there is little reason for an organization to support shared governance.

Restructuring

One of the ways that organizations are approaching improving nurse and patient satisfaction and decreasing the cost to the organization is through redesign of the work on the unit. Many of the early models were dyads, in which the registered nurse worked with a support person to care for patients. This has evolved in recognition of the need for an interdisciplinary team to care for the patient. Some restructuring has enhanced the role of the nurse, but other efforts to restructure have left ambiguity regarding the role of the nurse and the nurse manager in these new models.

Differentiated Practice

Differentiated practice focuses on the structuring of roles and functions of nurses according to education, experience, and competence. As a philosophy, differentiated practice establishes that the domain of nursing practice is broad and has multiple responsibilities of varying degree and complexity. All practitioners are valued equally, and each has a separate and identified role in performing patient care activities. The implementation of differentiated practice has clearly defined the different roles of nurses in caring for patients and acknowledges that the provision of care to meet patient and organizational needs requires the broad scope of nurse education.

Summary

In the current environment of cost constraints and staff reductions, retention programs are being reviewed. The employee of today may be more interested in job security than the types of rewards that were offered in the past.

The challenge is to meet the needs of today's employees without overlooking the possibility of another nursing shortage in the future.

Staff Development

Components of an effective staff development program include orientation, inservice education, continuing education, and career development. Commitment to staff development activities in each organization depends on several factors: the philosophy of the organization, available financial and personnel resources, requirements of the Joint Commission on Accreditation of Healthcare Organizations, and community nursing standards.

Staff development is based on a continuous learning philosophy, which implies that there is always room for improvement regardless of career stage. Such a philosophy demands that employees participate actively in expanding their own skills because learning is an everyday part of the job. For staff development to be meaningful to both organizations and individuals, it must provide for individual and organizational goal accomplishment. Education activities are planned and developed to meet the needs of individual employees and the health care organization.

Because health care organizations work with adult learners, four important teaching principles are self-concept, experience, readiness to learn, and time perspective. Education programs need to be developed utilizing these principles.

KEY CONCEPT   • New graduates will learn to use life's experiences to reinforce their learning. Schedule time for learning. Use current clinical experiences to relate didactic learning.

Orientation

Orientation introduces new nursing personnel to the organization's philosophy, mission, vision, goals, policies, procedures, and physical facilities. The educational content is based on assessed learning needs and includes clinical work with a designated preceptor. Orientation can be of indeterminate length depending on the needs of the individual. With appropriate orientation, staff can begin patient care activities with professional confidence.

Inservice Education

Inservice education maintains and increases nurses' clinical competence in the provision of nursing care. This includes updating knowledge in general nursing practice as well as learning concepts and skills in specialized areas. Inservice education consists of activities having to do with pertinent new developments in patient care or deficiencies in knowledge as monitored through the CQI process.

Today, another important component of inservice education is cross-training. Because of the constant fluctuation in patient census, staff are required either to decrease their hours of work or to work in another area. Cross-training is a didactic and clinical education program for staff members who are assigned to, or want to work in, areas where overlapping skills and knowledge are required. For example, in settings where family-centered maternity nursing is practiced, nurses may be educated to work in all mother–infant areas. One of the newest efforts in cross-training focuses on patient care in the same unit but schedules staff to work in different hospitals in the same corporation. The long-term effectiveness and satisfaction with cross-training programs has not been measured.

KEY CONCEPT
- The broader the skill and knowledge level of the nurse, the more secure the job.

Continuing Education

Learning is a life-long process, a continuum. Continuing education begins after initial preparation for practice is complete. Continuing education consists of planned educational activities that build on the educational and experiential base of professional nurses for the enhancement of practice, education, administration, and research. In some states, contact hours for relicensure can be obtained from continuing education programs. Continuing education needs are identified by input from management and clinical staff, community needs, and new developments in health care.

Career Development

Career development is a method that the nurse manager can use to help professional nurses achieve career satisfaction. This involves helping nurses clarify their career goals and guiding them in making a plan to achieve those goals. The nurse manager can either structure a unit's learning environment to meet the goals of the staff or advise the nurse to use his or her network to facilitate goal achievement in another area of the organization.

Individual employees are responsible for initiating their own career planning. Employees begin by identifying their present knowledge, skills, abilities, interests, and values to set goals and develop career plans. The following is a series of questions that need to be addressed with the appropriate mentors:

- Where am I in the process of my professional career?
- What type of professional commitment do I plan in 1 year, 3 years, and 5 years?

- If I were to make a change in commitment involving time, emotional energy, and income, do I have the self-discipline and motivation to meet the demands required by the degree of change?
- If I decide to further my education or select a career change, can I accept the loss of income or loss of seniority?
- Do I have the support systems and or significant interpersonal relationships that will help me in the new situation?
- What are my marketable skills? How do I identify them?

KEY CONCEPT
- Employees need to use various resources to support their career development planning. Human resources departments, nurse managers, and senior staff nurses can serve as mentors for new professional nurses.

LEARNING CHALLENGE
1. When the evaluation is not congruent with the expectation of the position description, how would you address this issue?
2. If the evaluation process does not include self-evaluation or peer review, what suggestion would you make to change the process?
3. What do you do if your input into decision making regarding patient care is ignored?
4. When you have a limited orientation and feel uncomfortable in the environment, what are your resources to ensure that you maintain standards of care?
5. How does the use of human resources affect the cost and quality of the organization if people are its most valuable asset?
6. When an organization states that it is customer focused and that patient care is its business and number 1 priority, is that mutually exclusive to the importance of the employee and the employee's environment?
7. How do professional and continuing education prepare nurses to function in the team setting so that they can accept accountabilities for patient outcomes?

RESEARCH FOUNDATION
Dutcher, L.A., & Adams, C.E. (1994). Work environment perceptions of staff nurses and aides in home health agencies. *Journal of Nursing Administration, 24* (10), 24–30.

Registered nurses and home health aides in three nonprofit home health agencies that are Medicare certified and have visit volumes greater than 40,000 per year were surveyed to identify their work environment perceptions. Seventy staff nurses and 35 home health aides who had been employed for at least 6 months provided demographic information and completed the

Work Environment Scale (WES) . The WES measures three work environment dimensions: relationship, personal growth, and systems maintenance–systems change. Data analysis revealed that the nurses had a higher level of education than the home health aides and that the aides had more years of experience in home health. The nurses perceived significantly higher levels of involvement, peer cohesion, and work pressure than the aides. The home health aides perceived significantly higher levels of control and clarity. The groups did not differ significantly in perceptions of supervisor support, task orientation, autonomy, innovation, and physical comfort. Nurse managers who understand how perceptions of staff nurses and home health aides may be different can create innovative, collaborative work environments.

REFERENCES

Blouin, A. (1992). Exempt salary administration. *Journal of Nursing Administration, 22* (6), 24–28.

Curran, C. (1991). Why can't they be like we were? *Nursing Economics, 9* (4), 220, 231.

Deming, W.E. (1993). *The new economics for industry, government, education.* Cambridge: Massachusetts Institute of Technology.

Donovan-Sierk, T. (1994). Implementation of a salary model for staff nurses. *Nursing Management, 25* (1), 36–37.

Eubanks, P. (1992). Work redesign calls for new pay and performance plans. *Hospitals, 66* (19), 56–60.

Fosbinder, D. (1990). *Nursing care through the eyes of the patient.* Unpublished doctoral dissertation, University of San Diego.

Fosbinder, D., & Vos, H. (1989). Setting standards and evaluation of nursing performance with a single tool. *Journal of Nursing Administration, 19* (10), 23–30.

Haddon, R.M. (1989). Nursing resource management. In M. Johnson & J. McCloskey (Eds.), *Changing organizational structures* (pp. 178–203). Redwood City, CA: Addison-Wesley.

Husted, G.L. (1991). Ethical questions nurses can ask potential employers. *AORN Journal, 53* (3), 791–792.

Katzenbach, J.R., & Smith, D.K. (1991). The discipline of teams. *Harvard Business Review, 71* (2), 111–120.

Peters, T.J., & Waterman, R.H. (1982). *In search of excellence.* New York: Harper & Row.

Rajokovich, M.J. (1987). Voluntary and involuntary termination. In E.M. Lewis & J.G. Spicer (Eds.), *Human resource management handbook* (p. 205). Gaithersburg, MD: Aspen.

PART III

The Future of Health Care

Planned Change Outline

Aloma Gender

CHAPTER OBJECTIVES

At the completion of this chapter, the beginning professional nurse will be able to:

1. define planned change and describe its purpose
2. describe the role of the professional nurse in the planned change process
3. examine various change theories
4. explore strategies for change and change tactics
5. describe the role of a change agent
6. describe impediments to and acceptance of change and define techniques for dealing with resistance

CRITICAL   A 55-year-old married man with a history of chronic obstructive pulmonary
THINKING   disease is admitted to the hospital in respiratory failure. He has smoked
CHALLENGE   three packs of cigarettes a day for the last 30 years. On the second day of
                  hospitalization, he tells his nurse that he recognizes the need, and has the
                  desire, to quit smoking. His nurse initiates a care plan to enable him to
                  change his smoking behavior by using the principles of change theory.
                  Identify the actions that the nurse should implement to effect this change.

THE MEANING OF CHANGE

In 1514, Machiavelli wrote in *The Prince*:

> It should be borne in mind that there is nothing more difficult to
> handle, more doubtful of success, and more dangerous to carry
> through, than initiating changes. . . . The innovator makes enemies
> of all who prospered under the old order, and only lukewarm sup-
> port is forthcoming from those who would prosper under the new.
> Their support is lukewarm partly from fear of their adversaries, who
> have the existing laws on their side, and partly because men are
> generally incredulous, never really trusting new things unless they
> have tested them by experience. (p. 51)

Machiavelli was referring to changes in government, but his comments apply
to the initiation of any new order. Change is a part of the cycle of life and a
principle basic to the universe (DeFeo, 1990). To be alive is to change, yet
the word is often accompanied by adjectives such as *anxious, threatened,*
and *fearful* when it is mentioned. Phrases such as "Don't rock the boat" and
"If it isn't broken, don't fix it" are in common use in American culture. People
generally enjoy doing things the way they have always done them. They resist
change and are threatened by it. Yet change is occurring in society today at a
frenzied pace. To survive in such a rapidly evolving environment, one must
have the capacity to adapt and adjust to quick and sudden innovation.

In the field of nursing, as in the time of Machiavelli, a person may experience change as a target, as a participator, or as an instigator of change
(Langford, 1981). The nurse may be going through change individually, may
be trying to change a patient's health habits, or may be experiencing reorganization in the work environment.

This chapter explores the process of change and planned change theory.
Strategies for implementing successful changes in nursing and the health
care environment are discussed, and methods for successfully coping with
change and for initiating change are examined.

Change is defined as something taking the place of something else, altering or transforming, passing from one phase to another, or substituting something in favor of something else. Havelock (1973) defined change as "Any sig-

nificant alteration in the status quo . . . an alteration which is intended to benefit the people involved" (p. 4). If viewed from an evolutionary standpoint, change is inevitable, yet it is difficult to operationalize because it is a potentially painful experience (Sheehan, 1990). Change means introducing the unknown, and people often fear what is unknown (Laughlin, 1989). Individuals have trouble overturning their habits or assumptions in favor of a new way of thinking or behaving.

Change and the Nursing Profession

DeFeo (1990) describes the phenomenon of change, as it relates to the human experience, as a central concern of the profession of nursing. Nursing is a helping profession, and nurses assist patients in making changes that will restore their health, maintain their current status, or lead to a higher level of wellness. DeFeo likens nurses to the symbol of the ferryman in Buddhist literature: "Humbly, without preaching, the ferryman offers the passenger a ride from shore to shore across the river of life" (p. 93). So, also, do nurses help patients bridge the troubled waters that occur in their lives.

Change and Nursing Theory

The process of change can be seen in the works of nursing theorists. They address change in human life in their models of nursing care. Roy and Roberts (1981) view the individual as a dynamic, open system responding to changes internally and externally. Change is adapting and coping with the environment. Rogers (1992) says that change is continuous. Her three principles of homeodynamics deal with the nature and direction of change. King (1987) views humans as existing in the midst of unceasing change. Individuals are creators, not passive observers of change, and are time oriented. Nurses help clients with the attainment of goals when they are unable to cope with changes in daily activities. Orem (1985) describes individuals functioning within stable and changing environments. Her theory views self-care as a learned behavior and as an element of the day-to-day living of individuals. Patients need nursing when their self-care requisites exceed their self-care capabilities as a result of changes in their health status.

Health Care and Change

The health care industry has been a field of rapid growth and technological change for decades (Langford, 1981). Today, it is in a constant state of reorganization from both national and local forces. Hospitals and other health care agencies must adapt to a rapidly changing world to survive. The nurse is in the middle of this turmoil and therefore must be able to understand and handle change in a positive, proactive manner.

All change, however, involves loss. This loss may be in the form of persons, place, status, vested interests, money, or function. Grieving accompanies this loss (Bushnell, 1979). How can this feeling of harm and sorrow be mitigated or eased? Planned change is one method.

Purpose of Planned Change

Any proposed change should be worthwhile, logical, and ethical (Sheehan, 1990). Organizational changes need to be fast enough to ensure survival but not so fast that they disorient or demoralize the workforce (Gillies, 1994). Change for its own sake is meaningless. Change has value only when it is being accomplished to achieve a defined end (Stevens, 1977). A proposed change should therefore be important for the people for whom the change is planned (Sheehan, 1990).

The process, or how the change is going to be implemented, is critical. Planned change is a method used to enable people to act with anticipation toward a new order and to help people cope with the new situation (Laughlin, 1989). Havelock (1973) defines planned change as "change or innovation which comes about through a deliberate process which is intended to make both acceptance by and benefit to the people who are changed more likely" (p. 5).

Components of Planned Change and Planned Change Theory

Planned change has several interacting components that need to be considered (Pierce & Thompson, 1976):

- the environment in which the change is to occur
- the procedural or technological variation from what currently exists to what is desired
- the human element, or change target, that needs to be modified
- the change agent, or the person who initiates and eases the change process
- the means for promoting and maintaining the new plan

There are many models or theories of how a planned change should be accomplished. A theory is a set of concepts that presents a systematic view of phenomena (Tiffany, 1994). A planned change theory, then, is "a unified collection of concepts about consciously designed and implemented social system modifications" (Tiffany, Cheatham, Doornbos, Loudermelt, & Momadi, 1994, p. 55).

A planned change theory accomplishes several things. First, it furnishes general guidance for the efforts of the change agent. Second, it gives a mechanism for diagnosing social system problems. A third benefit is that it provides a means for selecting or developing an innovation. Fourth, it places major emphasis on the plans for the change and the implementation of strategies and maneuvers designed to cause the new order to occur. Finally, it provides a means to evaluate the planned change event (Tiffany et al., 1994).

Planned Change and the Nursing Process

Planned change theories use steps similar to those in the nursing process (Table 11–1; Gillies, 1994; Laughlin, 1989). The assessment phase begins when there is an increased awareness of the inadequacies of the current system. During the planning step, what needs to be changed is identified. Objectives for the change process are outlined, and a course of action is chosen. During implementation, individuals are assigned various actions to complete by certain deadlines. The evaluation phase examines both the change process itself and the effectiveness of the new state (Gillies, 1994).

The Nurse's Role in Planned Change

Planned change is part of the leadership role of today's nurse, no matter what position he or she holds. The ability of each nurse to identify and achieve change is vitally important to meeting the needs of clients. Thoughtful use of planned change by nurses promotes quality nursing care (Welch, 1979).

Nurses and nursing leaders need to evaluate and select their planned change theory carefully to choose the concept that is most appropriate to the specific situation (Tiffany et al., 1994). The circumstance could be a clinical

Table 11–1 Planned Change Theory and the Nursing Process

Nursing Process	Planned Change
1. Assessment	1. Awareness of inadequacies of the current system
2. Planning	2. Identify what needs to be changed, develop objectives, and choose a course of action
3. Implementation	3. Achieve objectives by predetermined deadlines
4. Evaluation	4. Examine the change process and the effectiveness of the new state

change, such as preventing pressure sores in a spinal cord–injured patient by incorporating daily skin inspections into the patient's life style. Organizational change, such as carrying out staff self-scheduling, could be occurring. The change could involve staff development, such as converting from using needles to a needleless intravenous system. The change could be with the professionalization of nursing, such as the requirement of a bachelor's degree in nursing before a nurse takes a specialty certification examination. The theory selected must be critically evaluated in terms of whether its assumptions and characteristics will work for the desired situation (Tiffany, 1994).

KEY CONCEPTS	• The phenomenon of change is a central concern of the profession of nursing.
	• The process of change is seen in the works of nursing theorists: Roy, Rogers, King, and Orem.
	• Planned change is a method to enable people to cope with a new situation and to act with anticipation toward a new order.
	• The interacting components of planned change are: the environment, the procedural or technological change, the change target, the change agent, and the method of implementing and maintaining the new plan.
	• Planned change theories use similar steps as the nursing process.

CHANGE THEORIES

General Systems Theory

The phenomenon of change is embodied in the elements of **general systems theory** (Sheehan, 1990). A system is a whole comprising interdependent parts or subunits. The whole is greater than the sum of its parts because there is dynamic interaction among the parts. Langford (1981) gives the example of a car. The parts of a car, by themselves, are nothing, but if assembled in a way that allows them to work together they create a moving vehicle. So, also, does a group of nurses working together on a unit become a caregiving system that is greater than each individual nurse alone. Any system is also a part of one or more larger systems. For example, a patient as a system is part of a family, which is part of a larger system: the community in which the family lives. The variables surrounding a system form its environment.

A system is either open or closed. Open systems have constant interchange between the environment and the system. Inputs or stimuli from the environment are received and responded to across the system's boundaries (Laughlin, 1989). A change in any element of an open system produces changes in the other elements of the system. When a change occurs, the system will seek a point of equilibrium or balance among its forces (Langford, 1981; Laughlin, 1989). A closed system has well-defined boundaries between it and the environment (Sheehan, 1990).

Another aspect of general systems theory is the phenomenon of input, throughput, and output. A system receives input, processes it, and produces output, some of which is directed back into the system via a feedback loop for self-correction (Figure 11–1). All systems change with time (Langford, 1981), and both open and closed systems need constant input, or change, to be maintained (Sheehan, 1990).

To put general systems theory into action when planning a change, one would first select the target unit as a system. This unit could be a person, group, organization, or community. Next, the change agent locates the boundaries of that system. What is part of the system, and what is in the environment? The environment is analyzed. If a factor does not make a difference in achieving the change objectives, then it is outside the boundary and does not need to be dealt with in the change process. If the factor does make a difference in the change objectives but the change agent cannot do anything about it, then it is still placed in the environment to be taken care of later but is not directly addressed in the interventions (Chin, 1985). The change agent must also examine the input, throughput, output, and feedback loops of both the present system and the system that is planned for the future (Gillies, 1994). Appropriate interventions are then developed for changing the system and/or the environment to achieve the new desired state (Chin, 1985). Refer to Chapter 2 for more information about systems theory.

Lewin's Change Theory

Social scientist Kurt Lewin is considered the classic change theorist. Much of his work was done in the 1940s. Lewin identified three stages of change: unfreezing, movement, and refreezing (Figure 11–2; Lewin, 1951).

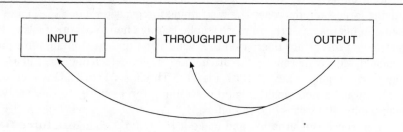

Figure 11–1 General Systems Theory.

**FORCE FIELD
ANALYSIS**

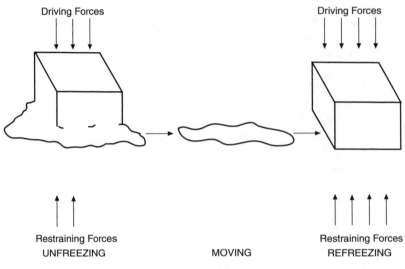

Figure 11–2 Lewin's change theory.

Stage of Unfreezing

In the **unfreezing** stage, a motivation to create some kind of change occurs. The client system is aware of the need for change or for a better way to accomplish a task. Group life, according to Lewin (1951), is viewed as a social field. If the present condition of a social field is a status quo, then the driving forces (those that are toward or away from something) and the restraining forces (those that oppose a change) are in a state of equilibrium. For a change to occur, either the driving forces must be increased or the restraining forces must be decreased, or both can be accomplished (i.e., increase the driving forces and decrease the restraining forces; see Figure 11–2). Lewin found in his research that a more stable, lasting change occurs if either the restraining forces are decreased or both driving and restraining forces are changed. Merely increasing the driving forces alone does not result in a lasting state of change (Lewin, 1951; Pierce & Thompson, 1976). Driving forces push toward a new position, and restraining forces mitigate this push by maintaining the status quo (Langford, 1981).

To unfreeze the situation and make it ready for a change, a **force field analysis** must be done on the driving and restraining forces. Driving forces must be strengthened or added. They can be increased in a positive manner, such as by providing a reward if a change occurs, or they can be increased in a negative manner, such as by taking away rewards if the move toward change does not occur (Langford, 1981).

Driving forces may be internal or external to the system. External forces could be economic, social, or political, such as the health care reform movement causing a need to reduce hospital costs. Another example is state non-smoking laws placing negative social pressures on smokers. An internal force for change might arise from quality assurance indicators (Gillies, 1994), such as the need to improve hospital services based on patient satisfaction scores, or it may be health related, such as the need for an individual to quit smoking because of shortness of breath (Vanetzian, 1988).

Restraining forces, or those that are preventing a change, must be weakened. According to Lewin (1951), three mechanisms can be used to help with this:

1. *Lack of confirmation or disconfirmation.* With this approach, a person becomes aware of the need to change because expectations accompanying the current state have not been met. A new nursing documentation system, for example, may be heartily embraced by a nursing unit if the current system is taking too much time.

2. *Induction of guilt or anxiety.* In this situation, a person feels uncomfortable enough about his or her current action or lack of action to want to change. An example might be the diabetic individual who is now ready for diet counseling because his or her current eating habits are causing hypoglycemia.

3. *Creation of psychological safety.* A former obstacle to the change is removed with this mechanism. An example could be an overweight individual who has wanted to participate in a fitness program and now has the funds to join a gym.

The unfreezing stage is completed when the individual or group is aware of the need for change or recognizes that there is a problem or a better way to accomplish a task. The second stage then begins.

Stage of Moving

During the **moving** stage, the change itself is planned out in detail and then initiated. Information is sought to clarify and identify the problem. Information can be gathered from a knowledgeable or respected peer or sought from a variety of sources. Cognitive redefinition, or looking at the problem from a new perspective, occurs during this stage. The actual changing or moving happens when new responses are developed based on the collected information (Welch, 1979). Once the change is implemented, the third stage begins.

Stage of Refreezing

During the **refreezing** stage, the new changes are integrated into the system and stabilized. The new concepts are incorporated into the individual's or group's value system. The change is perpetuated because it is now part of the value system in which the person or group operates (Lewin, 1951; Welch, 1979). Permanency of the refreezing stage implies that the new force field of restraining and driving forces is relatively secure against change (Lewin, 1951). Lewin states that, when refreezing occurs, the equilibrium of the former force field has been supplanted by moving its equilibrium point to a desired new level (see Figure 11–2). It is easier to change the status quo, according to Lewin, when there are many disturbing or disrupting elements in the situation than it is when things are going smoothly. Refreezing can be hastened when the change targets are rewarded promptly, such as with more interesting assignments, money, or evidence that the change is working (Gillies, 1994).

Models Based on Lewin's Change Theory

Other models for planned change based on Lewin's change theory have been developed. The models of Rogers (1962), Havelock (1973), and Lippitt (1973; Exhibits 11–1 through 11–3) all have their foundations in the works of Lewin. The change process may flow back and forth between any of the stages in the models. The mechanism may move rapidly from one stage to another, or it may get stuck at any point in the operation (Welch, 1979).

Exhibit 11–1 Rogers's Theory of Change

Unfreezing	Moving	Refreezing
Awareness	Interest	Adoption
	Evaluation	
	Trial	

Source: Reprinted from L.B. Welch, Planned Change in Nursing: The Theory, *Nursing Clinics of North America*, Vol. 14, No. 2, p. 310, with permission of W.B. Saunders, © 1979.

Exhibit 11–2 Havelock's Phases of Change

Unfreezing	Moving	Refreezing
Building a relationship	Choosing the solution	Stabilization and
Diagnosing the problem	Gaining acceptance	self-renewal
Acquiring relevant resources		

Source: Reprinted from L.B. Welch, Planned Change in Nursing: The Theory, *Nursing Clinics of North America*, Vol. 14, No. 2, p. 313, with permission of W.B. Saunders, © 1979.

Bhola's CLER Model for Change

Bhola's CLER theory of change has a 25-year history of development and is a general model that is useful for problem solving within open systems (Bhola, 1994). *CLER* stands for four concepts:

- *C, Configuration of change.* Change occurs in many different, often overlapping configurations, not just one. There are four basic social configurations: individuals, groups, institutions/organizations, and communities/subcultures/cultures. Each of these can be a planner or an adopter of change (or both). The change agent, or enabler of the change, must begin by defining the relationship among the configurations involved in a change episode. For example, is the configuration between two individuals, as in the nurse–patient relationship, or is it

Exhibit 11–3 Lippitt's Stages of Change

Unfreezing	Moving	Refreezing
Diagnosis of the problem	Selecting progres-	Maintenance of
Assessment of the motiva-	sive change	the change
tion and capacity for	objectives	once it is
change	Choosing an	started
Assessment of the change	appropriate role	Termination of the
agent's motivation and	for the change	helping
resources	agent	relationship

Source: Reprinted from L.B. Welch, Planned Change in Nursing: The Theory, *Nursing Clinics of North America*, Vol. 14, No. 2, p. 313, with permission of W.B. Saunders, © 1979.

between an individual and an institution, such as a nurse administrator in a large hospital?

- *L, Linkages.* Linkages are both formal and informal, horizontal and vertical ways of carrying communication between and within the planner and adopter systems.
- *E, Environment.* Environments are inside and around the systems involved in the change transaction. Environments can be inhibitive, neutral, or supportive. They can be deliberately manipulated. The planner system and the adopter system will not necessarily be responding to the same environment.
- *R, Resources.* Resources are used by the planner system to enable implementation of the change. Resources are used by the adopter system to incorporate the change. There are six types of resources: cognitive, which aids in understanding the substance and process of the change; influence, which arises from power and goodwill; material, such as cash or supplies; personnel; institutional; and time.

This model assumes interrelationships and interdependencies among social cultures and social systems. It accepts the basic concepts of systems theory. Change is not seen as something given by the planner to the adopter but rather as something mutually invented. Collaborative action and participative decision making are needed by the planners and the adopters. Bhola (1994) states that the model should fit with nursing because nursing is a nurturing profession. Change strategies result from using the four basic categories of the model first to describe the change situation and then to design the social interventions needed to make it happen.

To exemplify this theory, a cardiac rehabilitation nurse plans to incorporate an exercise program into the life style of a patient after myocardial infarction. The nurse first describes the situation according to Bhola's theory. The configuration is a nurse–patient relationship. The linkages are informal, with one-to-one conversations, and formal, with a series of group educational classes. The environment of the change situation is the hospital setting. The resources to be used are cognitive, in terms of exercise physiology theory; influence, in terms of the nurse, the physician, and peer support from other cardiac patients; material, in the form of written handouts; personnel, which includes the nurse and primary physician; institutional, such as the cardiac exercise equipment and running track; and time of the nurse.

The nurse then designs the social interventions that are needed to make the change occur. In the configuration of the change, the nurse must consider the family, outside groups, and community/culture of the patient. How will these social configurations hinder or support an exercise program? Will there be time in the day to accomplish what is needed? Will the family members support a change in the patient's living and dietary habits? Linkages will also need to be made with the patient's family members. They will need to hear the same information. The patient's work and leisure schedule will need to be carefully analyzed in terms of the environment. The resources of the patient need to be examined. What is the reading and educational level of the patient and family? Who in the family has the most influence over the change process? Will an ongoing change necessitate extra expenses for the patient, and will the patient be able to afford it? Does the patient have time in his or her day to incorporate the proposed changes? If not, what modifications can be suggested? These are some examples of the aspects of a change process to consider with Bhola's model.

STRATEGIES FOR CHANGE

Once a theory is chosen for the change process, a strategy must be developed for use throughout the model to minimize the resistance to the proposed change and to maximize commitment to it. The dictionary defines a strategy as a plan designed to lead to a favorable or advantageous outcome. Chin and Benne (1985) describe three types of change strategies that can be used individually or in combination, depending upon the type of change to be accomplished.

Empirical–Rational Strategies

Empirical means that something is derived from experiment and observation. **Rational** means that something is logical. This approach to change uses general education and dissemination of research and knowledge to convince people to incorporate a change. It assumes that humans are rational and that they will act in a reasonable manner and follow the best course once the plan is revealed to them. An example is the research and education used to convince people to be immunized against polio. Another example is the research showing that smoking is directly related to lung disease, which is influencing the number of individuals who currently smoke. This strategy does not work as well where research has not definitely proved that a change is better. When one is using this approach, giving information in both verbal and written forms helps people see the logic of the change (New & Couillard, 1981).

Normative–Reeducative Strategies

Normative means a response to social pressures from within groups. **Reeducative** means the teaching and learning aspects of the proposed change. This strategy suggests that the way people act and practice is supported by sociocultural norms and by commitments of individuals to these norms. The attitudes and values of individuals support the norms. Change will occur only when people change their normative orientations to old patterns and develop commitments to new ones. This involves changes in attitudes, values, skills, and significant relationships, not just a change in knowledge or rationales, as with the first approach. There is no assumption with this strategy that more information will cause the change to occur. The power of this approach rests with the individuals and groups making the change rather than in the knowledge itself. For this strategy to work, active participation in the change by the individuals involved needs to occur.

With this approach, a change agent plays a big role in helping people develop more self-awareness and understanding of how the target for change will address their values and norms. The change agent works collaboratively with the client to problem solve, analyze the current and proposed change, and generate workable solutions. Unconscious elements that impede problem solving must be brought into consciousness and openly examined and reconstructed. Personal growth must occur with the target group. Experience-based learning is the key to an enduring change with this approach.

An example of this strategy is a pediatric nurse teaching a series of parenting classes. During these sessions, old patterns of behaving and learned familial values must be replaced by new approaches. The parents must become aware of how they learned their old beliefs and must participate in generating new ways of functioning.

Power–Coercive Strategies

In this method, the impetus for change is generated from someone or something in authority or with legitimate power, such as the law. The emphasis is more the political and economic sanctions of power rather than the influence of one person over others. The change in behavior is brought about by decreasing pain rather than gaining pleasure: If change does not take place, either negative sanctions will occur or positive sanctions will be lost. This strategy uses moral power, such as guilt and shame; political power, such as the law; or economic power, as in managed health care companies forcing hospital cost reductions in their contracting for lower fixed rates.

KEY CONCEPTS	• Change theories
	  1. General Systems Theory: input, throughput, output, and feedback loops
	  2. Lewin's change theory

    — Unfreezing: force field analysis conducted on driving and restraining forces
    — Moving
    — Refreezing
  3. CLER model for change
    — Configuration of change: individuals, groups, organizations, cultures
    — Linkages: communication
    — Environment
    — Resources: cognitive, influence, material, personnel, institutional, time

- Strategies for change
  1. Empirical–rational: general education and dissemination of research and knowledge to convince people to change
  2. Normative–reeducative: change occurs when people change their normative orientations to old patterns and develop commitments to new ones through a change in attitudes, values, skills, and significant relationships
  3. Power–coercive: impetus for change is generated from someone in authority or with legitimate power

BARRIERS TO CHANGE

In using any change theory or strategy, it is important to understand why people resist change and what makes them more susceptible to and accepting of a new direction. This understanding is necessary in the planning phase of any change project. Some of the reasons for **resistance to change** are as follows:

- *Threatened self-interest.* Individuals may fear the loss of a job, status, or money with an impending change. They may believe that more work will be required or that their social relationships with peers will be disrupted. They may believe that the personal cost of the change is greater than the personal benefits (New & Couillard, 1981). A spinal cord–injured man may refuse to perform self-catheterizations, for example, because he sees it as more work.
- *Inaccurate perceptions.* Individuals may not understand the change correctly. They may feel that it is not to their benefit (New & Couillard, 1981).
- *Objective disagreement.* Individuals may resist the change because they place the organization's or their family's interests above their own

and feel that the change will not be of benefit to the organization or to their significant others. In some cases, these individuals may be correct (New & Couillard, 1981).

- *Psychological reactance.* With a change occurring, there may be a feeling that the freedom to engage in particular behaviors will be threatened or eliminated. These behaviors then become even more desirable because they are being threatened and people attempt to reestablish them (New & Couillard, 1981). An example of this might be cross-training an individual to do several tasks. By doing more work, there may be less time for breaks, which may have been a desired behavior. Another example might be the fear of giving up the social aspect of smoking with friends for a person contemplating a program to quit smoking (Vanetzian, 1988).

- *Low tolerance for change.* Many organizational changes require rapid attitudinal and behavioral shifts. Although a person may intellectually understand the new order, he or she may not be able to make the transition emotionally because of low self-confidence, aversion to risk, or low tolerance for uncertainty (New & Couillard, 1981). People differ in their ability to tolerate change. Generally, those individuals with a high need for novelty welcome frequent change (Gillies, 1994).

- *Change runs counter to current trends.* If the change does not go along with what is happening at other institutions in the industry or runs counter to current thought patterns, there will be more resistance. For example, if a hospital plans to use more nursing assistants when the trend is for all registered nurse staffing, there will be resistance (New & Couillard, 1981).

- *System has been stable for a long time.* Resistance is high when a system has been stable for a long time. Personnel tend to be well satisfied with the current situation (Gillies, 1994).

In summary, with all the possible impediments to change, resistance has less to do with the substance of the change generally than it does with the perceived net value of the change for the individual (Langford, 1981). This resistance can arise at any point in the change process.

ACCEPTANCE OF CHANGE

Acceptance also depends on several factors. There are aspects to consider in facilitating **acceptance** of a new situation. First of all, if people believe that the change is their idea, they will go along with it more readily. If the change is supported by their significant others or by peers and if they see the change as decreasing their burdens or problems, it will be easier for them to adapt to it. If autonomy and security are increased with the new order or if the change is in accordance with their own values and ideals, resistance will be less. Finally, if people are a part of assessing and diagnosing the steps in the change process and agree on the basic problem and alternative solutions, they will accept it more quickly (Laughlin, 1989).

Another tactic to aid in acceptance might be to introduce major ideas informally and/or on a one-to-one basis to assess the reaction. Starting a change project with those individuals who are the most receptive can also ensure success (Gillies, 1994). Providing training in new skills as well as giving positive reinforcement and considerate treatment with regular meetings help ease discomfort (Gillies, 1994; New & Couillard, 1981). When a person is required to demonstrate a specific behavior consistently, his or her attitude shifts from a negative to a positive one to decrease cognitive dissonance (Gillies, 1994). Gradually introducing an organizational change by doing a pilot first may also decrease resistance. Providing positive reinforcement of new practices and support for the individual further aids in acceptance (New & Couillard, 1981).

KEY
CONCEPTS
- Impediments to change
  1. Threatened self-interest
  2. Inaccurate perceptions
  3. Objective disagreement
  4. Psychological reactance
  5. Low tolerance for change
  6. Change runs counter to current trends
  7. System has been stable for a long time
- Facilitating acceptance to change
  1. People believe that it is their idea
  2. Change is supported by significant others
  3. Change decreases their burdens
  4. Autonomy and security are increased
  5. Change is in accord with their own values and ideals
  6. People are part of the change process and agree on the solution
  7. Training in new skills and positive reinforcement are given

THE ROLE OF THE CHANGE AGENT

Havelock (1973) defined a **change agent** as a person who facilitates planned change. Change agents prepare the way for the change, serve as facilitators to enable it to happen, and identify and repair breakdowns when they occur (Sheehan, 1990). Havelock (1973) defined four main roles for change agents (Figure 11–3).

A change agent in an institution can be in a line or staff position and can work from below or above on an organizational chart. It helps to be in a formal position of authority and to work from above, rather than from below, because of the legitimate power assigned to the position, but a change agent can be effective without this. The change agent must understand the process of change, who the influential players are to approve and facilitate the change, the most effective channels to go through, and the best time, place, and circumstance to bring about the change (Havelock, 1973). Nurses are natural change agents for their patients. Their position as nursing experts gives them formal authority within the health care system.

Catalyst

Usually a person becomes a catalyst because he or she feels deeply about an issue. Such people may be visionaries or intrapreneurs (i.e., employees of an organization who are able to take an idea and implement it within that organization; Manion, 1990). As catalysts, they help overcome the inertia of a status quo system. They prod the system and pressure it to be less complacent.

To be effective in this role, a catalyst must be sensitive to the process of change and be able to see the point of view of the client or of the existing leadership in an organization to win their support. Catalysts must have a good sense of timing. Activities must be planned to maximize their effectiveness. As stated earlier, systems in crisis are more likely to be unfrozen than stable ones with no unrest.

Solution Giver

In this role, the change agent has solutions to problems but also knows when and how to offer the solutions. The needs of clients are ascertained before solutions are offered. Innovations must be adapted to fit the client system. Solutions must be flexible. Clients must be helped to be a good judge of innovations so that they can evaluate and decide which ones should be adopted. As a solution giver, the change agent must be open and authentic with the client system.

Process Helper

In this role, the change agent shows the client or group how to recognize and define needs, diagnose problems, and set objectives. He or she assists in

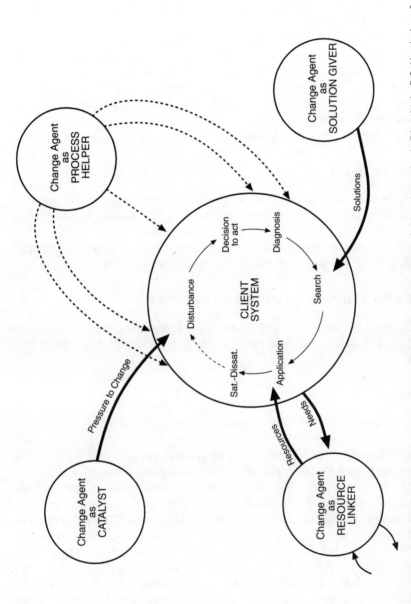

Figure 11–3 Four ways to be a change agent. *Source:* Reprinted from *The Change Agent's Guide to Innovation in Education* by R.G. Havelock, p. 8, with permission of Educational Technology Publications, © 1973.

acquiring resources, selecting and creating solutions, adapting and installing the solutions, and evaluating them to determine whether they are working and/or satisfying needs.

To be effective, the change agent must build a relationship with the client. Change agents must help clients be aware of their needs and help them generate and select solutions. Acceptance and adoption of the solutions are aided by the change agent openly discussing and/or demonstrating the change. The innovations are stabilized by the change agent encouraging clients to be their own change agent and to continue to work on solutions in a similar way so that the relationship can eventually be terminated.

Resource Linker

In this role, the change agent brings together needs and resources. This can be knowledge, people, money, time, and so forth. As a linker, the change agent brings people together and helps clients find and make the best use of resources inside and outside their own systems. To be effective, the change agent must be a good listener and a two-way communicator.

ORGANIZATIONAL CHANGE AND CULTURE

When one is making a change within an organization rather than with an individual or group, specific areas of knowledge are required to achieve success.

Culture

Each organization has its own **culture** (Sovie, 1993). Culture helps determine the success of an institution (Gillies, 1994). Culture is a pattern or measure of shared values, beliefs, thoughts, feelings, and behaviors that direct the perception of, and the approach to, the work that is to be done (Thomas, Ward, Chorba, & Kumiega, 1990). Culture affects how the work is done (Snyder, 1985; Sovie, 1993; Thomas et al., 1990).

There are also subcultures that develop within groups. They influence how their members approach and fulfill their roles and responsibilities (Sovie, 1993). Different shifts and different units can have different cultures. Cultures develop to solve work-related problems and to help employees survive in their jobs. A nursing unit, for example, often reflects the character of the manager who opened the unit. Over time, workers bring their own values, personalities, and customary behaviors to the organization. These workers' norms and preferences become incorporated into the group culture. Cultural values can support an innovation or restrain it if there is conflict between the desired state and the culture (Coeling & Simms, 1993).

When one is attempting to change group behavior, some aspects about culture need to be considered. First of all, culture is broad and has an impact on almost all behaviors and changes. Second, it is powerful because it is what staff believe they must do to survive. The group must therefore agree to change before any change can occur. Third, each work group culture pattern is unique, and therefore any given innovation must be implemented in a different way for each unit or department. Just as patients are assessed before a nursing intervention is individualized and implemented, so must the culture of each work group be assessed, cultural barriers to change be identified, and the interventions be individualized (Coeling & Simms, 1993). Refer to Chapter 1 for a detailed discussion of organizational culture.

Methods exist for understanding organizational culture. These consist of direct observation by an external agent, use of questionnaires, examination of facility or unit documents, or direct assessment by members. The last of these can be the most successful. Snyder (1985) suggests that questions can be asked to ascertain the culture of a group, such as: What type of people succeed here, and what type of people do badly? Who are the heroes of this organization, and who are the villains? What rituals are obligatory, and what topics are taboo? What are the most critical events of the organization's history, and what stories are told about these events? Snyder states that, without knowledge of cultures, a person may be led astray in his or her change efforts. With this knowledge, the person is in a better position to reinvent the future strategically.

Internal and External Change Agents

At times, organizational change is more effective with an internal change agent; in other situations, an outsider is able to see aspects more objectively. The advantages of **internal change agents** are as follows (Havelock, 1973):

- They know the system. They know where the power lies and can identify the gatekeepers.
- They speak the language. They understand the ways in which members discuss things.
- They understand the norms. The commonly held beliefs, attitudes, and behaviors of the group are understood by insiders, and they probably also believe in them.
- They identify with the system's needs and aspirations. They feel the problem and the pain deeply themselves, and there is a personal incentive for helping.

- They are a familiar figure. Most of what internal change agents do is understandable and predictable. They do not pose a threat.

The disadvantages of internal change agents include the following (Havelock, 1973):

- They may lack perspective. They may not be able to view the client system as a whole because of their place in the organization and their perspective from that vantage point.
- They may not have the specific knowledge or skill necessary for the desired innovation.
- They may lack an adequate power base to implement the change.
- They may have to live down past failures.
- They may not have the independence of movement. Their time and energy may be limited.
- They may face the difficult task of redefining ongoing relationships with other members of the system.

Using **external change agents** has the following advantages (Havelock, 1973):

- They can start fresh and are not burdened by negative stereotypes.
- They are in a position to see the problems of all members equally.
- They are independent of the power structure and are not threatened by superiors. Outsiders are free to work in a variety of ways with different members of the system.
- They can bring in new ideas.

The disadvantages of an outsider are the following (Havelock, 1973):

- They are strangers and may represent a threat.
- They may lack knowledge of the norms and values of the system.
- They may not identify with or feel the pain of the client system.

A combination of both an internal and an external change agent capitalizes on the advantages and avoids the problems of both. The outside person can provide some expert legitimacy for the efforts of the insider (Havelock, 1973).

Managing Organizationwide Change

When one is instituting change that will affect an entire organization, there are other aspects to address in addition to culture and the type of change agent. For the necessary resources to be obtained to move the project along, the project goals should be congruent with the organization's strategic plan. Budgets are usually tied directly to this plan. The leader of the project must be someone who is able to communicate the vision effectively to all levels of the organization and to devote the amount of time that is necessary for the daily coaching and nurturing of groups and their leaders. Commitment to the project must be obtained from the key stakeholders at all levels of the organization. Objectives for the change must be specific and measurable. They must be defined for each work group in terms of how this change will affect patient care. Individuals from all levels of the organization should be involved, and work groups should be established to complete specific objectives. The past efforts and successes of the organization should be built upon for the new change. Finally, top management should deliver the message about the project directly so that everyone understands the commitment. Communication regarding the project needs to be comprehensive and ongoing (Bolton, Auden, Popolow, & Ramseyer, 1992).

Assessing Readiness for Change

Giving up the comfortable old for the questionable new is risky (DeFeo, 1990). Resistance, as has already been mentioned, is normal. Given this fact, there are some questions that must be asked before an organizational project begins and answers that must be obtained to ensure success (New & Couillard, 1981):

- Which individuals are affected by the change? What are their numbers, and what is their power in the organization? Are they willing (and do they have the ability) to contribute to the change effort?
- Who is likely to offer resistance and why?
- How much time is available for the introduction of the change?
- How important to the organization is the planned change? The more important the change, the more critical it is to develop a strategy to deal with resistance.
- To what extent is there mutual trust and cooperation among the members? Without trust, some change techniques will fail because of resistance.

Each employee looks at change from his or her own self-interests. The change agent can anticipate the questions that might be asked by putting himself or herself in the employee's place and asking questions such as these (Stevens, 1975):

- Will the change alter my role in the organization?
- Will it alter my job content? Will I be adding tasks?
- Will it change the way I do my job? Will I have more or less freedom?
- Will it affect the conveniences or inconveniences of my job? Will it add more restrictive rules or lessen them?
- Will it affect my salary and status now and in the future?
- What advantages does it offer me, and what benefits does it take away?

PHASES OF CHANGE

If a planned change theory is followed, the barriers to and acceptance of change are analyzed, and the change agent is chosen carefully, any innovation, whether minor or major, can be successfully managed and implemented. Understanding how the phases of change affect individuals and how to evaluate a change project completes the process.

Human emotions run through many spectrums when a change process occurs. The organization and/or the change agent must deal with these emotions if the new desired state is to be effective. The energy and personal resources of the individuals involved in the change need to be channeled appropriately to accomplish the end result. Perlman and Takacs (1990) describe 10 phases that individuals go through and what interventions are effective for each step. These phases cross all the steps of a change theory and involve the feelings of those going through the process. They are not unlike the stages of death and dying that psychologist Kübler-Ross (1969) describes because change involves the death of the old way of operating or doing business.

1. *Equilibrium:* Many employees or individuals have contributed to the status quo in their organization or their lives. They are comfortable, content, and emotionally in a state of equilibrium. Many of their personal and professional goals may have been met with the current state. To help change this equilibrium, the change agent must make the employee or client aware of the need to do something different.
2. *Denial:* During the denial phase, employees and patients actively resist the change. By listening to the change target and being supportive, empathic, and nonjudgmental, the change agent can assist with this stage. It's important for the change agent to learn what part of the reorganization or change the client accepts and to build on that.
3. *Anger:* During the anger phase, clients begin to blame others. The change agent must recognize the symptoms and use active listening and problem-solving skills to work through this stage.

4. *Bargaining:* Clients enter into agreements with others to prevent the change during this stage. They may agree to compromise if the employer or nurse will also make a change in his or her plans. The change agent must focus on the needs that are threatened by the change. Once these are identified openly, both sides can explore how the needs can be met without damaging the end result.

5. *Chaos:* During the chaos stage, there is a feeling of powerlessness by the client, and his or her energy is diffused. The change agent must let the client know that this is to be expected and that it will pass, that not knowing the current direction and structure is all right.

6. *Depression:* During this phase, clients experience a sense of nothingness, having no energy left to produce results. They spend time remembering the past and wallowing in self-pity. The change agent must tell the clients as much as possible about the change and allow them to express their pain and sorrow. An increase in sick time and turnover and a decrease in productivity may be seen in an organization. Patients may refuse to participate in therapies and isolate themselves.

7. *Resignation:* Clients begin to accept the change and no longer resist. It's important, at this stage, to allow them to move at their own pace and to expect them to be accountable for their reactions and behavior.

8. *Openness:* During this stage, clients are able to proceed with growth in a new direction and are able to take the lead from their managers or nurse. To facilitate this stage, education regarding the change must be repeated.

9. *Readiness:* Clients exhibit more energy during this stage and are more willing to do what is asked of them. The change agent can be more directive with change targets at this phase and assign them specific tasks.

10. *Reemergence:* At this point, the change is fully operational as the client lets go of the old ways, both emotionally and intellectually. New identities and meanings have been developed with the new state. The interventions for this final phase are to redefine goals for the patient or the mission, culture, and career paths in an organization and to reach a mutual understanding of new roles and identities.

KEY CONCEPTS

- Four roles of a change agent:
  1. Catalyst
  2. Solution giver
  3. Process helper
  4. Resource linker

- Aspects to consider with organizational change:
    1. Culture
    2. Type of change agent (internal, external, or both)
    3. Congruence of project goals with the strategic plan
    4. Commitment from key stakeholders
    5. Staff involvement at all levels
    6. Delivery of the message about the change project by top management
- The phases of change are similar to Kübler-Ross's stages of death and dying.

EVALUATION OF CHANGE

Evaluation confirms the extent to which a change has been effected and the degree to which the expected results have been achieved (Langford, 1981). Specific measures or outcomes to evaluate a change must be established at the beginning of the project. Areas to examine are, first of all, the effectiveness of the new state. Was the desired end result achieved? Second, the efficiency of the new system should be analyzed. Are outcomes achieved in the most economical way, conserving time, cost, and resources? Finally, satisfaction should be evaluated from the perspective of all the customers. Are people pleased (Stevens, 1977)? Members of the target group should be involved in the evaluation process. As the results emerge, the change begins to be recognized as a real part of the system. The change begins to be transformed from something new and possibly temporary to something completed and accepted (Langford, 1981).

The change process itself should also be assessed. What energies and resources were required to reach the end results, and by what means? Was the end result worth the price? Was it reached with a minimum of trouble, confusion, and resentment? If it solved one problem, did it create new ones? The final assessment of any change cannot be made until a state of refreezing or equilibrium has been achieved. At this point, the change is perceived as the new continuity (Stevens, 1977). With any change, follow-up must be done if the change is to be maintained. Unexpected consequences must always be watched for (Stevens, 1975).

CONCLUSION

LaBeur (1993) states that one can either welcome change or protest against it. Burying one's head in the sand will not stop change from occurring. "Refusing to accept the inevitable will result in tire tracks across our faces as the wheels of change grind forward" (p. 74).

The individual nurse can be a forecaster and innovator of change and can also support a climate of change in whatever facility he or she works. Manion

(1990) describes the role of intrepreneur. An intrepreneur is one who takes hands-on responsibility for creating innovation within an organization as opposed to doing so from outside, as an entrepreneur would do. Manion states that for American businesses, including health care enterprises, to survive, the creative potential of employees must be capitalized upon. Nurses are key stakeholders in the future of health care because they are its largest group of providers and are in direct and continuous contact with the health care consumer. Nurse intrepreneurs, then, are essential to the successful future of the health care field (Manion, 1990).

To be a forecaster, catalyst, or intrepreneur for change, nurses must keep up with the news and pay attention to current issues at local, national, and international levels. Reading books and periodicals helps an individual predict what changes may occur or will be needed based on the information gathered. By joining a national nursing organization, nurses can obtain information about changes in a specialty area of practice and at the professional nursing level (LaBeur, 1993). Becoming involved in community programs and agencies and attending workshops are also ways to gather ideas for innovation and change.

In the work setting, a climate of change can be supported by developing in each nurse a self-directing capability. Mutual confidence and trust as well as free-flowing communication and information must be established. Decision making should be encouraged at all levels of staff. Employees should be rewarded for innovations even if they fail. Independent action and cross-disciplinary problem solving must be recognized. Finally, staff can be educated during a change process about new insights, skills, and methods that they can use in later change efforts or that will help them become innovators of future change (Gillies, 1994).

Continual change is present in every aspect of an individual's life. Implementing change in a patient or group is a part of the role of the professional nurse. By using change theories and change strategies, the nurse can implement successful planned change that will result in a higher level of wellness for a patient or for an organization. The nursing profession is in an excellent position and in a unique role to influence, and to make alterations that will benefit, a variety of change targets.

KEY CONCEPTS

- The new change and its process must be evaluated in terms of:
  1. effectiveness
  2. efficiency
  3. outcomes achieved
  4. satisfaction of all customers

- The nurse must be a forecaster and innovator of change and support the climate of change by:
  1. reading books and periodicals
  2. knowing current local, national, and international issues
  3. joining a national nursing organization
  4. becoming involved in community programs and agencies
  5. attending workshops and inservices
  6. being an intrepreneur

LEARNING CHALLENGE   Identify the appropriate change theory and steps of the change process that you would use to implement the desired action or behavior in the following situations. Include analysis of culture, change strategies, force field analysis, change tactics, overcoming resistance and enhancing acceptance of the change, and choice of change agent(s) when applicable to the situation.

1. As a new nurse, you read an article on staff self-scheduling and would like to implement this on your unit.
2. A female patient with a stroke has loss of sensation on the left side of her body. You need to teach the patient's husband how to inspect her skin daily to prevent breakdown, but he is reluctant to be involved in any of her care.
3. The nursing documentation system where you work is repetitive and time consuming. You have an idea for new forms, but this would involve a change for three other nursing units besides the one on which you are working.
4. A newly diagnosed diabetic girl, 10 years old, is assigned to you as a primary patient. She will need to learn how to self-administer her insulin injections but prefers to have her mother do this. Her mother works two jobs and will not be available during all the times when the insulin injections will be required.

RESEARCH FOUNDATION   Thomas, C., Ward, M., Chorba, C., & Kumiega, A. (1990). Measuring and interpreting organizational culture. *Journal of Nursing Administration, 20* (6), 17–24.

Thomas et al. (1990) describe a research study that measures organizational culture before a change process. The Organizational Culture Inventory (OCI) was used in a metropolitan community hospital with 225 nursing personnel; 56 nurses completed the inventory. The OCI consists of 120 questions that describe behaviors or personal styles that might be expected of members in an organization. The tool measures the ways in which members of an organization are expected to think and behave in relation to their tasks and to other people. The questions result in 12 scales that correspond to three primary cultural styles: constructive, passive/defensive, and aggressive/defensive. Participants plot their own results on a polar graph. Aggregate results are also profiled. Benchmark scores are available that represent the ideal nursing culture that "should be expected to maximize organizational performance, quality of care, and individual motivation and satisfaction" (Thomas et al., 1990, p. 19). Gaps between ideal scores and actual scores represent potential areas for organizational change and development.

The study results revealed that the culture in the hospital was weak. Scores were further examined by looking at staff nurses versus administrative nurses. The nursing administrators reported slightly higher expectations for achievement and self-actualization than the staff nurses. The results indicated that these styles were not being encouraged at the staff nurse level. Furthermore, staff nurses had significantly weaker expectations for competitive and power behaviors than the administrators. Day shift nurses had scores closer to the ideal scores, with stronger achievement, self-actualizing, humanistic-encouraging, and affiliative scores than nurses on the other shifts. Although this was not unexpected, it raised the question of the need for adequate communication with the other shifts.

In summary, this tool was able to identify areas that needed development and change to help the organization function more efficiently.

REFERENCES

Bhola, H.S. (1994). The CLER model: Thinking through change. *Nursing Management, 25* (5), 59–63.

Bolton, L.B., Auden, C., Popolow, G., & Ramseyer, J. (1992). Ten steps for managing organizational change. *Journal of Nursing Administration, 22* (6), 14–20.

Bushnell, M.E. (1979). Institutions in transition. *Perspectives in Psychiatric Care, 17* (6), 260–265.

Chin, R. (1985). The utility of models of the environments of systems for practitioners. In W.G. Bennis, K.D. Benne, & R. Chin (Eds.), *The planning of change* (4th ed., pp 88–105). New York: Holt, Rinehart & Winston.

Chin, R., & Benne, K.D. (1985). General strategies for effecting changes in human systems. In W.G. Bennis, K.D. Benne, & R. Chin (Eds.), *The planning of change* (4th ed., pp. 22–45). New York: Holt, Rinehart & Winston.

Coeling, H.V., & Simms, L.M. (1993). Facilitating innovation at the nursing unit level through cultural assessment, part I: How to keep management ideas from falling on deaf ears. *Journal of Nursing Administration, 23* (4), 46–53.

DeFeo, D.J. (1990). Change: A central concern of nursing. *Nursing Science Quarterly, 3* (2), 88–94.

Gillies, D.A. (1994). *Nursing management—A systems approach.* Philadelphia: Saunders.

Havelock, R.G. (1973). *The change agent's guide to innovation in education.* Englewood Cliffs, NJ: Educational Technology Publications.

King, I.M. (1987). King's theory of goal attainment. In R.R. Parse (Ed.), *Nursing science: Major paradigms, theories and critiques* (pp. 107–113). Philadelphia: Saunders.

Kübler-Ross, E. (1969). *On death and dying.* New York: MacMillan.

LaBeur, M.S. (1993). Forecasters of change. *Nursing Management, 24* (6), 74.

Langford, T.L. (1981). *Managing and being managed—Preparation for professional nursing practice.* Englewood Cliffs, NJ: Prentice-Hall.

Laughlin, J.A. (1989). Rehabilitation: Unlocking the gates to change. In S. Dittmar (Ed.), *Rehabilitation nursing: Process and application* (pp. 528–540). St. Louis: Mosby.

Lewin, K. (1951). *Field theory in social science.* New York: Harper & Brothers.

Lippitt, G. (1973). *Visualizing change: Model building and the change process.* La Jolla, CA: University Associates.

Machiavelli, N. (1981). *The prince* (G. Bull, Trans.). London: Penguin. (Original work written 1514)

Manion, J. (1990). *Change from within. Nurse intrapreneurs as health care innovators.* Kansas City, MO: American Nurses Association.

New, J.R., & Couillard, N.A. (1981). Guidelines for introducing change. *Journal of Nursing Administration, 11* (3), 17–21.

Orem, D.E. (1985). A concept of self-care for the rehabilitation client. *Rehabilitation Nursing, 10* (3), 33–36.

Perlman, D., & Takacs, G. (1990). The ten stages of change. *Nursing Management, 21* (4), 33–38.

Pierce, S.F., & Thompson, D. (1976). Changing practice: By choice rather than chance. *Journal of Nursing Administration, 6* (2), 34–39.

Rogers, E. (1962). *Diffusion of innovations.* New York: The Free Press of Glenco.

Rogers, M.E. (1992). Nursing science and the space age. *Nursing Science Quarterly, 5* (1), 27–34.

Roy, S.C., & Roberts, S.L. (1981). *Theory construction in nursing. An adaptation model.* Englewood Cliffs, NJ: Prentice-Hall.

Sheehan, J. (1990). Investigating change in a nursing context. *Journal of Advanced Nursing, 15* (7), 819–824.

Snyder, R.C. (1985). To improve innovation, manage corporate culture. In W.G. Bennis, K.D. Benne, & R. Chin (Eds.), *The planning of change* (4th ed., pp. 164–175). New York: Holt, Rinehart & Winston.

Sovie, M.D. (1993). Hospital culture—Why create one? *Nursing Economics, 11* (2), 69–75.

Stevens, B.J. (1975). Effecting change. *Journal of Nursing Administration, 5* (2), 23–26.

Stevens, B.J. (1977). Management of continuity and change in nursing. *Journal of Nursing Administration, 7* (4), 26–31.

Thomas, C., Ward, M., Chorba, C., & Kumiega, A. (1990). Measuring and interpreting organizational culture. *Journal of Nursing Administration, 20* (6), 17–24.

Tiffany, C.R. (1994). Analysis of planned change theories. *Nursing Management, 25* (2), 60–62.

Tiffany, C.R., Cheatham, A.B., Doornbos, D., Loudermelt, L., & Momadi, G.G. (1994). Planned change theory: Survey of nursing periodical literature. *Nursing Management, 25* (7), 54–59.

Vanetzian, E. (1988). Force field analysis: A person-centered approach to behavioral change. *Rehabilitation Nursing, 13* (1), 23–28.

Welch, L.B. (1979). Planned change in nursing: The theory. *Nursing Clinics of North America, 14* (2), 307–321.

CHAPTER 12

Building Shared Visions

Jim O'Malley

CHAPTER OBJECTIVES

At the completion of this chapter, the beginning professional nurse will be able to:

1. describe characteristics of dysfunctional organizations and reasons for organizational dysfunction and failure of health care systems
2. identify strategies to create, communicate, and implement shared visions
3. describe a planning design that facilitates and integrates the planning process and strategic thinking
4. examine steps to becoming a visionary leader and characteristics of leaders who build shared visions

CRITICAL THINKING CHALLENGE

Create a hypothetical vision with your classmates for the work group or patient care unit where you are having clinical experience. Paint a clear picture of what the work group or unit will be like in 3 years. Describe what steps need to be taken to implement the vision and what barriers might affect its implementation. Identify strategies to build, communicate, and implement the vision that might enhance success in operationalizing the vision.

THE DYSFUNCTIONAL NATURE OF ORGANIZATIONS

Historically, health care systems in general and nursing services in particular have tolerated a significant degree of dysfunction characterized by operational inefficiencies and cumbersome bureaucracy. The reasons for organizational dysfunctions and failures of health care systems are multifactoral and complex in nature. They include:

- the complexity of services provided
- excessive specialization and compartmentalization
- a high degree of external regulation
- cost-based reimbursement systems
- historical traditions of the American hospital

Our tolerance for this level of organizational dysfunction has been directly linked to the static structure and environmental conditions within which the health care system has lived. With the recent array of rapid and complex changes facing the health care industry, there is now much concern about the dysfunctional nature of health care organizations. Clearly, the development of health care organizations from a functional perspective is not where we had hoped it would be.

Most health care organizations, and acute care hospitals in particular, have been paralyzed by the call for major health care reform and operational restructuring during this time of unprecedented change. Among the most significant failures has been their inability to create clear and bold shared visions that provide their work force with the required inspiration to achieve organizational excellence (Roberts, 1994). From a management development perspective, when one analyzes the processes for creating visions and the systems for integrating and articulating them, the nature of the problem becomes readily apparent. The visions of most organizations, if they exist at all, have usually been created by a single individual or a small group of individuals at the top and then systematically imposed.

WHAT IS A VISION?

By definition, a **vision** is a mental image created by one's imagination of what is going to happen. It is a mental journey from the current state to a desired state, from the known to the unknown, and from the present to the future. Visions provide organizations with clarity about purpose, focus, and direction. Visions have the ability to unify processes, services, and systems at all levels of the organization so that extraordinary levels of organizational performance can be achieved. Senge, in his important work on the art and practice of the learning organization, describes a vision as a picture or image that individuals carry in their heads and sometimes in their hearts. He further describes visions as being among the most powerful of all human forces, capable of unifying and mobilizing people to unprecedented levels in achieving superior performances (Senge, 1990). The powerful impact of visions is derived from a combination of factors, including the nature of the vision's content, the process by which it was developed, and the methods by which it is to be operationalized (Whiteley, 1991).

Senge provides us with the following analogy to the film *Spartacus* that dramatically demonstrates the powerful impact that visions can have on both individuals and collective groups:

> You may remember the movie Spartacus, an [adaptation] of the story of a Roman gladiator/slave who led an army of slaves in an uprising in 71 B.C. They defeated the Roman legions twice, but were finally conquered by the general Marcus Crassus after a long siege and battle. In the movie, Crassus tells the thousand survivors in Spartacus's army, "You have been slaves. You will be slaves again. But you will be spared your rightful punishment of crucifixion by the mercy of the Roman legions. All you need to do is turn over to me the slave Spartacus, because we do not know him by sight."
>
> After a long pause, Spartacus (played by Kirk Douglas) stands up and says, "I am Spartacus." Then the man next to him stands up and says, "I am Spartacus." The next man stands up and also says, "No, I am Spartacus." Within a minute, everyone in the army is on his feet. (Senge, 1990, p. 205)

The impact of loyalty and commitment to a vision created by one individual and then shared collectively by a larger group can be every bit as powerful and dramatic as the inspiration created by Spartacus: the belief that the slaves could be free people. Clearly, the power of shared visions is derived from a common sense of caring about an idea from everyone in a larger group.

Wheatley (1992), in her work on searching for simpler ways to lead organizations, challenges our current thinking about visions and suggests that we begin to think about visions as a destination for the organization. She hypothesizes that the level of clarity of the image of this destination has a direct relationship to the amount of influence the future will exert on the present in pulling it into the desired future location. The idea of vision as a place as opposed to a process or product brings into being a whole new set of ways to look at desired future states and their accompanying variables and opportunities. In short, visions are nothing more than a clear understanding of where we are and where we would like to be. Exercising vision, both as an individual and as an organization, is a here and now challenge. It has become increasingly clear that the quality of the decisions we make today is ultimately what will create our desired future state (Cox, 1990). Visions are what unite strategic directives with organizational culture building in ways that affect achievement of organizational excellence. They serve as the foundation for an organization's strategic planning process and, from a tactical or business planning perspective, as the spark plug or the driver for the implementation of all operational initiatives.

KEY   • Visions are mental images of a preferred future.
CONCEPTS   • Visions are the foundation of strategic planning and operational
             activities.

WHAT IS A SHARED VISION?

Visions become shared when two or more individuals have a similar mental image or model and are committed to each other having this vision; in contrast, personal visions are those for which the commitment is to oneself or one individual holding a vision. Shared visions connect individuals and bind them together by similar or common aspirations. Visions that are shared derive their power from a sense of common or community caring. This need to be connected may be one of the primary reasons why individuals seek to build shared visions. Senge (1990) hypothesizes that shared visions are a prerequisite for the creation of an environment that supports organizational learning. He suggests that, in a generative sense, they provide the energy and the focus for organizational learning. **Generative learning**, or expanding one's ability to create, occurs when individuals are committed to accomplishing something that matters to them, hence the importance of being excited and having a passion for the vision. Without individuals being excited about organizational visions, the reality of generative learning would be empty and meaningless, and organizational learning, if it occurred at all, would be merely adaptive in nature (Senge, 1990).

By their very nature, shared visions make organizational accomplishments a reality. Although personal visions created by leaders within organizations are important, it is only when they are shared at all levels of the organization that their impact can be fully realized. They literally have the ability to focus the talent and energy of thousands of individuals working within the same organization by creating a common sense of identity and purpose across an enormously diverse work force. Although shared visions may be extrinsic, it is usually the intrinsic shared visions that create that special energy, that spark and excitement, that have the ability to transform a mediocre organization into an excellent one.

The presence of a shared vision significantly changes the relationship that each individual has with the organization at large by facilitating people working together for a common purpose. The building of a shared vision is an important step in improving trust among employees and across departments and organizational levels. Maslow's pioneering work on high-performing work teams demonstrated that shared visions have resulted in increasing both individual and group sense of purpose, focus, and underlying operating values (Senge, 1990). In the health care environment of today, the nurse will be an important member of a high-performing work team. Sharing a vision is essential for the team's success.

The transition from personal visions to shared visions is contingent upon an organization's willingness to let go of the assumption that visions must be created by, and only by, the chief executive officer or his or her senior executive team. This historical approach has been minimally effective in transforming organizations. Specifically, this top-down approach has carried with it three significant limitations: It is a singular, one shot approach to defining organizational purpose; it usually is the result of a desire to create a strategic vision and, as such, is not built upon an individual's personal visions; and it is frequently developed as a solution to an existing problem (Senge, 1990). Although shared visions may well emanate from the top or from any other level of the organization, the important concept is that they only become shared when they are built on the interactions of personal visions and are shared by the organization as a whole. This process requires ongoing dialogue in which individuals feel the freedom to articulate their dreams and listen to the dreams of others, culminating in new insights that eventually create a shared vision for the organization. Development of shared visions is the effect of transformational leadership. See Chapter 4 for further discussion of leadership.

THE IMPACT OF SHARED VISIONS

The underlying values of shared visions serve as the foundation for developing meaningful and productive relationships within and across an organization. Successful leadership in building a learning organization is contingent on one's ability to build broad-based agreement on common values while simultaneously recognizing and honoring the diversity of an organization's various constituencies. Shared visions provide the common language by which individuals and groups within an organization communicate and collaborate with one another. The presence and use of a common language results in an increase in energy, enthusiasm, drive, and commitment and a decrease in tension and stress. It also increases levels of satisfaction and effectiveness by providing a reason for people to care about their work, their jobs, and the contributions they make to the organization. Kouzes and Posner (1993) report a series of benefits to the organization when shared values are in place: an increase in loyalty to the organization by employees, an increase in employee innovation and creativity contributions, an increase in the quantity and quality of employee communication, and an improvement in the integrity of shared decision-making processes. These benefits are the direct result of individual contributions that people experience when their values and those of the organization are in synch and when they as individuals feel part of a larger, organizationally based team.

THE ART OF BUILDING A SHARED VISION

Executing vision is an integrative skill that, when effectively utilized, can position an organization both to create and to take advantage of future opportunities. As such, visioning can be viewed as a defensive as well as an offensive skill. Building a shared vision not only can assist an organization in developing a blueprint for the changes necessary for achieving a desired future state but also can enable an organization to make the necessary adjustments in response to external environmental changes (Hickman & Silva, 1984). The processes utilized to build a shared vision should focus on creating a sense of wholeness for an organization while incorporating all its diverse components.

Among the most common organizational mistakes in endeavors to create common sets of values and visions is the tendency for senior management to define and prescribe from the onset what are the important or necessary values. Although this approach was commonplace in the old command-and-control bureaucratic structures and hierarchies, in which managers told and sold the values and the vision, it is destructive to the overall vision-building process in contemporary, highly diversified learning organizations. The process of creating and operationalizing a shared vision flows from an underlying commitment to finding common ground by including a broad representation of diverse values, which ultimately enables both leaders and constituents to speak with one voice (Kouzes & Posner, 1993). Irrespective of how the process is designed for building shared visions, there are two fundamental questions that will need to be addressed: What are the most deeply held values by the various constituents, and what impact do these values have on internal organizational work processes and the overall delivery of organizational products?

In recent years, within management development circles an array of techniques and processes has emerged to facilitate the building of shared visions. Clearly, the common theme or trend for these processes has been the creation of opportunities for participation in building organizational shared visions by large numbers of individuals from all levels of the organization. The predominant approach, with a variety of design and process variations, has two primary components: the development of a corporate mission and vision by board members and the senior executives of the organization, and broad-based consultation and consensus building about the organization's mission, values, and visions with large numbers of employees within and across the organization.

The second component of this approach is a significant departure from business as usual in that it brings together large numbers of diverse workers to consult initially with the organizational leadership and later to build consensus regarding organizational mission, values, and eventually shared visions. This step of the process is usually structured in a way that facilitates active participation by literally hundreds of employees within the organization. The design is structured to address a series of issues, including the following:

- How does the organizational vision fit with your personal vision?
- How does the organizational vision fit with what you stand for?
- What do you like about the vision?
- What do you dislike about the vision?
- What does the vision do for you?
- Is there anything missing from the vision?
- What would you like to change about the vision?

Usually, this process is structurally designed over 2 to 3 days at a meeting held off site that engages participants in a series of small group activities to facilitate listening, talking, and discussion of the central themes and issues. The small groups usually then report back to the larger group, where additional consultation and consensus building occur, ultimately resulting in the building of a shared vision for the organization. Although these processes are extremely labor, time, and money intensive, the accompanying results are overwhelmingly impressive. Andrea Zintz, Vice President for Human Resources at Ortho Biotech, where this approach was utilized in 1992, reported that "Creating a company where everyone can contribute their best is important to our long-term success. It helps us attract and retain the best people in our industry, and when people feel good about where they work, they can perform their best" (Kouzes & Posner, 1993, p. 128).

Kouzes and Posner (1993, pp. 146–152) have identified a series of practical steps to follow when the above described approach to building shared visions is utilized:

1. *Get together to start drafting your group's credo.* Soliciting people's ideas and listening to their concerns are critical. At the early stages, look for feedback; it is not the time for yes or no decisions.
2. *Make sure there is agreement on values.* Focus on understanding shared values. Ask constituents to write down what they believe are the key values of the team. How much agreement is there? Clarify what is vital, and determine what is secondary.
3. *Conduct a values survey.* The best way to know what people think is to ask them. Send out a survey and find out what they think. Analyses help pinpoint particular problems and opportunities.

4. *Connect values with reasons.* The importance of certain values may seem self-evident, but we have seen that commitment is facilitated when people know that the values are not just their own, individually, but are shared by others.

5. *Structure cooperative goals.* Discuss the team's vision, and have members explore how the vision can be best achieved by everyone working together. Encourage cross-functional and interdisciplinary learning.

6. *Make sure everyone knows the business.* Get a cross-section of people together, and see if they can answer the following questions: Who are our toughest competitors? What do our customers see as our differential advantages in the marketplace?

7. *Be an enthusiastic spokesperson for shared values.* Speak enthusiastically about shared values. Let people know that everyone is in this together, that what they are doing is important, and that their contributions make a difference.

8. *Accumulate yeses.* The key word in agreements is *yes.* It is a magical word and a powerful tool for bringing people closer.

9. *Go slow to go fast.* Keep the importance of making it easy for people to say *yes* firmly in mind. Start where people are, with the easiest issue for them to agree with. Move progressively from the easiest to the more difficult issues.

10. *Establish a sunset statute for your credo.* It may be a good idea to rethink your team's credo periodically. Although certain values will endure and others will change, the process of reviewing and prioritizing can only reinforce the team's unity . . . to its shared values.

LEARNING CHALLENGE   Review the vision of the organization where you are having your clinical practicum. How does the organizational vision fit with your personal vision for health care and nursing? Discuss your ideas with your peers. Ask the staff with whom you are working to describe the organization's vision for health care and nursing. How does the staff implement the vision in their clinical practice?

TRANSFORMING SHARED VISIONS INTO REALITY

The building of shared visions serves no useful purpose unless the visions become the foundation for everything that happens within an organization. Shared visions are created out of a consensus-building process from a multitude of personal values and become a set of shared values; as such, they become the cornerstone for establishing everything, from an organization's goals, to its strategic plans, to setting priorities for its operational initiatives. They become the gold standard against which the value of all organizational behavior and activities should be measured.

FROM STRATEGIC PLANNING TO STRATEGIC THINKING

Historically, planning as a management tool has been nothing more complicated than a set of functional activities designed to determine present and future actions and a process for evaluation based on defined goals. Two types of planning are commonly identified in the literature: tactical planning and strategic planning. By definition, "strategic planning is long-range and encompasses ends as well as means," by contrast "tactical plans look at shorter time frames, have a narrower scope, and focus in more detail" (Arndt & Huckabay, 1980, p. 67). Strategic planning as a process determines organizational goals and major initiatives, which in turn are supported by more specific and detailed tactical plans. Arndt and Huckabay (1980) identified a seven-stage strategic planning process for nursing administration that utilizes a systems approach (Figure 12–1).

In this era of organizational transformation, a transition in focus has emerged from developing strategic and tactical plans to learning how to think and manage strategically. As ironic as it may seem, strategic plans have often become an obstacle to the very purpose for which they were developed. In many organizations, strategic planning as a process has become bureaucratic and overly structured, resulting in excessive dependence on a formal, written planning document. In this time of rapid change, many organizations are building a false sense of security on a plan that is at risk of becoming outdated shortly after its development (Hickman & Silva, 1984). Within the context of thinking strategically, shared visions are providing the frame-breaking change for creating a new mindset for health care organizations in the current turbulent environment. Shared visions are the driving force in the necessary transition of health care organizations from a product orientation to a market orientation, from a caretaking mentality to a risk-taking mentality, and, most important, from operational management to strategic management (Shortell, Morrison, & Friedman, 1990).

Vail (1989), in his work on new ideas for a world of chaotic change, provides us with a model for the strategic management process. He labels this model the **inward-outward-forward scheme**. In this model, the word *inward* is used in reference to values, feelings, and commitments; the word *outward* refers to all external and environmental factors; and the word *forward* is used for the issues of movement through time into the future. Vail

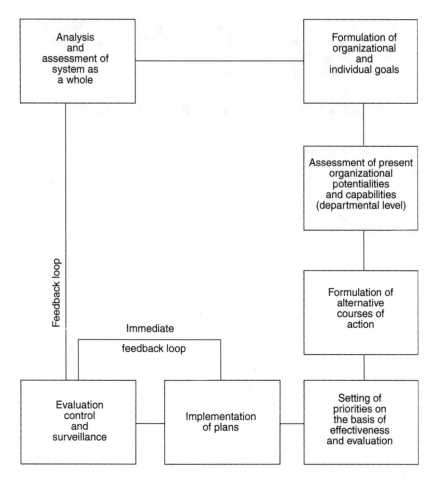

Figure 12–1 Systems approach to the planning process. *Source:* Reprinted from *Nursing Administration: Theory for Practice with a Systems Approach* by C. Arndt and L. Huckabay, p. 69, with permission of Mosby-Year Book, © 1980.

reminds us that within the context of strategic planning and strategic management, although block diagram models and all the accompanying steps and functions are useful, it is the implementation, the doing of the strategizing, that is the hard part. He refers to strategy as "the conduct of some whole unit in relationship to its environment" (Vail, 1989, p.162). He further suggests that strategies as acts of leadership are initiatives, consciously thought-out choices, that when operationalized become an organizational change process; that is, a strategy statement is merely a statement of the intent to change the organization in a particular direction for a particular reason.

KEY CONCEPT
- Strategic planning refers to long-term planning; operational or tactical planning is short term.

LEARNING CHALLENGE
Identify one element of the strategic (long-term) plan of your organization. Identify one element of the operational (short-term) plan of your organization.

THE ART OF VISIONARY LEADERSHIP

During this period of major organizational transformation, the role of leadership is more about visualizing what could be than analyzing what is. Within this context, shared visions become the target that calls forth or drives all the decisions we make today. Bellman (1992) articulately describes the leadership challenge in transforming visions into reality as providing "the clarity of what could be combined with an awareness of the resources that are available now to help you get there and to convince and motivate others to do what must be done today to move toward tomorrow" (p. 18).

How one positions oneself and the organization to create and take full advantage of future opportunities is a direct result of how skillful one is at facilitating the building of shared visions. Clear vision results from a profound understanding of an organization and its environment. Visions that effectively blend strategy and culture result in organizational excellence. Hickman and Silva (1984) have identified the following three primary steps in becoming a visionary leader.

Recognizing Vision

The first step in becoming a visionary leader is recognizing vision and developing the skill to distinguish between those with vision and those without it. More than anything else, philosophy, values, and management style differentiate a visionary executive from a nonvisionary executive. It is commonplace for the nonvisionary leader to spend the day meeting formally with employees and in general to have a calendar filled with meetings that do not allow for squeezing in another appointment. The overloaded schedule has strapped the leader into what feels like a straitjacket. On the other hand, visionary leaders will truthfully admit that they have a few crucial appointments scheduled on the calendar (certainly never taking up more than 50% of the day) and will spend much of the day making informal contacts with employees at all levels of the organization. Nonvisionary leaders spend their day solving daily problems, making decisions at the operational level, and almost never talking about philosophy; the visionary leader takes advantage of every informal opportunity to dialogue about philosophy, mission, corporate direction, and values that will move the organization ahead. The nonvisionary leader functions from a position of mistrust and as such focuses on weaknesses (e.g., poor performance and policy violation). The visionary leader's focus is developing staff and supporting risk taking and authenticity in the workplace. The nonvisionary is aloof, rational, critical, and sometimes even cold; the visionary has an open, expressive, supportive style and people and ideas ignite him or her. The nonvisionary leader lives in or is trapped in the present; the visionary leader is a skillful strategic player and operates quite differently from one who is merely trapped in a role.

Hickman and Silva (1984) have identified some key areas to measure one's visionary ability. A leader with vision:

- considers many ideas and concepts until a clear vision crystallizes
- communicates the vision in easy to understand terms that are consistent with the plans and cultural values of the organization
- motivates employees to embrace the vision through example
- evaluates the impact of the vision on all levels of employees
- supports team building around implementing the vision
- helps employees personalize the vision
- remains involved with implementing the vision
- evaluates the success of the vision and modifies it where needed

Organizational Introspection

The second step in becoming a visionary leader is taking a hard look inside oneself and the organization, a process called organizational introspection. This requires developing skill in objectively weighing every possible factor that can influence the future, including environmental dynamics as well as industry trends. It is a process that strives to create a clear vision, not fantasizing or desperately seeking a flash of blinding insight. Simply knowing yourself is not enough; to achieve clear vision, it is necessary for you to come to know the full complexity of your organization and its environment. The process includes exploring the answers to a series of questions that will begin to shape the nature of an organization's vision (Hickman & Silva, 1984) :

- What are the critical dynamics of your environment? How do things really work? How does your organization make money?

- What trends are changing the nature of your industry? How would you describe the state of the art in your industry? What are the potential opportunities or threats?
- Who are your competitors, and what are they doing? Are they gaining a competitive advantage at your expense? How are you seeking new ways to regain the advantage?
- What do your customers really want? How do they value what you offer? How can you add value?
- What is the image of the organization? How do people feel about who you are? Are they clear about your purpose?
- What makes your organization distinctive and unique? Does your distinctiveness afford you any opportunities?
- What are your most important capabilities and skills? With whom have you formed your most important relationships? Do you sufficiently understand them?
- What is your full potential as an organization? What is possible now and in the future?
- What determined your success in the past? Do you really understand the nature of your successes?
- Why have you failed in the past? Do you understand the real reasons for those setbacks?

Scenario Building

After reflecting on the crucial questions about the past, present, and future of your organization and its environment, your next step is mentally creating the future. This step is appropriately called scenario building. This process moves you from the world of introspection to the world of projection. Projection provides a means for testing your vision before you fully commit your organization to it through mentally creating the future by building a series of scenarios. This step assists you in providing further clarification about your vision and minimizes costly trial and error. It should not be confused with planning. You should move away from the tendency to overanalyze or overplan ("analysis paralysis") because recent experiences have demonstrated that an action orientation and an "experiment with it" attitude result in faster and more lasting results than the time-consuming and too often artificial "analyze it and plan it to death" routine.

Scenario building is a four-stage creative thinking process (Hickman & Silva, 1984):

1. *Defining the vision:* a thorough yet simple description of the vision, including its philosophy, strategic direction, and cultural values
2. *Determining opportunities and dangers:* a careful identification of all the positive and negative potential outcomes of the new vision, including an analysis of the best and worst possibilities
3. *Listing key success factors:* a thorough evaluation of all the factors involved in implementing the new vision, with special emphasis on a handful of key factors that will ultimately determine success or failure (such factors, along with political issues, include people, money, resources, and expertise)
4. *Sequencing major events:* a logical progression of benchmarks that should occur during vision implementation and the likely impact that any one event will have on other events

The primary purpose of scenario building is to increase the probability of successfully achieving your vision; as such, it becomes important to account for every possible opportunity or danger. Only then will you really learn something from mentally "test-driving" your visions. Some questions to test how well your scenarios are developed include the following (Hickman & Silva, 1984):

- Can someone unfamiliar with your business understand your vision?
- Does your scenario identify all the potential benefits and liabilities?
- Are you realistic about the costs of your scenario?
- Have you clearly identified and prioritized all indicators of success and failure?
- Have you properly sequenced all events to ensure maximum impact on the outcome?
- Is your scenario adaptable to changing conditions?
- Can you commit your scenario to paper for future review and development?

CONCLUSION

As facilitators of the processes that will create tomorrow's visions, leaders will need to be clearly focused and solution oriented. They will need to build partnerships with staff that result in increased levels of empowerment and interstaff support. As empowerment facilitators, leaders of the future will build strong organizational cultures that encourage risk taking and innovation at all levels. Transformational leadership skills are the key to operationalizing shared visions effectively by managing corporate culture, strategy, and change. Transformational leaders are truly powerful and know how to implement change by creating a vision in the minds and hearts of others. They view risks as opportunities and empower staff at all levels of the organization to be creative and innovative. As masters of managing change, they have the ability to commit people to action and to convert followers into leaders. There is a spiritual dimension to this kind of leadership that is founded on trust and characterized by a sort of magical, charismatic, enlightening quality. Transformational leaders do not force events or control people. Their style is characterized by trust and empowerment and is best seen in their artistic approach to communication (O'Malley & Cummings, 1993).

In summary, there are several key characteristics that describe the inherent qualities of leaders who are charged with building shared visions (O'Malley & Cummings, 1993, pp. 136–137):

- *Trusting subordinates.* Generally, if a manager believes in and trusts subordinates, they will go all out for the manager. Conventional management structures with responsibility and authority residing at the top of a pyramid are fast giving way to high-commitment organizations with high-performance teams. A high-performing team's success is based on trust and a partnership among leaders and all levels of their staff.
- *Remembering to relax and keep cool.* The best leaders excel under fire. How one capitalizes on the opportunities presented in crises is the acid test for true transformational leadership.
- *Developing a passion for encouraging risk taking.* Effective leaders encourage staff not only to take risks but also to readily accept error. Fear of failure should never be the reason not to try something new.
- *Having an obsession for being an expert.* From the transportation aide to the clinical nurse specialist to the executive in the board room, everyone needs to know that the nurse manager knows what he or she is talking about. Leaders need to do their homework. Staff follow a lot more willingly if they are confident that their leader knows what he or she is doing.
- *Inviting dissent and creating a little controversy.* Effective organizational leaders create environments where constructive dissent is supported. Staff members are not giving their best if they are afraid to speak up. The higher you get in an organization, the more important it is to have people who will tell you when you are right or wrong. If you have "yes people," either you or they are redundant.
- *Developing an ability to simplify.* Leaders should not get done in by the details. Effective leaders can see the global picture and develop

pragmatic solutions to complex issues. They zero in on essentials, are clear about outcomes consistent with desired direction, and are effective at keeping the details at bay.

In the final analysis, the challenge for nursing leaders during this period of major organizational transformation is to be a visionary yet a realist, to be sensitive yet demanding, and to be innovative yet pragmatic.

RESEARCH   Hertzel-Trexler, B.J. (1994). Permeation of organizational level strategic
FOUNDATION   planning into nursing division level planning. *Journal of Nursing Administration, 24*(11), 23–29.

This study examined the relationship between organizational strategic planning, operating profits and loss, and the permeation of organizational level strategic planning into nursing planning. Fifteen acute care hospitals in the Northwest participated in a 1993 study that addressed the following problem: Does strategic planning that has permeated to the nursing division level affect operating margins? The sample of participating hospitals, located in metropolitan, urban, and semi-urban settings, ranged in size from 30 to 450 beds. Hospitals were nonprofit independents, nonprofit multihospital system members, and for-profit system members.

This descriptive study used Drucker's model of linked mission and objectives converted to action through strategies. Data were collected by structured interview. The hospitals' mission and objectives and strategic planning documents, if they were available, were compared to determine linkage of concepts. The 10 hospitals with strategic planning documents were slightly better off financially than the 5 without strategic plan documents.

The value of strategic planning was also evidenced by those hospitals that had a negative operating margin loss that they changed to a positive operating margin profit after they implemented strategic planning. For the five hospitals where strategic planning permeated the nursing division, the nursing division objectives reflected the value strategic planning can have on the whole organization.

REFERENCES

Arndt, C., & Huckabay, L.M.D. (1980). *Nursing administration* (2nd ed.). St. Louis: Mosby.

Bellman, G.M. (1992). *Getting things done when you are not in charge.* San Francisco: Berrett-Koehler.

Cox, A. (1990). *Straight talk for Monday morning.* New York: Wiley.

Hickman, C.R., & Silva, M.A. (1984). *Creating excellence.* New York: New American Library.

Kouzes, J.M., & Posner, B.Z. (1993). *Credibility.* San Francisco: Jossey-Bass.

O'Malley, J., & Cummings, S. (1993). Planning and developing a professional practice model. In E. Berkhart & L. Skeggs (Eds.). *Nursing leadership: Preparing for the 21st century* (pp. 111–140). Chicago: American Hospital Publishing.

Roberts, K.H. (1994). Functional and dysfunctional organizational linkages. *Journal of Organizational Behavior, 1*, 1–11.

Senge, P.M. (1990). *The fifth discipline.* New York: Doubleday.

Shortell, S.M., Morrison, E.M., & Friedman, B. (1990). *Strategic choices for America's hospitals.* San Francisco: Jossey-Bass.

Vail, P.B. (1989). *Managing as a performing art.* San Francisco: Jossey-Bass.

Wheatley, M.J. (1992). *Leadership and the new science.* San Francisco: Berrett-Koehler.

Whiteley, R.C. (1991). *The customer driven company.* Reading, MA: Addison-Wesley.

CHAPTER 13

The Changing Role of Technology

Becky DeVillier

CHAPTER OBJECTIVES

At the completion of this chapter, the beginning professional nurse will be able to:

1. identify implications for nursing care delivery and patient outcomes that are a direct result of applied technology in diagnostics and intervention
2. describe the impact of an informed patient population on the nurse's role in patient teaching
3. describe how the relationship among the concepts of applied technology, economics, nursing practice, and patient needs affects work redesign
4. identify the implications of bedside mechanical devices on nursing practice
5. identify the difficulties that health care workers experience in dealing with bioethical issues
6. describe the impact on the nurse's role in cases where the patient, family, and/or significant others are participating in decision making about the patient's death
7. describe the nurse's responsibility in working with computerized systems that interface with bedside monitoring equipment

CRITICAL THINKING CHALLENGE As a staff nurse, you have been selected as a member of the planning committee for a new children's hospital. You must help decide what technology is essential. What components must be in place to maintain confidentiality? What elements of the medical record are essential to automate? How will you decide on cost versus need? How will you ration the use of the new technology that is available? How will you coordinate care of the child after he or she leaves the acute care setting?

The last three decades have witnessed a technological explosion that has profoundly influenced all aspects of health care. From electronic thermometers to artificial hearts, advances are being made on almost a daily basis.

Nurses are constantly faced with decisions about the use of technology. The beginning nurse especially will be faced with many technological innovations. Technological advances make all areas of health care far more complex and challenging. Patients who a few years ago had no chance for survival are living productive lives as a result of new technology.

The beginning nurse needs to understand the changes in practice that will be occurring during the next few years because of the technological advances of today and those on the horizon. The mere availability of new technology gives rise to many ethical and legal questions, such as the following:

- What patients receive the new technology?
- Does every health care facility provide all new technology?
- Can we afford all the new technology?
- How do we protect confidential information?
- How do we ration health care?
- Who decides how far we should and will go with genetic screening?
- What is the definition of brain death?
- When should we stop treatment?

Advances in technology continually expand the body of knowledge for which nurses are responsible. It is important to understand the role that nursing plays as health care changes due to new technology occur.

Changes in technology will force constant review and revision of individual paradigms, the rules and regulations through which one sees the world. It is important to be open to new ways to view the world and technology. One's openness to new paradigms can multiply the ways in which new technology is used.

THERAPEUTIC INTERVENTION

Clinical Technology

Laparoscopic Surgery

The term *minimally invasive surgery* applies to any procedure that decreases patient risk and healing time. Laparoscopic surgery is one of the best developed minimally invasive surgical techniques. The laparoscope is a long tube that allows the surgeon to enter a body cavity through a small opening. The laparoscope can be connected to a video system via a video recorder at the tip of the scope. The image from inside the body can be projected onto a video screen and magnified for better visualization and surgical technique.

The scope also accommodates tiny surgical instruments that are passed through it and manipulated. Small organs and tissue can be removed using this instrument. Repair of all types of tissue is often easily done via a laparoscope. The result of laparoscopic surgery is less trauma to the patient's physiological system and shorter healing time.

The use of laparoscopic equipment has allowed surgeons to increase greatly the number of surgical procedures that can be done on an outpatient basis. The video recordings may also be used for diagnosis and comparative studies. For example, a lesion can be recorded on tape and compared with a recording done at a later date. This is a useful technique in tracking certain types of tumors.

Laparoscopic surgery results in larger numbers of outpatients and fewer hospital days and requires more follow-up in the home. It is one of the techniques that is shifting the focus of nursing care from the acute setting to the home. The nurse will need assessment skills for these patients ranging from acute care to home visits. Patient teaching will be even more critical because much of the recovery period is in the home.

Laser Technology

The word *laser* is an acronym for *l*ight *a*mplification by *s*timulated *e*mission of *r*adiation. The concept of the laser is often attributed to Albert Einstein, but it was not until 1958 that laser technology was first used in a medical-surgical setting (Maley & Epstein, 1993). Much of the early work with lasers involved ophthalmic surgery.

Most modern operating suites are equipped with carbon dioxide lasers. These are the most common type of laser used in health care. These instruments amplify a beam of light to a high electrical level. The light beam then burns through tissue, coagulating blood as it does so and producing a clean, almost bloodless incision.

The laser's beam of light can be used much like a scalpel. Because it is such a highly intense beam of light, however, it requires additional skill by the surgeon for operation. Nurses in the operating room must become familiar with use of the carbon dioxide laser because it will be used in more and more surgical procedures.

Laser technology instruments are expensive to purchase and require additional training of both physicians and nursing staff. The cost of laser surgery has been generally well accepted because it is offset by smaller incisions, fewer bleeding problems, and overall shorter operative times. As a result, patients heal faster and require shorter hospitalization. A patient who is too physiologically compromised for conventional surgery and anesthesia may be a candidate for laser surgery.

Researchers are continuing to expand the types of surgery in which the laser can be used successfully. New types of laser devices are being developed. Lasers will have an even greater impact on health care as researchers find new uses for them.

Biotechnology

Biotechnology is the term used to define different types of technological products that mimic body functions. Biotechnology includes therapeutic agents, artificial body parts, and mechanical assist devices.

Biotechnology drugs are being developed at a rapid pace (Huber, 1993). One issue in biotechnology drug development is the high cost. Drugs are being developed that often are phenomenally expensive. One dose may cost as much as several hundred to several thousand dollars. They are able to produce results that were not possible with older technology, however.

Much of the current biotechnology research is focused on finding a cure for AIDS. Many scientists believe that biotechnology research will produce a cure for this disease, which claims thousands of lives each year (Kiplinger & Kiplinger, 1990).

Other biotechnological advances include production of functioning artificial body parts. The use of artificial limbs has provided options for many individuals with handicaps. Biotechnology developments include artificial hands with computer chips for more normal functioning of the wrist and fingers.

Researchers have been attempting to perfect an artificial heart for almost three decades. The major problem in designing an artificial heart has been the size of the device. The hearts are too big. Currently, the artificial heart must be connected to a large external power supply system. While the device is in place, a patient is confined to a wheelchair or has limited mobility. Computer technology will make it possible to design an artificial heart that can be contained within the chest cavity.

The Food and Drug Administration (FDA) regulates the use of newly developed artificial organs in humans. Research products must get FDA approval, which can take as long as several years. Restrictions on new products are more stringent in the United States than in other countries. Although this protects individuals, it may also lead to delays in availability of new technology.

Biotechnology research in cancer care is making rapid advances. Treatment is changing from radiation and chemotherapy to targeted, tumor-specific drugs that boost the immune system. This type of treatment will affect the way cancer is treated in the future (Lumsdon & Anderson, 1992). The use of these drugs may also affect a patient's psychological response to cancer by providing more hope for recovery.

The nurse will be responsible for helping the patient understand biotechnology alternatives. The potential outcomes are exciting, but many ethical issues will arise related to cost and availability. These are discussed later in this chapter.

Reproductive Technology

Successful in vitro fertilization, which is essentially fertilization of a human egg in a test tube, was first done in Great Britain in 1970. Since the 1980s, this procedure has been done in a large number of health care settings (Lumsdon & Anderson, 1992). The procedure involves removal of the eggs from the mother, usually with a laparoscope. The eggs are incubated in the laboratory along with semen to allow fertilization to occur. When the fertilization is successful, the embryo is transferred to the mother's uterus in the hope that it will implant and grow. Success of this procedure varies; some centers report a pregnancy rate as high as 20%.

In vitro fertilization has also been utilized when preimplantation testing is desired, especially for detection of genetically linked disease. For example, before implantation an embryo could be tested for cystic fibrosis. The ethical issues associated with this technology are staggering. This technology provides the basis for genetic screening. If not carefully handled, it could result in unscrupulous selection of embryos for implantation.

The mid-1980s saw the development of the gamete intrafallopian transfer (GIFT) procedure. GIFT is accomplished by placing sperm and eggs into a fine pipette and inserting them into the fallopian tube via a laparoscope. This procedure has a higher success rate than in vitro fertilization because of the more natural transition of the embryo into the uterus. GIFT has been further modified to the zygote intrafallopian transfer (ZIFT) procedure, in which the eggs are fertilized in a test tube and the resulting embryo is placed in the fallopian tube. The GIFT and ZIFT procedures result in pregnancy 40% to 50%

of the time. This is an astonishing success rate because the conception rate among healthy fertile couples is only 25% (Jones, 1993).

Surrogate motherhood is another result of technological advances in reproductive medicine. In this case, a woman is artificially inseminated and carries the child to birth. The surrogate mother agrees before the procedure to surrender the child at birth for adoption. In the early 1990s, the legal and ethical issues related to this procedure made the headlines on several occasions when the biological mother and adoptive parents battled for custody of a child.

The nurse will play a key role in patient education in reproductive technology. Nurses may be specially trained to assist with these procedures and conduct genetic counselling.

Transplantation

Organ transplantation has become possible as a result of technological advances in immunosuppression and donor matching. In 1983 the FDA approved the use of the drug cyclosporine in this country. This drug decreases the risk of tissue rejection in most patients. The proliferation of transplantation procedures can be directly traced to the use of cyclosporine (Lumsdon & Anderson, 1992).

The major organs being transplanted today are the heart, liver, lung, and kidney. In the early 1990s successful organ transplant began to be performed on neonates. The waiting list for all types of organs for transplant lengthens on an annual basis. The United Network of Organ Sharing (UNOS) is a nonprofit group that helps provide consistency in organ transplantation. UNOS requires its members to list all potential donors with local and national organ procurement organizations.

In addition to organ transplantation, many people benefit from tissue transplantation. As many as 70 individuals may benefit from the tissue of one deceased person. Tissue transplants include corneas, skin, bone marrow, bone, heart valves, and veins.

It is the physician's responsibility to discuss organ donation with the patient's family, but the nurse is often involved in further explanations and providing support for the family. Nursing can play a key role in encouraging the family to consider organ donation.

Transplantation has brought many new challenges to health care professionals. The early days of transplantation saw great fear and anxiety as a patient awaited a donor organ. Today some of the stress related to speculating about organ availability has been relieved via computerized databases of potential organ donors, such as UNOS. The selection of recipient patients and the potential rationing of organs to certain patient populations, however, have resulted in ethical issues that are extremely difficult. This area is discussed in more detail later in this chapter.

Advances in Neonatology

In recent years technical advances have led to many changes in neonatal intensive care. Neonates who had little chance of survival a few years ago now survive on a routine basis. Some of the most common and severe problems experienced by premature infants have been successfully treated via advanced technological devices.

Frequently the premature infant is unable to produce surfactant, which lubricates the lung alveoli, a deficiency known as hyaline membrane disease. Without surfactant, the infant rapidly develops massive pulmonary problems that lead to death. The advent of artificial surfactant has greatly improved the viability of many of these infants, even those with very low birth weights.

A developing area of technology for neonatal care is liquid ventilation (Greenspan, 1993). To date, research in this area has been confined to animals. Early studies indicate that it has potential benefit for the infant with respiratory distress syndrome (RDS).

Most premature infants require some level of ventilatory support immediately after birth. Ventilators are available for neonates that are capable of delivering up to 900 breaths per minute. These are highly advanced ventilators and have saved many infant lives. They have also become more accurate in delivering low tidal volumes and are smaller in overall size than they once were as a result of technological research.

A limited number of centers across the United States offer extracorporeal membrane oxygenation (ECMO) to treat infants who have advanced RDS. ECMO is based on the cardiopulmonary bypass machine used in open heart surgery. The procedure involves ligating the internal jugular vein and shunting the blood to the bypass machine, where it is oxygenated and returned via a cannula into the common internal carotid. This procedure provides oxygenation to the neonate's blood supply while the lungs rest and mature. ECMO is a controversial treatment because it requires so much time, equipment, and personnel (Maley & Epstein, 1993). Most neonatal centers rely on more conventional and less expensive measures to treat RDS. Advances in drug therapy may one day eliminate the need for ECMO, but it has been a life-saving measure for a number of infants.

Another of the major areas of physiological support needed by neonates is thermal regulation. Premature infants are not able to sustain their body temperature in the normal range. Technological advances have provided improvements in both incubators and radiant warmers. Incubators have been used for many years, but new improved incubators provide temperature monitoring and automatic adjustment to maintain a preset temperature level. These incubators may also have built-in scales for daily weight monitoring.

The radiant warmer is an open type crib with heat lamps built into an overhead device. These warmers provide a crib rather than an incubator atmosphere and allow easy access to the infant. The mother can easily touch her infant. The warmer allows staff to gain access to the infant for routine care as well as for the application of life-saving devices when necessary.

The use of home apnea monitors and home ventilators is an outcome of technological advances in neonatal care. Neonates are often discharged to home with apnea monitors that alert parents to decreased respiration rate. The use of home apnea monitors not only saves lives but also decreases the length of hospital stay. Early discharge leads to improved psychological development of the neonate and decreased hospital cost. Funding is a major issue with neonatal intensive care, and early discharge contributes to decreasing costs.

Technology-Dependent Children

There are children who grow up in a hospital because their medical condition requires a level of technology that is simply too complex to administer outside a specialized unit. The survival of these children depends on constant access to the latest technology. The number of these children is increasing, and they present unique challenges, such as providing an environment that assists growth and development, providing normal life experiences, promoting positive self-image, promoting independence, providing opportunities for learning, and providing exploratory experiences.

A family-centered approach can help these children adjust to a technology-dependent environment. It can also assist in earlier discharge of these children. As these children mature, they will need support from a variety of sources. The nurse can coordinate services with social work and other organizations to improve the quality of life for these children. Technology-dependent children can benefit greatly from a case management approach. The complexity of their illnesses requires that many services be coordinated on a routine basis. A case management model provides the integration needed to move these children along a predetermined critical path.

KEY CONCEPTS
- Patients' operative risks and healing times have both been decreased as a result of minimally invasive surgical techniques based on technological advances.
- Body functions can be imitated and artificially reproduced via biotechnology developments, such as therapeutic agents, artificial body parts, and mechanical assist devices.

- Several different fertilization techniques allow more women to experience motherhood.
- Many persons' lives are prolonged because organs and tissues can be transplanted, including heart, liver, lungs, kidney, corneas, skin, bone marrow, bone, heart valves, and veins.
- Many premature neonates survive today because technology has provided solutions to the major problems they face, including thermal regulation, ventilatory support, and surfactant therapy.
- Infants and children are frequently discharged home on complex technological devices that parents or caretakers must learn to operate.

LEARNING CHALLENGE

1. You are taking care of a child in whom brain death has been determined. How would you relate to the family? What questions would you anticipate? What would be your role in organ donation?
2. You are working in a neonatal intensive care unit with a child who requires ECMO. How would you prepare the family for this treatment? What is your role in managing the care of this child?

Diagnostic Technology

Computed Tomography and Magnetic Resonance Imaging

Computed tomography (CT) scanners are devices that measure physiological variations in the density of bone, blood, and tissue. Images are taken before and after a contrast medium is injected into the patient's bloodstream. The computer subtracts the original image from the postinjection image. The result shows the distribution of the contrast material. Analysis of this distribution can identify tumors or other abnormal tissue. These devices were first introduced in this country in 1972 (Maley & Epstein, 1993). CT scanners provide cross-sectional images and increased contrast ability. They are particularly helpful in neurological, spinal, lung, and abdominal imaging. New software development provides three-dimensional images.

The next step in CT scanning will probably be ultrafast scanning. This new technology will be particularly useful in cardiac-related diagnosis. The use of CT scans improves diagnostic speed and accuracy.

In 1981, patient studies using magnetic resonance (MR) imaging began. This technology places the patient in a magnetic field and exposes the body to energy in the radiofrequency range. As a result MR can detect small physiochemical changes that indicate disease or abnormal tissue.

MR is a rapidly growing form of patient diagnostic and evaluation technology. It presents interesting challenges for the nurse. Patients must remain absolutely still for long periods of time (sometimes hours) surrounded by a huge magnet in a tunnellike configuration. The patient cannot move any body part and cannot see outside the device. Appropriate preparation of the patient to decrease anxiety during the procedure is important. This may include remaining with the patient and supporting him or her by maintaining physical touch to an exposed body part, such as the foot. If the patient moves at all, the procedure will have to be repeated.

One of the challenges with both CT and MR is monitoring the patient. The nurse may need to accompany the patient to remote sites to ensure an acceptable standard of care for the patient. This may involve ambulance transportation and monitoring during the procedure and return to the point of origin. It is important that the nurse maintain the same standard of care for patients in any health care setting. Technological changes can produce fragmented care if the nurse does not address this issue. Large hospitals often have nurses working in radiology for monitoring and assessing patients during these procedures. It is important, however, that care of the patient be coordinated from the time he or she leaves the unit, during the testing, and until he or she is returned to the patient room.

Frequently, patients are given medication to make them more relaxed during a procedure. This practice is known as conscious sedation and is a major issue associated with many diagnostic procedures. It is the nurse's responsibility to assist with monitoring these patients while they are sedated. Conscious sedation has become a controversial and risk management issue at many health care facilities. During the late 1980s and early 1990s, numerous deaths resulted from conscious sedation. The Joint Commission on Accreditation of Healthcare Organizations makes this issue a priority when it conducts site visits. Strict guidelines are now required for all patients undergoing a procedure that involves conscious sedation.

Teleradiology

Teleradiology is the transmission of digital radiological images to computer workstations. This technology allows X-ray images to be transmitted to various locations and viewed on any computer terminal that has high-resolution graphics capabilities. The images may be enhanced (made larger or turned to various angles) to improve their diagnostic yield. The images from these devices can be viewed at more than one location at the same time. This technology eliminates the need for traditional X-ray film.

Computer software is being developed to assist with the assessment of radiographic images. This software can also assist with comparisons for differential diagnosis as the patient's condition changes.

KEY CONCEPTS

- Patients can undergo fast and accurate diagnostic procedures via CT scanning, which measures density of bone, blood, and tissue, and with MR imaging, which detects small physiochemical changes in the body.
- National or international specialists can be consulted and view diagnostic results via teleradiology technology.

LEARNING CHALLENGE

You are preparing a patient for an MR scan at another facility. What information would be essential for the patient and family? How would you manage the transport of the patient to ensure continuity of care?

Self-Care Aspects

On-Line Information

Patients today have access to vast amounts of information. One of the growing arenas for patient education is on-line information services, usually databases that can be accessed via a computer modem. There are numerous dial-up information services or networks that provide health care information. Each one begins its session with a disclaimer of responsibility. The information tends to be general in nature, but it does reach a large number of consumers. Eventually these services will result in a more informed consumer population.

One dial-up network is CompuServe, which provides the Healthnet database as part of its basic access service. Healthnet allows the user to access general information about disease processes, surgical procedures, and drug actions. The user can also find information about nutrition and exercise.

Another system that has been developed is HouseCall. This is an on-line program that consumers can call to record their symptoms. Once the symptoms are recorded, the database provides a list of all possible causes. Thus the caller is able to obtain a large amount of information about his or her symptoms before actually talking with a physician or nurse practitioner.

HealthDesk is another on-line system that allows the consumer to record personal and family health history, to update the information, and to view it on screen. This has been shown to be an effective method for chronically ill populations to track their own health care needs.

CD-ROM

Another growing method of information access is CD-ROM devices. Many CDs can be used either in an audio CD player or in a computer CD player. An audio CD provides voice only, but computer CDs provide vivid graphics with sound, color, and motion. It is possible to play back a videotape recording through a CD-ROM device.

The technology available with CD-ROM will have a dramatic impact on the amount and type of information that is available to patients. Because CDs store vast amounts of information, they make interactive teaching a reality. Via computer input devices (e.g., keyboard and mouse), patients can pose questions and receive moderately individualized responses. This technology could be applied to preoperative teaching, culminating in a fully informed patient who is ready to sign an informed consent form.

The graphics capabilities of CD-ROM provide unlimited possibilities for teaching and learning tools for both patients and health care workers. The use of CDs could lead to better understanding of health issues, disease processes, and treatments. The CD may well be the textbook of the future. For example, the *Mayo Clinic Family Health Book* is currently available as an interactive CD. This type of reference will become available to many families as the use of CD-ROM continues to increase. Another interactive CD, the *Wellness Checkpoint*, helps the consumer maintain a healthy life style by allowing him or her to set healthy life style targets and to monitor individual progress in achieving them.

The nurse will be called upon to clarify and reinforce the information obtained from these sources. The nurse will often need to help patients interpret general information supplied by these resources as it applies to them individually. These materials will help produce a more informed consumer of health care.

Self-Testing

Self-testing technology continues to advance and become increasingly available as our population becomes more independent and demanding of these methods. Currently, self-testing products include pregnancy tests, glucose monitoring, and cholesterol monitoring. Technology has also made it simple for a patient to monitor his or her own blood pressure at home.

Current research is being done on noninvasive diagnostic devices that would eliminate the use of urine and blood samples in many cases. These devices perform diagnostics by reading physiochemical levels through the skin. As these systems are perfected, more self-testing may become available. Encouraging self-care also may have a positive effect on the cost of health care.

The result of self-testing will be a better informed patient. As patients increase their information base, however, they are apt to seek more specialized knowledge from the nurse. The nurse is in an excellent position to help patients understand their options. It is always better for the patient to be more informed than less informed.

**KEY
CONCEPTS**

- Generations growing up playing video and computer games and using computers in their elementary through high school education will have little difficulty in taking advantage of on-line computer databases of health care information.
- People will demand that the multimedia technology of computer games be applied to education, and CD-ROM technology will be used to teach health care providers as well as recipients.
- Society is accustomed to fast as well as quality services and will continue expecting these in health care by demanding fast, affordable, easy-to-use at-home devices that produce quick and accurate self-testing results.

**LEARNING
CHALLENGE**

1. You have been asked to coordinate a patient teaching program at a home health agency. How would you utilize computer-generated information in your program? How would on-line information affect your patient population?
2. Someone you know has been recently diagnosed with diabetes. How would you use computer-generated information to assist this individual? What changes will new technology make in the management of his or her care? How would you encourage self-care?

Automation of Function

Supply Delivery

How do we get supplies to the nurse and other health care workers in the most cost-effective way? For many years, we have used tube systems and dumbwaiters to deliver supplies, but these have not proved to be totally satisfactory. Ineffective vertical and horizontal delivery systems are one of the more common problems facing health care facilities. Changing technology greatly affects the delivery of supplies.

Many institutions are experimenting with robotics. It is difficult and costly to add robotics to existing facilities, however. Therefore, this technology is most frequently seen in newer facilities.

Supply dispensing devices are being used more frequently. For example, there are devices that are similar to vending machines that dispense supplies or medications. These systems are computerized and can record the item used on the patient's record and also on the patient's bill. Pharmacy systems such as these are particularly helpful. Narcotics and other controlled substances can be safely and accurately dispensed (Frick, Rein, & Parks, 1993). These systems not only reduce staff time but also increase the accuracy of transactions.

Communication

Technology is changing the way we communicate. Electronic mail, voice mail, beepers, answering machines, cellular telephones, and fax machines have made their mark on health care. It is possible to speak only to machines for all types of important communication.

Electronic communication can produce anxiety in both consumers and health care providers. Although it provides increased access on one level, the human element is often missing. Message systems save time but can potentially lead to misunderstandings. Health care providers must be constantly aware of this potential problem.

Numerous companies offer nurse call systems that provide improved communication. Some of these systems provide each nurse with a two-way communication system that he or she can carry for immediate response. These systems can lead to quicker staff response time and less disturbance of patients by eliminating the need for overhead pages. The system is not without its downside, however, and the nurse needs to be aware of the problems and interruptions that instant communication can create.

Home health workers find cellular phones and dedicated communication devices beneficial. With the help of a wireless modem, the home health nurse can access patient information and treatment protocols from any location.

Emergency care now makes use of global positioning satellite systems to pinpoint accident sites. When combined with a computerized map, this system can lead emergency workers to precise accident locations. This results in reduced travel time to the accident site and more rapid onset of emergency measures.

KEY CONCEPTS

- New supply technology is difficult to incorporate into already built facilities.
- The technology that brought food, drink, and money dispensing machines is bringing supplies, medications, and linens to health care workers in a fast, safe, and cost-effective manner.
- Learning to use cellular telephones, wireless modems, and satellite technology will be part of the curriculum for many health care providers.

LEARNING CHALLENGE

1. Think of five ways that new technology will affect your role as a beginning practitioner.
2. You are working in an ultramodern hospital with all the latest technology. How would you ensure that the personal touch remains? How would you help the nursing assistant understand the value of personal communication?

Bedside Mechanical Devices

Monitoring

Intensive care units were designed to provide intensive nursing care as well as intensive technology. A patient in the intensive care unit is often surrounded by much of the latest technology. On a routine basis in most intensive care units, the patient is monitored for heart rate and rhythm, breathing, arterial blood pressure, central venous pressure, and blood oxygenation. The number of bedside body function monitoring devices continues to increase.

The beginning professional nurse may be overwhelmed by the amount and complexity of technology in the intensive care unit. Still, the technology is easier to master than the relationships with patients. It is important for the nurse to focus on the patient rather than the technology. The art of nursing is caring for the patient's emotional needs amid the ever-increasing technology.

New technology allows many patients to be monitored at home. As mentioned earlier, apnea monitors are common in children with respiratory problems. The use of home monitoring equipment can lead to earlier discharge, requiring more patient teaching and follow-up.

Care Assist Devices

Intravenous (IV) infusion pumps are one of the most commonly used care assist devices. These machines monitor and regulate the amount of fluid a patient receives. IV pumps have become commonplace in the health care setting. These devices increase the accuracy of fluid delivery and will also sound an alarm if the fluid source is depleted or the port becomes obstructed. In the fluid-sensitive patient, IV pumps have become a necessary piece of equipment.

A computer system developed in the late 1980s automated temperature, pulse, and respiration monitoring and documentation. In the future, a specialized system such as this will become part of a clinical information system (CIS).

Other care assist devices include automatic blood pressure monitoring, electronic thermometers, hydraulic lifts, and electronic scales. Progress in the development of devices to assist nurses in providing care has not been as rapid as in other areas of technology.

Diagnostic Devices

Automated glucose monitors continue to become smaller, easier to use, and more accurate. The newer devices require only one small drop of blood, which does not touch any internal mechanisms, and are almost foolproof in their operation and results. Other devices are addressed in the section on self-testing, above.

KEY CONCEPTS
- The beginning nurse's focus on the patient should not be overshadowed by attention to technological monitoring and recording devices.
- Future high-technology devices will be small multifunctional or networking devices but will not negate the need for high touch.

LEARNING CHALLENGE As a nurse in an intensive care unit, you are caring for a patient with numerous monitoring devices. The equipment indicates that the patient's heart has stopped. What would be your first course of action as you enter the room?

TECHNOLOGICAL ADVANCES

Information Systems

Evolution of Information Systems

Hospital information systems have advanced from the early financial systems to sophisticated clinical information systems. The CIS will be at the core of the computerized patient record.

Mainframe Computers

Mainframe computer systems are at the core of most hospital information systems. Early mainframe computer software focused on financial and admission-discharge-transfer data. Data entry was often via lightpen technology. These systems were designed to crunch numbers for billing, and they did that very well.

The flexibility of mainframe computers has actually increased over the past few years as a result of the microcomputer. Most hospitals still have substantial investments in large, fairly inflexible mainframe computers, however. It is difficult to adapt mainframe systems to more user-friendly environments, and even the more flexible mainframe computers often fall short in the area of CIS development.

CISs are computer systems that automate all the functions associated with the patient and the patient record. These systems vary in levels of sophistication from systems that provide a complete, on-line patient record to ones that record only limited information, such as vital signs.

Basically, two different approaches have been used in developing CISs. One approach was based on the early mainframe financial systems with modifications made to accommodate clinical information. This approach proved to be extremely complex and difficult. It resulted in systems that were slow and cumbersome to use.

The second approach to CIS development grew out of the critical care areas and made the patient's record the focal point of the system. Work continues on these newer mainframe-based systems, known as second-generation CISs. These systems are becoming increasingly usable. As technology advances and is continually refined, these systems offer the promise of more speed and ease of use. The systems developed using this second approach will win out because the core of a true CIS must be the computerized patient record.

Computerized Patient Records

The computerized patient record consists of all patient information online, including all physiological function monitoring data, professional progress notes, orders, medication administration records, and diagnostic test results. CISs interface directly with physiological monitors, ventilators, gas monitors, IV pumps, and other bedside equipment. The interface allows data to be sent from any device to the computer record. The nurse will always have the opportunity and responsibility to verify the data before they are recorded in the patient's record. For example, once verified, the heart rate can be recorded directly from the monitor into the on-line patient record. These systems will increase accuracy by transferring data directly to the patient record.

Direct order entry is a key component in any CIS. When the physician writes an order, it is sent directly to the appropriate department. For example, when the physician orders laboratory work, the laboratory is notified directly of this order. The whole transaction takes a matter of seconds. All pertinent patient information is online and available for laboratory technicians to access. Once the specimen is obtained, the medical technologist selects the appropriate machine for analysis. The laboratory equipment is also interfaced to the CIS for results reporting. Thus laboratory values are available at the bedside as soon as the machine completes its analysis. Alarm systems can be used to notify the nurse that new laboratory results are available. Special alarm codes indicate laboratory results that are urgent or out of the normal range. In addition, upon completion of the laboratory analysis, all laboratory data can be transferred directly to the patient record via the use of a CIS. Electronic transfer of data saves time and decreases potential errors in transcription of information.

When medications are ordered, the CIS can check for appropriate dosage, allergies, and incompatibilities before accepting the order. Many systems also have built-in dosage calculators. Once accepted, the order is sent directly to the pharmacy for dispensing. The transaction takes only seconds. Electronic verification decreases the risk of errors in both ordering and transcribing. The CIS can automatically assign administration times to each medication. The CIS can also alert the nurse via an audio signal or electronic mail that there is a new medication order.

On a daily basis, the CIS can print a task list for each nurse. The data can be formatted in almost any manner, thus allowing the system to generate an individual version of the list. The task list prints the times at which treatments, medications, and procedures are to be completed. The nurse can even chart completed tasks directly from the list.

Other hospital departments, such as dietary, respiratory therapy, nuclear medicine, and radiology, will be able to receive orders and provide results and to access and distribute information on these systems. Documentation can truly be interdisciplinary as a result of the ease of access.

The CIS's ability to cross-reference information is limitless. Some systems even use a weight system to calculate urine and other types of body fluid loss and then use the calculations to establish a fluid infusion program that replaces fluid volume milliliter for milliliter.

CISs can automatically generate care plans based on the diagnosis and the acuity of the patient. These care plans can be modified to meet the individual needs of a given patient. Many of these systems contain databases for selection of critical paths. Also, data from previous admissions can be stored and readily accessed, allowing comparisons against a baseline.

Computerized patient records will allow immediate access to pertinent information in emergency situations. An electrocardiogram stored in a computer, for example, could readily be sent to another hospital emergency department. Also, by interagency and intraagency sharing of computerized records, patients could be spared redundant questioning by several health care professionals. This would also help speed the admitting process.

Another distinct advantage to using a computerized patient record is that more than one individual will be able to access the chart at the same time; also, patient records can be accessed from remote locations. A physician, for example, could have direct access to the chart at his or her office. The physician could review laboratory work and vital signs and then write orders without leaving the office. The orders would be sent immediately to the appropriate departments for filling.

The goal of the future is to have a totally paperless chart. Computer experts have learned, however, that it is much easier to get people to relinquish their pens than their paper. Most people still need the security of a paper chart. For this reason, most of the systems in use today print out the patient record at a specified time, usually at the end of the shift or the end of the day.

Confidentiality will be one of the major issues in using these systems. The nurse will need to be aware of this and assist in ensuring a confidential record (Youngberg, 1993). The nurse will need to understand the importance of computer security and protected passwords for computer access. Electronic signatures will replace conventional signing of records. At present, state laws govern the use of electronic signatures. Not all states allow their use, but this is likely to change as more health agencies are able to afford this technology. Refer to Chapter 6 for a more detailed discussion of confidentiality.

In January 1992, the Computer-based Patient Record Institute was founded. This organization is dedicated to promoting routine use of computerized patient records. It comprises work groups from numerous and diverse organizations (Milholland, 1993).

Point-of-Care Technology

Point-of-care technology refers to computer data entry at the point where care is given. Point-of-care technology allows data entry wherever the patient is located, obviating the need to write information on a piece of paper for later transfer to the computer. A point-of-care system may be a hand-held device that the nurse carries or multiple devices located throughout patient care areas.

Technology in this area is advancing rapidly. Devices the size of a pocket calculator are available to provide computer input at any location. These devices can read bar codes and identify some handwriting styles (Betts, 1994). They are light and durable for use by the nurse at any location.

One issue in using small, hand-held devices is their disappearance from the agency. Although they are not of use outside the original setting, their size makes it easy for people to walk away with them.

Research Implications

CISs provide data for endless research possibilities. These systems will allow staff to download volumes of information about numerous patients. Manual chart audits will become obsolete with CISs. Through the use of this technology, it will be possible to answer research questions much more quickly. In addition, each nurse will have more of an obligation to look at the data available before making a decision.

A term coined in the 1990s is *analysis paralysis*: There is so much analysis being done that there are no actions being taken. With so many data available, it will be easy to allow this to happen. The nurse will be faced with data overload on many occasions. One of the challenges will be to use the information to improve care rather than having the data become an obstacle.

As a beginning professional nurse, you should be aware that more data are not always better. Map out the question that you want to answer, and collect data that are most relevant to that question. Stay focused on the issue at hand. Constantly ask the questions: What is the outcome that is desired? Is the information pertinent? What are the essential components of the question?

Local Area Networks

Many health care settings are using personal computer local area networks (PC LAN) as the platform for an information system. The PC LAN links a number of PCs together so that information can be shared by a number of users. Although a PC is certainly not as powerful as a mainframe, it offers a great deal of flexibility in a cost-effective manner. PC-based systems provide ease of use and power for smaller applications. The PC is a familiar machine to a growing number of people, and its learning curve is decreasing.

The use of a LAN has become popular in nursing service administration. Scheduling, acuity systems, and electronic mail are among the most popular applications. These systems allow nursing management to maintain databases of demographic data, skills competencies, and evaluative information about nursing personnel.

The beginning nurse will find computer skills a necessity in modern health care. Nurses are expected to be able to use a keyboard, mouse, and lightpen as part of daily activities. Much of the technology today involves the basic understanding of word processors, spreadsheets, and databases. General knowledge of major software applications has become essential, although knowledge of specific software is not. Computers are continually affecting more and more areas of nursing. Much of the equipment used in health care is actually a small computer of some type.

Micromedex

Micromedex is a database that is available on a type of mainframe computer system known as computerized CIS. This database contains a computerized version of the *Physician's Desk Reference* as well as a number of other databases, including Poisndex, Drugdex, Emergidex, Identidex, Tomes, and others.

A feature of the Micromedex system is its ability to access and print aftercare instructions. Patient instructions on a wide variety of conditions and subjects can be printed out. These are comprehensive instructions aimed particularly at emergency care center patients. The instructions can be customized by the hospital staff to meet individual patient needs.

Nursing and Medical Databases on CD

Most libraries associated with teaching hospitals have the *Cumulative Index to Nursing & Allied Health Literature* and MEDLINE available on

CD (Dyer, 1990). Originally, these databases were available only through a service accessed by telephone. Now, the use of CD-ROM technology makes it possible for a library or health care facility to buy CDs from the original service and then have unlimited use of them. Students also can use the CDs, usually at no cost.

These CD databases include abstracts, just as the telephone-access systems do. Topics in these databases can be searched in just a few minutes. Upon completion of the search, the information can either be printed on paper or written in a text file to a floppy disk.

KEY CONCEPTS
- As CISs become more user-friendly, each professional caregiver will enter data into the system at any appropriate place, and nurse stations as we now know them will not exist.
- The accuracy of data in a computerized patient record will always be the responsibility of the professional health care provider.
- In the future, a professional nurse will consider an individual hand-held computer a basic piece of equipment.

LEARNING CHALLENGE
1. Identify three key security issues with the automated patient record. As a beginning practitioner, how will you deal with security issues?
2. How will password signatures affect nursing documentation?

Future Technology

Voice Activation

Voice activation technology will allow users to input data and activate systems with voice commands. Speech recognition by a computer system in a hospital is difficult because much of the language used is jargon and because often many dialects are spoken within an institution. Issues with voice activation technology that need to be resolved include speed, confidentiality, training, and other human factors. Most of the systems now in use have a steep learning curve. It takes time to learn to use the system and follow the patterns that are programmed into it. It has been predicted that technology for voice activation will be perfected by the end of the decade.

One of the advantages with voice activation, from a risk management point of view, is improved documentation. Voice activated systems generally prompt the user for information and reduce the risk that important information will be omitted. In addition, voice activation may provide a more user-friendly interface for the computerphobe. A related application of this technology is the use of digitized systems by medical record departments, which automatically convert dictation to the written word.

The beginning nurse will need to be aware of the hazards of voice activation in maintaining patient confidentiality. Sensitive information may best be entered via a keyboard or mouse. The nurse will also have to use caution so as not to record inappropriate information inadvertently.

Virtual Reality

One of the most exciting areas in computer health care is the use of virtual reality. **Virtual reality** is the simulation of real-life events by means of sight, sound, and touch to make the experience as real as possible. Generally, the user places a shield with a miniature video screen over his or her face. This shield or helmet provides visual and auditory input to the user. A glove or pair of gloves worn by the user provides tactile feedback to the computer and gives the user a sense of control. With the shield and glove(s) in place, the user experiences the video images as if they were real. The computer sends visual and auditory stimuli to the user and reacts to the input from the glove device, making the experience seem quite real.

This technology allows entrance into the world of three-dimensional computer applications. Virtual reality can provide experiences far beyond those available in the traditional classroom. For example, the user can do surgery or miniaturize himself or herself and travel through the circulatory system with amazing reality.

Some of the early work in virtual reality was done in amusement parks. Although this may seem unrelated to the health care setting, researchers are using techniques learned in the parks to develop many health care applications.

According to Satava (1993), it will take less than 40 years to develop virtual reality surgical simulators that will be used as much by surgeons as flight simulators are being used by pilots. This technology will allow surgical residents to practice even the most delicate procedures with the aid of a computer.

Movement simulation is another area of development that relies on virtual reality. Simulation of motion will allow research in orthopedics to make advances in prosthetic development and joint illness treatment (Thalman, 1994).

Psychiatric uses for virtual reality focus on behavioral and knowledge-based animation. Virtual counseling sessions are available and may be used more frequently in the future. The possibilities are limitless for research and experimentation.

Virtual reality is currently being combined with robotics to develop new minimally invasive surgical procedures. Small robotics instruments can be coupled with virtual reality to perform surgical procedures that were previously impossible. This precise instrument will produce less surgical trauma and therefore decrease the amount of time for healing.

The applications of virtual reality in health care seem to be endless. For example, virtual reality may be the method of choice for keeping a patient occupied during the long time periods required for MR studies. It can be used to practice all types of manual skills in a totally nonthreatening, risk-free environment. Patient education in both concepts and skills will be greatly improved using virtual reality. For example, a diabetic could learn to give himself or herself injections with appropriate virtual reality software and hardware.

As health care changes and new skills are learned, virtual reality will play a key role for nurses in learning these skills. A virtual reality skills laboratory could be easily accessed for practice and demonstration of nursing competencies. Virtual reality will also provide a tremendous opportunity for practicing skills that are used infrequently.

Wireless Communication

Wireless communication is advancing rapidly. The cellular telephone has already changed much of the way in which we communicate. Other wireless devices are beginning to crowd the airwaves. This may create some interesting problems for health care. Many facilities are experiencing dead areas where beepers and other equipment will not work because of the density of electronic equipment. Also, wireless systems in health care settings will need to use nonpublic frequencies as a security measure to prevent inadvertent reception of confidential information.

The Internet

Much has been written in the 1990s about the information superhighway. The Internet opens the possibility of interfacing huge health-related computer systems. As technology progresses in this area, health care will continue to be affected. The information superhighway will provide immediate access to all types of information that previously took months to distribute. Again, legal and risk management issues will arise and will need to be addressed carefully.

Robotics

The use of robotics continues to increase in health care. Robots are being used to deliver supplies and to perform surgery. Another use for robots may include transport of patients and/or health care workers.

Patients with all types of impaired mobility will benefit from the use of robotics. Not only can robotics be used in artificial limbs, they can serve as retrieving devices for the immobile patient.

Robots will be increasingly used in the transport and preparation of hazardous material. They can be a great help to the nurse in daily activities of delivering supplies and transporting specimens.

KEY
CONCEPTS

- Each professional caregiver will be able to input his or her patient care notes with voice activated documentation systems.
- Each professional nurse will have the opportunity to develop adequate clinical skills using virtual reality technology.
- As a beginning professional nurse, you may be assigned a robot as your dyad team member.

LEARNING
CHALLENGE

1. You are working with a nurse who has no hands-on clinical experience. This nurse learned all her skills via virtual reality. How will this affect your working relationship with her? What will you want to be certain that she knows as a member of the health care team?
2. Identify five clinical uses for virtual reality.

Financial Impact of Technology

New technology is exciting and offers many opportunities as well as challenges to the beginning nurse. It is not without costs, however. For years, health care providers have been hesitant to discuss the cost of health care. It seemed uncaring to put a price tag on someone's health, or cure, or life. In reality, and in silence, we do that every day we practice.

Not everyone has access to the latest technology. Most often this occurs by default rather than by plan. The latest technology may not be available at a certain health care facility for that one patient who is there and needs it.

Management must address the issue of the cost of new technology. There is a limit to the resources that are available, and funding is becoming an increasingly important issue. Rarely is reimbursement based on charges. For many health care facilities, reimbursement is on a per patient day basis or by diagnosis-related group. This type of reimbursement structure is clearly a disincentive to the acquisition of new technology.

All new technology will be evaluated on a cost basis. If a technology can improve outcomes and reduce cost, it will have a much better chance of being installed and surviving. We cannot choose to disregard the financial side. Ultimately, someone has to pay for new technology.

The cost of care often creates a dilemma for the nurse. Nurses have been taught to do everything possible for the patient. If a hospital is forced to close as a result of financial failure, however, nurses will not have the opportunity to treat the patients whom the hospital had served. It is therefore important to provide quality care in a cost-effective environment. As a profession, nursing is continually becoming more cost conscious.

KEY
CONCEPT

- As a beginning professional nurse, you will play an active part in the competitive game of quality care and cost every day that you practice.

LEARNING
CHALLENGE

You are the newest member of the committee responsible for limiting the use of technology given financial constraints. How would you evaluate technology as it relates to cost? How would your committee play a role in the rationing of health care?

ETHICAL AND LEGAL CONCERNS

Bioethical Issues

As technology advances, bioethical issues increase. Bioethics relates to biological ethical issues. Many health care providers rely on ethics committees to help them deal with these issues. Ethics committees are multidisciplinary in their membership and approach and provide a forum for ethics discussions. The process of ethical decision making requires the use of reason and intellect. Ethical decisions and moral choices are necessarily influenced by individuals' values and world view. Ethical issues are often difficult for the health care team because there is usually not a single right answer.

One of the frequently debated ethical-technological questions is the high cost of health care. Technology is expensive, which could lead to rationing of certain types of care or treatments. In 1993, infant Siamese twins joined at the heart and liver were surgically separated at a phenomenal cost. This incident sparked numerous ethical debates about how much money should be spent when the chance for a successful outcome is extremely small. In this particular case, both infants died within months of the surgery. On the other hand, those in favor of the surgery argued that much was learned from the performance of the procedure.

Bioethical issues frequently debated include Do Not Resuscitate orders, withdrawal of life support, abortion, assisted reproduction, neonatal intensive care, and organ transplantation. All these issues have arisen as a result of advanced technology.

KEY
CONCEPTS

- The downside of a technological advance is a bioethical dilemma.
- A bioethical issue is a field of gray shades.
- Consensus on a bioethical issue should be developed through a synergy of patient, family, community, and health care provider perspectives and concerns.

LEARNING
CHALLENGE
A child who is terminally ill is being kept alive by artificial means. You and other members of the staff believe that this child is suffering and has no hope for recovery. What would be your first step in resolving this ethical dilemma? How would you get an ethics consult? Should the family be involved?

Legal/Risk Management Issues

Liability

Technology is advancing so rapidly that most health professionals do not understand how many highly technical devices work. These devices are often used based on anticipated results rather than on a working knowledge of the technology. If a health care worker does not understand the technology, he or she may feel insecure and may focus on the technology and not on communicating with the patient. As a result, the patient may not develop a sense of trust in the staff. This can create a greater risk because a patient who feels less trust is more apt to bring legal action (Youngberg, 1993).

Using technological devices increases the risk for liability exposure. Therefore, it is important that risk management and quality assurance issues are carefully considered when modern technology will be in use. Liability is usually related to negligence (Youngberg, 1993). The most frequent areas of concern are the following:

- misdiagnosis or failure to diagnose
- use of defective equipment
- misuse of equipment
- absence of appropriate equipment
- improper selection of equipment or tests
- improper inspection, maintenance, or repair of equipment
- lack of informed consent

In legal terms, negligence liability occurs when it can be shown that duty was owed, that duty was breached, that injury occurred, and that the injury was a result of the duty breached (Youngberg, 1993). In other words, something could have been done for the patient, it was not done, thus harm was done, and the harm was a direct result of what was not done for the patient.

Another area of liability often related to modern technology is product liability. This type of liability is most often related to allegations of defective products in that the product is said to be dangerous or does not do what it claims to do. Product liability places both the manufacturer and the hospital at risk.

The nurse may be asked to testify or serve as an expert witness in negligence liability cases. In some cases the nurse may be the defendant. Certain actions by the nurse will decrease the risk of negligence liability. Accurate, timely documentation is one crucial factor. Another is good rapport with the patient. When a patient trusts the health care system and health care personnel, he or she often has a better understanding of events and outcomes and may be less likely to pursue legal action.

Another area of risk management for the future will involve the availability of technology. Are we obligated to have the best technology available? Is the latest technology always the best? What happens when we are not trained to use new technology? These are some of the questions that will face today's beginning practitioner.

Brain Death

Brain death is not only an ethical issue but also a medical-legal issue. Brain death has been redefined several times in the past few years. Redefinition has been necessary because the high-technology environment has made it difficult to delineate brain death. The definition is generally determined by the state and interpreted by the health care facility (Youngberg, 1993). The following definition of brain death is used in the state of Alabama (Kowalsky, Willard, Jackson, & Troxell, 1990, p. 24):

> A person is considered medically and legally dead if, in the opinion of a medical doctor licensed in Alabama, based on usual and customary standards of medical practice in the community, there is no spontaneous respiratory or cardiac function and there is no expectation of recovery of spontaneous respiratory or cardiac function.
>
> In the case when respiratory and cardiac function are maintained by artificial means, a person is considered medically and legally dead if, in the opinion of a medical doctor licensed in Alabama, based on usual and customary standards of medical practice in the community for the determination by objective neurological testing of total and irreversible cessation of brain function, there is total and irreversible cessation of brain function. Death may be pronounced in this circumstance before artificial means of maintaining respiratory and cardiac function are terminated. In the case described in this subsection, there shall be independent confirmation of the death by another medical doctor licensed in Alabama.

Advance Directives

The Patient Self-Determination Act went into effect in December 1991 (Allen, 1993). This act requires that all hospitals and nursing homes receiving federal funds inform each patient about advance directives. An **advance directive** is a document filed by an individual giving direction about medical care in the event that the individual can no longer make his or her wishes known. This act has been difficult to implement, but it has provided a mechanism for patients to make their wishes known.

One of the legal issues surrounding an advance directive occurs when the family is not in agreement with the directive. In most cases, the family can overrule the individual's advance directive.

Do Not Resuscitate Orders

The decision not to resuscitate a patient must be made by the health care team and the family. An advance directive may give guidance in some cases, but it is generally a decision that is based on the health care team's assessment of the patient's potential for recovery.

Once resuscitative measures have been initiated, it is often difficult to reverse the situation. It is often more difficult for the health care team to withdraw life support than it is to withhold treatment. It can be argued that there is no legal or moral difference between the two situations, but most members of the health team are more reluctant to discontinue support once it has begun. It is of extreme importance that decisions not to resuscitate are well thought out by the family and clearly documented in the patient record by members of the health care team.

The nurse, having spent a great deal of time with the patient and family and having established rapport with them, has the opportunity to counsel the family in this decision-making process. Often the family will ask the nurse about the Do Not Resuscitate issue. The family members may be divided as to what course of action to take. Often they are seeking information and will have many questions. The nurse can play a key role in helping them reach a decision by being supportive of their wishes and coordinating access to information from the physician, spiritual supporter, or other members of the health care team.

KEY CONCEPTS

- Doing the right thing well always includes a nurse's accurate and timely documentation.
- A nurse should know the definition of brain death in the state in which he or she is practicing.
- Frequently, family members as well as health care providers find it difficult to accept the legal choices a person has made about his or her final destiny.
- Assisting family members in dealing with the issue of Do Not Resuscitate orders may involve more caring than later assisting them in dealing with the issue of withdrawal of life support.

**LEARNING
CHALLENGE**

1. As a beginning practitioner, what is your role in dealing with advance directives? What role does the family play? How would you explain an advance directive to the nursing assistant working with you?
2. You are asked to be an expert witness for the prosecution in a negligence case against a nurse. How would you decide whether to be a witness? What information would be essential in your decision?

CONCLUSION

New technological breakthroughs are occurring on a daily basis, and it would be impossible to address all of them in a single chapter. This chapter has summarized the most critical areas related to technological advances that are affecting health care.

New technology is exciting and stimulating. Although it presents new challenges to health care, it also gives new hope. The future in health care will be more exciting than the past because of technology. The nurse's challenge will be to keep technology and caring in the proper balance. The machines of the future will be able to accomplish unbelievable tasks, but they will never be able to provide the human touch and understanding of the nurse.

REFERENCES

Allen, A. (1993). Issues of consequence . . . rapid advances in scientific knowledge and technology engender ethical and moral concerns. *Journal of Post Anesthesia Nursing, 8*, 353–354.

Betts, M. (1994). Designing doctor-friendly systems a chore. *Computerworld, 12*, 76.

Dyer, H. (1990). The effects of CD-ROM on library services. *Health Libraries Review, 7* (4), 196–203.

Frick, T., Rein, A., & Parks, V. (1993). Benefits of an automated narcotic retrieval system. *Nursing Management, 24* (7), 57–59.

Greenspan, J.S. (1993). Liquid ventilation: A developing technology. *Neonatal Network, 12* (4), 23–24.

Huber, S.L. (1993). Strategic management of biotechnology agents. *American Journal of Hospital Pharmacy, 27* (2), 1–3.

Jones, S.L. (1993). Genetic based and assisted reproductive technology of the 21st century. *Journal of Obstetric, Gynecologic and Neonatal Nursing, 23* (2), 160–165.

Kiplinger, A., & Kiplinger, K. (1990). 90's technology will cure many health care ills. *Hospitals, 64*, 1–8.

Kowalsky, A.D., Willard, S.C., Jackson, W.L., & Troxell, T.R. (1990). *Code of Alabama* (Vol. 14). Charlottesville, VA: Michie.

Lumsdon, K., & Anderson, H.J. (1992). Cancer at the crossroads. *Hospitals, 66*, 22–30.

Maley, R., & Epstein, A. (1993). *High technology in health care.* Chicago: American Hospital Publishing.

Milholland, D. (1993). Privacy and confidentiality of patient information: Challenges for nursing. *Journal of Nursing Administration, 24* (7), 19–24.

Satava, R. (1993). Virtual reality surgical simulator. The first step. *Surgical Endoscopy, 7* (3), 203–205.

Thalman, N. (1994). Towards virtual humans in medicine: A prospective view. *Computerized Medical Imaging Graphics, 18* (2), 97–106.

Youngberg, B.J. (1993). *Quality and risk management in health care.* Gaithersburg, MD: Aspen.

SUGGESTED READING

Belton, K., & Dick, R. (1993). Voice-recognition technology: Key to the computer based patient record. *Journal of the American Medical Record Association, 62* (7), 27–32.

Bertolini, C. (1992). Ethical decision making in intensive care: A nurse's perspective. *Intensive Critical Care Nursing, 10* (1), 58–63.

Bleecker, G. (1993). Reimbursement and pharmaco-economic perspectives in biotechnology. *American Journal of Hospital Pharmacy, 7,* 27–30.

Bond, N., Phillips, P., & Rollins, J.A. (1994). Family-centered care at home for families with children who are technology dependent. *Pediatric Nursing, 20* (2), 123–130, 132–133.

Casey, M., & Savelle-Dunn, J. (1994). Sketching the future: Trends influence nursing informatics. *Journal of Obstetric, Gynecologic and Neonatal Nursing, 23* (2), 175–182.

Clouser, K.D., & Gert, B. (1990). A critique of principlism. *Journal of Medical Philosophy, 15* (2), 219–236.

Farrell, M., & Lewis, D. (1993). Brain death in the pediatric patient: Historical, sociological, medical, religious, cultural, legal and ethical considerations. *Critical Care Medicine, 2* (12), 1951–1965.

Furst, E. (1994). Cardiovascular technology: The Safe Medical Act. *Journal of Cardiovascular Nursing, 8* (2), 79–85.

Godde, C., & Hahm, S. (1993). Oocyte donation and in vitro fertilization: The nurse's role with ethical and legal issues. *Journal of Obstetric, Gynecologic and Neonatal Nursing, 22* (2), 106–111.

Harms, D., & Giordano, J. (1993). Ethical issues in high risk infant care. *Issues in Comprehensive Pediatric Nursing, 13* (1), 1–14.

Iserson, K.V. (1993). A simplified prehospital advance directive law: Arizona's approach. *Annals of Emergency Medicine, 22* (11), 1703–1710.

Lynch, D., & Kordis, P. (1988). *Strategy of the dolphin: Scoring a win in a chaotic world.* New York: Fawcett Columbine.

Minnick, A., Pische-Winn, K., & Sterk, M.B. (1993). Introducing a two-way wireless communication system. *Nursing Management, 25* (7), 42–47.

Quimby, C. (1994). Women and the family of the future. *Journal of Obstetric, Gynecologic and Neonatal Nursing, 23* (2), 1113–1123.

Schenker, J. (1993). Pre embryo: Therapeutic approaches. *Annals of Medicine, 25* (3), 265–270.

Simpson, R. (1993). Managing innovative technology. *Nursing Management, 24* (10), 18–19.

Slomka, J. (1992). The negotiation of death: Clinical decision making at the end of life. *Social Science and Medicine, 35,* 251–259.

Sulmasy, D.P. (1992). Physicians, cost control, and ethics. *Annals of Internal Medicine, 116* (11), 920–926.

Tonges, M., & Laurenz, E. (1993). Re-engineering: The work redesign technology. *Journal of Nursing Administration, 10,* 15–22.

CHAPTER 14

A Glimpse over the Horizon: The Future of Advanced Practice Nursing

Tim Porter-O'Grady

CHAPTER OBJECTIVES

At the completion of this chapter, the beginning professional nurse will be able to:

1. define the context and the changes in health care affecting the role of advanced practice nursing
2. identify three emerging characteristics of advanced practice affecting the future delivery of health services

3. outline the basic elements and characteristics of advanced practice nursing within the format of a continuum of care over the next two decades

CRITICAL THINKING CHALLENGE What are the possible emerging service models that will facilitate the use of the role of nurses in advanced practice? What kinds of partnerships will emerge that will include nurses in advanced practice? What will the continuum of care look like, and what positioning will nurses in advanced practice have within it? What is the relationship of nurses in advanced practice with other nurses along the continuum of care?

There are enormous forces affecting the delivery of health care services in the current marketplace. These forces are affecting every aspect of the delivery of health care and will challenge basic notions regarding health care and service delivery for at least the next two decades (Anderson, 1993). Although every aspect of nursing practice is being challenged by the changes occurring in the economic, social, and technological arenas, none is more dramatically affected than the role of the nurse in advanced practice. Economic influences alone have driven significant changes in the mix and role of providers, requiring a number of different responses to health service change and providing the foundations for a different focus for the delivery of those services (Brown & McCool, 1990).

Physician-driven medical care processes have determined the delivery of health care services for most of this century (Starr, 1992). Much of the institutionalization of health care has been a result of medical model approaches to the delivery of health care services (Johnson, 1992). Patients have come to hospitals for the purposes of receiving physician services and for 24-hour observation based primarily upon medical protocols and plans outlined for those patients. Although nursing clearly has had a knowledge base and practice framework of its own, nurses have been subordinated historically in institutional models to those of physicians (Ashley, 1976).

Increasingly, in the modernization of health care, medical intervention and other sickness-based approaches have come under significant examination and closer scrutiny (Relman, 1988). Newer approaches and different kinds of models of health care have emerged in response to the need for a much more extensive and comprehensive approach to individual and community health. Along this pathway, the role of other providers, either as extenders of physician services or complementary to medical practice, has become of serious interest to the leadership in the health care system. It is within this context that the role of the advanced practice nurse has emerged. The two primary pathways, nurse specialization and nurse practitioner, have been the context for much of the functional role of advanced practice nurses for the last two and a half decades. The primary roles that have emerged are clinical specialists, nurse practitioners, certified nurse-midwives, and certified nurse anesthetists.

The unfolding of these roles has not been without its challenges. Although there has been a specific need for the kinds of services these providers offer, others (predominantly physicians) have had some difficulty with the unfolding character of the roles in terms of health care delivery. Increasing dependence on the permission and approval of physician practitioners has limited the full expression of the roles within the context of the nursing frame of reference. As a result, much of the perception and indeed many of the activities of these practitioners do appear to be predominantly subsets of medical practice.

Although conceptually and theoretically unfounded, the perceptions of the advanced nursing practice base and expectations from physicians, other health care providers, and the community related to the activities of nurses in advanced practice point toward seeing advanced nursing practice as a subset of medical practice. This has created some critical challenges with regard to the legitimate and viable role of nurses in advanced practice, resulting in some confusion and uncertainty about the character of the role in the following areas:

- The parameters of nurses in advanced practice with regard to practice and competence limits are unclear.
- The legal framework for advanced practice focuses on function rather than role.
- The functional authority for the patient of nurses in advanced practice is subordinated to medical authority.
- Existing physician, patient, legal, and structural requirements limit the ability of the nurse practitioner to establish an independent role in relationship to patient care.
- Many functional components of the role of nurses in advanced practice cross or affect medical boundaries of practice, creating conflict between the roles.
- The role of the advanced practice nurse creates confusion in the nursing discipline itself. Relationships, roles, partnerships, and specified functions among practitioners are unclear, depending on the character of the organization and the nature of the relationship among the various nursing roles.
- There is uncertainty about the specific character of nurses in advanced practice, especially those in nurse practitioner roles. Because of the

large functional content of practitioner roles, it is unclear whether they are a functional subset of the medical frame of reference or an extension of the nursing practice framework. That lack of clarity creates confusion in the discipline and affects support for it.

Many of these conflicts relate to dramatic changes in the expectations for and impact of the nurse's role in the delivery of health care services. Because many of the primary care services for patients in managing their life processes are not provided by physicians, some bridge between managing life processes and medical interventions is certainly needed. The integration of nursing-based roles related to the life management process and medical roles related to diagnosis and intervention has resulted in the advanced practice nurse being a key player in bridging these two elements (Flynn & Kilgallen, 1993).

As a result of these key characteristics, nurses in advanced practice have provided a wide variety of roles both inside institutions and in the larger community. From the role of specialty expert to practitioner roles in clinics, rural settings, and urban, institutional, and work settings, there is ample evidence of the broad base of utilization for the role of the nurse in advanced practice (Newman, Lamb, & Michaels, 1991).

The **clinical specialist in nursing** is an advanced practice delineation that indicates a higher intensity of knowledge in a specific specialty area and has unfolded mostly as an institutional practice. These primarily hospital-based specialists focus on some element of nursing care in an advanced practice format in a wide variety of specialty areas. Often, there are as many clinical nurse specialists in specialty practice delineations as there are divisions of practice. These individuals focus on a higher level of complexity and frequently play out the expert role in the delivery of these highly specialized clinical services. Therein lies the challenge of the role as well.

Clinical nurse specialists have been looked at by hospitals as a luxury rather than as a requisite for high-level, high-quality, complex care. Even though care has become more intense and increasingly complex in institutions, the role of the clinical specialist has not been greatly expanded. Often because specialization and advanced education in nursing practice are not of value to the institution, these roles have not been integrated into the nurse staffing process in unit-based clinical care. Furthermore, the use of clinical nurse specialists has often been predominantly for roles other than in-depth practice activities. In many ways, the specialist has been taken away from advanced expert practice and placed into roles related to special programming, delegated functional management, quality improvement activities, and education and development as well as a host of special projects and support activities. The problem with this is that the nurse in advanced clinical specialty practice should have a primary focus on patient care. His or her frame of reference and functional value are in roles specific to patient care services. The use of these practitioners for other activities has made it challenging to define specifically their value within the context of patient care.

THE NURSE PRACTITIONER ROLE

On the other hand, the **nurse practitioner** role has unfolded primarily as a response to the need for community-based practitioners either in areas that are underserved by physicians or as an extension of the physician role. The nurse practitioner is predominantly grounded in clinical practice with a solid relationship directly with the patient. Little of the expectation for the nurse practitioner role relates to meeting organizational or institutional needs. Therefore, there is a perception of a more independent role for the nurse practitioner than for the clinical nurse specialist. The practitioner's primary function has also been related more clearly to the patient than to the organization. In this way, the functional characteristics of the role are more clinically oriented (Diers, 1993).

The education and development of the nurse practitioner have also paralleled more closely the medical model clinical approach. Although the clinical content of the preparation of the clinical nurse specialist may be as intense, the focus and function of this role are more developmental and less interventive. The nurse practitioner role focuses on specified clinical activities meant to relate particularly to patient populations in an intervention framework. Therefore, it has more of the character of medical practice than it appears to have of traditional views of nursing practice. It is nevertheless founded on the principles of nursing practice. Its application and expectation come out of a nursing frame of reference. Its value to the community, however, is often seen by both health practitioners and patients in the community within the medical frame of reference.

This therefore creates an increasing source of frustration and conflict between the two major nurse advanced practice roles. Furthermore, because of the difference in the preparation of each role, the relationship between these two advanced practice categories is relatively weak. They are often seen as separate from each other with almost no connection They are rarely seen as roles that have a common theoretical, conceptual, and contextual bond in the advanced nursing practice arena.

At the same time, physicians and other primary health care decision makers have a difficult time sorting out their relationship to the advanced nurse practice role (De Angelis, 1994). Because nurses in advanced practice act under the auspices of a separate legal entity that is not accountable to another discipline (e.g. medicine), the trust between the nursing advanced practitioner and physicians and other disciplines is not sufficiently developed. Their role is not universally perceived as a benefit to the delivery of health care services. Furthermore, the normative perception of the nurse's role in relatively institutional frames of reference does not make it possible to obtain the breadth and intensity of support from nursing colleagues that could strengthen and clarify the character of that role within the nursing frame of reference. Frequently the role of the nurse in advanced practice, most notably the nurse practitioner role, exists "between the devil and deep blue sea." These nurses lack active support from physician colleagues, who may see them as a possible threat, and from nursing colleagues, who may see them as disconnected from the nursing mainstream. This creates essentially a no-man's land for any solid role identification for nurses in advanced practice and especially for nurse practitioners (Fagin, 1992).

CRITICAL CHALLENGES

The current conflicts in the roles of advanced practice nurses have many implications (Exhibit 14–1) and lead to the following conclusions:

- There has been a concerted and determined identification of a need for nurses in advanced practice in both institutions and the community.
- The categorization of nurses in advanced practice—clinical nurse specialists and nurse practitioners (including midwives and nurse anesthetists)—creates conflict between the roles with regard to the parameters and perceptions of each.
- The relationship, practice parameters, and interaction of nurse practitioners with physicians and other disciplines create challenges regarding values and role identification. Problems emerge with regard to positioning of the nurse practitioner between nursing and medicine. Concomitantly, the role of the clinical nurse specialist is viewed as a luxury rather than a requisite for expert practice, thereby limiting access of clinical nurse specialists to the health care system as well as circumscribing their desirability and employment opportunities.

KEY CONCEPT
- The role of the advanced practice nurse is growing. It will become increasingly important. This new emphasis will require more focus on the role and will raise questions about how it fits into a primary care health model and how it relates to other disciplines in providing service.

Exhibit 14–1 Role Conflicts: Implications for Nurses' Action

Clinical Nurse Specialists

- Define more clearly the role of expertise within the context of nursing practice.
- Provide a stronger knowledge base for nursing-defined practice within the institutional model.
- Increase the character of the learning continuum for nursing along a novice-to-expert pathway.
- Contribute significantly to the knowledge and development of the scientific and practice base of nursing, especially within hospital institutions.
- Expand the perception of the contribution that nursing makes to patient care delivery by virtue of the expansion of clinical knowledge.

Nurse Practitioners (including Nurse-Midwives and Nurse Anesthetists)

- Provide a nursing frame of reference to clinical intervention and practice in community models.
- Strengthen the interdependent role of the nurse as a primary provider of clinical services.
- Move the focus from medical intervention to life management processes within a contextual frame of reference.
- Meet a defined need for health care practitioners in communities and locations where such health care services were not otherwise available.
- Develop clinical role and a specific nursing identity within the patient services community with a high level of acceptance and evaluation with the patient and provider community.

LEARNING CHALLENGE

1. How does a focus on primary care change the opportunities for nurses in advanced practice?
2. What is the difference between nurse practitioners and clinical nurse specialists and how can they be bridged in a primary care delivery system?
3. What is unique about nursing that differentiates nurses from other providers in a multidisciplinary practice environment?

NEW CONTEXTS FOR HEALTH CARE SERVICE DELIVERY

There are significant changes emerging on the health care horizon. The introduction of major initiatives for health reform in the mid-1990s has led to increased transformation in all health care services. Some changes are being driven by legislation, others by economic realities, and still others by advances in technology (Buerhaus, 1994).

Social Forces

On the verge of the new century, Western civilization is at a major paradigmatic moment. Social and economic forces are converging to create new social and financial imperatives for a global economy (Barnet & Cavanagh, 1994). The globalization of strategies and activities in a much broader social context is influencing the delivery of health care services just as it is having an impact on every other arena of social life (Toffler, 1990).

The globalization of society, driven by the possibilities inherent in communication technology, is creating a new reality for everyone. National boundaries are shifting, political and social relationships are changing, and social strategies of the Cold War era are adjusting to new configurations and relationships unfolding on the global stage (Belli, 1991). The impact of these shifts is changing the very nature of competition and the activities of the workplace in a number of different settings around the world.

The regionalization of international society and international competition has changed the social climate for work. Research reflecting relationships between workers and their workplace reveals the need for a much stronger relationship at the point of service and productivity. Workers have an impact on the goals, purposes, and outcomes of every organizational system. Strategies such as total quality management, continuous quality improvement, work redesign, shared governance, integration of the organization, and service- and product-focused strategies have changed the very character of the workplace and have affected every social configuration. Downsizing, reconfiguration of work, technological retooling, integration of organizational systems, mergers, and national and international partnerships all reflect the changing social character driving much of the social influences governing every system (Hammer & Champy, 1993).

Health care is influenced by this social change, resulting in the creation of an impetus for integration, linkage along the continuum of care, building of the continuum process, abandonment of institutional models for providing health care services, structuring of health care around the point of service, and creation of partnerships between providers and services (Conrad, 1993). These are all examples of the major thrusts toward community-based health services driven by social change.

This new social compact is challenging the very character of health care service delivery. The medical model, no longer a realistic and applicable model for defining the nature of health care, is being challenged in a number of subtle and not so subtle ways (MacDonald, 1994). Diagnosis of and interventions for sickness as the predominant clinical strategy no longer represent an effective way of managing the health care of society. This new paradigm challenges the very character of the relationship between the health care system and the greater society within which it unfolds.

Integration has become an imperative for the delivery of health care services, such that every practitioner plays a role along the continuum of care. Delineating the role and relationship of practitioners along the continuum of care becomes critical to the success of the clinical provision of services.

Health care organizations are attempting to address all the components of care delivery to ensure that the full range of benefits, processes, and activities that relate to the health of society operates under one umbrella. This effort means that providers also are being linked with and integrated into the delivery system, such that independent relationships in health care have become less viable. This means essentially that physicians and other practitioners will no longer be the independent, entrepreneurial providers of health care services they once were. Such a reality thrusts the providers together in an integrated organizational system, unprepared to deal with the noise associated with linking disparate players along the continuum of care (Meighan, 1994).

This process forces physicians into a partnership with other health providers, challenging them to create new, interdependent relationships among the various entities offering health care services along the continuum of care. This challenge is directed at other practitioners as well, including nurses in advanced practice. Indeed, the current social climate has created a crisis in traditional definitions of the advanced practice role and challenges the role to make the transition to a newer definition, linking and integrating the players along the continuum of care in a multifocal, multidisciplinary delivery system (Porter-O'Grady, 1994).

Economics

Providing the backdrop to many of the challenges of integration is the economic retooling of the nation. Driven by huge aggregates of debt accelerating over the last 30 years, the availability of economic resource has declined radically (Calleo, 1992). At the same time, an increase in the percentage of the Gross Domestic Product devoted to health care has robbed the nation of dollars required to attend to other social and developmental issues (Friedman, 1994). The more dollars spent on health care, the fewer dollars available to challenge and change society to reflect emerging new social paradigms.

The crisis that results from the current economic configuration is reflected in higher crime rates, increased poverty, lower levels of educational outcomes, and ethical, moral, and legal crises on a number of fronts within the social system (Jacobs, 1991). A growing emphasis on health care services has been the response to the products of the nation's social ills: violence, poverty, homelessness, and abuse.

To control the deficit and to gain more accountability for expenditures, the public sector has focused its attention on the health care delivery system and the number of dollars it takes to support it. In every venue, attempts to control the number of dollars going to health care have had a major impact on the availability of resources, the distribution of those resources throughout the health care system, and the kind, quality, and quantity of health care services being delivered.

The economic challenge has changed the very nature of the way that health care is provided through many more capitated and cost-managed approaches. The delivery system has been experimenting with radically different designs of health care services to reduce the total utilization costs associated with providing these services. Managed care, health maintenance organizations, capitated plans, and integrated health systems all represent the variety of strategies being undertaken to address this complex set of economic circumstances (Beckham, 1994a).

Embedded in this is the utilization of the role of various providers in the delivery of health care. Although financial constraint has been a major bane of the front-line practice of nursing in institutions, the change in the economic model has created a boom in the growth and value of advanced practice roles. The emphasis on advanced practice, primary care, preventive services, case management, and managed care strategies is a classic example of the economic refocusing on community health care to gain control of costs and to influence the character of health care delivery in the United States (Altman, 1990).

Economics and finance will have an impact on the configuration of health care for some time. Increasing concerns with the amount of money spent on health care and the availability of health care services to all Americans have placed a major political and economic conflict on the American agenda (Coile, 1993). Many attempts to reform the American health care delivery system have resulted in heated dialogue, polarization, and a wide range of political strategies whose outcome has been at best uncertain.

It is in this context that the role of the advanced practice nurse takes on special significance. Because of the overriding belief that the advanced practice nurse provides a wide range of viable, valuable, and cost-effective health care services, there is increasing interest in this role as a major provider in the emerging health care system.

In capitated approaches, the goal is to keep people from using high-intensity, illness-related services. Therefore, increasing the focus on wellness, prevention, nonintense clinical services, early intervention, and nonhospital activities will increase the viability of the advanced practice roles within the primary care framework (Coile, 1994). Because advanced practice nursing roles are relatively inexpensive compared with physician costs, the viability of these roles and their past evidence of efficacy and quality make them of increasing interest to policymakers, politicians, and payers.

Technology

There is probably no greater driving force in health care, pushing providers into the new paradigm, than technology (Rheingold, 1993). The burgeoning of technology has had the greatest impact on the kind and content of health care delivery, moving it in two decades toward what could not be achieved in the preceding century of medical practice.

Technology is making health care increasingly portable and noninstitutional. Through chemical, therapeutic, and technological equipment enhancements, the ability to undertake activities in a portable fashion has increased the mobility and flexibility of health care provision. Outpatient services in hospitals have grown at 18 times the rate of any other sector of health care (Nauert, 1992). Increasingly, technology has made bed-bound care obsolete in the treatment of and interventions for patients. At one time, treatments and interventions were only obtained through admission to the hospital. Today, through the use of laser therapy, antibody therapy, and chemical, mechanical, and computer technology, many of the procedures once done in the hospital are no longer necessary or are done in a far more flexible and fluid manner than in the past. Most of these procedures no longer require that the patient be admitted to the hospital, thus reducing the focus on hospital inpatient services as both the source of revenue and the place of care delivery in the health care system.

This challenge has serious implications for the health care professions, especially nursing. Because 68% of nurses practice at the bedside at a time when hospitals are moving away from bed-based care, the challenge for nursing is related directly to its mobility and ability to move quickly and with fluidity into new roles and practices in the health care delivery system (American Nurses Association, 1991).

Technology is also leading to renewed emphasis on the role of primary care services in preventing and alleviating the problems of illness before they become serious, requiring higher levels of intervention. Through enhanced diagnostic capability, health professionals are able to identify problems long before they become critical and require more expensive and intensive therapies and interventions.

Furthermore, as mentioned earlier, technology is making health care exceptionally portable, such that most of the technology is highly mobile and can be utilized in a number of settings simply by moving it there. In this way, rural and urban settings can have as much access to the technology of health care as the wealthier suburban settings, where such services are readily available (Tan, 1994).

Technology will continue to make health care increasingly portable and less intensive. The flexibility and variety of services that are available in a number of settings and the mobility of those services will create a new framework for health care delivery (Tonges & Lawrenz, 1993). This indicates a need for more flexible and fluid providers of health care services who can move into a variety of settings quickly to render health care services. Indeed, providers will need to bring those services to the community so that, through advantaging of people, the community can attain a higher level of health (Barger & Rosenfeld, 1993).

Here again, technology is making health care more accessible, affordable, and broad based. It is creating a decreasing dependence on institutional models and structures, however. As previously indicated, the majority of nurses practice in institutions. Therefore, it is critical that nurses become flexible and mobile in their response to the application of technology if they are to be able to address their own future viability in a radically altered health care system. Increasingly, this means deinstitutionalizing health care and bringing those services to where the patients are. In fact, it means making health care more "community-friendly" and accessible.

Summary

The preceding discussion has several implications for advanced practice nurses (Exhibit 14–2):

- Health care is being dramatically affected by social, technological, and economic forces.
- Social forces are creating a much more integrated, community-based approach to providing health care services.
- Economics is constraining the use of financial resources and capping dollars available for health care, thus forcing organizations to address more critically and specifically the costs associated with delivering health care services.
- Technology is increasingly making health care services portable, flexible, and customer- and community-friendly, thus changing the primary location within which health care services will be offered.

Exhibit 14–2 New Contexts for Health Care Delivery: Implications for Nurses'
Action

- Nurses will need to reflect on the deinstitutionalization of health care services and the movement toward a continuum of care.
- Job competence must be quickly replaced by career planning as the primary concern as nursing practice moves away from hospital-based systems.
- Nurses will need to be computer and technology literate as technology increasingly drives the framework and the architecture of health care service delivery.
- Social forces are converging to require that nurses advance their practice, develop broader-based skills, and respond more strongly to the primary care, noninstitutional, continuum-based activities that will become the centerpiece of health care delivery in the future.

KEY CONCEPTS

- The forces of change are creating a transformation in health care. This transformation is parallelling all the other changes affecting the globe.
- The view of the nurse in advanced practice must unfold within the context of these changes.
- The responses to change must always be seen through the lens of the new paradigm, not the framework out of which the changes are taking us.

LEARNING CHALLENGE

1. How does the transformation in health care affect the practice of every nurse?
2. What potential new roles emerge in a health system that is not focused on the hospital's role in service provision?
3. Do nurses make an economic or financial contribution to health services? How do you know, and what does it look like?

BREAKING THROUGH THE PARADIGM: CREATING A NEW FOUNDATION FOR ADVANCED PRACTICE

The emerging focus on the continuum of care in an integrated health care system creates a new range of opportunities for advanced practice nursing. Indeed, the economic and social changes are creating a strong foundation upon which advanced nursing practice can unfold. There is a need to understand what advanced practice will mean in this new setting, however.

The advanced practice of nursing requires a much broader definition and an understanding of the impact of advanced practice in the clinical setting.

As deinstitutionalization continues to unfold, institutional models of services for advanced practice become increasingly less viable (Vautier & Carey, 1994). Therefore, the old distinctions between clinical specialists and nurse practitioners become decreasingly viable as separate definers of the role of advanced practice. As a result, the need to integrate the educational development of advanced practice nurses into compatible tracks becomes important. The dramatic change in health service forcefully influences the design of curricula and the preparation of advanced practice nurses. There are elements in the clinical nurse specialist role that need to be in the nurse practitioner role, and vice versa. As subscriber-based approaches to health care continue to develop, however, changes in the content and character of both roles are indicated.

Preparation of the nurse in advanced practice must be broader based than currently defined. Although the diagnostic and therapeutic interventional skills and talents of the nurse practitioner continue to be essential, embedding the developmental, educational, and research base of the clinical nurse specialist into the role also becomes important. Therefore, it is not an "either–or" set of circumstances that must be considered in the preparation of the advanced practice nurse. Indeed, as integration of the skill sets found in both pathways becomes critical to the provision of good health services, the success of the nurse in advanced practice depends more on their successful application.

Primary care, with its continuous focus on early identification, prevention, and intervention, requires stronger skills in life management than those currently incorporated into the nurse's role. Diagnostic and therapeutic intervention has been a strong value in nurse practitioner education. Challenging that as a fundamental core in the redesign of curricula will also be the influence of preventing illness and early introduction of health-based activities into the lives of subscribers to the health plan.

This means essentially that the skills of value in a health-based delivery system relate to social, community, and early preventive strategies that help the members of the community develop basic skills in healthy living and learn health-based habits that will ultimately result in less intense requirements for health care services. This will be more clearly reflected as the continuum becomes a more comprehensive framework for health care delivery.

THE CONTINUUM AS THE FOUNDATION FOR HEALTH RELATIONSHIPS

When the continuum becomes the focus of health care delivery, advanced practice takes on a different character. A system based on providing a continuum of services should prevent the need for high-intensity services. Within this continuum framework, institutional care services currently located in hospitals should be the court of last resort. Because these high-intensity, high-intervention services are exceptionally costly and will put a drain on capitated payments for health care, the goal of health care providers is to prevent people from ever having to use resource-intensive services. This means that the nurse in advanced practice has a fundamentally different focus in the application of his or her role:

- The goal is to avoid using health care services, keeping people as independent as possible.
- Subscribers must become more accountable for identifying activities that place them at high risk.
- The subscribers' culture and environment become the locus of control for ensuring health.
- The provider's role is to assist subscribers in maintaining the highest level of health to prevent the use of high-cost interventions.
- The provider must be more broadly based with a more sophisticated understanding of life management issues as a backdrop to addressing health care needs.

Increasingly, because of the need for a larger number of point-of-service players in the community, there will be a demand for a higher level of interdependent functioning on the part of the nursing professional. There simply is not a sufficient number of physicians to manage the primary care component of health care delivery. The transition of physician development and education toward preparing sufficient numbers of providers will take a significant period of time, longer than the health care system can afford to wait. Therefore, it is obvious that primary providers who are already prepared, licensed, and on a pathway that can accelerate their availability should be able to address health service needs. This is where nurses in advanced practice have special value.

The flexibility and fluidity of nurses in advanced practice in a wide variety of settings make them a valuable resource as case managers and continuum of care integrators along the patient pathway. Because of their location, viability, and flexibility, these practitioners provide a valuable resource in a community-based, noninstitutional continuum of care. Where utilized, they can actually reduce the total number of dollars expended in provider time in rendering care services through good clinical management of the patient. These providers focus on the management of life processes, thus controlling the use of high-cost resources.

In this framework, it is becoming increasingly visible to policymakers and the leadership in health care that nurses in advanced practice are a significant alternative to current practitioners (including physicians) in a much more point-of-service, primary care–driven health care system (Mundinger, 1994). The challenge of the times is not moving the system in the direction where need for services will accelerate but rather preparing the nurse in advanced practice to fulfill the requisites of these emerging roles.

NEW FOCUS FOR PLANNING FOR FUTURE NURSING ROLES

Clearly, in a movement to a noninstitutional continuum of care, bed-based service structures will have less impact on service. Therefore, continuing to prepare for nursing roles that are fundamentally institutional in focus is no longer a valid nursing resource strategy. Much of the growth in nursing practice in the future will be located in decentralized, community-based settings. This also indicates an increasing need for advanced preparation in nursing at an accelerated rate. The five new areas of major growth in nursing practice in a primary care environment are family health, adult health, care of women, care of children, and gerontology. Clearly, these five major growth areas indicate a thrust in nursing practice that represents more primary approaches to health care delivery than the old generalist/specialist, institutionally driven educational model for nursing evident in the old hospital service paradigm. Included in the above five major areas of emerging practice focus for the education of nurses are psychiatric/mental health nursing practice and preparation of nurses in advanced roles in administration. Increasing focus on psychiatric and mental health services and the administration of decentralized emerging health care models at the point of service is quickly accelerating as a point of emphasis in the transforming health care delivery system.

This increasing focus on advanced preparation in primary care arenas has many implications for advanced practice nurses (Exhibit 14–3). For one it means reallocating the development and education dollars from basic nursing education toward advanced practice preparation. Managed care strategies and management of care along the continuum will require accelerating levels of preparation for more interdependent roles in a noninstitutional framework. Nurses will establish much stronger partnerships with other advanced practice players in pharmacy, therapeutics, a variety of technologies, and other health intervention roles. This will require a level of articulation from nurses that is not currently realized in nursing preparation. The ability to integrate, dialogue, negotiate roles and relationships, and manage the continuum of care with other disciplines in a collateral and collaborative manner will require accelerating levels of preparation comparable to those of other disciplines. Nursing professional preparation currently does not provide the level of graduate preparation that is already available to other disciplines in clinically based or noninstitutional practice arrangements. Managing the continuum of care and associating with a multidisciplinary, multifocal managed care environment challenge the current competence of nurses at all levels of preparation, including advanced practice nurses.

Although nurse practitioners are prepared in advanced practice for clinical intervention, their social negotiation, interaction, and collaborative skills still may be less developed than they need to be for these nurses to integrate well within a team-based approach to the continuum of care. The preparation of these kinds of practitioners will have to accelerate by at least three times the current rate. At the same time, the number of beginning practitioners will have to be reduced so that nursing resources reflecting the level of current demand are utilized.

KEY CONCEPTS

- The new role of the nurse in advanced practice challenges older configurations and uses of the role in transforming the health care delivery system.
- Advanced practice roles require a stronger focus on integrating traditionally disparate practice delineations.
- The continuum of care requires the deinstitutionalization of nursing roles and relationships, demanding the reduction of bed-based nursing services.
- Preparation of nurses in advanced practice roles for the primary care continuum of care environment requires the comprehensive integration of nurses in advanced practice roles.
- Retooling educational preparation of nurses, deemphasizing beginning practice, and reemphasizing advanced practice will require a shift in resources and focus:
  1. reduce the number of basic practitioners prepared for hospital-based practice
  2. significantly diminish the numbers of associate degree nurses to a level appropriate to technical, highly structured roles
  3. reduce the total number of undergraduate nurses prepared to more directly parallel demand over the long-term economic and demand cycle
  4. increase dramatically the number of graduate programs in advanced practice, especially in primary care roles

Exhibit 14–3 Planning for Future Roles: Implications for Nurses' Action

---

- The continuum of care expands the role of the nurse and places him or her at the center of the delivery of health care.
- Nurses in advanced practice will be required, in increasing numbers, to provide services along the continuum of care.
- The continuum of care focuses on health, prevention, and life management strategies reflective of nursing preparation.
- The new focus on the continuum of care reemphasizes the role of the nurse as case manager and clinical integrator of provider services.
- New opportunities will emerge for the delivery of clinical care services in the primary care setting for which a wide variety of nurses are and can be prepared for the future.

**LEARNING
CHALLENGE**

1. What is different about the community that will require different preparation for nurses?
2. How will nurses adapt to a noninstitutional practice for nursing when the majority of nurses now practice in hospitals?
3. What roles appear to be emerging for nurses in advanced practice that are different from those currently available?

EMERGING ROLES OF NURSES IN ADVANCED PRACTICE

As a new focus emphasizing the continuum of care unfolds in the health care delivery system, opportunities for better defining the roles of the advanced practice nurse will emerge in the health care delivery system. Many of these roles will represent some of the characteristics of the current roles. Most of them, however, will reflect a different set of relationships in the health care system. These relationships now exemplify a different paradigm for both practice and the organization in a continuum of care delivery system.

The continuum of care is not focused especially or essentially on hospital-based services. Therefore, admission and discharge relationships between patients and providers are not critical to the success of the patient–provider relationship. Indeed, the emphasis in the new system will be avoiding such relationships. This means that the patient–provider relationship must be more focused on long-term strategies of health care than it is currently (Beckham, 1994b). Increasingly, as life management becomes the primary thrust of preventive and health maintenance services, a focus on establishing a relationship with the patient along the life continuum becomes critical to the success of the nurse in advanced practice.

Increasingly, the nurse in advanced practice will be a primary connection point between the provider and the consumer. Because subscriber-based approaches will essentially drive the marketplace, developing a relationship with the subscriber and maintaining that relationship over the long term will be essential to the economic and service viability of the system. The ability to intervene early in the delivery of health services when such intervention is necessary is also a fundamental component of an effective system (Fries, 1993). Therefore, the advanced practice nurse's primary task is to develop a relationship with the consumers in a given health system. Exhibit 14–4 lists some of the prerequisites for accomplishing that task.

The movement from health organization to health plan, representing a comprehensive array of responses to a predefined benefit package, means that a set of services will be determined in advance. Although these services initially may focus more on the illness end of the continuum during the transitional period, increasingly, as health care becomes focused on life management, higher levels of the patient–provider relationship based on healthy functioning will emerge in the advanced practitioner's role.

At the point of access, the consumer must continually be assessed with regard to health status and health service need. The role of the nurse in advanced practice in these settings will often be that of gatekeeper in conjunction with other primary providers, including the primary care physician. Because the goal is to avoid high costs in the maintenance of the relationship between the subscriber and the health professional, there will be an increasing desire to limit the amount of physician exposure that a particular subscriber might have. Increasing physician-driven clinical activity leads to an increase in costs. Therefore, the role of the advanced practice nurse is to provide care in a way that does not necessitate physician intervention until that intervention is essential. In this way, the lowest cost is engendered at the front end, and high-cost services are not utilized until they are needed.

This relationship between the primary provider (advanced practice nurse) and the subscriber means a number of changes for the nurse in advanced practice. Clearly, establishing healthy and viable relationships with a number of practitioners who may be assessing the patient along the continuum of care, without physician intervention, means that the nurse must be able to refer independently and interdependently to other practitioners across the continuum of services. Given the growing set of choices in health plans whose benefits are designed to facilitate the consumer's health, a range of health practitioners not currently covered by payment may be included in the health plan. This comprehensiveness of services becomes the critical competitive variable with regard to the viability, success, and desirability of any given health plan or service framework.

Exhibit 14–4 Emerging Roles for Nursing: Implications for Nurses' Action

- Preparation in advanced practice is the emerging arena of opportunity in nursing.
- Nurses now must focus on career development rather than job proficiency.
- Building partnerships with other disciplines in an interdisciplinary clinical relationship will be important to the future viability of nursing roles.
- Academic institutions must make it easier for basically prepared registered nurses to move quickly toward advanced practice roles in a user-sensitive educational pathway.
- New payment structures will require increasing accountability for the outcomes of service. Focusing on outcome must replace nurses' attachment to process if the discipline is to have an impact on value.

Of course, this will have an impact on state, federal, and accreditation regulations. The current legal framework for practice inadequately addresses the emerging reality. Nurses will have to focus more of their energy on reworking practice acts and relationships with other providers and regulators so that a more accurate legal and regulatory structure emerges for the changing health care field. This has already affected hospitals that are moving to broad-based, integrated health plans. Old constraint of trade laws and federal barriers to relationship building are quickly collapsing to accommodate the newer structures for health care services. Nurses must be as active in revising the limitations to adequate use of their services and resources, too.

The physician and other members of the health team meet to assess the activities of groups of patients or clinical activities within a specific benefit program of the health plan to determine viability, efficacy, and impact on the patient population. Therefore, team-based activities in advanced practice relate more to delineating the framework for practice than to focusing on any one particular event of practice. This will give the nurse in advanced practice much more liberty in the future with regard to guiding individual choices that the consumer might make for use of identified clinical resources. The primary role of the nurse in this scenario, besides providing services in managing lives, is to determine at what point an intersection with other health professionals needs to occur, what health professional needs to be seen, and at what level of intensity intervention is required. Also, the collaborative and collateral role of the nurse in advanced practice with the physician helps maintain the fluidity of clinical activities between both providers.

Facilitating this emerging role for the nurse in advanced practice are new payment models that look toward paying for services rather than for providers. Increasingly, as physicians become integrated with health plans and systems, individual physician payments for specified interventions will diminish. Payment for defined services will become the predominant mechanism for allocating financial resources. The intensity of the relationship between the health plan and the individual physicians will accelerate over time, creating a framework of relationship that provides no incentive to the physician to make unilateral intervention decisions for his or her own economic advantage. Increasingly, the goal of the payer will be to provide a range of services that keep the patient from higher intensities of care and to share the revenue enhancements that come from providing services at a lower cost. This ultimately expands the margin between what it costs the health plan to do business and the amount of income it retains from the plan's cost-effective management of its subscribers.

SUBSCRIBER ENROLLMENT AND IMPACT ON ADVANCED PRACTICE

The goal of health systems in the future will be to provide a comprehensive range of health services. The nurse in advanced practice will be the gatekeeper and moderator of the kinds and numbers of services provided. Also, the intensity of service requirements will be managed by the nurse in advanced practice to ensure that the highest level of service is provided at the lowest point of need. The advanced practice nurse's focus must also reflect sensitivity to maintaining the goal of highest level of independence of the patient to ensure that patients do not need to utilize high-cost, high-intensity services of the health plan until necessary in light of their needs. As a result, the nurse must perform the following key functions:

- continuously assess a defined group of patients along the continuum of care to determine their status and to maintain service within the context of their highest point of health
- continually define with the subscriber the kinds and levels of need that the subscriber has at any given time to obtain those needs and thereby maintain the highest level of health
- build a defined and effective relationship with other partners along the continuum of care to whom the subscriber can be referred to address any specified health needs
- maintain a continuing and ongoing relationship with the physician and other team members to assess the series of activities necessary to maintain the health of the subscribers

- intervene and or refer to other points in the system when the patient's health circumstance or illness condition demands a higher level of intensity or a broader-based approach to services

KEY CONCEPTS

- Nurses will have a stronger relationship with other disciplines and will practice in new arrangements and settings.
- Nurses must be prepared to exit hospital-focused practice in greater numbers, looking to other opportunities for building their skills and competence.
- The hospital will not be the only major place where opportunities for beginning and advanced practice are located.
- The focus for nursing practice must now be broad.
- The primary role of the nurse in advanced practice is imbedded in the continuum of care. Developing relationships along the continuum will be critical to the success of the role.
- Defining stronger relationships with the other health professions will be important to the success of the nurse in advanced practice. Building those relationships will be critical to managing the continuum of care.
- All care services will be moderated to the culture of the consumer. Adapting care to the consumer's context will be a major element in the role of the nurse in advanced practice.
- Nurses in advanced practice will become gatekeepers at a number of different points along the continuum of care. Connecting those points to maintain a seamless set of services for the consumer will be important to the viability of the health plan.
- Accountability will demand that the nurse in advanced practice be clear regarding the contribution he or she makes to the patient–provider relationship. Services rather than providers will be paid for, and therefore the outcome value of the service will be critical to the provider.

LEARNING CHALLENGE

1. What kinds of business skills will nurses in advanced practice need to succeed in the corporate world of health care?
2. What is the difference between an employed advanced practice nurse and an independent or contracted advanced practice nurse?
3. How do nurses in advanced practice indicate their value when there are many others who do not believe there is any distinctive value for nurses in advanced practice?

ACCOUNTABILITY AND THE ROLE OF ADVANCED PRACTICE

Historically, accountability for health services and the health system rested in the hands of administration and management leadership. Increasingly, as care becomes decentralized and service roles shift to point-of-service designs, accountability becomes an increasing obligation of practitioners at that point of service. Accountability is about outcomes, not process. Therefore, there must be some clear contributions to which the nurse in advanced practice commits as the new role unfolds in a continuum of care delivery system.

There are more diverse expectations of nurses in advanced practice, depending on the clinical service framework within which they find themselves. As those frameworks become better defined and the role becomes more critical to the management of patients, the nurse in advanced practice will have to indicate more clearly what his or her value is to the organization. Accountability is about value insofar as it indicates that there is a quid pro quo between cost and the functions and activities of any given role. If the nurse in advanced practice is to be viable, economic and financial value must also be indicated in his or her role. This will not be an accidental determination.

Increasingly in health care delivery, there are few functions and activities that are not related to some value to the organization. Rewards in the form of salary and hourly wage determinations are no longer a viable way of allocating fiscal resources in health care. In those older models, there is simply no relationship between the work and the products of that work. As service provision and the payment system that supports it change the nature of the interaction between work and payment, new reward approaches must be undertaken.

Nursing has historically had a poor relationship between what it does and how much its members get paid for work. Increasingly, as we move to point-of-service designs, the economic contribution and value of every nursing role will be critical to the success of the system. Payers for health care services will be interested in the real value of those who provide care and in relating what they are willing to pay for health care to what they feel they have a right to get in return. This is important to nurses because how much the payers are willing to provide influences the number and kind of health workers the system can support.

The nurse in advanced practice must engage the financial and economic processes in a way that results in determining the essential value of advanced practice nursing to the delivery of health care services. Value is critical to the effectiveness of the system. Increasingly, health plans will compete with other health plans for the kind and volume of subscribers whom they can serve in any given period of time. Two indicators will measure the outcomes of care: cost measures and quality indices based on national standards of comparison among providers and plans. Included in those comparative data will be the activities of the nurse in advanced practice and the value of that role's contribution to the bottom line of the organization as well as to the quality and comprehensiveness of its services. Nurses can no longer assume that they do not represent economic and financial determinants of value. Increasingly, the relationship between service and payment is critical to any single discipline's contribution to the health care delivery system.

There is clearly no doubt that nursing is a good value with regard to qualitative outcomes. The doubt arises when that value is translated into financial terms. Because there are generally poor measures of the financial contributions of nurses in advanced practice, the need to define these contributions will accelerate in managed care and capitated, subscriber-based approaches to the delivery of care services.

Through the use of a variety of techniques, including measuring work content, the needs of patients, the number of patients served, and what care providers do with patients, the nurse in advanced practice can begin to get at the essential value that he or she brings to the financial table. It is just as important for the nurse in advanced practice to know his or her economic contribution as it is for anyone else. In this frame of reference, the total cost involved in rendering care can be more accurately determined, and the percentage contribution to those outcomes of any given provider can also be effectively obtained.

Unlike the case with previous nursing roles in the old paradigm, it is vital for the nurse in advanced practice to begin to determine the value of the role in comparison with that of other roles. Value is a major indicator of relationship and power in the health care delivery system. If nurses in advanced practice are to accelerate their significance in the decision-making framework, a determination of their economic contribution must clearly precede any dialogue.

The critical pathway becomes the most successful vehicle in determining the relationship of providers to outcomes. Each of the providers participates in defining the critical elements along a clinical pathway for which mutual intervention and activity are required. Particular providers who made a contribution to the clinical outcome identify their role, their contribution, and their relationship to other providers along the clinical pathway. Identifying the critical relationship of each of the players, evaluating clinical outcome against individual activities, and dividing aggregated dollar values by the time, intensity, and volume contributions of each of the members result in the percentage contributions of each to the critical path. In this way, the nurse in advanced practice can determine his or her piece of the financial contribution to the continuum of care and to the bottom line of the organization supporting it.

In the old hospital model using nurses in advanced practice, institutions or physicians simply employed nurses in advanced practice and therefore subjugated their practice to the practice of the institution or service. Often physician practices or public health services have employed nurses in advanced practice, again subjugating nurses' practice decisions to those who own the practice or administer the service.

More often in the future, partnerships between practitioners and a health plan will mean negotiated roles and relationships rather than predefined and employee-based functions. To manage these new relationships, nurses in advanced practice must also learn negotiating skills to negotiate roles, responsibilities, and value, in terms of both economic and service, with physicians and other players within group practice arrangements (Kritek, 1994). Increasingly, as plans are integrated and physicians are a part of the plan, nurses in advanced practice will need to contract for their services within the context of the plan and its relationship with other providers. These contractual relationships define a much more partnered base for building the role of the nurse in advanced practice within the framework of the organizational system.

Also, nurses in advanced practice will find that relationships among entities along the continuum of care will be contracted relationships. Often, individual entities providing services at specific points along the continuum will have a contractual relationship with other members along the continuum. Increasingly, as the financial viability of purchasing or owning all the service arrangements along the continuum becomes less financially wise, more contractual and partnered relationships will emerge between and among the providers.

These partnered relationships will provide an opportunity for nurses in advanced practice to establish partnership relationships with other providers along the continuum of care. These partnership relationships may mean that nurses in advanced practice will create a corporate or contracted relationship with each other. Through the comprehensive aggregation of nurses in advanced practice, their corporate entity can contract collectively with a health plan, medical plan, or service delivery system for the full range of services offered.

Becoming a provider along the continuum of care within an incorporated nursing structure creates a stronger foundation for nurses in advanced practice as new practice models and arrangements are created through the use of their corporate structure. Because integration, relationship, and partnership are moderators of the kind and character of interactions along the continuum, it is as appropriate for nurses in advanced practice to offer a contracted corporate relationship as it is for physicians and any other providers. Although building the continuum of care may be some time away in the unfolding of the future of the health care delivery system, it becomes an effective framework for defining the relationship between nurses in advanced practice and other players in the continuum-based health care delivery system.

BUSINESS CONSIDERATIONS FOR NURSES IN ADVANCED PRACTICE

Of growing importance is the recognition that nurses in advanced practice must join with each other to provide a business relationship. This relationship will form the basis for contracting with other practitioners in a health plan. Nurses in advanced practice will need, in growing numbers, to form practice arrangements and corporate structures with each other and to contract collectively for relationships with other players or plans along the continuum of care. Building those structures and the business models necessary to enable them to be successful will require specific strategies that help the nurse in advanced practice maintain independence (Exhibit 14–5).

Building a Corporate Structure

Incorporation at the state level is not a difficult process. Most state corporation commissions have a process that allows groups or individuals to incorporate. Finding a name, filling out the application, and filing a fee generally are always required in building a beginning corporate framework. It is recom-

---

Exhibit 14–5 The Business of Health Care: Implications for Nurses' Action

- Partnership roles in primary care and health plan practices are emerging as a real opportunity for nurses in advanced practice.
- Corporate formation of groups of nurses in advanced practice can have major implications for the strength of nursing's contribution to health plans and clinical service structures.
- Physicians are now partners in health service delivery. Building successful relationships with them will be important to the success of advanced practice nurses.
- Close attention to the financial relationships in new practice arrangements is important in determining how professional practice is rewarded. Knowledge of the market and the financial circumstances of a partnership or employment opportunity is important to the advanced practice nurse's future success.

mended that an attorney be utilized to ensure that the basic contents of the corporate structure are in place. Advanced practice nurses who are intending to join together in corporate arrangements must be fairly clear about their goals, mission, and purposes. Agreements regarding roles and relationships, officers of the corporation, and functions and purposes of the corporate entity will need to be clear before incorporation occurs. A set of bylaws that govern the relationship among the providers, issues related to economic configurations, and the options and opportunities toward which the corporation seeks to direct its energies are critical components of initial dialogue regarding the incorporation.

It is important that agreement and understanding among the members of the corporation be apparent at the outset. Trying to deliberate roles and relationships after legal arrangements have been established is a much more difficult proposition than dealing with those issues before legal formation. The roles, relationships, and operational processes essential to ensure the integrity of the corporate entity need to be clarified at the outset of the relationship. Accountabilities of the members and the roles and contributions that each make to the enterprise also need to be clear at the outset.

The size of the membership, the character of the corporation, and the forming or owning/partner relationships must also be addressed at the initial stages of corporate formation. Building the relationships among the key players at the outset and identifying the expectations of their leadership roles will help ensure that all the elements necessary to maintain the corporate identity are addressed by the parties to it at the outset.

Business Plan

No new venture should begin without specific plans related to its activities being identified in advance. The purposes and direction of the organization are critical to its success as it begins to undertake its work. Nurses in advanced practice in incorporated or partnered relationships are going to need to articulate clearly the kinds of roles and services they expect to initiate in the course of their relationship. Because incorporating helps define the relationship among the members of the corporation and integrates their commitment to a common set of initiatives and goals, it is important that those be clear at the outset.

A business plan, which is a statement of intent, budgetary considerations, financial goals, and the activities related to achieving them, is an important first stage once the members of the organization have made the commitment and are clear about their desire to provide service. The business plan gives form to the framework for service. Many professional practice arrangements do not have business plans. As a result, their strategies, activities, intent, and direction are not clear to the members, and therefore process gets negotiated "on the go." The problem with this is that as opportunities and challenges arise, the organization, not having an established course of action and a clear set of directions enumerated for all the players, can begin to disintegrate, resulting in internal conflicts among the members of the practice arrangement.

Negotiating for Relationships

Whether the nurse in advanced practice is a member of a corporate group or negotiates individually, having a negotiating strategy and a clear set of parameters at the outset with regard to the relationship he or she wishes to establish is critical to long-term success. Understanding the market and the characteristics of the relationships in the market in which the nurse in advanced practice seeks opportunities is a critical prerequisite to negotiating roles in that market.

Recognizing opportunities for employment, contracting, or corporate networking is an essential first step. Knowing the marketplace and the relationships that are possible in it becomes a solid baseline upon which to plan one's connection to the marketplace. Also, focusing on the skills one brings to the market and the career opportunity they represent helps focus one's vision to those areas where there is a stronger potential for building a successful relationship.

Negotiating corporate, partnership, or employee contracts takes a basic level of skill. It is always wise for the nurse in advanced practice to engage in a course, program, or seminar on negotiating skills if he or she expects to market his or her skills to full advantage. Understanding the fiscal, service, and competitive characteristics of the individual market within which a nurse in advanced practice seeks a relationship sets a baseline for building a successful negotiating strategy. Here again, negotiation is dependent entirely upon how well one knows what the other person's position is, what his or her arguments will be, and how broad the range of his or her parameters or constraints might be going into the negotiation. Knowing as much as you can about the party with whom you are going to negotiate provides a strong knowledge base upon which to build those negotiations.

For the most part, nurses in advanced practice will be negotiating with health plans that are related to a hospital framework or to a physician or medical framework. It is important for the nurse in advanced practice to recognize the breadth of opportunities available within the entity with whom he or she is negotiating. There is a great need for primary care providers in advanced practice in a wide variety of settings. Therefore, the marketplace is anxious to have a relationship with available nurses in advanced practice. It is also clear that unique and creative arrangements are being explored in a number of different settings in the health care delivery system. As health care entities build along the continuum of care, newer kinds of relationships and creative contracts can generally be negotiated. This means that there is room for innovative approaches to establishing relationships between the nurse in advanced practice or an incorporated group of nurses in advanced practice and a health plan, physician practice plan, corporation, or other service entity.

Sharing risks as well as rewards is a strong position to take in negotiating. If the nurse in advanced practice is willing to share financial risks, the opportunity for increasing the availability of rewards and expanding the viability of the relationship is enhanced. Also, ensuring outcomes, both quantitative and qualitative, helps strengthen the negotiating position between nurses in advanced practice and the entities with whom they might relate.

There is increasing pressure on health care organizations to focus on value. The relationship between cost and quality is an important one. The more clearly nurses in advanced practice can identify their impact on both cost and quality, the better they can identify their value to any practice arrangement. The more clearly the nurse can identify the functions and activities that he or she will perform in relationship to the outcomes he or she will achieve, the more viable his or her negotiating position. The health care delivery system is increasingly capitated, so that the only controls available are managing the costs of doing business or providing service. The clear understanding of that relationship on the part of the nurse in advanced practice is important. Commitment to facilitating the relationship between cost and quality will make an important contribution to the negotiation with potential partners or employers. The value that the partner and employer will be looking for is the ability of the nurse in advanced practice to contribute to the fiscal viability of the organization as well as to high-quality patient service.

Physician Relationships

Regardless of the historical character of the interaction between nurses in advanced practice and physicians, it is now important to develop strong relationships. Physicians are becoming partners in an emerging continuum of care system. The primary partner with the nurse in advanced practice in primary care clinical settings will be the physician. The ability to interact in a balanced and assertive way with practitioners in medical practice will be critical to the initial success of the nurse practitioner in a health plan in either contracted or employee relationships.

Physicians are journeying toward partnered relationships with great difficulty. It is not something to which they come comfortably. Medical practice historically has been highly independent and entrepreneurial in nature. Now, as more collective and team-based approaches to clinical delivery become the norm, building partnered relationships with physicians becomes increasingly important, albeit sometimes challenging. This will require the nurse in advanced practice to focus on some specific issues:

- The character of the relationship between the physician and nurse must be clear. The physician's position and feelings regarding the relationship with the nurse in advanced practice should be determined as soon as possible.

- The performance expectations and role content of the nurse in advanced practice in relationship to the physician must be clarified as soon as possible.

- The legal, regulatory, and relationship components of the interaction between the physician and the nurse in advanced practice should be elucidated as soon as possible. Knowing what the constraints and possibilities are in the relationship between the physician and nurse helps define more clearly the parameters and expectations that both will have between them.

- An agreement that elucidates the role relationships and performance expectations for the nurse in advanced practice should be obtained in advance of his or her accepting either a contract or an employment relationship. Knowing that the expectations are clearly elucidated in advance, either in a letter of agreement or in a set of performance expectations, helps facilitate the nurse's integration into the system.

- Elucidation of the financial relationship between the physician and the nurse in advanced practice before any agreement is signed is essential to the success of the interaction. That dialogue should be frank, open, and concluded before any agreement is closed.

- Any duties, responsibilities, tasks, or functions not traditionally viewed by the nurse in advanced practice as a part of his or her role should be clarified early in the process so that no surprises and uncertainties about that role arise after the relationship is initiated. Clarity at the earliest point possible with regard to the full range of functions and activities helps facilitate the exercise of accountability once the relationship has been initiated.

- Any supervisory functions or activities related to the work of other players in the workplace should also be defined before the relationship is accepted. Knowing the obligations for the work of others informs the nurse in advanced practice of the time and role commitments involved in the new relationship.

The Business of Health Care

It is important for nurses in advanced practice to recognize that there are major financial considerations with regard to the provision of health care services. In the United States, health care is primarily a private sector economic enterprise. Therefore, the financial interactions and relationships between the players and the payers are critical elements in the successful implementing of health care services.

Nurses in advanced practice should be clear about value, costs, reimbursement, and the different approaches to paying for services. They should understand the economic and financial relationships in the service entity of which they are going to become a part. Financial value may be defined through corporate relationships and networking, through partnerships, or through an employed relationship. The nature of the contribution of the nurse in advanced practice, the economic viability of that contribution, and the value relationship between what the nurse in advanced practice does and the return on that activity are critical elements affecting the financial and service viability of the whole practice. Recognizing the total value of the practice entity of which he or she is a part and articulating the specific contribution made to that begins to delineate critical value in the role of the nurse in advanced practice.

KEY CONCEPTS

- In the evolving health care system, there is increasing focus on value. This means that nurses will have to relate more directly to the cost of nursing care and the benefit achieved by offering it.
- Nurses' roles in patient care, in community care, and with other providers in rendering cost-effective services will be emphasized. If value (cost and quality) cannot be defined, nurses will be negatively affected.
- Advanced practice is a business enterprise. Understanding the nature of the business is essential to success.
- Negotiating skills are essential to finding a meaningful role in the many arenas of advanced practice.
- Defining value and determining the relationship between cost and quality are essential to success in advanced practice arrangements.
- Developing a good business relationship and attending to the details prevent problems in the relationship from developing later on.

LEARNING
CHALLENGE

1. How will nurses in advanced practice be used differently from how they practiced in the past?
2. What innovative business arrangements can be created that allow the nurse in advanced practice to partner with others without necessarily being employed by others?
3. How should nurses and physicians relate to each other in a primary care arena in a way that respects the contribution of each to health care?

NURSES IN ADVANCED PRACTICE AND MARKET RELATIONSHIPS

The more nurses in advanced practice are integrated into the subscriber-based delivery system, the more accountable they will become for the satisfaction of subscribers. They must be cognizant of their service and the continuing factors influencing the business of health care. Arrangements between providers and payers, businesses, and other subscriber aggregates will increasingly depend on the intensity of commitment between groups of subscribers and providers. It is to be remembered that the subscriber in the future delivery system will have the final choice as to whether he or she remains with a given plan or moves to another arrangement. The role of any health plan is to keep its subscribers with it as long as possible. A long-term relationship is necessary to maintain the service continuum that is essential to attending to subscriber health needs and to maintaining cost effectiveness.

It is clear that out of this business arrangement nurses in advanced practice, like other providers, must be aware of the market implications of their own practice and their relationships with consumers. In capitated systems of care, payment and operating funds are based on the volume of enrollment. Maintaining sufficient enrollment and growing the enrollment base are essential components of success. Two factors will influence enrollment volumes: the cost of care in enrolled continuum of care practices, and the quality of services provided as perceived by the consumer of those services. Both will have to be addressed with equal intensity to ensure that subscribers stay with the health care system with which they have contracted.

The tension for the nurse in advanced practice is maintaining the balance between service capacity and revenue maximization. Clearly, the intent of the system is to provide an excellence of services that keeps as many patients as possible from having to use high-intensity, high-intervention costly services. Therefore, the fewer costly services are utilized, the more likely it is that revenue will be available to expand the benefits program, enhance the quality of services, or intensify the providers' rewards. The balance between the volume of subscribers and the cost of the program is critically determined by the services provided and the quality of those services along the continuum of care.

Affecting this relationship is the health plan's ability to increase the sophistication of the consumer, provide a broader range of health-prescriptive rather than sickness-driven services, and maintain the general health of the subscribers over the long term. Doing this essentially reflects the contract relationship between the nurse in advanced practice and the plan, system, or program of which he or she has become a part.

Contractual relationships also mean being able to self-market, to project the contribution one makes to a system, practice, or relationship. The value of the partnership is not automatically apparent, however. The critical part of exemplifying that value is the time spent by the nurse in advanced practice in determining and articulating his or her value to others. Nurses historically are not experts in self-promotion. Their focus on their work and the activities related to it has precluded them from taking the time to promote themselves as a viable option and alternative to the traditional medical delivery of health care services. Thus their market value and market relationship are often undefined. Increasingly, as nurses move to interdependent practice roles, determining their value as members of the team becomes more difficult but is still a part of the obligation of team membership.

The nurse in advanced practice therefore must develop some skill in self-promotion and marketing which will be critical to his or her viability and to the value of the practice arrangements that he or she has created. The elements related to **marketing** that are important to the future of advanced practice nursing thus include the following:

- defining the unique characteristics of the role of the nurse in advanced practice that lend value and viability not only to the consumer but to other providers in the health care system as well
- determining the cost effectiveness that nurses in advanced practice bring to the service relationship so that economic and financial viabilities are clear before negotiation
- determining the outcome value of the nurse in advanced practice either in comparison with other practitioners or as a result of defined functions and activities
- identifying the levels of satisfaction that consumers have with the role of the nurse in advanced practice or with a system using such roles; customer satisfaction is a strong indicator of continuing value in plans whose future depends on the degree of customer satisfaction with service

- joining with other health professionals in a comprehensive approach to marketing a package of relationships and services, which strengthens the viability of any one of the discipline members; the viability of the team is thus exemplified and reflects positively on the role of each member, including the nurse

COMMUNITY SUPPORT

Clearly, nurses in advanced practice and the value of the profession cannot be advanced without a partnership with consumers. The primary purpose of nursing practice and nursing roles in the future depends on the kinds of relationships that are formed between the nursing discipline and the community it serves.

Nursing is fundamentally a social contract. The fulfillment of that contract rests in the commitment of nurses to the care and safety of those whom they serve. Because nursing historically has focused on the health of the consumer and has always facilitated health-based practices, moving into this broader frame of reference is not an overwhelming change for nurses.

It is important, however, that nurses recognize that an interdependent team-based practice is the future of health care. The value of the contribution of nursing as a part of the team is now a more important identifier of the character of the relationship with consumers. Increasingly, as health care moves to the continuum of care and into the community, nursing partnerships with community members are going to be valuable in building healthy communities. Because the goal of the subscriber-based system is to maintain the health of its subscribers, closer interaction with the community and the workplace, the home, the community center, schools, and other places where the community defines itself will be critical to the success of health care practice. It is in the best interest of nurses to be seen as advocates and leaders in creating the foundations for healthy communities.

Nurses who commit themselves to improving community health will find it an increasing requisite to identify with the community and to identify the contribution that nursing makes to the community's health. The closer the discipline gets to the community and the more advanced nurse providers partner in creating the community's health, the more viable the vision and image of nursing as a community resource will be.

Community vision and value for nurses in advanced practice will depend on several factors:

- the ability of nurses to identify for the community their specific contribution to the community's value for health

- the visibility of nurses in advanced practice in the forums of health care to which the community looks for advice and counsel with regard to its ongoing health
- the ability of nurses in advanced practice to use the media and other public vehicles for communication to convey the message of the contribution of nurses in advanced practice to the delivery of health care services and in building toward healthy communities
- the degree to which the nursing profession is seen as a key resource in the delivery of health care services so that it is sought out as a primary source of information, support, and partnership in attaining the community's health
- the ability of nurses in advanced practice to define clearly their position and location in the health care delivery system as primary care providers; providing health–care focused activities outside the medical model creates a new paradigm for developing an independent health care relationship with the consumers of health care services

Nurses in advanced practice in the future will have a viable and important role to play in the delivery of a consumer-based continuum of care. The role of the nurse as it emerges in this frame of reference provides a broad base upon which to define future opportunities and activities for the nursing profession.

Nurses in advanced practice in integrated practice arrangements become a key provider role equal to other disciplines and roles in the continuum of care. The opportunity for increased visibility and viability in relationship to other providers and in direct relationship to the consumer of health care becomes a more viable possibility.

The challenge for nursing, on its way to increasing both its numbers and the quality of nurses in advanced practice, is readiness for the challenges that lie ahead. Clearly, during a major paradigm shift, there are great losses. The losses associated with the reduced number of bedside nurses can certainly overwhelm individuals, thereby limiting their perspective of their own future possibilities and opportunities in health care. It will be a grave injustice if the future of the health care system develops without major contributions from nurses.

In the new paradigm, it is no longer about jobs but about building careers. Job focus and job orientation are characteristics of the industrial age, now fast fading into yesterday's landscape. More and more, the challenges that lie before us demand broader competence, mobility on the part of nurses, primary care roles at the point of service, and broader-based nursing education and development for roles that will partner with other players in the health care delivery system. Increasing mobility with regard to health services increases the opportunities for nurses in transforming health services.

The real challenge for the nursing profession is whether nurses are prepared with a broad-based perspective, a strong sense of their location in the delivery of primary care services along the continuum of care, and an increasing commitment to community-based approaches to unfolding nursing practice. Future preparation of advanced practice roles and the expanding definition of what those might be, the flexibility of the profession in responding to demand, and the fluidity of the discipline in its ability to move to where health care demands are all converge to create a base of opportunity for the growth and development of the future of the practice of nursing. Advanced practice nursing is bound up in that challenge. The future is bright. It is wise to remember that opportunity never waits for readiness. The future of advanced practice nursing depends on the profession's readiness for an exciting opportunity and for writing the script for the future.

CONCLUSION

The role of the nurse in advanced practice is changing rapidly. As the health care system shifts and adjusts to new realities, so also must the nurse in advanced practice. Critical changes are unfolding every day. The ability of the nurse in advanced practice to be fast, fluid, and flexible will be critical to his or her success.

Basic principles and foundations for the role of practice in the future marketplace are already unfolding as the new paradigm becomes clearer. The four principles—partnership, equity, accountability, and ownership—are emerging as the foundation for the new work relationships not only in health care but in the global workplace as well. Using these principles as a template for looking at the kinds of changes that are occurring can be helpful to nurses in advanced practice as they begin to plan their own future activities.

This chapter leads to the discussion of several questions with regard to the future of advanced practice; these questions provide a framework for further dialogue in pursuing a deeper understanding of the application of the role of nurses in advanced practice:

- What is the public's perception of nurses in advanced practice? How much does the public know? What would enhance that perception? What can nurses do to advance the visibility of nurses in advanced practice?

- What might be ways to integrate the otherwise disparate roles of the clinical nurse specialist and the nurse practitioner (including nurse-midwives and nurse anesthetists)? What is the contribution that each can make to the other's role? What would an integrated curriculum look like for preparing a nurse in advanced practice?

- How can the relationship between nurses and other providers be enhanced? What are the major barriers to building a stronger relationship with other health professionals? What is it that nurses in advanced practice should do to facilitate their relationship with other providers? What changes will have to occur with the physician relationship to build a stronger partnership between nurses in advanced practice and physicians?

- What new kinds of business arrangements can nurses in advanced practice create? What would a corporate structure look like? How would nurses incorporate their relationship with each other? How would they then negotiate relationships with health care providers and payers? Should nurses have nonemployed, contracted relationships with service providers?

RESEARCH FOUNDATION   Bear, E. (1995). Advanced practice nurses: How did we get there? *Advanced Practice Nursing Quarterly, 1* (1), 10–14.

Bear describes the historical underpinnings for the development and progress of advanced practice nurses. She articulates clearly the foundations for advanced practice and specifically outlines the development of the role of a number of advanced practice nurses. Her review of the origins of advanced practice form the framework for viewing the advanced practice nurse from the perspective of today.

Bear enumerates the development of advanced practice beginning with the certified registered nurse anesthetist, the first nurse to play an advanced practice role as a licensed and formalized practitioner. She proceeds through each of the developments in advanced practice and gives an insight into the processes associated with the expansion of the various roles. Bear concludes with the challenges faced in developing the advanced practice role and identifies some of the implications for the future of the role. This historical research helps provide a baseline for understanding the development and value of the advanced practice nurse. Understanding the history of the role helps anticipate and broaden the application of the role for the future.

REFERENCES

Altman, S. (1990). Health care in the nineties: No more of the same. *Hospitals, 64*, 64.

American Nurses Association. (1991). *Nursing's agenda for health care reform*. Washington, DC: Author.

Anderson, R. (1993). Nursing leadership and healthcare reform. *Journal of Nursing Administration, 23*, 8–9.

Ashley, J.A. (1976). *Hospitals, paternalism, and the role of the nurse*. New York: Teachers College.

Barger, S., & Rosenfeld, P. (1993). Models in community health: Findings from a national study of community nursing centers. *National Study of Community Nursing Centers Report: National League for Nursing, 14*, 426–429.

Barnet, R., & Cavanagh, J. (1994). *Global dreams: Imperial corporations and the new world order*. New York: Simon & Schuster.

Beckham, D. (1994a). Building the high performance accountable health plan. *Healthcare Forum Journal, 37*, 60–67.

Beckham, D. (1994b). The power of primary care. *Healthcare Forum Journal, 37*, 68–74.

Belli, P. (1991). Globalizing the rest of the world. *Harvard Business Review, 69*, 50–55.

Brown, M., & McCool, B. (1990). Health care systems: Predictions for the future. *Health Care Management Review, 15*, 87–94.

Buerhaus, P. (1994). The economics of managed competition and consequences to nurses. *Nursing Economics, 12*, 10–17.

Calleo, D. (1992). *The bankrupting of America*. New York: Morrow.

Coile, R. (1993). *Revolution: The new healthcare system takes shape*. San Francisco: Grand Rounds Press/Wittle Books.

Coile, R. (1994). Transformation of American healthcare in the post reform era. *Healthcare Executive, 9*, 8–12.

Conrad, D. (1993). Coordinating patient care services in regional health systems: The challenge of clinical integration. *Hospitals & Health Services Administration, 38*, 491–508.

De Angelis, C. (1994). Nurse practitioner redux. *Journal of the American Medical Association, 27*, 868–871.

Diers, D. (1993). Advanced practice. *Health Management Quarterly, 15*, 16–20.

Fagin, C. (1992). Collaboration between nurses and physicians: No longer a choice. *Nursing & Health Care, 13*, 354–363.

Flynn, A.M., & Kilgallen, M.E. (1993). Case management: A multidisciplinary approach to the evaluation of cost and quality standards. *Journal of Nursing Care Quality, 8*, 58–66.

Friedman, E. (1994). Bury my heart at Jackson Hole. *Health Management Quarterly, 16*, 11–14.

Fries, J. (1993). Reducing need and demand. *Healthcare Forum Journal, 36*, 18–23.

Hammer, M., & Champy, J. (1993). *Reengineering the corporation: A manifesto for business revolution*. New York: Harper Business Books.

Jacobs, M. (1991). *Short term America: The causes and cures of our business myopia*. Cambridge, MA: Harvard University Press.

Johnson, R. (1992). The entrepreneurial physician. *Health Care Management Review, 17*, 73–79.

Kritek, P. (1994). *Negotiating at an uneven table*. San Francisco: Berrett-Koehler.

MacDonald, A. (1994). Integrating management of physician groups and hospitals. *Topics in Health Care Financing, 20*, 48–54.

Meighan, S. (1994). Managing conflict in an integrated system. *Topics in Health Care Financing, 20*, 39-47.

Mundinger, M. (1994). Advanced practice nursing—Good medicine for physicians. *New England Journal of Medicine, 330*, 211–213.

Nauert, R. (1992). Planning an alternative delivery system. *Topics in Healthcare Financing, 18*, 64–71.

Newman, M., Lamb, G., & Michaels, K. (1991). Nursing case management: The coming together of theory and practice. *Nursing and Healthcare, 12*, 404–408.

Porter-O'Grady, T. (1994). The real value of partnership: Preventing professional amorphism. *Journal of Nursing Administration, 24*, 11–15.

Relman, A. (1988). Assessment and accountability: The third revolution in medical care. *New England Journal of Medicine, 319*, 1220–1222.

Rheingold, H. (1993). *The virtual community: Homesteading on the electronic frontier.* New York: Addison-Wesley.

Starr, P. (1992). *The logic of health care reform.* Knoxville, TN: Whittle Direct Books.

Tan, J. (1994). Integrating health care with information technology. *Health Care Management Review, 19*, 72–80.

Toffler, A. (1990). *Powershift.* New York: Bantam Books.

Tonges, M., & Lawrenz, E. (1993). Re-engineering: The work redesign technology link. *Journal of Nursing Administration, 23*, 15–22.

Vautier, A., & Carey, S. (1994). A collaborative case management program. *Nursing Administration Quarterly, 18*, 1–9.

Index